Backstairs
at the
White House

Backstairs at the White House

a novel by
Gwen Bagni and Paul Dubov

PRENTICE-HALL, INC.
Englewood Cliffs, New Jersey

The story of the lives of
Lillian Rogers Parks
and her mother,
Maggie Rogers

Based upon
My Thirty Years Backstairs at the White House
by Lillian Rogers Parks
with Frances Spatz Leighton
and authors' taped interviews with
Lillian Rogers Parks

BACKSTAIRS AT THE WHITE HOUSE

All rights reserved.
Copyright © 1978 by Ed Friendly Productions, Inc.;
copyright © excerpted material from "My Thirty
Years Backstairs at the White House," 1961,
used by permission of Fleet Press Corporation.
This book may not be reproduced in whole or in part, by
mimeograph or any other means, without permission.

ISBN 0-13-056341-2

Library of Congress Catalog Card Number 78-73717

10 9 8 7 6 5 4
Published simultaneously in the United States and Canada

PRINTED IN THE UNITED STATES OF AMERICA

To Lillian Rogers Parks,
who lived it . . .
and to Ed Friendly,
whose dedication made the mini-series
and this book possible.

Backstairs
at the
White House

PROLOGUE

⊠ ⊠ ⊠

Keswick, Virginia 1907

The spavined horse, sway-backed, of undistinguished
ancestry, turned its ears, listening to the melody of
Lillian's young voice. " 'At's my darlin', 'at's my darlin' . . . you be a Derby horse for sure . . ." At the
nudge of her tiny heels, beast and ten-year-old rider
went plodding down the path and across the stream,
little Emmett running alongside, demanding "My turn,
Lil'yan, my turn . . ." They disappeared into a tangled
stand of buckthorn and willow oak, the children's
voices staying a moment in the still, hot air.

Maggie smiled at the joyful sound of her children.
Hitching the sacklike dress to her belt to keep it free of
scrub water she got up from her knees and leaned
into the open window and breathed in the fragrance
of dogwood, pine, and wild petunia that grew around
the weathered little farmhouse with the same luxurious
abandon as that lavished by nature on Thomas Jefferson's place Shadwell, not a mile away, and on
Monticello, she'd heard, although she'd never been that
far down the road. Maggie thought of the single gera-
nium struggling for life on her windowsill back in the
city and felt grateful to have gotten her children away
if only for this brief time from alleys and garbage;

I

from the congestion of carriages, broughams, and those dangerous new motorcars, that were a threat to life and limb.

A quick stabbing sensation in her toe brought the realization that she'd picked up a splinter from the rough board floor. With forefinger and thumb she pulled it out of her bare foot, squeezing hard.

"What'd you do?" Gran'mama asked without looking up from the washtub.

"Just a sliver."

"No need you down there, scrubbin' that old floor, Maggie. I could wipe it up myself. Don't even need a pail, water runs 'tween boards right on the ground."

"My kids doin' the trackin' up, Gran'mama . . ."

"Good to have children 'round, doin' the trackin' . . ."

It was the most they'd said to each other all morning, both knowing that their minds turned on the single thought: Emmett was coming home. Neither woman spoke his name, but his presence was in the room with them, in the air of expectancy tempered with caution. The children's first words, on awakening yesterday in Washington, were "Papa's comin' today . . ." On the train ride to Keswick it was all they talked of, and when Maggie had gone out into the barnyard to help Gran'mama wring the neck of an old hen for the stew-pot, they could hear Lillian's bright young voice reassuring her younger brother not to fret, that Papa was sure to show up, and this time he would stay . . .

Gran'mama washboarded a pair of white duck riding pants with homemade yellow laundry soap, dunked them into the rinse tub, wrang them out. Maggie helped her carry the heaping laundry basket to the yard where they hung the dozen pairs of pants and shirts. It was a common sight along the byways of the horse country of Keswick, women washing riding clothes for the landed and the blooded who were always getting ready for a show in Upperville, Middleville, Berryville, Middleburg, and sometimes all the way up to New York.

They went back into the house, Gran'mama filling time by patching the children's worn garments, Maggie attacking floorboards with brush and suds. How many times had they waited for him, as they were doing now. Yesterday, at the depot . . . having to explain to the children that their papa must have just missed the train, he'd be on another one. And hope and pray it was true.

Being married to Emmett Rogers for going on eleven years had taught her that living was a seesaw. Never just plain wake-up-content, go-to-bed-sleep-easy. Away from him she could settle in her mind what was right and sensible. On the verge of seeing him face to face, of accepting the demands of her own pent-up need for him, the torment was upon her.

"Woman, you a fool . . ." The words escaped on their own.

"You say somethin'?"

"Nothin', Gran'mama . . ."

Gran'mama walked out early every morning to cook for the Randolphs, whose plantation was down the road, always returning with a large basket of laundry to be done. She grew and sold vegetables, tilling the soil herself. Not yet fifty, an overlay of gray-ash pallor already dulled the once warm cocoa of her skin. She had a name, Isabel Moore, but no one seemed to use it. Her son Emmett had grown to manhood barely knowing his father, whose stern blue-eyed visage looked down from a framed photograph on the wall; he was always referred to as Captain Rogers, and he had another family in the town.

The cold truth was, Gran'mama and her son were the "other" family. The one in town had a marriage recorded in the family Bible, a house, carriage and horses to carry them to church of a Sunday. Captain Rogers had never carried Gran'mama anyplace people were likely to see them, yet Maggie had often observed her wiping off the glass that covered his picture. That Emmett bore his father's name was enough for Gran'mama. He wasn't to go through life with her name, which she got from her mother who was given it by the slave owner who fathered her. As young as Lillian and little Emmett were, they'd already heard it time and time again, "We come from some of the best blood in Virginia."

Maggie, born Margaret Williams, was of many bloods. While her color tended more toward cream than coffee, and her eyes were startlingly blue, a breadth of nose and texture of hair announced her African heritage. It was these characteristics, rather than those of the Roanoke Indian or Italian somewhere in her background, that determined for her the path her life would take. She didn't bear her father's name but knew his credentials to be City Sergeant, Real Estate Agent for the City of Salem, Virginia. When she married, her mother had persuaded her to write her father, who had dredged up enough paternal responsibility to write back and urge her not to marry so young, but to get an education. The advice came a little late. In order to keep body and soul together and send a few dollars home to an ailing mother, Maggie had been working for better than two years as nursemaid for the children of Major Slack of Dupont Circle. It was while the major's family summered at White Sulphur Springs that she first laid eyes on Emmett Rogers, with his dazzling smile and silken ways and already a headwaiter at nineteen. There had been no turning back for her.

Maggie shook the scrub water off the brush and put the brush on the windowsill, bristles up, to dry, wondering how it was possible at age twenty-eight to feel so old. Gran'mama, with her gnarled knuckles and bunioned feet, had once been a beauty—if you could trust the testimony of the daguerreotype in the trunk. Her life had gone to working, waiting, being left behind.

Maggie vowed her own life would not go that way . . .

The train's far-off, plaintive whistle announced the four forty pulling into the station. It would stop in Keswick to take on water, maybe a passenger or two, what little mail and freight the insignificant hamlet extruded. And (*Good Lord willin'*) to drop Emmett Rogers.

"Children," Maggie shrilled across the field, "hurry
... Papa be here."

They rode up on the old horse, with Lillian, the el-
der, clearly in command. "I want to ride alone. Can't I
ride alone, Mama?" little Emmett begged, looking im-
ploringly at Maggie with the same sea-blue eyes. In
spite of the fair skin he'd inherited from the man in the
photograph, there was enough of Maggie in his face to
relegate him going through life with Jim Crow.

"Later," Maggie promised him, rushing both children into the house, pausing on the threshold to wash
their feet so as not to track up the floor again. It would
take their papa only fifteen-twenty minutes, if he was
lucky enough to hitch a ride from somebody with a
wagon. Half an hour at most, if he was to walk. Between Gran'mama and Maggie, the children were
stripped and given spit baths. As Gran'mama helped
little Emmett clean his ears, Maggie brushed the bram-
bles out of Lillian's long, silky, curling chestnut hair.

It was Lillian who was the fairest of all, with velvet
skin light as a peanut shell and limpid brown eyes.
Picked up and put down some place away from all of
them, she could have been taken for a child of Medi-
terranean background.

After the young ones were dressed and set to wait
on chairs so as not to dirty up again, Maggie took the
basin and washrag into the bedroom, slid out of Gran'-
mama's old work dress, sponged her body, and put on
a petticoat and camisole, pausing to look at herself in
the tarnished, distorting mirror. Not a beauty, she admitted, but a fine, strong straight body. Comely, with a
proud head, full breasts, slim waist, and a glow to her
cheeks that hadn't been there until that train whistle
told her that Emmett could be near. She hurried now,
pulling on black lisle stockings, buttoning high-topped
shoes, a fresh-ironed shirtwaist, skirt cinched in with a
belt. She gave her hair a quick brush, secured the hair-
pins. As she closed the top button of her shirtwaist
she could see the pulse throbbing in her throat.

A shout from outside brought them all to the door.

"Ho-ooooo," his voice reached them. "Where my babies, where my loveys?"

Emmett Rogers came up the path, wicker suitcase in hand. The finest of striped silk shirts, white stiff collar. Trim-fitting Palm Beach suit, its stylish lines unable to completely conceal his lithe sensuality. Straw skimmer atilt, reminding Maggie of the way he looked the first time she saw him. It brought a smile and an ache, because when his hat was at that rakish angle it meant he had something to hide.

The children went in a dead run down the path and grabbed him around the legs. Gran'mama, as was her way, stayed back. Maggie took a step toward him. He dropped the suitcase and as though no one else were there, grabbed her in hungry embrace. "Missed my Maggie somethin' fierce, somethin' fierce . . ." It was a moment so private for both of them that Gran'mama looked away. It took the combined efforts of both children to pull them apart. Without releasing Maggie, he bear-hugged both youngsters to him. "Think I didn't see you, hm? I saw you . . . rec'nized you right off, said to myself, now they's two the finest-lookin' young-uns ever set eyes on, jus' like their daddy . . ." With two fingers, he stretched his mouth into a comic face that set them all to laughing. His all-inclusive embrace drew Gran'mama into the group, her joy at having him home so great she didn't know what to do for him first. "Come on in . . . rest . . . settle . . . eat."

Emmett's presence made the gut-pinching poverty of the house seem less evident. He had that way about him, of life being always going off to a carnival. It was the coming home with no prize under your arm that he'd never quite learned how to handle.

The children tumbled over each other, staking claim to their father's attention.

"Look'a me, Papa, how I growed . . ." This from little Emmett, stretching to his fullest.

"My stars and body, you sure did . . . legs gettin' so long, first thin' you know, you be taller'n me . . ."

"Mama, I'm goin' be taller'n Papa!"

And Lillian, pirouetting for him: "Want to see what I learned at dancin' school, Papa . . . want to see . . . ?"

"Now that is somethin' worth comin' all this way on a train for. I most surely do want to see . . ."

And again, from little Emmett, as he pulled up his sleeve and flexed his muscle, "Feel how strong I be, Papa?"

"How's the job comin' on, Emmett?" Maggie took him by surprise. For a fleeting instant he was unmasked. "Fine . . . fine . . ." was all he said, then, "Go on, Lil'yan, let your daddy see you dance."

Lillian said she needed music. No problem. Emmett Rogers knew a brand-new song, "Love Me and the World Is Mine." He spoke the words of the title as a plea to Maggie, but she didn't turn her head toward him.

"It's got to be ballet-dancin' music, Papa," Lillian insisted. "Teacher always plays a piece called Hoo-mor-esque . . ."

"Well now, why didn't you say so? I know that song."

"You do, Papa?" Lillian said in wonder.

"Why sure now, your papa knows most everythin' . . . Those string quartets play that Humoresque music all the time for the rich folks when me and my men servin' 'em tea at that fine hotel up there to White Plains."

Maggie spoke again. "How many men you got under you now, Emmett?" He ignored the question. "You dance now, Lil'yan, I sing for you. Dum-da-DUM-da-DUM-da-DUM," he intoned. "Too slow for you? Okay, darlin', how this . . . DUMdaDUMdaDUM . . ." He sang faster, moving with the jerky gestures of a character in a nickelodeon picture show, and had the children holding their sides. Even Gran'mama laughed, but an ache was growing in Maggie's chest.

"No no, Papa, that too fast."

"Hold it." Raising his hands in the manner of an orchestra conductor, he gave a downbeat. Then, sitting straddle-legged while little Emmett climbed to a seat on his shoulders, Emmett Rogers cradled an imaginary cello between his knees and solemnly sawed away, humming the music at a tempo pleasing to his daughter as she danced.

They ate their meal, Emmett Rogers regaling them with stories of the swells at the hotel. "You know, they come out there an' hide all day under their big umbrellas so's they don't turn dark to be the fine color we be . . ."

"When do you have to go back to the job?" Maggie asked.

"Oh, one these days," he evaded, "take my time, take my time."

For the first since Emmett had come up the path, Gran'mama gave Maggie a look that admitted she, too, had caught the tilt of his hat and understood its meaning. But how could she not, she who had raised him, and remembered his deep hurt at learning that even his light skin didn't open the door to his father's house.

Perfecting a kind of mocking challenge to charm generous tips out of those he served, at sixteen he was a wine boy; at twenty, a maitre d'. At twenty-four he had forty-seven men working under him. At thirty he was a drunk who couldn't hold on to a job and who came a day late to his family because he'd had to stop off someplace and sweat the stink of booze out of his skin.

"When we goin' back to live in Cape May, Papa?"

"That what you like to do, Lil'yan, baby?"

"Oh, yes, Papa."

"Well, I tell you, my dancin' girl," Emmett promised Lillian. "You want to go back to Cape May, your papa do his best to get that for you . . . yes, sir," he assured all of them at the table, "they liked me at that hotel—I was head man—liked me a whole lot. Yes, that be nice, you children playin' at the seashore all day, your mama not havin' a livin' thing to do, jus' watch you grow. Remember that, Maggie?"

Maggie remembered how the fancy society folks carried parasols and were pushed along in beach chairs the whole length of the boardwalk. But there were isolated beaches where any of God's children could go. Miles of wide, white beach; waters lapping at your feet as you walked along. Cape May "diamonds" scattered everywhere, big, crystally chunks smoothed off and thrown up by the sea, sparkling in the sun, just waiting to be picked up. And the hotels . . . nothing finer in Newport or Atlantic City. They said the Presidents always went there, way back as far as President Lincoln and Grant. The first year of their marriage, Emmett had worked steady, winters, at the Normandie Hotel in D.C., in command of the dining room. Summers, when Capitol Hill emptied and Washington got too hot to endure, they would pack up and go to Cape May where he came to be important enough for Commodore Vanderbilt to ask for him by name. Yes, they were beautiful days, out there in Cape May with their babies —first Lillian, then Emmett—playing in the sun, shoveling sand into little tin buckets painted red and blue, running from the water's edge, squealing like little piglets as foamy chunks of ocean nibbled at their feet.

Angry at herself for letting a stale dream overtake her, Maggie shoved back her chair and started clearing the table. Emmett grabbed her around the waist and tried to pull her down into his lap. "Come on, darlin', let the dishes be." She looked into his guileless eyes and firmly removed his hand from her body. The children kept at their papa to share more of the magic of the world that seemed to be peculiarly his, but Emmett Rogers' well of whimsies had suddenly run dry. As soon as the dishes were wiped, Gran'mama, sensitive to the rising strain, urged the children to come along and share her bed.

There were kisses and promises all around. Would Papa still be here in the morning? Yes, he sure as shootin' would be here. All the high-steppin' horses in Virginia couldn't drag him away from seeing his children in the morning. And would he be coming back to Washington with them, like he did last winter?

They'd talk about that in the morning.

Emmett and Maggie talked of it that night. They walked away from the house and on down the rutted road, surrounded by the cloyingly sweet scent of night-blooming jasmine. Rotting pippin apples, fermenting on the ground, brandied the air. They kept their distance, neither reaching out for the other. Maggie finally said what she'd instinctively known from the first glimpse of him, with his smile ablaze and tilted hat: "You fired again."

In the gloom of early evening the Blue Ridge Mountains cut a huge black swatch into the sky. In awhile he said, "Let me tell you how it happened, Maggie."

"No need to tell me." She'd heard it enough times to recite from memory. He'd got his pay. In the waiting-around time between serving lunch and dinner, his money found its way onto a table with chips and playing cards, and his glass never stayed empty. "You only thirty years old . . ." She said it more in sorrow than in condemnation. "Not a man o' color in the South wouldn't change places, all the opportunities you had . . ."

"I never look at another woman, Maggie," he offered as the only palliative he had. "You the onliest one, Maggie."

"I know that, Emmett, I know that . . . but you drinkin' your life away sorrows me jus' as had you another woman."

"God, Maggie, God . . . what am I goin' do . . . ?" Leaning against the sagging fence, he closed his eyes tightly in despair. "Don' want to drink, tries hard not to . . . First day I worked as wine boy, knowed I had the taste for it . . . I fights it . . . every single day . . . fights it like it was the devil hisself . . . God, the money I made, and nothin' to show for it but the blue shakes, mornin' after, and IOUs . . . Wanted to come to you and the younguns this time, bringin' you everythin' . . . had 'most two hundred dollars, clear . . . was goin' bring rent money, and presents . . ." His words broke off in convulsive sobs. Her fingers found the tears on his face. She held him as though he were another of her children.

All Maggie had to her name were the curling irons in a black satchel that she carried to the homes of

Washington society ladies. When income from hair-dressing wasn't enough, there were office floors to scrub at night. In this tenuous way, she had kept her family together, hoping that Emmett, by some miracle, could break his craving for the bottle.

Together, their arms tight around each other's bodies, they retraced their steps back to the bed Gran'mama had made up for them in the little add-on room where Emmett had slept from babyhood until that night, at fifteen, when he had listened to the siren song of the train whistle and followed it.

They lay in the bed, his body fitting the identical arc to hers. Baskets of fingers held her breasts. "Give me another chance, Maggie . . ." There was no clock in the room, but the clack of wheels on track and whistle blast told them that the eleven twenty was going through. Maggie had a ticket for herself on the five ten and the children would ride free. The porters on the B. & O. were usually good for a complimentary ride to the serving fraternity; chances were Emmett would have no problem.

"I'll make it this time, Maggie. Sell my silk shirts for the rent. They'll take me back to the Normandie. 'Course, may have to start down a ways, not as a good a job as I had, but I'll work my way back up to head-waiter again. Always have . . ." In the dark, burrowed together in the feather bed, it seemed possible. At any rate, she couldn't tell him no, when with all of her being she had just told him yes. She fell asleep in his arms. He lay awake the rest of the night, fighting a desperate thirst. They left Gran'mama's while it was still dark, each carrying a sleeping child. Emmett picked up Maggie's suitcase. His own suitcase he had strapped to his back. Gran'mama kissed them both, kissed the sleeping children, walked down to the road with them and waited until they were well out of sight before she cried.

They stopped several times during the walk to town to shift the weight of their children. Passing on the way the estates of the Ingersols, the Beaucocks where, as a boy, Emmett had helped whitewash fences and repair

paddocks. The sun came out just before they reached
the Keswick depot. Maggie boarded with the children
and found seats in the first car behind the engine, designated for "coloreds." Since a supervisor was on this
particular run, the porter advised Emmett to sneak on
just as the train started. He hung out on the jolting platform between cars, taking the wrenching of each curve,
until the porter came with word that the supervisor was
at breakfast in the diner. Emmett walked on up to the
car that carried his family and found the children were
awake and eating the baking powder biscuits Gran'-
mama had given them for the journey.

With all the stops, the trip to Washington took a
tedious three hours. Maggie rode most of the miles
looking out the window, but all she saw or heard was
Emmett promising his children the world. ("Wait till
you see the fine place I'm goin' get us to live.") Soot
and cinders whipped back at them through the open
window, fit to make you go blind, but to close the window was to suffocate. At the Culpepper stop, the local
Negro women were at the train, as always, carrying
their wares on trays on their heads that were level with
the windows, walking along the track calling "Sweet
'tato pie . . . fried chicken . . ." The children's papa had
his moment of pride. What did his babies want? Well,
that's what his babies would have. With the last nickels
he had to rub together in his pocket, Emmett bought
legs and pies. The final Virginia stop was Alexandria,
then on to the District of Columbia.

When they got off at Pennsylvania Station, Emmett
apologized for not being able to take them right home
to the rooming house, but he had an important stop to
make. Maggie didn't have to be told what the stop was.
When he did join them, hours later, in the small room
that would house them "jus' till things get better,"
there was one less silk shirt in his wicker suitcase and
his bourboned breath was heavily camouflaged with the
smell of mint leaves.

In the spring of 1908 the talk around Washington
was whether or not the Democrats would choose

William Jennings Bryan for a third try at the presidency. And if they did, could he defeat Teddy Roosevelt's rumored hand-picked successor, William Howard Taft?

"What if the convention doesn't pick Taft? Or if he doesn't want the job?" asked a portly gentleman with a flat Nebraska accent. He had ordered the T-bone well done with lyonnaise potatoes. His congressman, relishing the oysters Rockefeller, replied that he hoped the Democrats *would* run Bryan again. "Then we're a cinch, no matter who we pick. Silver-tongued orator, my foot . . . to me, Bryan's nothing but a big bag of wind. You hear what he's after? *Equal rights to all. Special privilege to none . . .*"

Both men took hot Parker House rolls from a silver tray offered by Emmett Rogers, who stepped back a respectful distance from which he could observe the needs of the three tables in his station.

"We're damned if we do, and damned if we don't." The Nebraskan, a man of cattle and railroads, made it clear he didn't think much of that trust-busting Roosevelt in the White House, even though they were of the same party—and he was afraid that Taft would be more of the same. "Mine workers allowed to strike. Regulation of railroads . . ." he deplored. "And what are you going to do about that infernal packinghouse inspection bill?"

"Nothing I can do. Already signed into law."

"That's not what we sent you to Washington for."

The esteemed congressman, losing his appetite, snapped his fingers. "Waiter," he called to Emmett. "More wine."

"Yes, sir."

Emmett lifted the napkin-wrapped bottle from the wine cooler and deftly poured a finger and a half of the rich red port into each of their glasses. "More," said the gentleman from Nebraska. Emmett added another finger and replaced the bottle, but not before the maitre d', an eagle-eyed mulatto, observed that Emmett had spilled a drop of the ruby fluid on the pristine white tablecloth.

Emmett served the other tables in his station, vaguely aware of the Washington gossip: The President's
daughter Alice had shown her ankle in public, had
driven her runabout over thirty miles an hour down
Pennsylvania Avenue, openly smoking a cigarette. . . .
There was a regular menagerie over at the White
House: a live bear, somebody said, and the Roosevelt children, completely out of control, had pony
races in the East Room.

Emmett's head was thudding. He could feel cold
sweat forming under his collar. As, one by one, his tables cleared, he removed plates and silver to a tray to
be carried to the kitchen. He dropped a fork. It fell on
the thick fleur-de-lis of the carpet without a sound, but
the maitre d' heard it and glared at Emmett across the
room.

"What is Roosevelt sticking his nose into the packing business for, anyway?" reiterated the Nebraskan.
"Let him go back down to Panama and help dig that
damn ditch of his and leave business alone!"

Emmett brought desserts and refilled coffee cups,
vaguely aware that they were discussing Teddy Roosevelt's wasteful spending of government money in re-
decorating the White House: ". . . and building those
two office wings . . . if it was good enough for Lincoln
to conduct the business of the presidency out of his
house, it should be good enough for the Rough Rider."

Emmett's consuming attention was on that wine
bottle. His waiter's ethic told him that whether they
drank it or not, he should at least make the gesture
of refilling their glasses, no matter how little remained
in the bottle.

The gentlemen finished the meal. Emmett presented
the bill on a silver salver. The congressman studied it,
laid a paper dollar and some coins, which included the
tip, on the plate, and left with the Nebraskan. Emmett
was acutely aware that there were still two fingers of
port left in the bottle . . . and the maitre d' was supervising a flambé at a table beyond the potted palms.
Need was too great for caution. Placing the bottle on
the tray of used dishes, Emmett backed into the kitch-

en, where he shoved the tray across the counter. Before the scullery boy could move from the garbage pail, Emmett had the bottle stuck underneath his white coat and was hurrying through a door and down a flight of wooden steps to the employee area. His locker was at the far end of the dank cavern. Sometime back he had realized that there was just enough space between it and the wall, if he stretched his arm to its fullest, to place a bottle. There were three bottles back there now, a finger or two of wine left in them, and one almost a quarter full of bourbon. A quick gulp of the port calmed him. The urge to consume it all was powerful, but if he did, he rationalized, he'd go blotto again. He was on his third hotel since coming back to the capital with his family, and he would not, *would not,* he swore to himself, lose this job! He permitted himself one more slow swallow, letting the wine drip into his throat. Just enough to hold himself together. He added the bottle to his cache, and chewing on Sen-Sen, went up the stairs. The maitre d' was just coming through the swinging doors, looking for him, as he reached the top.

"Where your checks, Rogers? And your money? You supposed to be at your station." Emmett, managing to avoid face-to-face contact, emptied his pockets of checks and money, which the maitre d' quickly counted. "Where you been anyway, Rogers? You didn't get permission to leave the floor."

"I had to make a visit to the commode. Or they passed a law against that?" He shouldn't have spoken that way to a superior, but it was galling to be dressed down by this man, who had fewer in staff than he himself had commanded, at hotels far finer than this one . . .

"Did you wash your hands?" the maitre d' demanded.

"I washed my hands, *sir.* Always wash my hands. My mother taught me." Emmett walked back to the dining room, greatly offended to be spoken to as though he were an ignorant field hand who had never seen an inside commode. Why, he had learned manners from some of the finest: the Astors, the Goulds. He had served them all. *And to be asked by a common maitre d' if he had washed his hands . . . He, who had some of the finest blood in Virginia in his veins . . .*

During the rest of the luncheon hour he showed them all what real style was: pulling back chairs for the ladies, lighting the gentlemen's cigars, deftly suggesting the most sophisticated dishes. He could hold a job with the best of them . . .

The final guest left the dining room. Luncheon cloths were replaced with dinner cloths and the lights were dimmed. Deliberately the last waiter to leave, Emmett was proving to himself that he didn't have to run to the bottle with his tongue hanging out like some boozehound. With unhurried pace, he walked through the swinging door, through the kitchen, down the steps.

And there was his locker, pulled from the wall. All the other waiters, standing around, watched as the maitre d' took the precious bottles he had squirreled away and emptied them into the sink.

He was given his pay and told he was through.

The "fine place" that Emmett Rogers had secured for his family was on an unpaved lane in a decrepit neighborhood aptly named Foggy Bottom. Its main advantage, as he told Maggie when first he brought her to see it, was that it was close to everything. Mostly it was close to the river. A boggy heaviness that never seemed to leave the atmosphere penetrated the walls, taking up permanent residence in quilts and mattresses. In the summer mosquitoes bred in obscene numbers; during the spring and fall—TB time—the funeral wagon was no stranger to the area.

Emmett Rogers wrapped himself around the tilted pole that held the E Street sign, took several deep, head-clearing breaths, and started out again; clinging with desperate fingers to the last moment before relinquishing the pole's support. Two liquid hours and a week's pay had passed since getting fired. He had fallen several times on his lurching way home. His trousers were muddied, one knee was ripped. Somehow two buttons had departed his shirt front. He struggled to remember how it had happened. Oh yes . . . in the beefy fist of a mahogany man who had him by the shirt and flung him out of the saloon into the street when his money ran out, calling him "yella-skin mongrel nigger . . ."

His rocky journey ended at number 24. Shuffling up the weed-grown path to the broken stoop, he stumbled against the door, which hung slightly askew on its hinges, and was in the one-roomed shanty. Rags were stuffed into cracks in the walls, a potbellied stove provided heat and cooking, and a blanket, hung on a rope, divided the room into sleeping areas. Grateful to find the house empty so he could clean and sober up before the family got back, he went to the stove to reheat the strong day-old coffee. And realized he wasn't alone.

Maggie came out from behind the blanket partition, in fresh shirtwaist, trim tailored skirt, pulling on a pair of immaculate white gloves. They looked at one another.

"Thought you be to work by now," he said.

"Jus' leavin'."

"Middle of the day, Sat'day . . . where the children be?"

"Emmett to the picture show. Lil'yan to her dancin' class."

"A nickel for the show, nickel for dancin' lesson?"

"I earned both those nickels."

He grabbed at her arm, "Let me tell you how it happened, Maggie."

"I got to go to work. Customers waitin' for me." The day that had begun warm had turned chill. Maggie reached to the wall peg for the woolen capelet trimmed in passementerie that one of her society ladies had given her, and put it around her shoulders. She picked up her black case of hairdressing equipment and left him alone. Abandoned, Emmett seemed immobilized for a sodden moment; then he sagged to the floor.

The dancing teacher, a compactly built lady the color of a peach bruise who had once seen Isadora Duncan, tried to instill in her young pupils the discipline of the art. "It's not jus' dancin'," she said to them. "It's livin', it's lovin', it's life. When you not dancin', you jus' as well not be breathin' . . ." The upright piano had an E-flat key missing below middle C. The slightly wavy mirror behind the *barre* had come from a burned-out neighborhood saloon and still had char marks on one end. But the little girls who sometimes brought their nickels, and just as often said, "Can I owe you?" didn't notice these defects.

"Glis-sade, glis-sade . . . Re-levé . . ." and the little girls all went up on their toes. Lillian couldn't maintain her balance and grabbed for the *barre*. The lady at the piano turned a page, losing the beat, and continued with her pedantic version of "Humoresque." *"Glis-sade . . .* pick—it—up . . ." The teacher urged the pianist, "Fourth—position . . . Fifth—position . . . And *tour jeté . . ."* Lillian went into the whirl, stumbled, fell. "Everybody relax," said the teacher. Throughout the lesson she'd been especially observing Lillian, usually the most attentive of students, who today seemed strangely clumsy. She drew her over into the corner of the room and touched her forehead, "What's the matter, darlin'? Feelin' poorly?"

"No, ma'am, jus' fine." It wasn't true. Each time she stretched, her leg muscles cried out, but some of Maggie's indomitable pride was already part of Lillian's character, and to give up before the hour was complete was not in her nature. When the lesson was over and all the other little girls had left, the teacher offered to walk her home. She couldn't do that, she told her. She was under strict orders from her mother to wait for her brother.

"No need to fuss 'bout me, ma'am. He be right along . . ."

The teacher changed into her street clothes, turned out the lights, and locked the door, reluctantly leaving the child sitting on the cold stone step in front of the dark studio.

Daylight faded. The lamplighter, a Neapolitan, came along. He extended the long pole with its flaming wick to the gas. It sputtered, then caught. For reasons unknown to him, D.C. lamplighters were all Italian, which was good. A man could get right off the boat and come direct from Ellis Island and find a job, without even knowing how to speak, but he was proud of the English he'd learned and liked to use the new language. As the lamp flared, casting a cold bluish glow to the pavement, he saw the shivering child. He moved closer, concerned. He had kids of his own and didn't like the way this one looked. "Wha's-a matta you, kid . . . somethin'-a wrong, you? You no feel-a too good?"

"I'm all right, thank you."

When you come from proud blood, her mother had taught her, you don't take your troubles to every Tom, Dick, and Harry 'cause they most likely got troubles of their own. "My brother's comin' for me," she assured him.

"Okay, kid . . ." He looked back two or three times on his way to the next lamp. Another pool of gaslight flickered, then another. He grew smaller, and finally rounded the corner.

The tension in Lillian's legs had mutated to a frightening kind of burning that sent agonizing darts to every part of her body. Inside, she was on fire; outside, the bitter chill of evening and her threadbare sweater made her shiver so violently she could barely talk when little Emmett finally arrived.

"Where you been? You supposed to come long time ago . . ."

He had forgotten and had stayed through the nickelodeon show three times. "But it wasn't as funny as Papa," he said. "What's the matter with you, Lil'yan . . . what you shakin' so for?"

All she could say was she felt awful. Cold, and hurtin'.

"Well come on, don't jus' set there, let's get home."

"I cain't, Emmett . . ."

"What you mean, you cain't?"

The strange way she was crying, in bursts of strangled sound like a hurt animal, scared him. "You gotta come," he insisted, tugging at her arm. "Come on . . ." She tried to take a step, and fell, with a shriek.

"Get up," he insisted out of his fear. "Get up."

She couldn't. Something had gone all wrong with her legs. All she could do was lie on the cold sidewalk and moan. From somewhere in his terror, the nine-year-old boy found the strength to half-carry, half-drag his sobbing sister back home.

The street lamps that bordered Dupont Circle were more ornate than those on streets nearer the river. Town houses were of stone and red brick with filigreed iron fences and gates, curtains of Belgian and French laces framed windows of Tiffany stained glass. Maggie had been admitted into many of these homes, dressing the hair of ladies whose pictures graced the society pages.

Her last appointment for the day was the Colgate mansion. She had barely set up her equipment on Mrs. Colgate's inlaid chinoiserie dressing table when a discreet knock on the boudoir door preceded the apologetic butler. His practiced phrase "Beggin' you pahdon, ma'am" brought with it the distressing information that there was a young boy down at the kitchen door, claiming to be Emmett Rogers, Jr. Seemed there was trouble at home. Maggie better come, soon as she could. Something done gone wrong with her little girl . . .

The brougham was hastily brought around. Mrs. Colgate wouldn't hear of Maggie staying to finish her hair, but paid her nonetheless. It was only after Maggie and little Emmett were installed as passengers in the luxurious carriage that Maggie realized she still had the warm curling iron in her hand. To ride in a brougham had long been a secret wish of hers, but on the trip back to Foggy Bottom she gave no attention to the supple leather, burnished woods, the hood that surrounded them, or the liveried driver. "Tell me again, chile," she demanded of little Emmett over and over.

"Tole you, Mama, all I know. Papa, he run for the doctor and Lil'yan's cryin' somethin' fierce 'cause she cain't walk." The carriage came to an abrupt stop. The driver turned and looked down at them from his high perch. "Y'all can get out now."

"Maybe you didn't hear right," Maggie said. "We lives at 24 E Street."

"I heard," he said with the disdain of the long-tenured retainer. "This whole place down here too full o' chug holes and bumps for a fine animal and carriage. Step down now." He waited with obvious impatience for them to quit his vehicle. Little Emmett jumped, and Maggie's foot had barely reached the ground when the reins snapped and the brougham rolled away. They ran down E Street, Maggie in near panic, scalding lungs so in need of air that she was dry-heaving by the time she pushed open the door of number 24.

The blanket partition was pulled aside. Lillian lay on the mattress as the aging, poverty-worn doctor gently probed her legs. "That hurt? . . . feel that? . . . don't you cry, li'l one, don't you cry . . ." Emmett Senior stood helplessly by, hands clasping and unclasping. The shock of little Emmett dragging Lillian into the house, dirtied and sobbing, had done what bitter black coffee couldn't: sobered him. *God, make her well . . . I never touch drink again, long as I live . . .*

The doctor turned from the sickbed, with the dire words "Infantile paralysis." A scream welled up inside Maggie; she refused it utterance. Emmett's arms extended to her, but she would have none of him.

"Nothin' more I can tell you." The doctor's practice on these squalid streets had long since partnered him with despair. "Massage her legs a lot, 'specially that left one. Try to get some feelin' out of it. You know how to take temperature, Miz Rogers?" Maggie said she did. He left a thermometer with her. "You come get me now, it gets higher than it is, you hear?" With a shake of his head, he refused the dollar bill Maggie offered from her purse. "Pay me a quarter, that be fine. You goin' be needin' any money you got, to take care this child."

Maggie and Emmett sat at the bedside of their child throughout that night and many nights until one day the fever and pain were gone.

"That right? You never goin' walk no more?"

"They goin' cut your leg off?"

Little Emmett struggled to wheel Lillian through the swarm of curious, barefoot children gathering on the wooden sidewalk like flies to a plate of sorghum, as fascinated with her means of conveyance as they were with her infirmity. The cart of unraveling wicker was a hybrid of large perambulator and boardwalk chair that the junkman had given Maggie, declining the ten cents she begged him to take.

"You leave my sister be . . ." Little Emmett, fiercely protective, tried to force his way through them. Indifferent to his effort, they clung to the cart, impeding his progress, repeating with the cruel innocence of childhood, "Why cain't you walk . . . ?" "My mama says she seen the paralyzin' befo' . . . you ain't never goin' be able to . . ."

"Am too!"

"She is too," little Emmett defended; the chorus of "Is," "Ain't" continuing as they went up the street. "Nothin' the matter with me," Lillian insisted with bravado. "Jus' been sick some. 'Course I goin' to walk. Not jus' walk, dance!"

"You jus' talkin' . . ."

"Go on, le's see you do it."

Little Emmett tried to prevent her getting out of the cart. "Mama give strict order you jus' to set there . . ." but Lillian felt impelled, not only by the taunts of the children, but by her own growing fear that what they said might be true. During the past weeks, coming out of fever, getting back her strength, Mama and Papa, unbeknownst to each other, had separately stood her on her feet, extending their arms, coaxing, "Come on, darlin' . . . walk . . ." She had cried and shaken her head, begging to be put back in bed.

Using her arms for balance, Lillian thrust herself out of the cart and onto her feet. For an uncertain instant, she stood erect, awing her tormentors into respectful silence. With a swing of her right hip, she extended the right foot out into a firm, strong step. The spectators gasped with approval. She attempted a step with the afflicted left leg. It jerked uncontrollably, as though it had a mind all its own.

She fell. Cried. Crawled . . .

Maggie, rounding the corner, returning with her ubiquitous black case of curling irons from the day's work, found her daughter struggling to rise from a rancid puddle; ran to her, frantically gathering her up; a tigress, tongue-lashing little Emmett and the other children. "What you doin' to Lil'yan . . . Cain't you see my poor baby's crippled?" Maggie carried her back to number 24. Sat on the bed, holding, rocking her child.

"Am I a cripple, Mama?"

"Don' you worry now, darlin' . . . I'm goin' take care of you."

"What 'bout Papa? He goin' take care me, too?"

"Your papa do the best he can, best he can." Maggie would not be the one to give Emmett feet of clay. Every night on her knees she talked it over with her Lord and asked him to help Emmett find and follow the Way. If the blessed Jesus could endure the trip up Calvary, she could certainly carry the cross given her. The Lord knew Emmett was trying. The time immediately following Lillian's having been struck down, hadn't her papa sat by her bed, nights running into days, sponging away the fever, massaging, soothing; and when the pain was intolerable, walking the night away with the child in his arms. When Maggie's endurance cracked, setting her to trembling and crying as though she too were stricken, he had put her to bed and tended them both. It was he who had patiently helped quell the guilt in little Emmett that his sister couldn't walk because he had stayed too long at the nickelodeon. For a while there it had been Emmett's strength they all leaned on, his cheerful, joking voice they woke up to, his grits and chicory bubbling on the stove, his playing the butler for them. ("How will you take your breakfast, madam . . . On a silver tray, with a rosebud? I'm sorry, not the season for rosebuds . . . Got a big, fine sunflower, though . . . Kippers and eggs nice this mornin' . . . Jus' take you time, madam, make up your mind . . . Give you a little secret. Our chef here got no 'magination . . . makes everythin' out of grits . . .") But Emmett couldn't bring life back to muscles that had atrophied, couldn't make his suitcase bottomless. In no time at all his last silk shirt was gone, the silver cuff buttons he prized so and the watch chain went the way of his watch. All he had left of value was the velvet-collared Chesterfield overcoat he had once won in a poker game.

Maggie brought what money there was into the house, but summer was coming on, and soon Washington would be a ghost town. The privileged, including the ladies whose hair she dressed, were quitting the city for luxurious watering spots from Connecticut down to the Carolinas. Each week Maggie's clientele diminished until she was forced to her knees, scrubbing the floors of a hospital.

All this time Emmett had stayed clear of the bottle. There were times when the thirst was on him; she could always tell. But while Lillian burned with fever, some resource within him kept him dry. As soon as the child was only "sittin' up sick," he began to dress each morning in his Palm Beach suit, clean white shirt with starched collar, and go out looking for a job. At first he explained away his failure by the fact that the government was going into its summer slough, hotels were closing; there just weren't any jobs. Which, to a large degree, was true. "But I get me one today, you see . . ." were the words he left with each morning. Every evening he returned, his hat more and more atilt; on his breath, bourbon and mint leaves fighting for supremacy until finally the mint leaves lost. The evening that Emmett didn't come home at all, a porter, still in the uniform of the Baltimore and Ohio, delivered four dollars into her hand. "From you husband," he explained, uncomfortable to be the bearer of so personal a message. "Emmett, he gone off to

Kentucky. Heard they some jobs down there'bouts. Tole me tell you he loves you, loves the children; he'll send money soon's he can."

Grateful that the children were asleep, Maggie thanked the porter and closed the door, accepting the irreversible truth that there was no one to depend on but herself. Still holding the money in her hand, she became aware of the source of Emmett's four-dollar legacy. The velvet-collared Chesterfield was missing from its usual peg on the wall; replaced, no doubt, by a pawn ticket in his pants pocket that would, before long, find its way into the pot of a poker hand or the cashbox of a bartender, in exchange for a shot of raw whiskey.

The month of July was sultry and muggy. All along the Potomac, people suffering from heat sought the river. Small boys, including little Emmett (without Maggie's knowledge, of course), found surcease by diving off garbage scows. On that marshland westward between the White House and the river, there was no relief, night or day. Past sundown, the occupants of the shacks on E Street sat on stoops, feet bare, stripped to undershirts, pettiskirts, sucking on rags dipped in water, or, if by some miracle the wagon went by, a piece of ice. Dragging their quilts out of doors at night to share their bedding with cockroaches and mosquitoes, Maggie permitted Lillian and little Emmett to sleep in the open. While they slept she waved a makeshift fan, circulating the suffocating blanket of moist air above their sweating bodies. Come morning, no matter how little sleep she'd had, she was neatly dressed and on her way to the daily drudgery of floor scrubbing, always admonishing little Emmett before she left to "watch out for your sister now, don' you let her out of your sight . . ."

A world away, in Chicago, the Republican party —fired up by President Teddy Roosevelt's vigorous enthusiasm and with much shouting and waving of signs—nominated William Howard Taft on the first ballot to be their standard-bearer. Three weeks later, at the Civic Auditorium in Denver, Colorado, the Democrats—undoubtedly affected by the lack of oxygen at the high altitude—committed political suicide by a first-ballot choice of William Jennings Bryan, for the third time.

If Maggie, in her comings and goings, heard of these two events, she gave them no thought. Who occupied the White House meant less than nothing to her (except for what she'd heard about Mr. Lincoln). That brutally hot summer, her mind, time, energies were consumed by caring for Lillian. Three times a week the child had to be wheeled up to the doctor on Pennsylvania Avenue. Maggie, in her heart, never got over a basic but unvoiced fear of the machine they attached to Lillian's frail, withered leg. The ominous-looking black box, with dials that had numbers totally foreign to her, shocked electricity, that strange unseen force that until recently existed only in lightning, into the child. It felt something like needles, Lillian said. The whole procedure somehow conjured up to Maggie the image of voodoo. She tried to counteract this satanic influence by faithful visits to the Baptist Church. However, she was in no wise discounting the electricity, taking her blessings any way they flowed.

Lillian seemed to accept the role of invalid. Every morning Maggie helped her into her clothes, brushed her long, soft hair, and sat her in the cart that little Emmett would wheel. Soon her celebrity dulled and the neighborhood took no special notice of her. She would sit for hours, unable to move her cart about when little Emmett wasn't at hand, and watch the gymnastics of the other street children. Strong, bare brown legs, shoeless feet . . . running, jumping, climbing with an ease she dreamed of. Always the terrifying memory stayed with her—an inside scream—right leg forward, left leg, errant . . . *"Cain't you see my baby's crippled?"*

After each treatment the doctor stood her on her feet, arms outstretched, coaxing, "Come on, Lil'yan . . . walk . . . Try . . ." She would endure the charade, secure only when she was back in the cart, to be wheeled home. *"Glissade,"* the dancing teacher's voice reechoed in her mind, *"Glissade, glissade, tour jeté . . ."*

"You not said a word, chile . . ." Maggie guided the cart around a break in the sidewalk, "What you think-'in 'bout?"

"Nothin', Mama."

The passage of summer was marked by two letters that came in Emmett's fine handwriting (he had now moved on to Little Rock, jobs looked promising down there, hoped to have money to send soon, loved them all); by the way little Emmett shot up, a tall, thin weed of a boy; and by the futile visits with Lillian to the doctor. "Not right to keep takin' your money, Miz Rogers. Treatments not doin' her earthly bit of good . . . like pourin' water down a hole."

"Hardly pourin'," Maggie pointed out, "not with me back.-owin' you so much."

"Got to get her out of that cart, Miz Rogers. Cripple her mind right along with her leg. Get her movin' 'round, back into livin' like other children." He would send her to a man who made braces, he said, an understanding craftsman who would permit Maggie to pay over a period of time. With utmost care and gentleness the craftsman measured and fitted Lillian. When finally her leg was trussed up with leather and steel, he said to her, "Walk." She stood rooted, looking down at the ugly contraption. Encumbered by the weight and clumsiness of it, she took one step with her good right foot, and dragged up the left. *"Glissade, glissade . . ."*

Maggie took Lillian's outward lack of reaction to the brace as acceptance. Other matters pressed on her mind. It was barely possible to support her children odd-jobbing. Now with Lillian's continuing medical needs, there was no way to save a penny and get money ahead unless she altered her circumstances.

She wrote a letter to Gran'mama, and a week later received train fare to Keswick. Packing what few clothes she and the children had, she walked out, closing the door on the river bottom shack, never to return. The trolley carried them to Pennsylvania Station where she and little Emmett lugged the suitcases, and Lillian, by now proficient at the *step-lurch, step-lurch* of the brace, boarded the train. Fine steamer trunks, a number of them with Cunard liner labels, were being unloaded. The gentry were coming back in large numbers for the fall, to put their children in schools and pick up the social whirl of the capital. Ladies in lawn and dimity dresses and large flower-trimmed hats, their children, governesses, maids, being met by uniformed coachmen and chauffeurs.

Maggie and her children reached Keswick late in the afternoon. She unpacked their clothes but didn't stay for the evening meal. To leave her babies behind was hard enough and to stay through the night, as Gran'mama implored, would only make the parting that much harder. She kissed them goodbye, resolutely untangled their arms from her neck, and walked away down the road to the station. She was saved the price of a ticket back to Washington by a fortuitous meeting with a waiter friend of Emmett's who was serving meals on the train. She rode back to the city in the kitchen car, where the chef fed her. The talk among the waiters moving back and forth with trays was of who was likely to be the new President— Taft or Bryan. A goodly number of them seemed to favor a man by the name of Eugene Debs, someone Maggie had never heard of. "Don't stand a chance," Maggie heard one of them say. "Socialist. Don't nobody vote a Socialist into office . . ." But they'd sure like to see that Mr. Debs make it. No reason, " 'cep'n he was a railroad man."

It was nightfall when she got back to Washington. She slept in an unobtrusive corner of the depot, sitting up—coming awake twice during the night to move to a different location so as not to appear an itinerant. In the morning, she sponged herself best she could in the restroom for "coloreds," and ate the leftovers the B. & O. chef had given her. She bought a newspaper and soon found herself a job as a live-in nursemaid with extra money for doing the laundry for a well-to-do family in Annapolis.

To get her children back became her all-consuming

passion. The desire to communicate was acute but, as in all things, Maggie practiced a discipline worthy of Scripture. Once a week, on Sunday night, she wrote them each a letter. Between times, when emptiness became unbearable, she took to putting her thoughts in a note pad, never to be mailed. *Little Emmett, I know I been givin' lot of time to Lillian lately, but I don't love you none the less . . . You all be sweet now, you hear? . . . Read your Bible, mind your gran'mama, we find our way back together again . . .*

"Get my babies back" found its way onto the lined paper many times in Maggie's firm, thoughtful script. The dollar sign became a repeated symbol. Working as a live-in, her board and room taken care of, she permitted herself no indulgences whatsoever, hoarding every penny of her pay. Gradually the savings in the small drawstring purse under her mattress grew. Slowly passed the days, weeks. Months.

On the night of November 3, telegraph lines all over the country were jammed so that first edition newspapers could report William Howard Taft having won the election, forever putting to rest the presidential aspirations of William Jennings Bryan. It would be days or weeks before exact figures from all of the states came in, but the majority of popular and electoral votes was sizable enough to declare Taft the next President of the United States. Eugene Debs didn't carry a single state. And the political amusement park closed for the next four years.

Maggie's employers celebrated Taft's victory with a sumptuous dinner. They also celebrated Thanksgiving. Their Christmas festivities spilled over until Twelfth Day, and there was even a warm nightdress under the tree for Maggie, whom the children's mother, of British descent, called "Nanny," and the children's father, southern to the core, addressed as "Mammy."

Late in January a letter came from Emmett postmarked Miami (he had to have been in touch with his mother to know how to reach her). It told of the sun always shining down there, of the bright prospect for jobs, how he loved and missed them all and would send money when he could. Maggie could have read his letters in the dark, they were that much alike. His postscript noted that Lillian's birthday was coming up. She didn't need him to tell her that. February 1 had been looming on the calendar for days now—her baby turning eleven, and a mother not able to mark the day with her. It brooded on her so bad that Maggie asked for and got a day off to go across the river to her own church.

Sunday, the last day of January, she woke at 4:00 a.m., dressed, and hurried to the railroad station to board the first train. Rather than spend any more of her precious savings, she walked the slushy miles from the station on Sixth Street and, heart-heavy, sat in the familiar little clapboard church, seeking comfort in the pastor's message: "The Lord does not burden you with more weight than you can carry . . ."

"Speak to me, Lord," she asked in audible prayer, "show me the way to get my babies back . . ." but there was no answering flash of light. No burning wheel. After the service, Maggie sought out old friends and neighbors, asking if any of them heard of any kind of job where she could support her children and have them with her, please to keep her in mind. A tall order, but they would try. There was one lady who said she had a butler friend who seemed to know where every job was breaking. She would talk to him as soon as she could.

Little Emmett jumped for the overhead branch, swung his body in an arc, crawled onto the low limb of the tree, and hung by his knees. Somersaulting, he landed on his feet and ran off to shinny between the horizontal boards of the fence. The Calhoun boys from down the road, aping his every action, followed him through the contortions of the game, each shouting back to the one following, "Ketch me if you kin . . ." Just one step behind the smallest Calhoun brother, Lillian, undeterred by the brace, boosted herself to the tree with the aid of a fallen log, then grabbed the overhead branch and swung her body up. Since Lillian had to drag that brace everywhere, it was accepted as fair for her to have a little assistance. Crawling out onto the branch as Emmett and the Calhouns had done, she hung by her knees and felt the heady freedom of the pendulumlike action, swinging her head back and forth, her long hair cracking like a whip in the strong March wind.

"Here come Mama . . ." she yelled from her upside-down position, "Mama comin' . . ."

Maggie, riding up the winter-hardened road on the horse-drawn wagon of the friendly sharecropper she'd met on her walk from the Keswick depot, thanked the man, and with a shriek of anxiety ran to rescue her daughter.

"Oh no, Mama, I cain't get down till Emmett get me. I get down the wrong way, I lose. *Emmmmettt . . .*" she hollered, and young Emmett came running back across the field.

Nine months since she'd seen her children. Her arms ached to hold them, and here she was starting out with a scold. "What you doin', Lil'yan, up a tree? You know you not able to do roughhousin' . . . and Emmett, I told you, watch out for your sister, take care of her, she cain't take care of herself . . ." It shocked her to realize Emmett was already taller than Lillian. Time away had robbed her of the right to watch him grow. And Lillian, knees skinned, eyes bright, hair flopping like a small carefree gypsy, seemed a different child altogether from the wan little creature she'd brought here.

"Mama, we finishin' the game . . ." They pulled away from her intense embrace and were off, Lillian in *hop-skip* gait, trailing the boys. When she fell behind, Emmett stopped and carried her pickaback.

"Lil'yan, come back! You get yourself hurt!"

"Let 'em go, Maggie . . ." Gran'mama came hurrying out of the house, wiping her hands on her apron, to greet her. "They jus' havin' theirselves a little fun, let 'em enjoy it, they young . . ." She picked up Maggie's satchel. "Good, you goin' stay the night. Couldn't tell from your letter when you 'spected be here. I already done gone and fed the children but they's supper waitin' on you . . ." Unlike Gran'mama to talk so much. There was an unusual animation about her that Maggie didn't catch right off. The children were out of sight now, their rowdy voices calling out some kind of challenge.

"I'm goin' go get her . . ."

"Don't." Gran'mama's hand on Maggie's was a plea. "Don't make a cripple out of the chile . . ."

"She is crippled."

"Only she thinks herself that way. She got a bad leg," Gran'mama conceded, "but that leg got to take her through life. Best she get herself good and 'quainted with it . . . You sees how strong and bloomin' she come to look . . ." Maggie allowed herself to be urged toward the house, acutely feeling the nine months sliced out of her life. "You the one lookin' poorly, Maggie, powerful thin . . . do you good, you stays here some more than a day . . . sure pleasure me to have you, I already fed the children, got supper on the table for you . . ." And that was another thing Gran'mama never did: repeat herself. "I read in your letter you done gone and got yourself a good job . . ."

"Yes, I did, Gran'mama. Got myself a fine new—" Maggie stepped into the house and understood Gran'-mama's tension. Emmett Senior, wearing an anxious smile and threadbare Palm Beach suit that had lost touch with a pressing iron, stood just inside the door. Where once he had been lean, he was gaunt. Shadows, like smudges of charcoal, pushed bloodshot eyes deeper into his skull. His smile had the characteristics of a tic, deepening a line in his cheek until it appeared almost a gash. Nicotine-stained hands kept seeking each other, pounding in a continuous ballet of the jitters. One of his fine teeth on the farthest stretch of his grin, she noticed, was gone.

Should have known Gran'mama wouldn't let this opportunity for gettin' 'em together go by . . .

"How long you been here, Emmett?"

"Couple days."

Gran'mama, eyes darting from one to the other, sensed the unbridgeable chasm between them. "Maybe you want to rest up a spell, Maggie, 'fore you eat . . . I go out and round up the children . . . sundown comin' on." The door closed behind her.

"You been up here before." It was an accusation filled with resentment from Maggie, as though he was the thief who had stolen the nine months of her children from her.

"Time to time," he admitted.

"You drinkin' 'round the children," she said in disgust.

"No, Maggie, no . . . ain't had a drink all day. That bay rum you smell—went into town to the barber's . . . Well, you comin' back, wanted to look my best . . ." For a fleeting instant his smile was as ingenuous as a boy's, and his eyes filled with appeal. His hands, freeing themselves from their nervous compulsion, were on her arms, stroking from shoulder to elbow; on her waist, telling her the embers within were merely banked, could flare at his touch. She stepped away from him, went to the sink and washed her hands and face. "Children goin' back to Washington with me in the mornin'," she said.

"A man not seen his wife 'most a year, I was hopin' you might say 'Glad to see you, Emmett . . . missed you, Emmett . . . you lookin' good, Emmett'—well, I know that not true, but be nice you lied."

"The five ten." She dished up greens from stove to plate and began to eat.

"Maggie, I love you." His voice was a rasp. She nodded, absently. She knew all about love. All the fancy wrapping. Peel it all down, and all you got left is fear, and being alone. The Maggie who'd stood in front of the preacher with Emmett that day so long ago—that Maggie was gone. She would never come back. She broke the cornbread into small pieces and touched fatback to it.

"Maggie, you changed."

"S'pose so. Leavin' my children behind do that . . . watchin' 'em go hungry, and cold do that . . . And lame . . ."

"Lil'yan's gettin' better all the time, Maggie. You seen her when you come in. She climbin' trees . . . runnin' . . ."

"You think that what life is, Emmett?—climbin' trees? What's to become of her? Hard enough carryin' Negro blood without bein' the way she is. No one 'round to take care of her but me. Nothin' more goin' go wrong for my little girl . . . she not goin' be put out, one place to the other while I go off all hours, curlin' hair and nursemaidin' other people's children . . ."

"I get started again, Maggie . . . you see . . . Lot of places like me, lot of places . . ."

Unable to face his desperation, she carried her dish to the basin, washed it. "Goin' have my babies with me. Goin' see 'em every mornin' for breakfast, every evenin' for supper . . . Now on, Lil'yan's goin' be watched over right. Goin' keep her close with me, rest of the days I got . . ."

"Don't hold on to her too tight, Maggie." But she no longer heard him.

"Got me a fine job, Emmett . . ."

He knew he had lost her, lost them all. Here she was standing just across the room, not eight feet from him, washing up that plate and fork, but it was like she'd gone far, far away. "Fine job," she went on. "Come about, somebody at my church is friends with a butler. Job aready been offered to another woman, but she didn't want to leave her lady. So I carried myself on down to the Department of Interior and they read my references and sent me to a Colonel Brooks and he hired me . . . *Fine* position . . . permanent, they tell me, long as I do my work good . . ." He wanted to call out to her to turn time back, before the paralyzin' . . . before the boozin' . . . to go back with him and fill sand buckets at Cape May . . .

"I'm goin' be workin' at the White House, Emmett . . . can you 'magine that . . . the *White House!*"

When the children came in to be made ready for bed and Maggie said "Kiss your father good night," he held them fiercely to him, sensing it was for the last time, burning into his memory how they looked, felt, the smell of sweet sunshine on their hair. In the morning, when they dressed by candlelight, they wondered why their papa was not in the house, but they were used to his going his own way so it didn't seem to bother them excessively. The sharecropper's wagon was waiting at the end of the path to drive Maggie and her children, bundled up against the sharp gray day, into town. Through a chink in the barn wall, Emmett watched them go from the pallet he had shared with a bottle. Later that same day, he bade his mother goodbye and walked into Keswick, boarding the first train that came through, not even asking its destination. When he finally got off at Mobile, Alabama, it was already Inauguration Day in the nation's capital.

1

▨ ▨ ▨

Washington, D.C. 1909

The blizzard numbed the spectators who waited, some with mustaches and beards icicled . . . Women, hats held on by woolen scarves, received no quarter from the penetrating winds that swirled snow in blinding gusts. The new President, having moments before sworn to faithfully execute the office and to preserve, protect, and defend the Constitution, was heard to quip (on boarding his open carriage) that, judging from the hostility of the elements, the good Lord must be a Democrat.

"Can you see 'im . . . can you see 'im . . . ?" Lillian and little Emmett, bundled to the eyeballs, vied with each other for vantage point only to be met by the obstacle of tightly packed adult bodies that stood between them and the street. Through a forest of trouser legs and skirts, their only glimpses of the Inaugural parade were of horses' hooves and moving carriage wheels.

Maggie, pulling the inadequate capelet up around her chin only to suffer the merciless wind on her lower body, tried to keep up with her children as they trudged down the sidewalk, searching for a hole in the crowd.

"Lil'yan, careful how you walk . . . don't fall, child

37

. . . Emmett, watch for your sister . . ." She grabbed hold of Lillian's collar, but Emmett escaped her, and disregarding her admonitions, shoved his way through to the curb, calling back his observation. "He big and fat and got a mustache . . ."

All Maggie saw that morning of the twenty-seventh President of the United States was the top of a tall silk hat as it passed above the heads of those hardy souls in front of her.

On March 8—four days into the Taft administration—the blizzard had subsided but snow was still sovereign in the city. Huge drifts, no longer virginal, were piled high against the curb. Drivers maneuvered carriages with skittish horses, and motorcars crept along slickened streets.

Maggie stood outside the imposing grilled iron fence and looked at the White House. Clutched in her hand were the precious papers that gave her the right to walk up the path and enter the door designated for servants. Until this moment she hadn't stopped to contemplate just what entering this building would mean to her. She'd passed it many times on the way to her Du Pont Circle ladies. Occasionally she had paused and looked at it, marveling at its size. The two office wings that President Theodore Roosevelt had added to the residence made the building a block long. Now that she was on the verge of going into this formidable place, made even more startlingly white by the snow-blanketed ground, she felt apprehensive. Straightening her already neat skirt, capelet, and hat, she started up the walkway with measured steps, preparing herself to face the baptism of fire. She was unaware of the man coming up the walk until after he passed her, and then she only accorded him a casual glance, noting that he was an ordinary-looking fellow, darker than herself, of medium height and somewhere near her own age. Her interest was caught by the sight of a cow on the White House grounds, peacefully munching from a bale of hay. The incongruity of the barnyard animal in this setting of power made her smile, relieving some of her tension. Resuming her pace, she noted that the man, throwing an anxious look back, was walking faster now. Then, from behind her, a second man, taller than the first but of about the same age and color, came running by, passing her. Grabbing the first man by the arm, he whirled him around. "I tole you about this job," he challenged, "if you think you goin' cut me out of it . . ."

The first man shoved him back. " 'Cause you hear 'bout a job, you own it? They goin' pick the best man . . ."

"And he standin' right here in my shoes." Their accents, it seemed to Maggie, were Georgia. Or was it Carolina? Expecting fists to fly at any moment, she hurried on past them, their voices following her up the walk.

"Don' you play big man with me . . ."

"Who you think you roustin'?"

She hurried on through the little white iron gate, down the steps to the ground-floor staff entrance. "I have a position here," she told the uniformed policeman. "Miz Jaffray is expectin' me."

He nodded her in, gesturing vaguely. "Kitchen, servants' dining room down that way. Housekeeper's office someplace just across from there." The door closed behind her. It was a long hall. Her wet shoes made a squishing sound but she wasn't the first to track up the floor this morning, she noted, wondering if there was somebody in the White House whose exclusive job it was to wipe up muddy footprints. The aroma of fresh baked bread pulled her along in the direction of the kitchen. The fragrance of cut flowers brought her past a small florists' room where baskets and vases were being prepared for the day.

"Are you looking for me? Maggie Rogers?"

"Yes, ma'am," Maggie replied to both questions. It didn't occur to her to inquire if the handsome, well-corseted woman sitting behind the desk of the small, clinically furnished office was Mrs. Jaffray. A lady of conservative Victorian elegance, she was obviously a person of authority.

"Come in. Do you have dry shoes with you?" Mrs.

Jaffray inquired, as Maggie, carefully avoiding stepping on the carpet, handed over her application papers.

"Yes, ma'am, I do. Right here in this sack."

Mrs. Jaffray immediately launched into the catechism of employment. "The hours are six in the morning until four in the afternoon. You will work with the head maid, changing linen, making beds, dusting, cleaning. Mending. Any assistance required by the First Lady, you are to drop whatever it is you are doing and quickly, unobtrusively—that means without being noticed—perform whatever duties asked. Clear?"

"Yes, ma'am."

There was something very special about Maggie's job of which Mrs. Jaffray wanted her to be aware. No colored maid had ever before been employed on the family floor. Kitchen helpers, butlers' staff, coachmen —these were traditionally Negro. But to come into direct contact with the First Family beyond the action of serving a meal, opening a door, driving a carriage, or removing dishes had to this point been unheard of. "You understand the responsibilities of such a thing, don't you?"

Maggie did. Colonel Brooks who had interviewed her had told her all about that. Scrutinizing Maggie's papers, Mrs. Jaffray said, "You are being accorded this privilege, you understand, because your references say you are an excellent beautician." She paused. "Mrs. *Colgate?*"

"Of Dupont Circle."

"I am aware of who she is . . . Why did you leave her employ?"

"Society people go south in winter, across the water in spring, and off to resorts in summer. I got children."

"Yes . . . well . . ." Mrs. Jaffray put the papers into a file, the file into a drawer, and resumed the litany. "There will be no talking in hallways any more than absolutely necessary. No loitering. No gossiping. What is heard within these walls is to be forgotten. No information about the personal habits of the First Family to be repeated on the outside. Understood?"

"Yes, ma'am."

"The salary is twenty dollars a month."

"Twenty . . ." Maggie tried unsuccessfully to hide her disappointment. "I thought, bein' the White House, I'd do better."

"I remind you that twenty dollars from the White House goes considerably further than twenty dollars from, say, Treasury or Census. Here you wear government uniforms laundered with government soap and ironed with government irons. And while on duty your meals will be provided. Clear?"

"Yes, ma'am."

"Yes, *Mrs. Jaffray.*"

Maggie stood corrected. "Yes, ma'am, Miz Jaffray."

"You will change now." Mrs. Jaffray handed her a starched uniform on a hanger, mentioning that if it didn't fit correctly, Maggie could alter it in her spare time. She gave directions on how to find the women's changing room, and a locker key. "This key is given into your care. It is your responsibility to see that your uniforms are promptly laundered. Don't dawdle now, return here as quickly as possible. I want to be finished with you before I tend to my marketing." She picked up the telephone, holding the receiver to her ear as though she didn't totally trust it: "Have the carriage brought around. I will be ready to go to market momentarily."

The changing room, while it was on the same floor, had the isolated feeling of cellar about it—which, indeed, the ground floor was, the White House having been built flat to the ground. If Maggie had walked in the opposite direction she would have come to the magnificently appointed, oval-shaped Diplomatic Reception Room where state visitors entered through Teddy Roosevelt's remodeled door under the south portico, which, until Lincoln's time, had been the front entrance. This end of the floor, where Maggie changed into her uniform, was functional, unadorned except for wooden benches and a plain mirror over the long shelf that served as a dressing table.

She hung away her street clothes in the locker, pinned on the plain, white cambric cap, and tied on

the apron. The uniform was large for her, but regular
eating would help her fill it out. She locked away her
pocketbook, secured the key to the inside of her camisole with a safety pin, and retraced her steps to the
housekeeper's office. Mrs. Jaffray was at a mirror, carefully securing a Queen Mary hat to her pompadour
with a hatpin.

"Promptness is a virtue," she stated, adding, "the
First Lady will be pleased to have someone in the house
to do her hair."

"I be proud to," Maggie said.

"You will be expected to scrub down the grand
staircase each morning." Mrs. Jaffray tucked her
shopping list into her reticule and stepped into the hallway, pulling on her gloves. "Have you had breakfast?"
Maggie was following a deferential step behind. "Well,
have you or have you not? Yes or no?"

"No, ma'am, Miz Jaffray."

"You will eat. We all need our strength here." Moving a short distance down the dark, wooded corridor,
she waited, her back to Maggie, for the door to be
opened: thinking how different her life had become.
Five years back, a husband, home of her own, modest
staff of servants, social position. Then widowhood and
declining circumstances that finally put her into stew-
ardship of this cold stone mausoleum with orders from
Mrs. Taft to "make it into a home." Her private quarters, comfortable enough, were down a T-corridor on
the second floor, but she hadn't yet adjusted to living in
what felt like a hotel, or, at best, an embassy. And this
heterogeneous collection of servants, brought into the
White House under divergent administrations, could
only be described as a motley mosaic of creatures in
desperate need of training.

It took a moment for Maggie to realize that Mrs.
Jaffray expected her to open the door.

" 'Scuse me, ma'am . . . Miz Jaffray."

The dining room where the servants ate was as spare
as the changing room, but the long table, which could
easily seat thirty—and did, at least twice during the
day—belied the stark surroundings with linen table-

cloth and napkins, napkin rings, and stem glasses, bell-like when touched by a snapping finger. The plate and flatware didn't all match, but what there was, was of the finest. Which could also be said of the food.

As the door opened, those seated at table (nine, at this moment) turned and looked, as one. The tall man of color who was serving also paused and glanced their way. Maggie's first impression was that the table drew its own color line. Blacks sat with blacks (though there wasn't a true "black" among them), whites with whites.

"Our new second maid," Mrs. Jaffray introduced from the doorway. "Her name is Margaret Rogers."

"Miz," Maggie amended. "I be called Maggie."

"You will break her in, Annie." Mrs. Jaffray addressed the ruddy, strong-featured Irish woman sitting toward the head of the table, who didn't bother to hide her resentment at having her breakfast interrupted. "And when you have finished for the day," Mrs. Jaffray told Maggie, "I will have a manicure." With a quick glance around, checking on who might be loitering at table, Mrs. Jaffray left to be taken by carriage and coachman on her daily rounds—Center Market on Seventh and Pennsylvania for fine produce, meats, cheese, and butter, then on to Magruders at K and Connecticut for out-of-season foods. Where she was catered to with the same care lavished on the society ladies. It was a ceremony which offered succor to Mrs. Jaffray's wounded ego, since she, in truth, was a servant.

Maggie stood awkwardly, wondering what she should do next. Annie Gilhooley, who had been instructed to break her in, was taking her sweet time, washing down a last bit of scrambled egg with coffee.

Annie, employed at the White House since the time of President McKinley, hadn't been able to warm up to Mrs. Jaffray. There had been no formal housekeeper until the Tafts moved in, and Annie somehow felt her position was being undermined. Things had never been the same since Mr. McKinley (poor soul, burdened with an epileptic wife and then shot down in cold blood). Then that wild man, Teddy Roosevelt, tearing the building apart. Now the Tafts, with everything changing around faster than you could blink an eye. A housekeeper new to the job, and worse, a Canadian. Annie had trouble reconciling herself to "furriners," especially the British. Canadians, she figured, being kin, had to be of the same treacherous tribe even though an ocean separated them. Now this new maid—a heathen black—and her ordered to break her in. Annie knew little or nothing about those cursed by Cain, but she had heard some wild tales about British plantations in Jamaica, and in the African colonies.

She rose partly from her chair, then sat back down, indicating, rather than introducing, the various staff members.

"Coates . . . he's head butler."

By virtue of his position, Coates sat "high at the table," his forty years evident only in the touch of white creeping into the edges of his tightly crimped hair. He nodded, his demeanor announcing that he had been born in dignity.

"Dixon . . . third butler."

Dixon, who also wore the black coat, bow tie, and white shirt of a butler, was a paler version of Coates in all ways. A shade younger, shorter, lighter. Two seats down from the head of the table with no immediate companion on either side—a subtly felt difference between station and race—he nodded, mumbled, "Mornin'." Maggie, still standing, murmuring "How do" to each introduction, tried to hang on to identities. Names went by her. But a pattern was emerging to Maggie. Butlers, servingmen, coachmen—Negro. Housemen and gardeners—white. The Irish clumped together. Mrs. Feeney, first cook, wore her fifty years like a rock around her neck. Housemen: McKenzie, with a face straight off a toby jug and the hirsute hands of a longshoreman; Michaels, large, raw-boned, dark auburn hair slicked down with pomade, in his twenties and still with the shy look of a young farmer not yet used to city ways. Third maid, Maureen, not a day over twenty, endowed with milk-white skin, luxuriant hair, eyebrows and eyelashes the color of red clay. Her clear gaze and smile reached out to Maggie. " 'Tis a pleasure to make your acquaintance, Maggie, I'm sure." It was the first warm greeting from any of the group.

Two short, slight Filipinos sat halfway down the table in self-imposed isolation. Annie identified them as Lubau and Dolores, valet and personal maid to the President and First Lady. Hearing their names spoken they looked up, expressionless, then looked back down to their plates.

"And that there's Viola, third in service in the kitchen," Annie said with finality, glad to be shed of the chore.

Viola, bean-pot dark, gestured Maggie to join her with a finger as thin and bony as the rest of her. In lieu of kitchen cap, her hair was covered with a bandanna not unlike those Maggie had grown up seeing her mother and other house and field hands wear. "You new," Viola said to her. "You set heah'bouts with me. We low at the table."

Maggie pulled back the chair and sat. She'd seen the inside of many luxurious homes, had eaten in some fine kitchens, but to put her feet under a table so nicely appointed was a new experience. She looked around at the others, but they had all resumed eating. Slipping the napkin from its silver ring, she experimentally opened it, placed it on her lap, running her fingers over the hand-hemmed linen.

"Would Miz Rogers care for a popover?" Pleased to hear the melodious accent of a fellow Virginian, she looked up at the servingman. "I be known as Levi Mercer," he introduced himself, turning the coffee cup right side up on the saucer and filling it. She judged him, correctly, to be about thirty, within a few months of her own age. He had an extremely high forehead; he'd go bald early, she thought. Eyes, solemn until he smiled, then his warm copper face lit up. With the deference accorded a guest of an exclusive resort, he presented the napkin-covered bread tray. She accepted a popover, broke it open, buttered it. "And from the hot table," he said, "may I suggest coddled eggs, corned beef hash . . . Smithfield ham?" Unable to cope with the choice, Maggie said just anything would do. He moved the cream pitcher and sugar bowl closer, leaning in to confide, "Know how you feel, Miz Rogers, not been here too long myself. Now why don't you set and let me fix you somethin' nice?" He went off to the steam table with her plate. She could see a part of the kitchen through the curved archway that separated the two rooms. A row of shiny black coal- and gas-burning stoves, dozens of white enameled pans, all sizes, double-racked across the ceiling. Electric light bulb hanging on a long cord, a congoleum floor and an icebox you could walk into, built into the wall. All up-to-date.

"Sure set a groanin' table here . . ." The speaker, Maggie was surprised to notice, was the man who had hurried past her as she came up the walkway. For some moments she'd been vaguely aware of two men standing over at the steam table, filling their plates, but hadn't given them more than a passing glance. Now the taller of the two—the one who had threatened the other with bodily damage if he took away the job —joined the first with friendly insult. "Goin' to need a groanin' table, with you 'round." Both were in full livery: navy-blue trousers with silk stripe down the leg, cutaway tailcoat, striped waistcoat, white tie, and, extending from trouser pocket, white gloves. They announced that they were the new doormen just hired on that morning by the head usher, Mr. Ike Hoover because the new First Lady wanted colored footmen on the door instead of city policemen. Taking the nearest vacant seats, they quickly realized, from the cool looks, that they'd crossed the unseen line into the white section. Even their brethren, the butlers, looked askance at their jackadandy dress. Feeling the tension from both sides, the two rookie doormen picked up their plates and moved down to seats next to Maggie at the foot of the table. Again, forks were picked up and the silent breakfast ceremony continued.

"I'm Mays," the taller of the two confided to Maggie. "This fella here, he Jackson."

"Watch out for him," warned Jackson. "He sweet-talk you . . . don't know too much, but sure talk sweet."

Maggie was puzzled. Didn't she just see the two of them about to come to blows outside?

That was before they found out there were four job openings on the door. "The Pres'dent's lady wanted a welcomin' smile and a man that can really wear a uniform. Nacherly, took me," said Jackson.

"Hired me 'cause I got class," Mays allowed. "Him, 'cause they felt sorry for him."

"You got it backward, boy. Wanted quality on the front door, so they took me. Musta hired Mays for the back door." John Mays and Sam Jackson turned Maggie's mind back to a minstrel show she'd seen when she was a very small girl. In a special way, it bound the three of them together. Their "Mr. Bones, Mr. Interlocutor" quips kept her smiling, made the food go down easier, and kept Levi Mercer, as much an outsider as they with barely three weeks' service under his belt, near them, refilling their cups, wanting to be part of their camaraderie.

The silent Filipinos put down their napkins, pushed back their chairs, and left the room. The President's valet out of earshot, the conversational flood gates opened.

"A cow, of all things—on the White House lawn."

"Well, hardly more outrageous than the roller skatin' the Roosevelt younguns did in the East Room, ruttin' the fine floors."

"True, true, but that was inside the house . . . till reporters got wind of it. That cow's right out there for the world to see."

"You'd think the Tafts, used to palace life, would have more decorum." (Maggie wasn't sure which of the two butlers, so offended by the livestock, was which at this point.)

"Cream comes dear"—this from the Irish McKenzie —". . . might just be the lady's way of savin' money."

"Is it now?" Mrs. Feeney of the kitchen wanted to know. "And do you think they'll be after payin' us more?"

"Don't be holdin' your breath." This from Annie, who looked like holding her breath was a steady way of life. Mays informed the table at large that not since Andrew Johnson, and that nine—no, ten—Presidents ago, had there been livestock on these grounds. But then Johnson had been somewhat of a rustic.

Butlers, housemen, even kitchen helpers of longer tenure looked down the table at him. *A newcomer expressing an opinion?* Mays shrugged good-naturedly and resumed eating. "Jus' somethin' I read," he said.

There was a moment of silence, to put him in his proper place. Then the butlers, who obviously considered themselves the aristocracy of servants, aired their embarrassment over Mrs. Taft having stayed with the gentlemen while they had their brandy and cigars instead of retiring graceful-like with the other ladies. A trend that could bring nothing but censure to the White House.

"Well, somebody had to keep the conversation goin'," Coates (or was it Dixon?) replied. "Can't deny the Pres'dent did fall asleep at his own Inauguration party . . ."

This kind of talk seemed contrary to Mrs. Jaffray's strong admonition against gossiping. As Maggie followed the Irish contingent up the two flights of stairs to their duties, she expressed her puzzlement to Maureen.

"Heaven forbid, 'tain't allowed," Maureen agreed, "but sayin' what's been in the papers, now that ain't rightly gossip, is it?"

The back stairs originated on the ground floor right near the kitchen. They were narrow, of marble that tracked easily and had to be scrubbed often. The newly installed elevator with filigreed cage that would have made a fine aviary (thanks to Teddy Roosevelt) also originated on the ground floor, but no servant was to use it except to bring something up or down too bulky to lug by hand around the sharply turning corners and small landings. The elevator was the exclusive domain of the ushers. Permission had to be granted by that elite group, who maintained offices just inside the grand entrance, took their meals separately, and ushered up the President, his family, and other personages of note.

Both elevator and back stairs ended in a recessed corridor of the second floor (which was actually the third floor, there being the ground floor beneath the main floor). Maggie was to run into other enigmas before the day was over and she took her weary self home.

The day's work was to fulfill Mrs. Jaffray's prediction that "we all need our strength here." Carpet sweepers to run, beds to be made, stairs to climb, dusting, polishing . . .

"Never in my born days" were the words that escaped Maggie as she followed Maureen out of the backstairs corridor into what was known as center hall: a vast central space too long for its width to be considered a room, and yet too massive to be a mere corridor, it was huge, more than half the length of the building. Previous administrations had furnished it like a hotel lobby and called it a hall; the area was made even more awesome by two enormous sitting rooms visible through broad, arched doorways at the east and west limits. And high; two-three men standing on each other's shoulders high, it seemed to Maggie.

It wasn't the dimensions that drew the gasp from her. Middle of winter in Washington, D.C., and she'd walked smack into a jungle. Everywhere you turned were potted palms, tree ferns, orchids, bamboo, alocasia: exotic tropical foliage and flowers on every shelf and surface. The only time Maggie had seen anything remotely like it was a drawing of the Garden of Eden in her Bible. She could believe what one of the butlers had said in the dining room about the Tafts being used to a palace, what with all the oriental furniture, lacquered inlaid screens, tapestries, ivory, and jade about.

"Brought the whole thing, kit and caboodle, from the Philippine Islands, they did," Maureen informed her.

"Just where does this Philippine Island be?"

"Don't rightly know. Someplace far. Mr. Taft was gov'nor there, I think it was, and herself, mind you,

carried on like she was somethin' of a Queen . . ."
Catching herself in the act of spreading gossip about
the First Lady, Maureen quickly amended, "Well,
that's what it said in the papers."

First maid Annie Gilhooley, dispensing brooms and
mops from the service closet, prodded Maggie not to
just "stand there a-gawkin', there's work to be done."

"Yes, Miss Annie."

"And you've no need to be callin' me that. Or
'ma'am' neither. I work here, same as you." Annie
kept her distance from Maggie, fearful of contamination. Whenever she spoke to her it was through pursed
lips, as though she'd just eaten a quince. An overseer,
she was on Maggie's back from the word "go."

*Teak to be polished, until your arms threatened to
fall off* . . . "Ye missed a spot . . . where are your
eyes?" *Beds to be made.* Annie stood in the doorway of
the severely appointed room that Maggie learned was
Mrs. Jaffray's, watching as Maggie carefully tucked
corners, pulled the sheet as taut as skin, plumped pillows. When it was done, Annie took hold of sheet,
blanket, counterpane, and ripped it apart. Again, Maggie made the bed. Again, Annie tore it apart. "Do it
over. Right this time."

What she had sensed in the dining room was all too
clear; it was to be a tug-of-war between them. But
Maggie didn't bend or break easy. The months without
her children, the empty spaces with Emmett, the worry, had hardened her inside. *I can pull hard as you,
Miss Annie, so tug away.*

On hands and knees, Maggie and Maureen crawled
along the floor, rolling up sisal floor mats—the housemen poised with brooms and mops to sweep up the
dust that filtered through the woven straw, and to polish hardwood floors before they were put back down.
"Not straight." Annie derided Maggie's efforts.
"You're rollin' crooked, pullin' it all out of shape.
Roll it back, do it over."

Maggie and Maureen, hoisting the rolled mats between them, climbed the flight of steep stairs to the attic. "Don't let Annie rile ye," Maureen soothed. "She

ain't used to workin' coloreds. Meself, I've no objection. A person's a person." They came up out of the treacherously narrow stairwell into the cramped garret with its sharply slanting roof. The criblike cubbyholes were stuffed to the rafters with leftover furniture and household equipment. As they rolled the mats out onto the floor of the attic's center hall and started to sweep, Maureen wondered, "Would you be Catholic now?"

No. Maggie was a Baptist.

"Saints preserve us." Maureen expressed her distress for Maggie's soul by raising a cloud of dust enough to choke the devil. "I'll pray for you, darlin', just like I do for the President, him goin' the wayward way of the Unitarians."

That day, Maggie swept, scrubbed, polished, seeking no succor from Annie's prodding. Carried piles of used linen down flights of stairs to the laundry room, then all the way back up to the attic storage room for fresh linens, only to be sent back down to the laundry for a forgotten towel. Not once did she complain. Determined to learn everything she could, she kept eyes and ears open, and asked questions. Houseman Michaels appeared, by his frank open face, to be a friendly sort, but, outranked by McKenzie (who was a chip off of Annie's block), he refrained from any comment other than an occasional nod or shake of the head. Maureen, whose spirit didn't buckle to authority, was Maggie's most willing guide, helping her square away which was east and which was west in the center hall. Off the elegant east sitting hall were the "company" rooms where Kings and Queens had rested their heads. *Imagine.* Next to the mammoth Oval Room, which looked out on the sloping south grounds across the Ellipse and on down to the river, was the smaller Cabinet Room with its dark oak furniture and floor, imposing brass chandelier, and heavy picture frames holding faces of dignitaries unknown to Maggie. She paused in her dusting of the mantelpiece to read an inscription that said this room had served the cabinet for every President from Johnson on down to the year 1902. She didn't know where President Johnson fitted—whether before or after Lincoln (her only frame of reference for Presidents), but the room gave her a feeling of permanence. And that's what she was seeking for herself.

Off the corridor that T'd to center hall were the Taft children's bedrooms, but the three of them were away at boarding schools and college. Maggie scrubbed immaculate bathrooms that hadn't been used, with Annie surveillant in the doorway.

It was the west sitting hall that formed the nucleus of presidential living, the First Lady's rooms being directly attached to the hall, the President's room adjacent to hers. Maggie didn't see the President her first day, Mr. Taft having already left by way of the elevator for his office in the west wing annex before the staff arrived on the floor, but judging by the breakfast tray that was wheeled out of his room by the valet, the President was a man of gargantuan appetite. Mrs. Taft was still in her boudoir, being tended by her personal maid.

Annie found dust on the rubbery leaves of a potted tree. Set to wiping each separate leaf, Maggie foresaw an eternal chore in this dense foliage. But leaf wiping, no matter how tedious, was a prayer, according to Maureen, compared to dusting and brushing all the glassy-eyed hairy beasts that President Teddy Roosevelt had on the walls.

Annie found an errant fingerprint and set Maggie again to polishing teak. (It could have been Annie's, for all Maggie knew.) Maggie perched briefly on the edge of a mandarin chair to get easier leverage at her work. "Oh, don't you be sittin' down now," Maureen cautioned. "Never know when Herself is goin' to show up, lookin' over your shoulder . . ."

So there was more than Annie to worry about. There was also the First Lady . . .

The grand staircase was a broad, graceful escalier that began on the ground floor and swept up two flights to end directly opposite the Cabinet Room. President Garfield, felled by an assassin's bullet, was carried up these steps. Alice Roosevelt Longworth and Frances Folsom Cleveland descended to their weddings in the East and Blue Rooms. Union spurs nicked the edges of the stairs and Union sabers scarred the balustrades as their wearers hurried up with dispatches. Ball gowns swept the marble surface of the steps on their way down to galas remembered and forgotten. Teddy Roosevelt had restored this grand staircase to perfection. His children had polished the banister with the seat of their pants. Maggie's aching muscles soon discovered the width of it to be more than her two arms outstretched to their fullest. From wall to balustrade, each stair and riser required at least twenty-four strokes with a soapy brush and rinsing rag. Catch the drips . . . lug the bucket . . . move backward down the steps on your knees . . . *Twenty dollars a month* . . .

"If you work from the corner out rather than toward the corner, you will be more efficient."

Maggie, five steps below, arms soapy to the elbows, looked up at the woman who stood at the head of the stairs. Helen Herron Taft, daughter of the law partner to President Rutherford B. Hayes, twenty-three years the wife of William Howard Taft, former chatelaine of Malacañan Palace, now mistress of the White House, was a handsome woman, full-lipped with a cleft chin, unlined forehead, large expressive eyes, and chestnut hair piled high in a stylish pompadour. A diamond brooch held fresh violets to the shoulder of a mauve wool dress. A small woman, she stood tall, regal, looking younger than her forty-odd years.

"You are the new one." Her voice was mellow but there was no mistaking its ring of authority. Maggie was quick to her feet.

"Yes, ma'am, Maggie Rogers," she said, wiping her hands on the rinse rag.

"Oh yes." Mrs. Taft scrutinized her. "Mrs. Jaffray tells me that you do hair. Whose have you done?"

"Uh . . ." Maggie's tongue reached for the names. "Miz McLean, Miz Colgate, Miz Merriweather . . ."

Mrs. Taft's nod approved the pedigrees.

"And Miz Alice Roosevelt Longworth."

"Really?" Ice coated the word. "You must be a genius to be able to do anything with her hair. We won't mention that name again."

"No, ma'am."

"Do you have your curling irons with you?"

"No, ma'am."

"You will kindly bring them in the future."

"Yes, ma'am."

Mrs. Taft's attention was diverted to a potted banana tree that had been induced to procreate one small, hard, green banana, on which she found dust. "Annie . . ."

Annie came running, pulling a dustrag from her pocket. "Sorry, Mrs. Taft, mum, won't happen again." The First Lady turned away and disappeared into center hall out of Maggie's view. Annie rubbed her cloth over the offending fruit. Maggie, resuming her posture on her knees, went back to scrubbing. When she raised her eyes again to the head of the stairs, Annie was still standing beside the banana plant, looking balefully down on her.

Maggie carefully scrubbed, rinsed, wiped every stair. When she reached the main floor she stepped for a brief moment out into the grand hall. From where she stood, she was able to see into a parlor that couldn't be called anything but the Green Room. Walls, carpet, damask on French chairs, all in shades of green. A crystal chandelier hung from the high vaulted ceiling, catching the light in its hundreds of prisms; huge gilt-framed portraits of Presidents vied for attention. A fragment of the magnificent East Room, with its vast expanse of parquet oak floor, was visible through a stately, draped archway. At the far end of the hall she could see a portion of the State Dining Room, with opulent velvet draperies hanging from molded ceiling to floor.

Maggie continued on down until, finally at the ground floor, she reached the last three steps, which flared in a pleasing design. She scrubbed and dried them and sat down, eyes closed, scrub brush in her lap, wondering how many muscles she must have to set up such a concert of pain within her. Strangely, the most aggravating muscles were the ones in her cheeks, twitching away uncontrollably.

"Are you all right?" The voice, filled with concern, came from a tall man, hair slightly graying at the temples, of such dignified bearing he just had to be somebody important. "No, don't get up. Rest a minute," he said. But she got to her feet anyway, hoping to disguise the crick in her back. "You must be Maggie Rogers."

"Yes, sir, I am."

"Mrs. Jaffray told me you would be starting today. My name is Ike Hoover. I'm the chief usher." She'd heard the name throughout the day, learning that the position he occupied was even loftier than that of housekeeper. But Ike Hoover had not always worn the somber business suit that bespoke his office; he had once carried a lunchbucket and cutting pliers. Having started his tenure in the White House as an electrician during the administration of Benjamin Harrison, he had helped electrify this old building. Every time he turned on a switch and watched chandeliers, that for a century had held candles, leap to instant light, he marveled, and felt proud to have been a part of it. Many times in his own mirror he had seen the drained look of exhaustion that Maggie wore. He knew what it meant to put in a full day of grueling labor. His smile was full of understanding. "Welcome to the White House," he said.

The day was finally over. Maggie struggled back into her street clothes wanting only one thing: to get through the door, down the street, and home. It wasn't to be. Mrs. Jaffray's voice caught her just as she reached the exit. "You haven't forgotten my manicure, have you, Maggie?"

The word "undertaker" had come to be a beacon, as a lighthouse must be to a seaman. Every night when Maggie turned the corner onto Twenty-first Street and

saw it imprinted on the sign that hung over the small
storefront establishment, it told her she was nearly
home. These winter nights it got dark early. "The
hours are from six in the morning until four in the afternoon," Mrs. Jaffray had told her, but it never seemed
to work out that way. If it wasn't some extra job required by Annie, it was a last-minute coiffure for the
First Lady.

The low-watt bulb that burned in the undertaker's
window cast deep shadows on a coffin displayed there.
Without pausing, Maggie looked up at the lighted window directly over the undertaker's. On the sill she
could see a covered mason jar half full of milk and two
small, saucer-covered bowls, and immediately set to
worrying that her children hadn't had their supper. The
next door on the street was half wood, the upper half
glass with one word painted on it: ROOMS. It was never
locked. She pushed it open, quickly closing the chill of
winter behind her, and went up a steep flight of stairs
that was never much warmer than the street. More
accurately, she dragged herself, bone-weary, up to the
one room she shared with her children, finding the doorknob by feel in the unlighted upper hallway.

"You children should have had your supper." She
immediately regretted the sharpness in her voice, and
determined not to inflict her exhaustion on them.

"You said to wait for you, Mama." Little Emmett,
still wearing his outdoor sweater, was at the table with
his schoolbooks, reading by the wavering gaslight
that illuminated the room. Mr. Davis, the undertaker,
had not yet gotten around to electrifying his rentals.
Lillian, who loved warmth, had her little backside up
to the radiator, savoring the minimal heat it gave off.
Not a big room, but snug. And clean. The curtains
were lace, threadbare, but immaculate, and there was
a rug underfoot. Maggie was pleased. She'd gotten her
children up off the ground, away from the eternal mil-
dew, the constant sickness of the old place on E Street.
There was a cot for little Emmett and a three-quarter
bed which Maggie and Lillian shared. An upright pine

wardrobe which served as closet and catchall, a table, three chairs. Nothing extra, but it would do. One day, she vowed, she'd find them a better place, a home, with a real kitchen and a bathroom of their own. In the meantime, the windowsill was their icebox, a two-burner hot plate, their stove, and a basin, their spit bath. They would go down the hall to the commode, and on downstairs to Mr. Davis' to pump water and to use his big cookstove if there was something their burners couldn't handle.

Still wearing her wraps, Maggie threw open the window, quickly bringing in the milk and dishes from the sill, and as quickly closing the window to keep out the cold.

"Emmett, move your schoolbooks. Lil'yan, set the table." Maggie emptied the bowl of cold gravy into the chipped enamel saucepan, lit the burners with a match. She emptied the second bowl of cold cooked grits onto the table and began to cut it into slices for frying.

"You gettin' home later every day, Mama." Lillian pulled herself away from the radiator and went to the task of setting out the mismatched dishes, forks, and spoons. Maggie, observing how unselfconsciously the child maneuvered the braced leg, explained there'd been a tea party at the White House, it was her job to stay and help. "Emmett, stir the gravy so it don't stick."

"Ain't you goin' take your hat off, Mama?"

Maggie removed hat and wrap, hung them in the wardrobe. "Don't say 'ain't' . . . Emmett, buckle your knickers . . ." As he paused to do so, she stirred the gravy and placed sliced grits in the frying pan with pieces of side fat from a bowl. "My children not goin' to have street ways. I have you both to remember you got some of the finest blood in Virginia in your veins . . . One of our kin made it to the State House . . ."

"Why didn't Papa come up to Washington with us? When's he comin' back?"

Lillian's plaint threw Maggie off guard, ripped away the scab covering her own wounds. "Your papa have to find work, child." Abruptly she changed the subject. "You children come straight home from school, like you s'pose to?"

"No fun, jus' settin' in this room every day, doin' homework."

"Papa's goin' send for us to Cape May," Lillian assured little Emmett, who "allowed" that till Papa did, they were stuck here. Maggie bit back the words that Cape May was a pipe dream, like all the dreams their papa had put in their heads.

"An' you didn't disturb the people downstairs?" Maggie continued, as though no other thought had entered her mind.

"How we goin' to disturb 'em?" Emmett wanted to know. "They 'most all dead down there."

"Don't you go mockin' the dead now. Honest profession, undertakin' . . . You do well, Emmett, to get such an upstandin' position, time comes you to take care of your sister . . ."

"I'm goin' take care of myself. Papa say they's nothin' I cain't do, I want to . . . he say I can be anythin' anybody can be. Even a jockey, he said, should I choose . . ." Little Emmett took exception to this, Lillian being a girl. For himself, Papa had told him he could be a general . . .

"An' tell you what else Papa said," Lillian continued.

"Don't matter none what your papa said . . . he a moon away!" The cutting edge to Maggie's voice put distance between her and the children, pointing up the disparity between her exhausted, tense mothering and the remembered easygoing style of their papa. It set her to missing his fun, his laughter, his bed. How could she ever explain to them the complexities of Emmett Rogers? That last night in Keswick she had stood by and listened while Emmett filled their heads with impossible visions. (*"Don't you forget, my li'l Lil'yan, you can be anythin' you want to be, don't you let nobody tell you you cain't . . ." "Even a dancer, Papa? . . ." "That what you want, sweetheart? Well, you jus' keep on believin' . . ."*) When Maggie had taken him to task for it, he'd said, "It's all I got to my name to give the chile. Had to give her somethin' . . ."

Maggie dished up the food. The children ate, silently, obediently, showing little appetite, yet she knew them to be hungry. Regretting her irritability, she attempted to heal the breach by bringing to the table a small, napkin-wrapped package. "Brought you a little surprise . . ." She put it before them, disclosing two sweets. "Petits fours. Save 'em for dessert now."

"Fours?" Little Emmett puzzled. "They's only two of 'em."

"Well, that be the name of 'em . . . My, they was a hundred or more of them pretty little cakes at that party today . . ." She sat with them, but was too worn out to eat. Little Emmett stared at his plate, Lillian made gullies in the gravy with her fork. It would take more than a bit of pastry to unseat their papa from the table. Maggie wanted to shout *"Look at me . . . cain't you see I'm the one tryin' so hard for us?"* Instead, she blanketed her feelings with talk about the White House. Not the work and the fatigue, but the grandeur of it. "Fine, big rooms. Tall windows. I declare, some of those rooms I thought I was in one them fine churches in the picture books. Chandeliers shinin' like a pile of diamonds . . ." They listened politely, but not with the wonderment she'd hoped to instill. Their minds were back in Keswick, romping with their father. "They tell me over there I can bring you to the White House one day, soon as I get special permission. My, my, that party today in the Red Room . . . everythin' so fine . . ." Fatigue led her over to the bed. She sagged, eyelids shuttering. Still she talked. "Walls was red . . . carpet . . . silk wallpaper . . . and curtains . . . all the way . . . up . . . to . . . ceilin' . . . red . . . You children clean up, hmmm, you finish eatin' . . . you do that for your mama?" Her body gave up the struggle to remain awake. "Red . . . everythin' . . . red . . ."

She was asleep, the lower part of her body still sitting, the upper part fallen over onto the pillow. The children observed her for a moment, then pushed aside their plates and ate the petits fours. Later, she woke to find herself stretched out, still fully clothed. The dishes had been washed and put away. Emmett was already in his cot. The doors of the wardrobe were open, providing a screen of privacy for Lillian to undress. In the space below the doors, Lillian's feet and calves were visible. Scuffed, black high-topped shoes. Black stockings. The skirt of her nightgown dropped into sight, covering the ugly steel and leather brace. When she came to the bed, Maggie helped her remove it, noting as she did that Lillian was outgrowing the appliance. There would soon have to be money found from somewhere to replace it. Maggie tucked her children in, kissed them, blew out the light from the gas fixture, and undressed in the dark. Then she crawled into bed to lie awake beside her crippled daughter, worrying about making ends meet.

Life took on a pattern. Up before dawn. Dressing under the covers to keep warm. Getting little Emmett out from under the quilt to go down to Mr. Davis' furnace and put a scuttle of coal on the fire for the twenty-five cents a week the undertaker paid him. Preparing the morning grits, checking the children's clothing for the day; always leaving with the admonition to come straight home from school, do their homework, not bother the people downstairs, and never forget they "come from good blood." And Maggie would be off to the White House while streetlamps still burned, often having to forge a path through snowdrifts that had obliterated sidewalks during the night.

She developed endurance to Annie's dour countenance and critical eye, and to Mrs. Jaffray, who took to appearing when least expected, like an eagle focusing on a ground squirrel, especially when Maggie was at the daily drudgery of scrubbing down the grand staircase, and to the unremitting labor, although her muscles still told her "Enough, enough" at the end of the day. While she still sat low at the table, her reputation for hard work was gaining her respect from most of the staff.

Breakfast was probably the best part of the day. (*"Would Mrs. Rogers care for the blueberries this mornin'?"*) At first her guilt at eating heartily, even luxuriously, while her children were consigned to grits made it intolerable to put the food in her mouth. It was Mercer who informed that it was acceptable, even expected, to "tote"; elsewise, leftovers from banquets, dinners, and receptions got thrown out.

After that, she ate with relish, and began to fill out her uniform, and her children had supper every night.

It was also Mercer who put the hothouse rose beside her plate the first (freezing) day of spring. He'd got it from the florist room, he said. "It jus' goin' to get thrown out, I didn't put it beside somebody's plate."

"You know I'm a married woman, Mr. Mercer."

"Yes, Miz Rogers, I do believe I know that. What will it be this mornin' . . . a nice breakfast steak? Warmed up from last night's dinner party, but I assure you it's from a fine cut of beef . . ."

Mays and Jackson livened up the low end of the table with their morning funnin'. "I let in Mr. Philander C. Knox," Mays bragged, "and everybody who is anybody knows he is the Secretary of State."

"Well come now," Jackson countered, "I let in a cabinet member myself just yesterday. Mr. Charles Nagel, Secretary of Commerce and Labor. Now that is somethin' you wouldn't know much about, Mays—commerce and labor."

"You comin' on like that, Jackson, 'cause you jealous my cabinet member outranks yours. Naturally, such a high official would arrive when I be on the door. Style . . . gets 'em every time . . ."

A warm breakfast and a laugh helped prepare you for the long hard day that lay ahead.

"If I may say so, Miz Rogers, you lookin' much better these days," Mercer told her after she'd been there going on three weeks.

"Why, thank you, Mercer." She had pushed back her chair to leave the room, but he seemed to have something further to say, so she delayed until most of the others had left. "Wanted to tell you," he said, "we all proud you workin' upstairs. First colored lady to do that, you know."

"I know."

Mercer confided that he had ambitions himself in that direction: to be transferred upstairs as houseman, or valet.

"Hope it works out for you."

"Thank you, Miz Rogers." Again he found reason to detain her. "You ever seen the President? I never have. Been here six weeks now, never once did see him."

"Oh, I have seen Mr. Taft." Maggie realized she'd made it sound as though she saw that august gentleman every day. Being a woman of honesty, she couldn't let the untruth go by. "But barely," she amended (if the word "barely" could be applied to a man as huge as William Howard Taft). "Twice now, I have seen him —walkin' from his room to the elevator, goin' to his office, I guess. Was gettin' some cleanin' rags out of the supply closet, so I was right there beside the elevator. He said 'Good mornin' ' to me, pleasant as can be . . ." At the door, she said, "Mornin' to you, Mercer."

"Mornin' to you, Maggie."

Mrs. Taft sat at her dressing table, wisps of smoke rising from her hair. No matter how close to her scalp the curling iron came, she never flinched, so implicit had her faith in Maggie's ability become. It was always a welcome respite for Maggie to be called from her labors to the First Lady's suite. It smelled of perfumes, eau de cologne, and Chinese silks; everything in shades of plum and orchid. The Philippines, which seemed to mean so much to Mrs. Taft, were represented by heavy carved rosewood furniture. And twin beds, so up-to-date. First time they'd ever been used in the White House. Maggie learned to keep her black satchel of hairdressing equipment nearby, as a doctor would, enabling her to respond quickly to a summons. She was often called from breakfast to hurry up the stairs, through the west sitting hall with its Victorian velvets, to the First Lady's chamber to create or repair a coiffure while that elegant lady conducted her business. In delicate crepe de chine negligee, hair loose about her shoulders, the gossamer quality she projected seemed, to Maggie, in sharp contrast to her purpose and determination.

"You must realize"—Mrs. Taft spoke to a mirrored image of chief usher Ike Hoover—"that every move the President makes is written up by those dreadful newspaper people?"

"Yes, Mrs. Taft, I am aware." Ike Hoover stood before the fireplace in the First Lady's boudoir, replying to the voice that came to him from behind an ornate coromandel screen. From the opulent dressing room just off the bedroom she was able to see his profile by means of a series of strategically placed mirrors, but she herself could not be seen. It gave her the rather unique advantage of appearing to be omniscient.

"Mr. Hoover, we cannot have them ridiculing the President, you do understand that?"

"We do everything we can, madam. I assure you that none of the servants gossip."

Maggie waved the curling iron over a Bunsen burner to keep it hot while Mrs. Taft scrutinized the day's menu. "No, no, not fried oysters *and* rack of lamb," she reprimanded Mrs. Jaffray, who, being a woman, was permitted audience in the dressing room. "The President suffers from gout as it is. You have been made aware of that fact."

Mrs. Jaffray flushed at being corrected in front of the colored help. "Yes, madam."

And if any of the kitchen staff sneaked food again to the President, they were to be summarily dismissed. Was that clear? Mrs. Jaffray agreed that it was. "The newspapers, with all those dreadful cartoons about the President's weight . . . I can't bear to have him ridiculed that way . . ." Mrs. Taft's gold pencil briskly altered the menu. "Poached Nova Scotia salmon with egg sauce . . . game hens, consommé royal . . . The *simplest* of state dinners from now on, Mrs. Jaffray."

"Yes, madam."

"Mr. Hoover, are you still there?" Mrs. Taft queried the mirror.

"Yes, madam." Ike Hoover shifted position slightly to be better seen.

"You have a list of the President's appointments for the day, I hope. And you will see to it that he keeps them?"

He did, and he would. From his breast pocket he produced a folded sheet of paper which he held up for her to see. Never again would he be without a list. Not after the embarrassment of the previous day when the President, forgetting which visitor he was to meet in which room, had left them all cooling their heels and eventually been discovered by an ambassador napping in the Blue Room with the remnants of a smuggled meal before him. A breach of diplomacy certain to make the papers. Tongues were still wagging over Mrs. Taft's liveried doormen. (PRETENDERS TO ROYALTY, the newspapers put it. WHITE HOUSE NOT MALACAÑAN PALACE.)

"Are the men ready for inspection?" Ike Hoover assured her they would arrive momentarily, and left to expedite matters.

The grousing in the men's changing room never reached the second floor, but dissatisfaction was evident in their postures as they lined up in the west sitting hall. The housemen had never before been mummified in boiled dickey, waistcoat, tailcoat, and monkey stripe down the trousers. And white gloves? How were you supposed to scrub and clean in such a getup? The butlers, Coates and Dixon, who hadn't withheld their contempt for the new, overdressed doormen, now were eating their words. Ushers, who had always worn business attire, felt like circus ringmasters . . .

"Straighten up, men." Ike Hoover went down the line, adjusting a tie, shoving the hard edges of a dickey out of sight. "I know we're all a little uncomfortable, but we'll get used to it."

When Mrs. Taft finally emerged from her suite, coiffed and gowned for the day, fresh violets pinned to purple velvet, she moved along the line, a field marshal reviewing the troops. "Yes," she murmured, "oh, yes, that's more like it . . . *Now* the livery befits the dignity of the White House. Thank you, Mr. Hoover." He nodded dismissal and turned to follow the last man out. She signaled for him to remain. "The bald one with the beard," she said.

"Yes, madam. His name is Swenson. A new usher. Just hired on this morning."

"Dismiss him."

"Whatever you wish, madam." If Ike Hoover found the order unusual, he didn't comment. *Harrison, Cleveland, McKinley, Roosevelt, Taft.* Each administration had its own peculiarities, he had learned in the service of five Presidents and their ladies. An order was an order. For whatever reason, Swenson would go.

It was Maggie to whom Mrs. Taft confided her motive. More accurately, it was to her mirror that she spoke as Maggie reset a rebellious strand of hair. "They're bad luck, that's what they are. Won't have them in my White House."

"Ma'am?"

Mrs. Taft viewed the repair in a tortoiseshell hand mirror. "In the Philippines, we had a bald-headed servant with a beard. Tropical storm almost swept the palace out to sea, and us with it . . ."

"You don't say, ma'am."

"And another time, in Cuba, where Mr. Taft had gone to put down the revolution . . . There were bearded staff members there and the Marines had to rescue us from the rebels. I will not permit that kind of jinx following us into the White House . . ."

Spring was short and pleasant. Mrs. Taft received three thousand cherry trees as a gift from the mayor of Tokyo and supervised their planting along the Potomac. The newspapers said they would never grow. Evenings, the President and First Lady spent time out on the south portico to catch the breeze that came up from the river. Sometimes, having helped in the pantry, Maggie would leave after twilight. She would hear Mr. Taft's graphanola playing some of the new songs, "Meet Me Tonight in Dreamland" and "I Wonder Who's Kissing Her Now," and she knew that he and Mrs. Taft were dancing. Leastwise, that's what the butlers told her. She tried to picture that huge hulk of a man doing the fox-trot and one-step. But the butlers said he was light on his feet and the newspapers printed pictures showing his agility with golf club and tennis racket. Once she'd seen him out the window, cantering away on a horse. It was about as close as she ever got to the President.

Summer came, hot and unrelenting. The Taft children came home from schools and college. They were barely unpacked when trunks and suitcases were again brought down from the attic for the First Family to escape Washington's inferno at their summer home in Beverly, Massachusetts. Maggie and Maureen were delegated to find the electric fans—which were, of course, in the farthest corner of the last cramped, cluttered room in the attic. That seemed to be the unwritten law of the White House, that whatever you were scrounging for, you had to wade through every bit of stored furniture and tucked away, unwanted equipment to get to it. It was suffocatingly hot up under the sharply slanting roof. Both were almost to the point of heat prostration when they finally descended the steep attic stairs. "The Bible would have you believe Hades is the hot place," Maureen said. "I say, the devil's never been to Washington in summer."

Annie, who was waiting for the fans at the foot of the stairs, refused to touch the infernal machines. Nor would Maureen handle them beyond carrying them down, electricity being an instrument of Satan. It fell to Maggie to clean them off and plug them into the wall. Turning at full speed, they barely stirred the sluggish air, but what relief they brought was gratefully received. Housemen, washing windows, sweeping, cleaning, miserable in full livery, popped out of bedrooms into the center hall for a quick stir of air, then went back to their chores. The maids, no less uncomfortable in the prescribed long sleeves and buttoned-up necks, sweated profusely.

Finally, a parade of luggage was borne by Lubau, Dolores, housemen, and butlers out of the Presidential Suite. They descended the grand staircase with all the personal effects the family would require for the summer. Mrs. Taft, in a delicate summer gown and large leghorn hat, emerged from the room, followed closely by Mrs. Jaffray, whose clipboard had become as much a part of her costume as the stays in her corset.

"Helen . . . boys . . ." Mrs. Taft called out, as, from several directions, she was joined by daughter Helen, eighteen, with the promise of great beauty; twenty-year-old son Robert Alfonso, budding lawyer whom the White House would only see in brief forays from Yale and Harvard, and Charles Phelps, the same size and age of little Emmett, Maggie realized. She gave him a big smile. He surprised her by returning a wink. As the family and Mrs. Jaffray moved to the elevator where Ike Hoover waited to take them below, Mrs. Taft could be heard telling Mrs. Jaffray, "Now take good care of the President, and see to it that he eats sparingly . . . *sparingly!*"

The elevator mechanism connected. The *whirr* of machinery told them that the coast was clear. Work in the center hall came to a dead stop as housemen and maids emerged from bedrooms. The men stripped off livery: gloves, coat, tie, dickey, waistcoat, until they were down to their sweat-soaked undershirts; the women rolled up sleeves, opened necks. There weren't enough fans for all, but they took turns, stepping in front for an instant of relief, then back to work.

"Maggie, you'll be the one comin' back tonight," Annie informed her.

"Me? Why? What for?"

With half the staff off to Massachusetts, somebody had to turn down the President's bed and turn on all the lights, and it wasn't about to be Annie or Maureen, who hadn't left their superstitions behind when they came to these shores.

Maggie had hoped to spend the evening with her children. She wanted to sit on the curb with them as night fell and watch the stars. By the time she arrived home the sun was almost gone, but its heat lingered in the brick sidewalk, reflected off whitewashed walls. The undertaker's front door was open. The ice truck was backed to the curb, its horse seeming to sag underneath the ridiculous straw hat he wore. The iceman and Mr. Davis were each urgently carrying large amounts of ice into the morgue.

"Evenin', Mr. Davis."

"Evenin', Miz Rogers."

To the iceman she said, "You goin' be 'round awhile, I could use 'bout ten pounds." Mr. Davis was practically cleaning him out, he informed her, but he'd sure save her some. She climbed the stairs, went down the corridor to their door, pulling off her hat and opening her shirtwaist as far down as was decorous, calling, "Lil'yan . . . Emmett . . ." Neither was in the room. She called their names out the window. Mr. Davis, shouldering fifty pounds of ice on a gunnysacked shoulder, paused to inform her that he hadn't seen her children in quite a spell. Did see her boy goin' in and out, but hadn't seen Lil'yan since late afternoon.

Oh Lord, Lord, you tell 'em stay, they don't stay . . . Anxiety, coupled with the stifling heat, made the room unendurable. She doused her wrists in the galvanized washtub that sat on the table, where a dwindling chunk of ice cooled a mason jar of milk, a piece of fatback, some greens. At the first sound on the stairs she threw open the door, ready to chastise, " 'Bout time you children—" But little Emmett was alone, guilt written all over him. Barefoot, his shoes tied together and slung around his neck, hair slicked down, wet rolled-up knickers convicted him even before he was charged. He'd gone off to the river against all orders, and left his sister behind.

"Jus' went for a little while, Mama . . . told her I be right back . . . don' know where she be . . . been lookin' all over for her . . ." He could almost feel Papa's old razor strop in Mama's forceful hand on his bare behind. He'd almost welcome it to take away the awful feeling that if something was to happen to Lillian, it would be his fault.

She'd go to the river . . . fall in . . . her brace wouldn't take her across the street in time . . . somebody would run her over . . . The worry that Lillian couldn't take care of herself was always with Maggie. And the way little Emmett was trembling, the same fears had to be in his head. Maggie was torn between comforting the poor child and whaling the daylights out of him. But wasn't she the one to blame? Going off, leaving them from morning till night—him, just a young boy, asked to look after a crippled sister? Couldn't expect children to just stay cooped up in a room, 'specially in weather like this . . .

"You goin' to whup me, Mama?"

"I'm goin' out lookin' for your sister. You stay here, case she come back before I do. I'll figure out what to do about you later." He would have to suffer the torment of not knowing his punishment.

Quickly buttoning her shirtwaist, Maggie leaned across the bed to pick up her pocketbook from where she'd dropped it. Panic left her. Something even emptier took its place.

A length of pink ribbon extended from underneath Lillian's pillow. Maggie pulled on it, knowing what would be at the end. A small, worn ballet slipper. She hadn't seen it in over a year; had no idea where Lillian had kept it hidden. A day long past, back at the shack on E Street, replayed itself in her mind: finding the pair of ballet slippers thrown out for the junkman, of knowing it was Lillian who had abandoned them. Who had brought them back in? Her papa? That would be like Emmett, to keep a dead dream alive. And where was the other slipper? Had she kept just one? A child with only one good leg?

Maggie picked up the slipper and held it close to her. "Oh, my poor, poor baby . . ."

She found Lillian, as she knew she would, at the dancing school. It was unthinkable to her that anyone would dance on so blistering a day, but the teacher had transported her embryonic ballerinas into a state of euphoria that transcended weather, poverty, and minimal talent. It had even transcended Lillian's infirmity. There she was, right in the center of things, holding onto the *barre* with one hand, her movements made grotesque by the burden of the brace. Each little girl had a length of gauze dangling from one hand.

They were in a meadow somewhere, in a field of fragrant flowers.

"Feel 'em," said the teacher, "under your feet . . . point your toe . . . point it, feel it . . . Smell 'em, my, don't they smell grand . . . An' the breeze, wavin' your scarf . . . Let the scarf go with the breeze . . . arch your body . . . sway with the breeze . . ."

Sweat ran in rivulets down their faces, matted their hair to their heads. The dancing teacher's tunic was plastered to her body like she'd just been raised from a river baptizin'. The lady at the piano had her skirt hoisted way above her knees and alternately mopped her face and thighs with a rag at each measure's rest.

Maggie endured the last moments of the class, observing the grace of her child's hands and torso, the delicate way she held her head, the lovely extension of her supple young arms . . . while the braced leg bound her to the earth.

"Come, chile . . ." She extended her hand to Lillian, who obediently returned the scarf to the teacher. Before they left, Maggie opened her purse and found a nickel to pay for the lesson. In silence they walked back to the room over the undertaker's. Little Emmett waited in apprehension while Maggie helped Lillian wash and change into a fresh dress. Maggie kissed little Emmett, relieving him of his guilt. Then she and Lillian went back to the White House together.

2

William Howard Taft remained in the Oval Office well past the usual hour. Heat was an enemy to a man whose weight was in excess of three hundred and fifty pounds. Any unnecessary movement had to be well considered. Being first and foremost a jurist, he found arguing the case with himself a pleasant diversion.

With his family gone to the country for the summer, he could stay in his office far into the night. No obligation to sit down to a disciplined dinner, supervised by his loving spouse—but without her the place was so confounded empty. He had sent his good friend Archie Butt home, a decision he now regretted, but you couldn't impose on an aide to stay after hours just to fill up the empty spaces. Here he was in the highest office in the land. There were many who, at the drop of a hat, would gladly change places with him. But would any of them be so eager if they knew what a steam bath this White House could be? He smiled: Did it ever occur to the public that the President of the United States sweats?

Refusing to let any of his aides turn on the lights, he let night fall and sat in the dark, looking out the window to the sweeping south lawn, and wondered how

many Presidents had sensed the invisible bars at the
windows. Then he turned his mind to what he would
have for dinner.

Maggie brought Lillian back to the White House
with her as a protective measure, she told herself.
But the truth lurked in the back of her mind. It was
her own conscience she was assuaging. She had taken
this job to have her children with her, but she was able
to spend less and less time with them. As she switched
on the boudoir lamp that gave the presidential bedroom a soft rosy glow, and turned back the sheets in
the perfect V Annie had drilled into her, she wondered if she would be delegated to do this job all
summer. She plumped the President's pillows and returned to the center hall where Lillian perched on the
edge of one of the mandarin chairs, surrounded by
plants that so dwarfed her that she looked like a little
bug on the edge of a leaf. "Now you set there. Don't
you leave that chair now," Maggie admonished as she
prepared to go downstairs and turn on all the first-floor
lights. "I expect to find you where I leave you . . ."

"Mama, what's that over there?" Lillian had been
twisting around in the chair for minutes, trying to see
past a potted stand of bamboo to something large,
white and porcelain. And what was it doing in a jungle?

"It's a bathtub," Maggie confirmed. "For the President. Goin' to be installed tomorrow. None of *your*
business. Don't you move from there." After Maggie
disappeared through the foliage and down the grand
staircase, Lillian sat calmly for a while. Powerful curi-
osity to see that bathtub at close range overtook her.
With a glance around to assure she wasn't observed, she
slid off the chair and limped over to it. It was the biggest thing she'd ever seen. Longer by two feet and wider
by four than the bathtub downstairs at Mr. Davis' where
Maggie bathed her children once a week—bigger even
than the bathtubs she vaguely remembered from summers way back at Cape May. *Big as a boat* . . . With
that thought, she hoisted herself up onto the edge and

slid down into it. She was lying flat on her back, eyes closed, floating down a river, when the deep, resonant voice came.

"Well, well, well . . ." She opened her eyes and looked up at a behemoth of a man. From the depths of the tub he appeared to be a giant. His chuckling rippled a corpulent stomach. "What have we here, little lady in white—a ghost? It isn't often, you understand, that I find such a treasure in my bathtub." At her futile attempt to climb out, the giant set down the sheaf of papers he was carrying. "Allow me to assist you." He gently picked her up in his huge arms, conscious of her braced leg, and stood her carefully on her feet. "How do the newspapers do it?" he asked, as though he really cared for her opinion. "How in thunderation did they find out I got stuck in the bathtub and had to have a special one made? Oh, the cartoonists will have a field day with this one. Sixteen hundred Pennsylvania Avenue is just one giant sieve, you know that, don't you?"

Awed almost beyond speech, all she could articulate was, "You the Pres'dent . . ."

"At your service, mademoiselle." Lubau was at that moment arriving from the elevator with a rolling table that groaned with food. As it disappeared into the presidential suite, William Howard Taft offered his arm to Lillian. "Will you do me the honor of taking supper with me?" adding at her hesitation, "It's quite all right. My family is off to Connecticut. I could use some stimulating company."

"I'm not s'pose to get off that chair," she told him.

He took the matter under advisement. "Well now . . . to my legal mind it appears you were already off the chair, so the crime has unquestionably been committed. What you need is a good lawyer. And the condemned is always entitled to a hearty meal." She didn't understand, but there was no mistaking the gentleness in his tone, the wry laughter that lay behind his eyes.

For Lillian it was an evening of excesses. The biggest tub, the biggest man, the biggest meal. In the President's sitting room with its massive oak furniture, paneled walls, fine leathers—whole walls of books all in the same red binding—Lubau set out a staggering contraband repast: cracked crab on ice, cold roast tenderloin, lobster, glacéd ham, asparagus tips, German potato salad, a monument of molded ice cream, cakes, pastries, fruit, coffee, and a huge beer mug buried in ice.

The President held a chair for Lillian. "See . . . I couldn't possibly eat all this food by myself, although I would give it my best effort. Have I your permission to remove my coat, little ghost? And my tie?" At her nod he even removed collar button and collar, as he took his place at the table. "Hate the infernal heat," he went on. "Hot like this all the time in the Philippines. Loathed every minute of it. Mrs. Taft seemed to thrive on it. Never understood that about her . . ." Even in the direct air stream of the electric fan, the President continued to be uncomfortable, but the food served as a palliative. "What do you favor, my dear? Crab . . . lobster . . . éclairs? Hm . . . how about some ice cream? Lubau, give the lady some ice cream. No, no, Lubau, that's not enough for a fly." The President reached across and tripled the portion. Gran'mama had always said, when Lillian took too much on her plate, that her eyes were bigger than her stomach. Judging from what went onto Mr. Taft's plate, and the size of his stomach, Lillian figured he must have the biggest eyes in the world.

"So you're the ghost of the White House . . ." The idea seemed to please him. "I've heard they were in the walls, never saw one before you . . ." Between each sentence, he took a mouthful. "Hear them in the night, walking. They say the ghost of Lincoln is still in here. And Thomas Jefferson." He cracked a lobster claw and carefully removed the delicate meat, sucking the claw dry of its juices. "Why they'd stay around is beyond me. Anybody who holds down this job ought to be grateful for the chance to get away." With the intensity of a chess player he studied the platter and made his moves, replenishing his plate as he talked. "Thought of cornering one of them some night, to see

if they've got any answers about pleasing both business and the farmers on reduced tariff. The two percent
income tax—nobody's going to take kindly to me for
that. And my support for the labor movement. You
should hear what they call me!" For the first time his
fork was not in motion and he seemed to have lost his
appetite. But not for long. "Please forgive my bad
manners, my dear. Here am I with such a charming
dinner companion and I do nothing but complain.
I've not even asked your name . . ."

"Lil'yan, sir . . ."

"Pretty name."

"Thank you. My mother called me after Miss Lil'yan
Russell. She fixed her hair once."

Taft's eyes lighted in appreciation. "Now there is a
beautiful woman." As he drank a draught of beer he
smiled at her over the rim of the glass. "I wager you'll
be a beautiful woman when you grow up."

"Yes, sir. I'm goin' be a dancer."

Levity deserted him. "You be the best you can be,
my dear . . . be what you have to be."

"Yes, sir. My papa, he say I can do anythin' . . ."

He studied the ingenuous, trusting face. "Don't let
anybody, no matter how well intentioned, turn you
away from your rightful path in life . . ." For an instant, the words seemed directed to himself. A deep
sigh, then he was back to the joys of the table. "You're
not eating. Aren't you hungry, Lillian? All children are
hungry."

"Oh, yes, sir."

"Well then, enjoy it. Don't be shy."

Lillian had hungered for the ice cream from the moment she sat down, but timidity and astonishment at
being at the table with the President had held her back.
She dipped her spoon into it, carefully separating the
chocolate swirl from the other flavors. She had tasted
ice cream before. At Keswick, at the plantation house
of the Randolphs where Gran'mama once took her, she
had helped cut up the peaches and turn the crank to
freeze it. Late one night just after she got the paralysis,

when Papa hadn't the money for the rent, or to buy greens, he had brought home a quart of chocolate. They had all sat up in bed and eaten it.

The ice cream was thick and smooth in her mouth. She held it, letting it melt slowly, wanting to savor it a long time. Gradually hunger overtook her and she was digging into the plate with gusto when a polite knock sent Lubau across the room to open the door. Maggie stepped across the threshold. She'd been in this room almost daily, to clean, to wipe off the inkwells and pen-holders, and to assist the housemen in dusting all those books. She'd seen the President before, but always at a distance and always in passing. Their conversation had never progressed beyond an exchange of good-morn-ings. Now here sat her daughter, uppity as you please . . .

" 'Scuse me, Mr. Pres'dent . . . I apologize . . . Lil'yan, what on earth . . . I apologize, Mr. Pres'dent, for the chile's forwardness . . ." The storm clouds in Maggie's face got Lillian off the chair. Maggie's firm hand had hold of her collar. "I take her away now, sir."

"Must you?" The great man actually seemed sorry to see her go. "But not before she has a little tidbit, hm? Take something with you, Lillian. What would you like, my dear . . . lobster claw . . . how about a na-poleon, or some fruit?" Words father to the act, he began to prepare a packet of food in a large linen napkin.

"I got a brother, too," Lillian informed him.

Maggie thought she'd drop dead then and there. "Land sakes," she said, in mortification. But it seemed to strike the President as a pretty good joke. He laughed, a rolling laugh. "Good for you, missy . . ." He doubled the amount of food in the napkin, then rose from the chair and bowed solemnly to Lillian. "Thank you for your company, mademoiselle." To Maggie he said, "Let this little repast of mine be our secret, hm? Don't you go telling Mrs. Taft my menu now . . ."

"I didn't see a thing, sir."

The President remained standing as though they were special visitors. Lubau held the door for them. Maggie led Lillian out of the room, feeling somehow confused. How do you chastise your disobedient child when you've just been made to feel like some kind of ambassador, sharing a secret with the President of the United States?

Summer remained hot. Garages replaced stables at the White House, and motorcars, carriages. The indomitable Mrs. Jaffray stoutly refused to set foot in one of those sputtering machines, preferring to do her daily marketing by horse-drawn coach in the style of southern aristocracy. The President bought an automobile made by the Baker Electric Company of Cleveland, a stylish Landaulette. The newspapers made sport of the car as they had about his bathtub, one columnist hoping the driver's seat would be wide enough. The bathtub had made the front pages, with the four workmen who installed it sitting in it, two of them grinning like Cheshire cats. You could have heard Ike Hoover's anger all the way up to Capitol Hill. "You may be sure they weren't White House workmen, or they'd be picking up their walking papers!" The offending newspaper photograph was discussed in the staff dining room, in the kitchen, on the back stairs. Butlers and doormen, liverying up in the men's locker room, passed it from one to another. Coates, who had been present when Mr. Taft first cracked the paper open and saw his bathtub exposed to the world, said, "Hurts the poor man, know it does. Had to serve him lunch twice that day, he was that upset . . . and him in there with Captain Butt, frettin' 'bout how to get those Europe countries to talk, 'stead of always threatenin' war on each other . . ."

Mays fumed over the picture and passed it on to Jackson. "Hard as they be on Mr. Taft, Mr. Lincoln got the worst of the cartoonin' . . . though Mr. Grant was jabbed at pretty bad."

Maggie's concern, as summer moved from July into August, was as always for her family. Fall coming on, coal to buy, kids needing clothes, and Lillian outgrowing her brace.

Mercer, serving her at breakfast and lunch each day, had come to read her silences. "It be your children worryin' you, don't it? You want to talk, Maggie, I be right here, listenin' . . ." There weren't many at table, these days, with a good part of the staff off to Massachusetts with the First Lady. Mays and Jackson sat a few seats away, trading off sections of a newspaper with Coates, in his seat of power, high at the table. A kitchen helper and couple of men on the landscaping crew, finding the heat too much for conversation, ate in silence. Mercer had finished serving lunch except for an occasional coffee refill and felt free to sit in the empty seat beside her. His genuine concern made it easier to talk.

"Mercer, try hard as I can, I jus' cain't make it on twenty dollars a month."

"There be extras, you know. You can make more money." Mays spoke to her from behind the editorial page. Maggie hadn't meant to involve anyone else, but the provocative statement couldn't go by. "What extras?"

"You mean to say you haven't been collectin' for curlin' and fixin' Miz Taft's hair? And you been manicurin' Miz Jaffray every week for pleasure, all these months?" Mays picked up his coffee cup and moved to the empty seat on the other side of her. "Li'l lady, I goin' have to educate you."

"Educate me too, friend," Mercer urged.

"Well now," Mays expanded, "anythin' you do for the First Family, put in a voucher to Miz Jaffray—dollah here, dollah there, mounts up. Then they's the checkroom, can pick up good tips at parties. An' the ladies' powder room, though the ladies ain't ever quite so generous as the gentlemen." To Mercer, Mays recommended putting in for extra duty as part-time waiter for state dinners and doings. The First Lady would be coming back in a month and the social season would really take off. "Why, a body can keep goin' pretty good all winter on extras."

Mercer marveled. "How come you learn so much, Mays, the ins and outs. You come in just a short time after me, and same day as Maggie."

Mays grinned. "I'm a question-askin' man."

"All winter," Mays had said. The social season more than a month off, bills piling up on her, vouchers taking two-three weeks sometimes to collect . . . how was Maggie going to make do in the meantime?

"Mays . . ." Mercer leaned forward intently. "Cain't we get Maggie's boy a job? He come by here one day. I talked to him. Seems a smart boy . . ."

Maggie shook her head. "Gov'ment won't let you work till you twelve . . ."

"He look twelve to me . . . didn't he look twelve to you, Mays?" Mays immediately partnered in the conspiracy.

"He had long pants, he sure would look twelve . . ."

"You know I got no money for long pants," Maggie said, in exasperation. But they were carrying on a conversation of their own, with shrugs and looks toward the upper end of the table where Kearney, the head gardener, was taking a final swallow of coffee.

"Mr. Kearney," Mays inquired, "didn't I hear you say you be needin' a yard boy?"

Kearney, a taciturn man more comfortable with his hands in the earth than at conversation, drew heavy beetle brows together until they met over his craggy nose. "Don't remember sayin' it. Could use one, though. Fifty cents a day, providin' you know somebody's a good worker." Mays winked at Maggie and Mercer, waited until Kearney left the room, then called Jackson away from his newspaper. "Jackson, you got a boy . . ."

"Sure do. Fine boy. Goin' on thirteen, but he got hisself a job."

"What you do with his pants, he grows out of 'em?"

They stopped calling him little Emmett. Didn't seem proper, him working a full day at a man's wages. If his papa was to come back, Maggie rationalized, they

could always add "Junior" to his name. Until then he
would just be Emmett.

Emmett enjoyed the work. Aside from the river, it
was the coolest place in Washington. Trees, tall and
plentiful, gave shade, and the way the land fell away to
the Tidal Basin, there was sometimes a breeze. He liked
tending the flowers, and the smell of grass when it was
just mowed. Maggie would sneak a moment, two-three
times a day, to watch him. Not where he could see her,
of course. Made her proud. A neighbor lady, looking
in on Lillian for a few cents a day, gave Maggie
respite. There didn't seem much to worry about.

The First Family came back. The leaves turned.
Emmett showed up every afternoon, promptly, right
from the Stevens School. The long pants he'd gotten
from Jackson's son had been patched twice at the knees.
He hitched them up, tightening the cord belt that kept
them from sliding down around his hips. The more he
raked and piled, the more leaves seemed to fall. He
was stomping them down into a bushel basket one
afternoon when he became aware of the boy standing
there, watching him. Same size as himself. About the
same age.

"What's your name?"

"Emmett. What's yours?"

"Charlie."

In the wordless agreement of the young. Emmett
handed the newcomer the rake and went back to stomping leaves. They grinned at each other and worked in
concert for a bit, Charlie raking, Emmett filling baskets. Charlie fashioned a circle of leaves, but boredom
reared its playful head. He began to swing the rake in
an arc, scattering the well-organized piles. Finding that
too tame, he picked up a basket and dumped the
leaves over Emmett. "Hey, don't do that," Emmett protested, with no great conviction. A man's wages and
long pants notwithstanding, he was still a boy and the
temptation was more than he could resist. First, a fist-
ful of leaves. Then a basket, emptied over Charlie's
head. A second basket, and the boys flung themselves
onto the pile, a contorted mass of arms and legs,

wrestling. The wind joined the game, carrying leaves
aloft to fall back over the just swept lawn. It wasn't
long before Mr. Kearney came running and yanked
Emmett up by the collar.

"You want this job, boy? A day's wages, I expect a
day's work." He whirled around and had Charley halfway to his knees before realizing whom he had by the
scruff of the neck. "Oh, my . . . excuse me . . . sorry,
Master Taft, sir . . ." Kearney helped him to his feet,
brushed him off. Charlie had the good grace to insist it
wasn't Emmett's fault, that it was he who had started it
all. Mr. Kearney only wanted to get away from the
humiliation of having reprimanded a son of the President. "Yes, well . . . this boy's got his work to do.
Mind you," he shot back at Emmett as he walked away,
"do your work now."

Charlie Taft . . . In Emmett's view he didn't look any
different from any other white kid. Yet knowing who
he was put a crimp on their budding relationship.
Emmett soberly went about rectifying the havoc; Charlie pitched in to help. "What do you do when you get
through here?" Charlie asked.

"Nothing," Emmett said cautiously. "Go home."

They raked and stacked in silence. "Want to help
me put spitballs on Andrew Jackson's picture?"

Emmett knew he should let it go. "You mean, inside
the house—that big old hallway before you get to the
kitchen?"

Charlie chuckled, relishing the idea. "Make 'em look
like warts. Been drivin' the Secret Service crazy . . .
They don't know who's doin' it."

They found out. What was worse, *Maggie* found out.
Emmett's ear, in his mother's fierce grasp, preceded
the rest of him by half a foot. His feet barely touched
the ground as she led him down the street at day's end.
"Never so mortified in my life!"

"But Charlie Taft, he wades in fountains barefoot,
and ties people's shoelaces together at state dinners, he
told me . . . and nobody takes a strop to him."

"He the Pres'dent's chile . . ."

It was beyond Emmett's comprehension. " 'Cause I

got some the best blood in Virginia in my veins, *I*
ain't s'pose to do things like that. What kind of blood
Charlie Taft got?"

She would explain that some other time, she told
him. As they went up the stairs to their room, Emmett
frantically wondered if he could escape Maggie's eagle
eye long enough to stick something inside his pants.

Lillian was waiting at the door as it opened. "Mama,
I got a big surprise!"

"Not now, chile . . . Emmett—hate to do this to
you, but get the strop."

"Mama . . ." Lillian tugged at her sleeve. "Come
see what I got . . ." Excitedly, Lillian *hop-skipped*
back to the table. Emmett stood by, razor strop in
hand, but he might as well been all the way to Keswick for all the attention Maggie paid him. She stared,
transfixed, at Lillian's leg.

"Chile, why you be draggin' your foot so bad like
that."

"Mama, I want to show you . . ."

"Jus' turn 'round, walk back." The toe of the brace-
held shoe tilted strangely upward. Each step was a
slap of the heel, a *slide,* the toe never touched the
floor. Maggie's heart sank at the aberrant gait. How
long had it been this way, and she hadn't noticed?

"Mama, look see . . ." Lillian was waving five one-
dollar bills at her.

"How you come by this money, chile?"

"Oh, it come easy, Mama. You know that Mr. Elias,
caretaker downstairs? Well, he gone and taught me to
read the Armstrong's Scratch Sheet—got it over here on
the table, Mama, come see it—I had me three winners
today. Men on the street makin' a lot of money bettin'
the horses I pick for 'em, they give me a prize o' five
dollars . . ."

The devil's money . . . Maggie pulled it from Lillian's
hand as from the fiery furnace. "Oh, sweet Jesus!" she
said.

Never one to back off from a problem, one gray day
soon after that Maggie found herself standing in front
of St. Anne's convent, Lillian's hand in hers, a small,

scuffed suitcase on the sidewalk between them. It was a staggering decision for a Baptist with the ardor of the preordained. They went up the walk through the immense heavy door and into a monastic anteroom where a nun took their names and went away. In the hushed atmosphere they waited, their only companion a lifesize Christ in extremis. Lillian clung to her mother's hand as if to a lifeline. The Catholics, in Maggie's limited experience, were a mysterious group who crossed themselves, did their baptizing with only a flick of water, and answered their priest back in a foreign tongue. Nuns, she'd heard it rumored, shaved their heads; but no way to tell, with only faces showing in those starched white hoods. It was the echoing, hollow silence that made her the most uneasy. Hers was a vocal religion. You talked to the Lord, hallelujahed and amened as long as the spirit moved you. It would have been more comfortable leaving Lillian in the care of someone whose faith she more properly understood, but she'd exhausted every other course. There was no Baptist group anywhere nearby able to take her child in, full time.

The mother superior's gentle face and welcoming smile went a long way to dispel Maggie's misgivings. "She'll be happy here," she assured Maggie. "We'll take good care of her." Lillian clung to her mother until Maggie firmly released her.

"You be a good girl now, I come see you often as I can." The mother superior led Lillian away, down a long, cavernous corridor, the sound of Lillian's dragging footsteps echoing even after they were out of sight. Maggie stayed awhile with the nun at the desk, filling out papers. She paid for Lillian's first month's board, using all the voucher money she'd earned. About to leave, a nagging thought stayed her. From the inner recesses of her pocketbook she brought out a tightly wadded ball of paper money, Lillian's winnings. Carefully smoothing out the five one-dollar bills, she placed them on the desk.

"For the church, sister."

"Bless you."

Maggie's funds seemed to disappear down an insatiable maw, trying to maintain a roof over their heads and keep Lillian in the convent. The worsening leg was a constant worry; there would have to be a new brace, and perhaps an operation. Emmett contributed his earnings, but no matter how many vouchers Maggie turned in to Mrs. Jaffray it was never enough. Even with the brilliant social season underway in the White House, which provided Maggie with extra hairdressing for the First Lady, it seemed impossible to put aside a dollar.

Mrs. Taft's parties were dazzling affairs, always climaxing frantic behind-the-scenes preparations, with the meticulous lady finding dust no other human eye could detect. Her constant peering into pots and pans caused cooks to quit at the last moment. Maggie, whose culinary talents were limited to the simplest foods, even found herself pressed into emergency kitchen service when the special chef brought in for the occasion refused to do another earthly thing except prepare the terrapin soup for which he was famous. Mrs. Taft's habit of holding political discussions at the dinner table was the talk of Washington; her most recent involvement—writing to encourage the women in the Balkans in social reform—drew an exchange of diplomatic notes before the matter cooled down. Gossiping about the First Lady's "meddling in men's business" became the popular indoor sport. But "everybody who was anybody" vied for invitations.

That winter Maggie discovered you could get a voucher for working extra time in the pantry.

She placed lace doilies on china dessert plates and passed them along to Viola, who added crystal bowls filled with out-of-season raspberries and cream and passed them on to Annie, who added petits fours. The desserts accumulated at the end of the long counter where pantry boys placed them on trays, and Dixon, of the butler's staff, checked them for perfection before allowing them to be picked up by waiters and carried out to the state dining room.

There was a constant flow of traffic. Waiters (many

of them hired for the evening) moved in and out of the
swinging doors, leaving empty trays and dishes to be
sent down to the kitchen by dumbwaiter, and picking
up full trays of dessert to be served.

It was simple work, but it came at the end of a long
day and Maggie's feet had a tendency to complain. The
music, a soaring Strauss waltz played by a string quar-
tet somewhere beyond these doors, picked up her spirits
some, and it was good to be working alongside Viola.
Spending most of her days upstairs as she did, Maggie
had little daily contact with her own people, except at
breakfast and lunch. Viola had a nice quiet way about
her. Understood you even when you weren't saying
much.

"Miss your young'un somethin' fierce, don't you?"

Maggie nodded. The child had adjusted to convent
life better than expected. The last time Maggie had
brought her home for a visit, Lillian had actually been
anxious to go back, since there was going to be a
Punch and Judy show.

"Like to see the nice hand sewin' the nuns be teach-
in' her?" With shy pride, Maggie displayed a linen
handkerchief, hand-hemmed and embroidered, that
she kept neatly folded in her apron pocket. Viola ex-
claimed over it, allowing it was the best piece of work
she'd just about ever laid eyes on. Annie, just beyond
Viola, leaned in slightly, scrutinized the bit of fabric,
but made no comment. It still went against Annie's
grain to work with "coloreds." Maggie confused her.
From all she'd ever heard, they were lazy and shiftless, yet here was Maggie, one of the best workers in
the White House. She had to grudgingly admit a person
that would put her child in the hands of the Holy
Church had to have something going right inside. But
those blue eyes . . . Annie wouldn't permit herself to
think how Maggie came by those.

Again Viola sensed what was on Maggie's mind.
"Lil'yan's heel still draggin' so bad?"

"Worries me sick," Maggie admitted.

"If there's a miracle to be had for the child, the
nuns'll get it for her." It was the first Annie had spoken

to Maggie all evening. Surprised at compassion from this unexpected quarter, Maggie turned and smiled at her. "Why, thank you, Annie."

Annie reverted to vinegar. "Well, they're savin' her soul, ain't they?"

And that was another worry that had become a part of Maggie. What if the nuns converted Lillian? What if Lillian came out a stranger to her? What if—oh, sweet Saviour!—Lillian decided to put on those black robes herself?

Mercer, in full livery, backed into the pantry from the dining room with a tray of dishes, pausing at Maggie's station. "Never stepped livelier for an extra dollar."

As intended, it made her smile. "Mercer, you jus' spoiled."

" 'Spoiled' 's a kinder word than 'lazy,' thank you, ma'am." He leaned against the counter, lowered his voice. "Maggie, they be a fella out there in the dinin' room—waiter, fillin' in tonight. Say he wants to meet you. Got a message for you."

"Message? The man say what about?"

"Didn't say, Maggie." Mercer carried a full tray back into the dining room, sensing in Maggie a worry too private for her to verbalize.

The next time Mercer came through, the man was with him. Mercer introduced them. Soft-spoken, of middle years, he delivered the message guardedly. "Saw you husband few weeks back . . . in Hot Springs. Expectin' to get hisself located down there, say tell you he loves you, loves the children, goin' try to send some money soon as he can."

She should have thanked him and let him go. But he'd brought Emmett Rogers into the room and it couldn't be dismissed that easily. "How do he look?" she had to know. "He feelin' all right?"

"Oh, he lookin' fine . . . fine as corn silk . . . you know Emmett, he one fine-lookin' man . . . yes, ma'am . . . chipper as can be." It was painful to watch him struggle with the lie. Maggie nodded her thanks and released the man.

"My curlin' irons . . ." It was the only escape that

came to her mind. "Left 'em upstairs . . . you know how Miz Taft is about things left around . . . I be back." She fled the pantry. No one—not even Annie—looked up; they all wanted to avoid embarrassing her.

Sometimes Emmett was so strong within her she could almost hear him speak. Sometimes, when worries weighed her down, she couldn't quite call up his face. Then for days on end it would seem there had been no Emmett Rogers. But this stranger, who'd so recently laid eyes on him, whose kindness wouldn't permit him to speak the truth, ripped away all the defenses she'd built up over the months. Her knees felt weak, like she'd never make it to the second floor. Sheer will took her up the narrow, enclosed stairwell, across the deserted center hall, through the west sitting hall and the First Lady's bedroom into the dressing room. In this perfumed cocoon of silks she began to calm. Reluctant to tear-stain the handkerchief Lillian had made for her, she dried her cheeks with her hand. She was packing her curling irons in their case when she heard the voices. Her panicked eyes went to the only door through which she could leave the room. It led into the presidential bedroom, which the President and First Lady were at that very instant entering. Through Mrs. Taft's strategic placement of mirrors Maggie caught glimpses of them as they moved about. *Thank God, they couldn't see her.* Mrs. Taft was stunning in a plum velvet ball gown, the fire flashing from her eyes rivaling the glitter of diamonds at her throat; the President, in full dress, followed her with forbearance.

"How could you, William?" Mrs. Taft's agitation kept her moving in and out of the mirror. "In public! The President of the United States . . ."

"At a boring function, my dear, the President of the United States can fall asleep like any other mortal."

"In Manila," Mrs. Taft chided, "you fell asleep during a typhoon. *A typhoon* . . . Your chair was shaking . . ."

"I knew you had things under control, Nellie."

"Don't patronize me, William. Don't do that to me.

You know what the newspapers will make of your nodding off tonight."

"I noticed the British ambassador's head bouncing up and down like he was bobbing for apples."

"Your image, William . . . !"

The President patted his girth good-humoredly. "There's no denying my image. I don't give a hoot what people think, Nellie."

"You will, come reelection."

"Give you my word . . . I won't sleep a wink from the convention to election day, how's that suit you?" They were both gone from the mirror now, their voices indicating they'd moved into his sitting room. The pungent scent of tobacco announced that he'd gone in to his humidor for a cigar.

"Do this much for me, Will. Come back downstairs."

"Not tonight, my dear." They were back in the bedroom again. One of the small, damask boudoir chairs groaned under his weight as he sat on it and kicked off patent leather evening slippers. "Let me remind you, Nellie, I am in this house because you wanted it. Teddy would have made me Chief Justice, if you hadn't persuaded him otherwise. If Chief Justice Fuller had only retired before the convention, there would have been no doubt in my mind as to the course I should have taken. Want the truth? I don't think the Republicans ever really wanted me, but Roosevelt with his bullyboy charm had that convention in the palm of his hand. To this day, when somebody says 'Mr. President,' I look around for Teddy . . ." He loosened collar, tie, the buttons of his waistcoat. "I guarantee I wouldn't fall asleep on the bench."

"You'd come down to my party if Alice Longworth were here."

"Nellie, Nellie . . ." He laughed tolerantly, affectionately. "You have a vivid imagination . . . The lady wanted to see the Islands, who better to escort her than the governor?" He reached out for his wife's hand, but she withheld it. "Why are we going back over this old territory, anyway?"

Maggie stood pressed against the wall of the dressing

room. If they found her, she would surely be dismissed. Fear of being on the street, jobless, was as great as fear of discovery. For a moment there was no sound from the other room. Then a series of short inhalations, and she knew he was lighting the cigar.

When it was lit and drawing to his satisfaction, he looked up, distressed to find Mrs. Taft standing before him, wearing a slightly glazed look, both hands pressed to her forehead. With a cry of alarm he was on his feet, moving surprisingly quickly for a man of his bulk. "Nellie . . . what is it?"

In spite of her protestations that it was just a momentary dizziness, he eased her down into the chair he had just vacated. "Let me get you some smelling salts . . . or eau de cologne . . ."

Both were on the dressing table. Maggie stared at the crystal bottles filled with scent and unguents. *Oh, Lord, don't let him come in here* . . . For an instant, it seemed certain he would. Then, abruptly, Mrs. Taft appeared in the mirror above the fireplace. Erect. Alert. "No, no, William, please, I'm fine . . ." His image moved into the mirror with her. As long as Maggie could see them both, she felt safe. But she couldn't stay closeted like a fugitive forever.

"Come my dear, you're tired." Taft enveloped his wife in his arms. "Too many parties . . . too many late nights . . . Stay up here with me, we won't be missed . . ."

"No one is going to say the First Lady neglects her duties."

"You work too hard at the job, Nellie. Would I unduly offend you if I were to tell you it's an invisible job?"

Mrs. Taft pulled herself to her full height, which still had her below his chin. "Are you coming, Mr. President?"

"No. Here I stay with my graphanola where I can fall asleep without offending anyone except Caruso."

"William, I swear, you are hopeless."

"You should have been President. Suits you more than it does me."

"Mark my words, Will, there will be a woman President one day."

"You have my vote, Nellie." He leaned down, kissed her on the forehead, and went into his sitting room humming "Musetta's Waltz." Mrs. Taft studied herself in the mirror, patted her hair lightly, and left the room by way of the west sitting hall. It was minutes after the President put the graphanola record on and the passionate voice of Enrico Caruso poured forth Rodolfo's *"Che gelida manina, se la lasci riscaldar,"* that Maggie ventured a look. The door between the presidential bedroom and sitting room was wide open. Through it, she could see Taft overflowing his favorite leather lounge chair. He was in her direct line of vision, and she in his. Fortunately, his eyes were closed. Enthralled with the music? Or asleep?

Maggie didn't wait to find out.

The trolley jerked its way up Connecticut Avenue. The motorman, young and new on the job, alternately jabbed the car with too much current or too little, making Maggie nostalgic for the steady pace of the horsecars. It was usually a pleasant ride. From the window you could see what changes were taking place in Washington. Ladies emerging from the fashionable shops that lined the broad boulevard, having to be handed up into the new autos by their chauffeurs because of the latest fashion, the hobble skirt.

Five o'clock, and government workers were swarming out of the limestone buildings of Treasury, Immigration, Justice, Commerce, Labor, and the others like so many bees. Maggie, hanging on to the strap to survive the constant jostling, was thankful to Mays. Working on the door as he did, Mays seemed to get wind of things long before anybody else. He was the one who always knew when the President and First Lady were going to be guests away from the White House of an evening. It was invaluable information, since butlers and others could pick up extra work on the outside, waiting on tables at hotels and private parties. Mrs. Jaffray took a dim view of the practice, but closed her eyes to it since it meant fewer requests for raises to be turned down. For Maggie, on those rare occasions when she wouldn't be needed after hours at the White House, it meant an opportunity to augment her income with some of her former hairdressing clientele.

The only person to alight at Du Pont Circle, since government workers of any color could hardly afford to live in this rarefied atmosphere, she walked along the smooth sidewalk that fronted houses of notables—less impressive to her, now that she spent her days at the Executive Mansion. The thought caused Maggie to smile to herself: Was she becoming a snob? At any rate, Mrs. Colgate was easily her favorite client.

"The rumor's all over town," Mrs. Colgate said as Maggie laid in a perfect marcel wave with her irons, "that Mrs. Taft won't let her daughter Helen wear blue because of Alice you-know-who and her sweet little gown . . ."

"That a fact?" Maggie said laconically.

"Oh, now, Maggie, you are incorrigible. What's the use of having a hairdresser from the White House if you don't get a juicy tidbit now and then . . . ?"

"Did you enjoy Europe, Miz Colgate?"

"You know what's wrong with Europe, Maggie? You see the selfsame people over there that you see here. And hear the same tedious conversations . . . that Teddy Roosevelt's nose is out of joint because Taft is running the country without his advice, and that a break in their relationship has got to come." She waited expectantly for Maggie's response.

"The President don't usually consult me on those matters," Maggie replied with a slow smile. Undaunted, Mrs. Colgate elaborated on the question at hand: if a breach did occur between Taft and TR, that would put Captain Archie Butt, who served as aide to both, in an untenable position. Out of loyalty to Teddy, he would surely leave Taft in the lurch.

"Oh, ma'am, Cap'n Butt would never do that, he one of the finest gentlemen . . . devoted to Mr. Taft . . ." Maggie caught Mrs. Colgate's smile in the mirror. "Why, Miz Colgate, you tricked me into that . . ."

"Not really, Maggie. I'll tell you the truth. I don't give a tinker's damn, one way or the other. But in Washington, if you don't know the latest, what do you talk about at dinner parties?"

That was one problem Maggie didn't have. Those she *did* have lay close to the surface.

"Is it Lillian on your mind, Maggie? Her being in the convent? Or her leg?"

"Nothin' to worry you with, Miz Colgate."

"Maggie, we're friends." A simple, sincere statement, and Maggie found herself sharing fears about Lillian's foot turning up so bad. The nuns, as worried as she, had brought in a doctor. Without an operation, the leg would just keep getting shorter, but the surgery called for a special kind of doctor, "of muscles and things . . ."

"Why didn't you come to me sooner?"

Embarrassment burned Maggie's cheeks. She'd broken her cardinal rule never to inflict her problems on others, and for the instant had to battle her own unyielding pride.

"Maggie, I'm a rich woman. I donate to a lot of hospitals. It's time one of them did something for me . . ."

The speed with which Mrs. Colgate accomplished this was, in Maggie's view, nothing short of a miracle. Annie let her opinion be known to the White House staff at breakfast that it was all that praying by the nuns that had brought this blessed surgery about. Maggie kept her peace, and privately asked the sweet Jesus to bless Mrs. Colgate, whatever her church. And that lovely young Jewish Dr. Irving who had been alongside Lillian, holding her hand, as she was wheeled into the operating room. And was still in with her. To this point in her life, Maggie's only contact with the children of Abraham were the "Jew stores" on the corners. She found their accents strange and the smell of their foods different, but more than once, when she was in trouble, they'd let her owe for groceries.

Mercer came in off the street, unbuttoned his heavy coat and unwinding his muffler as he tiptoed deferentially to the desk and was pointed in the direction of the waiting room by the nurse on duty, who watched him go with some suspicion. He was the third colored, other than janitor staff, to enter their doors. First, a patient. The patient's mother. Now this one. Then she remembered: Dr. Irving was a Hebrew.

"Maggie, you still waitin'?"

"Still in the operatin' room," she told Mercer, surprised to see him wearing the white coat of the servingman as though he'd left in a great hurry.

His frown echoed her worries. " 'Most five hours you been here . . ." He sat beside her. "Maggie, I be awful sorry to tell you, but you goin' to have to come back to the White House . . ."

"Cain't, Mercer . . . cain't leave my baby . . ."

"Terrible thing done happened. Miz Taft had a stroke . . ."

"Oh, my God . . ."

"Cain't talk, keeps makin' signs 'bout her hair . . . wants you, Maggie."

But to leave, not knowing how her child had fared the dark hours under the knife! Mercer took her hands in his. "Lil'yan's not goin' be alone. I be here . . . An' Mays gets off the door, he goin' come, spell me . . . We family, Maggie . . ."

She felt lost, torn.

"The lady needs you . . ."

The President's Landaulette took her back. The waiting elevator, with Ike Hoover at the controls, rushed her to the second floor where Annie, Michaels, McKenzie, and Maureen all stood about in the hall, a sense of helplessness about them. Lubau, who held the door open for her, took her hat and coat.

Sickness had dulled the colors of the bedroom. The President, collapsed in despair beside the twin bed in which Mrs. Taft lay, murmured over and over, "Nellie . . . Nellie . . ." The right side of Mrs. Taft's lovely face drooped. Unformed, agitated sounds issued from her. A doctor and nurse consulted quietly in the background. As Maggie stepped into the room, Taft quickly rose and offered his chair. "She wants you."

Maggie sat beside her; held the useless right hand

in hers, stroking it. "Would you like me to brush your hair, ma'am?" A cry like a mewling baby's was the only reply. "There, there, you goin' get better, ma'am . . ." Maggie reached for the silver hairbrush that Mrs. Taft's maid Dolores had quickly fetched from the dressing room and began to brush the long, chestnut hair. In a while the sounds quieted, then stopped altogether. Some of the panic drained from Mrs. Taft's eyes.

Maggie's calm was deceptive. Only by suspending feeling could she put Lillian, lying there in the hospital beyond doors she could not enter, out of her mind.

When the telephone rang in Mrs. Jaffray's office, Coates, who had stationed himself in the corridor just outside the door, was quick to step into the archway. Mrs. Jaffray waved him back. "Yes," she said into the phone.

"Is it Mercer?" Coates overstepped himself to ask.

She nodded. Listened, as Mercer's relieved voice brought the news that the surgery was over, everything had gone well, that Lillian was back in her room. Inwardly, Mrs. Jaffray felt a surge of gratitude to the Almighty, but it wasn't in her nature to be effusive, especially with servants. "Thank you, Mercer," she said, "I'll see that she gets the message." She hung up and said to Coates, "The child is recovering."

A smile split his face in half. "Yes, ma'am, thank you."

"And you may tell Maggie that I am pleased."

"Yes, ma'am." He sprinted off, setting in motion a relay system. "Lil'yan goin' to be fine," he called up to Dixon waiting midway up the backstairs who extended the message to McKenzie who carried it to Annie. "Saints be praised," she said, as unused smile muscles found their way into the almost forgotten pattern. With a buoyance none of them had ever before seen her evince, Annie practically bounded across the center hall, to step respectfully through the door that Lubau held open for her. Maggie, gently brushing Mrs. Taft's hair, looked up to see a radiant Annie in the doorway, hands clasped under her chin, prayerlike. "Fine," Annie mouthed, "the child is fine."

Thank you, Jesus . . . "You goin' to get well," Maggie told Mrs. Taft. "Don't you worry, Mr. Pres'dent, we goin' to make her well in no time."

There was more wish than prophecy in those words. Months, during which Maggie's time and emotions were claimed at Mrs. Taft's bedside—and at Lillian's—with Mays and Mercer, on days she couldn't get to the hospital, acting as surrogates. It was Emmett who got the short end of her attention as she heavily involved him in obligations: to hear the alarm clock go off and rouse her; to put the grits on to cook; to clean the room; to go to school and to work; to be more without a mother than with one. One of these days, she promised herself, she'd give a whole Sunday to that young man. But that day just never seemed to roll around.

Lillian was to remain hospitalized longer than anticipated. Dr. Irving, unsatisfied with the first cast, structured a second. To prevent the leg from being shorter than the other, he wanted to closely supervise how she grew. Maggie shuddered to think what it was costing Mrs. Colgate, who refused to allow the subject of money to be discussed.

It was early spring by the calendar when Mrs. Taft's improvement began to be noticeable. Her smile still crooked, but a definite smile, she began to wake up hungry and to take an interest in which negligee was chosen for that day. She looked at herself in the mirror when Maggie brushed her hair, and accepted a touch of rouge to her cheeks, but still resisted her husband's attempts to get her to talk.

His time spent in the Oval Office was rationed. You could find him, day after day, at her bedside, prodding her to try to speak. Gently. Coaxingly. Insistently. Demandingly. Then gently again. "Nellie . . . say 'Nellie' . . . NNNNN . . . NNNNNellie . . . All right, then let's try Willllliam . . . Howwwward . . . You see, Nellie's easier. *Nellie . . . NNNNNNelllie . . .*"

The first warm day, Taft wheeled his wife over to feel

the warmth of sunlight through the open window. "Smell them, Nellie . . . your cherry trees . . ." A small lie. The three thousand trees the Japanese had sent as an official gift to the city of Washington had died of blight, frost, and transplantation. A new shipment was on the way, to form the bower that would, in later years, grace the drive along the Potomac. A small lie, but an inspired one: it caught her imagination, caused her tongue to seek the words. "Chee . . ." she said.

"Good for you, Nellie," he encouraged as, day following day, he brought her to the point where she could repeat a word or two after him. "Nellie . . ." he would say. "Nellie Taft's . . ."

"Nell-lie . . ." her words slow, slurred, with effort. "Taf . . . tttsss." Maggie was mouthing each word with her as though that would help her get it out easier.

"Bully," he said, using a hated word of his predecessor. "Bully. Now—*cherry* . . ."

"Cherrr . . . rrry . . ."

"Trees."

"Tree . . . eee . . . ssss."

"Marvelous, beautiful, isn't that just beautiful, Maggie?"

"Oh, yes, Mr. President . . . that jus' be beautiful . . ."

Captain Archie Butt sought an audience. Disquieting news had been received that Teddy Roosevelt, satiated with big-game hunting, was moving from one capital of Europe to another, leaving in his wake the rumor that he was considering challenging his good friend Taft for the presidency. But Taft couldn't be pulled from his wife's side to share Butt's concern for his political future.

"Let's try it again, my dear . . . *Nellie . . . Taft's . . .*"

"Nelll-lee . . . Ta . . . aft . . . sss . . ."

"Cherry . . . trees . . ."

So it went, until one day Mrs. Taft emerged from her bedroom in a day dress, hair simply coiffed, violets pinned to her shoulder. Putting aside her cane, she took the President's arm and walked, slowly, falteringly. Maggie remained near the doorway, smiling like a proud parent watching a child take its first steps. Mrs.

Taft's speech retained a slowness, her tongue not quite able to rouse itself to perform. But there was the ring of authority in her words.

"Nellie—Taft's—cherry trees—are—in bloom— a-long—the—" Both Taft and Maggie mouthed the next word with her. *"Po—to—mac . . ."*

"Superb, my dear, superb." The President kissed her hands as Mrs. Taft repeated, "Po-to-mac . . . Poto-mac . . . PO-TOMAC . . ." The three of them—the President, the First Lady, Maggie Rogers—were caught between laughter and tears over the joy of it.

Griffith Stadium was jam-packed. You couldn't buy a seat for love or money. Foot traffic, at the triangle of Florida Avenue, Seventh, and T, was so heavy the trolley, moving at a snail's pace, had to clang its way through the mass of humanity surging to the arena.

Opening day of the baseball season saw the Washington Senators, with Walter Johnson on the mound, facing the Philadelphia Athletics—an event the stadium owners could always count on to draw a crowd. But on this spring day of 1910, attendance went far beyond expectations because of the extra added attraction.

The big man in the bunting-draped box rose to his feet, rolled the baseball around in his hands, put the full force of his powerful body behind it, and threw it. The crowd went wild. It was the first time in the history of the United States that the President had tossed out the baseball to open the season. Walter Johnson pitched an inspired game. A shutout. 1–0. But it was William Howard Taft's day from the first inning to the last of the ninth.

Two months later in New York City, Theodore Roosevelt returned to his native shores and was greeted by tumultuous cheers and hysterical adulation. Some people said it wasn't confetti that stuck to him on that triumphal ride down Fifth Avenue, but the itching powder of power.

"Easy now, don't get too rambunctious, young lady . . ." But there was no stopping the pent-up energy

Lillian had generated in five endless immobile months. Now that the cast was off, she was off lickety-split down the hospital corridor, using the crutches like a pair of extra feet. Dr. Irving, watching her go, felt rewarded. Her legs would grow at the same rate now, not one shorter than the other as he had feared at first. His work as a surgeon was finished, but there were deep wounds he knew he could not heal.

"Have you talked to her?" he asked Maggie. She shook her head; she just couldn't bring herself to do it.

He had tried, several times. Lillian always listened politely, but heard only the words she wanted to hear. Maggie came from the closet with the leg brace. "No need packing that, Mrs. Rogers. Lillian won't be needing it ever again."

"An' when do I get shed of the crutches?" Lillian was in the doorway, face flushed with the exhilaration of newfound freedom, eyes alight. Waiting for him to promise the impossible.

"Lillian, we've discussed this, you and I . . ."

"I'm rid of the brace," she insisted. "My leg goin' to get strong now . . ."

Maggie, unable to face the desperation in the child, turned away and packed. Pedantically, patiently, the doctor explained it again, step by step: the problem with the heel was now corrected. Did Lillian understand that? She did. The operation had been to stop the foot from turning up, shortening the leg.

"You told me I was goin' to be better, you told me!"

"You are better. That's why we've kept you here, to make certain. I've explained that all along. But we can't bring back muscles that have lost their—"

"My papa said I can be anythin' I want to be . . ."

He tried to curb the hysteria he felt building within her. "Your papa's right. You can *be, do* anything you want, Lillian . . . providing you can do it on crutches."

"How long?" she demanded. "How long do I need 'em?"

"Lillian. I've tried to tell you . . ."

"HOW LONG?"

Her anguish was his. "Lillian . . . from now on . . . Probably for the rest of your life."

She shattered. Fragmented, like a fine glass goblet under a mallet. The cry that came from her was primordial. It tore at Maggie's soul to see the young face contort in brutish fury as Lillian hurled the crutches from her and sank to the floor, sobbing. Dr. Irving's words went unheard. "We did all we could, Lillian. All we could . . ."

Maggie dropped to the floor with her child, cradling, suffering with her. "I know, baby, I know . . . hard to set aside a dream when you so young . . ." Nothing would console Lillian. Not then, or for a long time to come.

1912

The storm in Chesapeake Bay reached its icy fingers into the usually calm, glasslike surface of the Tidal Basin, churning it with thousands of small, troubled whitecaps. Archie Butt stood on the Kutz Bridge and felt himself kin to the landlocked body of water. He was trapped, caught in a pincer between his friends Teddy Roosevelt and Taft. His life, usually calm as a millpond, organized, with duties clearly defined, now churned with the winds of dissension. The year of '12 was still newborn, to be nourished (or poisoned) by political conventions, elections, and problems of state. Soon it would no longer be possible to maintain a stance of neutrality. Sides must be chosen. He was either Taft's man or Teddy's. What had begun in '10 with TR hinting at another try at the presidency had taken on the quality of a crusade, with the Rough Rider, living up to his nickname, calling Taft, in private and in public, "inept," "hopeless," "well meant, but well meant feebly."

Archie Butt had far from casual relationships with these two men of power, having been quartermaster in the Philippines when Taft governed those islands, and again, during a revolution, with Taft in Havana. And for two years of Roosevelt's presidency, Butt had been his aide. Each laid claim to his loyalty. Tied to both their wagons, he felt himself drawn and quartered by the credo of noblesse oblige imposed on him by his Georgian heritage.

The wind scooped off his hat, which he rescued just short of the water. Smoothing his thinning hair, he set the homburg firmly on his head and started the long walk back to the White House, glad he had rejected Taft's offer of the chauffeured Landaulette. Perhaps with the wind at his back he could think out his dilemma. Crossing the broad Ellipse, he could see through the south lawn's winter-stripped foliage to the stark white building for which three Presidents had given up their lives and for which others would gladly offer up their eternal souls. The conflict was still on him as he paused to share a pleasantry with Mays at the door before being swallowed up by the building.

The year wasn't much older when Archie Butt left the country. Mays, whose talents extended beyond the door, cut his hair shortly before he left. "That man is sufferin' real bad," Mays told Maggie. "Jokes me like always, but his heart not in it." For some time Maggie herself had been worrying about Captain (now Major) Butt. Three, four times, when lights burned late in the Oval Office, he'd stayed the night on the second floor. Mornings, when she'd come to make up his room, she'd found him haggard from sleeplessness. His reasons for going abroad were widely debated. Some sources hinted that Taft had sent him to test the rumors of a war brewing over there. Others, claiming to be more in the know, insisted he had fled to keep out of the eye of the hurricane that was closing in on Taft and Roosevelt.

The day before he sailed, Archie Butt confided to Maggie as she made up his bed, "I feel so restless, like there's something hanging over me." The way he said it gave Maggie a chill that had nothing to do with weather.

In February, Lillian was fifteen; and Emmett, coming on fourteen, shot up a foot taller than she. They'd moved to a little house, closer to work—so Maggie could get home quicker though not any more often— and closer to Stevens School where Lillian got her eighth-grade diploma. Mrs. Jaffray, made aware of Lillian's talent with the needle, took to sending Maggie home with a sackful of White House napkins which, for a small fee, Lillian mended, reembroidered, and sent back. Her proficiency with the crutches grew. Mostly she only used one to bolster the withered leg. Her papa's prediction that she could do anything anybody else could was close to accurate, but offered little succor. After that one anguished explosion in the hospital, there seemed nothing left in Lillian but passive acceptance. Many times Maggie wanted to cry out to her to do something outlandish—some prank. *Make me scold you, sass me back!* Anything but that terrible, silent acceptance.

That spring, Mays and his barber shears went up the back stairs regularly. President Taft never said as much. but Mays had the feeling the President felt comfortable with him. Mays had come to like the big man and it pained to see him distressed. An avid newspaper reader, Mays knew these were bad times by the number of used dishes on the oversized tray that Coates brought down. Whenever newsprint was laced with bile, the President gorged.

"You see the papers?" Mays asked of Coates one morning.

"No. Why?"

"Extra on the street. Teddy Roosevelt comin' on strong about runnin' 'gainst the boss for Pres'dent."

Coates, who had served both men, found it hard to take sides. "They both the same party. Mr. Teddy sure say that hisself?"

"Accordin' to the paper, he say that do the Republicans want him at the convention, he come runnin'. He say he strong as a bull moose and ready to save the country from the do-nothin' we got in the White House now."

"Oh, my, that goin' hurt Mr. Taft somethin' fierce. Think he know?"

"Got to know. He read the papers."

President Taft had not only read the papers, he had seen the cartoons. One he had to admire for its ingenuity, and its prophetic truth: two big men, wearing his face and TR's, back to back in the same pair of britches, walking angrily away from one another. Sure to split the pants (labeled, for those dullards who couldn't get the point without help, "GOP Brand Trousers"—while a vulture waited on a signpost that pointed in both directions "To the Nomination"). Time, poets and philosophers would have you believe, heals all wounds and will rust the sharpest sword. But that was in the larger sense, his jurist's mind argued. With but sixty-five days left before the convention, time, in small chunks, could wither a man's soul.

Mays put the barber sheet around his ample patron and set out combs, powder, and brush. "I'm hopin' the First Lady findin' herself in good health, sir."

"Hm? Improving, thank you." Deep in his own gloom, Taft submitted to the haircut. Mays combed, snipped, and tried to distract him. "Sure must be enjoyin' the fine weather they be havin' in Massachusetts . . . Weather mighty nice in Washington for a change." Silence. "Mr. President, could I trouble you to sit up a little?"

The President obligingly altered his posture. "Yes, sir," Mays went on, "weather here in Washington best I can remember for April."

The President, surfacing from his thoughts, queried, "Were you in the house, Mays, when Mr. Roosevelt was here?"

"No, sir, you the first President I have had the pleasure of servin', sir."

"President Roosevelt was my friend." It was an epitaph.

"A man lucky to have a friend, sir."

"Caesar had a friend. His name was Brutus."

"Beggin' your pardon, sir?"

"It's a play."

"Yes, sir."

"I have another friend, though. Major Butt. There's a

man you can count on. Makes me feel better just to know he's coming back."

"Oh, that be fine, sir. Whole staff like the Major very much." Mays could feel the President relaxing under his hands.

"Can't wait to see him." A smile relieved the taut muscles in Taft's face. "Yes . . . everything will work out, soon as Archie Butt walks through that door."

"He be comin' back soon, sir?"

"Oh yes . . . very soon. Sailing tomorrow on the *Titanic*."

3

⊠ ⊠ ⊠

Excitement insulated her against the raw November day. The rope handles of the full shopping bag cut through the light cotton glove into her hand but she didn't feel it. Rounding K onto Nineteenth Street, Maggie stopped to shift her bundles and tried to remember how long it had been since she'd danced. Could you in all your born days believe it? The Marine Band to play for *them,* just like they did for the President. Just about the most joy-making thing, in Maggie's way of thinking, of her almost four years of service at the White House. Mr. Kearney had been working all day to fix up fine bouquets, same as he did for state dinners. Dress uniforms and dress clothes. Style and high-steppin'. The walls of the Odd Fellows' Hall would ring tonight. The thought occurred, though she didn't dwell on it, that the guests would all be Negro, and the band that would be playing for their pleasure, white. Now if that wasn't something to be esteemed about . . .

She hoped they'd play some of the new tunes she'd heard coming from the President's graphanola: "Alexander's Ragtime Band," "Waitin' for the Robert E. Lee," and one Maggie especially favored, "Melancholy

Baby." Mrs. Taft didn't dance since her stroke, but bought all the latest records for the President, to take his mind off his troubles. Poor man. One friend lost to the sea, one to ambition; and to the ballot box, the presidency.

Twilight was kind to the row of small old wooden houses which had long forgotten the taste of fresh paint. The smallest and narrowest house, in a block of small, narrow houses, was hers. A step up from the room over the undertaker's. A leap away from the river bottom shack. "Charmin'," she said of it as she turned through the low picket fence she and Emmett had built, and of the scrap of garden where, come spring, flowers would grow.

Little more than the width of a railroad car, the house had two rooms, one behind the other. "Evenin', Lil'yan," she called, as always taking care to sound cheerful (which tonight was no effort). Lillian held up her cheek to be kissed—"Evenin', Mama"—then turned back to the circle of light offered by the hanging overhead bulb and put a last few meticulous stitches in the White House napkin. The rip where the flatiron had pulled away the embroidered letters u.s. was closed. She bit off the thread, folded the napkin, and added it to the growing pile on the table, then picked up another and set about repairing it. That was her life these days. Not thinking back on the last napkin done, or ahead to the next. In that way, she'd trained herself neither to dream nor to wake up from dreaming.

Maggie carried the newspaper-wrapped food she'd toted behind the cretonne curtain with roses on it that divided the front room into parlor and kitchen, and laid it on the sink. "Didn't you go out at all today, chile?" she asked carefully.

"Nothin' to go out for, Mama."

Two years on the crutch . . .

"Brought you supper. It's here on the sink. You know I got to hurry tonight." Maggie pumped a basinful of water and carried it through the curtained doorway into the bedroom. Even smaller than the front room, but a room, with a bed for herself and Lillian, a chest of drawers, a closet, and a secondhand mirror she'd saved up for, that if you stood quite still you didn't set your image waving. Carefully, she washed and dried her hands before unwrapping Mrs. Taft's plum velvet ball gown. (*"You must wear it, Maggie. The color does lovely things to your eyes. Keep it. My husband will probably end up in the Supreme Court, which is what he wanted all along, I'm afraid. An off-the-shoulder gown would never do at one of their stuffy functions!"*)

"Miz Jaffray got a lot more sewin' for you, Lil'yan." Maggie, in her cambric camisole and pettiskirt, stepped into the doorway, sponging neck and arms with a washrag. "Admires your work very much. They's two dollars she sent you in my pocketbook."

"You keep the money, Mama."

"Why don't you come to the White House tomorrow, pick up the sewin', 'stead of me carryin' it . . . Everybody there always glad to see you . . . It's only five blocks, Lil'yan, you can walk that far, easy . . ."

"Don't feel like it, Mama." The tension in her voice sent Maggie, to avoid confrontation, back into the bedroom where she unbuttoned and removed the coarse-fabricked camisole she wore every day. She dipped the washrag and sponged her body. Four years of regular eating had rounded her contours. Seldom did she think of herself as anything other than jus' Maggie. Hair, skin, bones, flesh, not to be given, or taken. Lillian was a budding woman herself now, just two years short of the age Maggie had been when she married. What was to become of the child? An eighth-grade diploma hung on the wall, along with a certificate from typewriting school. ("A typewriter and me got nothin' to say to each other, Mama . . .") *Chile, you cain't live this way, cooped up in the house all the time. What you goin' to do with your life? Anythin' happens to me, what's goin' to happen to you?* But us usual Maggie left her thoughts unspoken.

Emmett came in from the street, slamming the front door. No matter how many times he washed his hands, he never quite lost the faint smell of formaldehyde that telegraphed his apprenticeship to the undertaker. "What's for supper?"

Lillian didn't look up from her sewing. "On the sink. Mama brought it."

The newspaper-wrapped package gave up the carcasses of two ducklings, one minus a breast, the other with a leg still shod with a ruffle of colored paper. "Duck again?"

From the bedroom came Maggie's voice: "It's duck or go hungry . . . And they's some of Charlie Taft's fine clothes in that sack I brought, underneath the napkins Miz Jaffray sent for mendin' . . ." Emmett lifted out the White House napkins and brought forth a pair of Brooks Brothers trousers of gray tweed, a cashmere pullover, and a shirt of Egyptian cotton. "I didn't hear you say that's very nice," Maggie's voice prodded.

"Very nice, Mama." He folded the clothes, put them aside on a chair, then went back to the sink and washed up again, but the smell was still in his nostrils. Lillian mended another napkin.

They both heard the horse's hooves in the street.

The hansom cab had rubber tires which absorbed the jolts. The driver, a man of color who lived in the neighborhood, was trepidacious about the fine cab he drove traversing these eroding streets. But his fares were friends: John Mays and Levi Mercer, dandied up in rented soup 'n' fish, and keeping him laughing all the way. Getting out of the cab was a satire of grand manners. "Kindly wait, my good man . . ." Doffing their silk hats, they "after you'd" each other all the way to the door. "Glad t'see you know your place," Mercer, who assumed the privilege of knocking, said to Mays. The driver, watching them be admitted, smiled. You did a favor for them, and one night they'd do a favor for you—like get you on at some big *do* over to the White House. A kind of unspoken law of the serving fraternity. He pulled his cap over his eyes and lay back in the seat to wait while they picked up the lady.

"Geez!" This from Emmett at first glimpse of their sartorial splendor. "You two sure look like swells."

"Let me present my friend, the Ambassador from Tokaboku," Mays said.

"Where's that?"

"Jus' south of New Jersey."

Maggie could hear Emmett's laughter. Thought she heard Lillian laugh once, but couldn't be sure. She stood for a private moment in front of the mirror. The rich plum of the gown was just a few shades deeper than the color excitement had brought to her cheeks. Hard work, even the daily scrubbing down of the grand staircase. hadn't yet bent her shoulders. Her neck was straight, head proud with its pile of dark brown hair arranged so stylishly. She looked, if she did say it herself, downright sparklin'. And something she'd forgotten she was: young.

Emmett was the first to see her as she came into the room. "Mama . . . never seen you look so grand . . ." Mays and Mercer, trying to outdo each other, struggled to their feet from the sagging daybed. "My, my, you somethin' . . ." "Goin' be the finest-lookin' lady there . . ."

"Lil'yan?"

There was a long pause. It wasn't pleasure on her face at seeing her mother looking radiant. Something closer to fear. "You beautiful, Mama."

A quick hug for her children. "Now you both know where to find me." They knew. Butlers' ball, Odd Fellows' Hall. Where they'd be doing the latest dancing rage, Mercer added, the turkey trot.

"Now you don't know how to turkey trot," Mays challenged.

"Mister, you talkin' to the turkey-trotter of the century. Madam, shall we promenade?" Both gallants offered their arms. To much bowing and scraping, Maggie was swept out the door. Laughter went down the walk with them. As the carriage drove off, Mercer could be heard singing at full voice, "When the Midnight Choo-Choo Leaves for Alabam'."

The room seemed hollow. Empty.

"Wonder where Papa is," Lillian said.

"Wonder."

She set the table. Emmett carried the remnants of duckling from the sink on the newspaper they'd been wrapped in. "What you goin' be when you all grown, Emmett?"

"Well, I sure not goin' stay in the embalmin' business. Never nobody to talk to." Lillian added some greens and they sat down to eat. "What you goin' to be?" Emmett asked.

"Don' know . . . jus' don't know . . ." Lillian placed a bird on each of their plates, then folded up the grease-stained newspaper to throw it away. Neither of them gave a moment's glance at the headline: WILSON WINS . . . TEDDY'S BULL MOOSE SPLITS PARTY—DEFEATS TAFT.

The winter of 1912–13 was a mild one. The four months between election and Inauguration Day passed without significant incident. Memory of the butlers' ball stayed with Maggie a long time; she would catch herself humming "The Memphis Blues." Once, while Maggie was scrubbing down the grand staircase, Mrs. Jaffray caught her at it and for a few hours, until Ike Hoover intervened, Maggie's job seemed in jeopardy. "I'd like to tell that woman she can scrub the stairs herself." Maggie spilled out her irritation to Mays, Mercer, and Jackson in the staff dining room.

"Take your blessin's where you can find 'em, Maggie," Mays solomonized. "Jus' be thankful to Mr. Teddy Roosevelt for remakin' this buildin' . . . 'cause they was *two* grand stairscases before then."

The day William Howard Taft was to give up the reins of office to Woodrow Wilson dawned crisp-cold and snowless.

Center hall was a shambles: walls bare, oriental furniture and plants gone, priceless bric-a-brac being quickly wrapped and buried in boxes and trunks. Draperies hung drunkenly from half-dismantled rods. The room had the look of a mansion being hastily abandoned, as it must have been in Atlanta, with Sherman on the outskirts.

Lubau and Dolores slipped out of west sitting hall carrying pieces of hand luggage and fled down the grand staircase with no glance for the staff, who took little notice of them.

Mrs. Jaffray clapped her hands. "All right, everybody." Those who served on the second floor, who'd been on duty around the clock, fell into an uneven line, like weary, reluctant troops: Coates, Annie, Dixon, McKenzie, Michaels, Maggie, and Maureen—the men in the livery so relished by Mrs. Taft, the women in their winter day uniforms. "Straighten up, everyone." Mrs. Jaffray attempted to present a proud, respectful facade to a defeated leader; but they straggled and grumbles were heard.

Emotion straightened the line.

President and Mrs. Taft emerged from their suite: he in cutaway and carrying the Inaugural top hat, she wan in velvet, violets pinned to her furs. The staff applauded—politely, at first, but four shared years refused to be trundled away like so many possessions.

The President's eyes grew moist as the applause grew. Pride and affection walked along with him as he nodded goodbye to each one: a hand shaken, a word of appreciation; Mrs. Taft fighting valiantly to hold back tears of defeat. As they reached Maggie, they stopped. Warm looks of deeply shared experience and a bond of affection flowed between these three. Mrs. Taft clasped Maggie's hand in hers, then the big man and his lady moved on to the elevator where Ike Hoover waited to escort them below.

The staff broke ranks, galvanized to action, the men quickly skinning out of livery, dropping full dress jackets into a waiting trunk. A remaining drape was taken down, a Persian rug rolled up, plants dollied away. *Out with the old, in with the new.* That day was Maggie's first experience with a change of administration. A scant hour in which to accomplish the impossible. The retiring President was at that moment stepping into the carriage with the incoming President . . . the ride up Pennsylvania Avenue . . . the swearing in . . . the speeches, the promises . . . the triumphal ride back . . .

The next time the elevator doors opened onto the family floor it was into a metamorphosed atmosphere of staid, serene New England, created by substantial oak, pine, chintz, and wicker furniture. Most of it had come out of the attic and bore the U.S. GOVERNMENT PROPERTY stamp; academicians like the new President were known to be of modest means.

"President and Mrs. Woodrow Wilson," Ike Hoover announced to the staff.

A severe looking man, at first glance almost formidable. Sharply featured patrician face, with a high forehead and long jaw that would be grist for the cartoonist's pen. Pince-nez pinched the bridge of his nose. Of modest stature, he created the illusion of height. Long tapering fingers held the Inaugural silk hat as he came into the corridor, studying his new surroundings.

"May I introduce your staff," Ike Hoover continued. "Mrs. Jaffray, the housekeeper. Our head butler, Coates—"

The First Lady, Mrs. Ellen Wilson, modestly gowned, of a pastel fragility that brought Gainsborough to mind, glanced with avid interest at the art displayed along the walls, since she herself painted, murmuring greetings in the warm accents of Georgia. Twenty-seven years married, content to have remained a professor's wife, barely adjusted to being the governor's lady of New Jersey, now suddenly thrust into the eye of the world in the White House—not by public acclaim, but by political accident of a split Republican ticket. It had all the earmarks of a back-door entrance . . .

"Housemen McKenzie, Michaels," Ike Hoover went on, "first maid Annie Gilhooley, Maggie Rogers, second maid . . ."

President Wilson held up a staying hand. "We will all come to know one another in time, I am sure." On the way to his suite he turned off every other lamp, pausing at the door to look back at the staff. His austere demeanor hadn't changed, but there was the slightest glint of humor in his eyes.

"Waste not, want not," he said, and followed Mrs. Wilson into their quarters.

Fix, mend, turn off, cut down . . . You felt the frugality of the Wilson White House everywhere, from the amount of sugar in your coffee to the amount of soap used in the laundry. "You hear the talk goin' round?" Mercer inquired of Maggie some weeks after the change of administration. "Mr. Wilson, he squeeze a nickel so tight, he make the buffalo holler . . . Well, that's what they sayin' in the papers . . ." The buffalo nickel, a newly minted coin, was often discussed these days.

Trouble was, the coin still only bought a nickel's worth.

For Maggie, the penny pinching brought an unexpected blessing. While only napkins had needed mending, she could carry them home. But the only place big enough to spread banquet cloths was the long table in the staff dining room. This called for Lillian to come into the White House, where Maggie could keep a proper eye on her.

The flatiron sizzled from a drop of saliva on Maggie's finger. When the surface was just the right temperature, she pressed flat with practiced hand a spot which Lillian had just meticulously rewoven. That child could work a miracle! Maggie would defy anyone to find where the damage had been. Moving the heavy iron back and forth across the fine linen fabric, she watched Lillian, sitting cross-legged on the table, reweaving a tear in the huge cloth that spread out before her the length of the table and two chairs beyond, working in a silence Maggie could never fathom. The flatiron cooled and had to be carried back to the kitchen to be exchanged for a heated one. A nuisance, but better than those new electric irons where you had to keep pulling the cord out to keep them from scorching. "You keep workin'," she told Lillian. "Be right back."

Lillian nodded. Put the needle into the cloth. Bring the needle out. Stitch, stitch . . . *What you goin' to do with your life?* Emmett was a boy, easier for him. He could get up and go after what he wanted. Didn't Papa go away every time he felt the need to? Mama was like the nuns in the convent, slaving all the time, day and night. That wasn't going to happen to Lillian . . . *Like to just lay down on this table and float away . . . up through the roof, across the sky . . . Free . . .* Stitch, stitch . . .

"Where you off to, chile?"

Impulse, as much as cramped muscles from the exacting work, moved Lillian to climb down from the table. "You not finished." Maggie pointed out a burn hole from a cigar ash and half a dozen more snags.

"Mama, I cain't jus' set and sew, got to walk 'round some . . ." She put on her shoes, tied the laces.

"Mind you now, you only here to help out with the mendin' . . . not free to wander where you not s'pose to!"

Crutch tucked into her armpit, Lillian swung out of the room and on down the corridor, bound for the door that would take her outside. But a velvet drape on the way tempted her like the serpent in Eden. She'd seen the draped opening every time she'd been brought to the White House. To her "What's behind it?" Maggie had always replied, "Not any of *your* business." Pulling the heavy velvet around her slight body, Lillian slipped into its folds and allowed herself a forbidden peek.

The long, broad corridor on the other side had a flourishing business of its own. A young white, uniformed guide, herding a group of tourists, was explaining: "This is not the original building, you understand. The British burned down the White House in 1814." At a portrait of a dark-haired lady with slumbering eyes, mocking smile, and décolletage, he said, "This is Dolley Madison, a woman of courage. You ladies will be interested to know she was a real heroine in that war . . ."

Lillian's interest was in three young women in summer frocks and hats, so close to the velvet drape that she could have reached out and touched them. As the tour guide moved his charges a little farther on, expounding on Dolley's courage in saving a portrait of

George Washington at the risk of her own life while the White House was burning, the three young women remained at the Madison portrait, scrutinizing it from every angle. "Sure better looking than those dreary *Wilson* girls," one of them said.

"Have you seen pictures of them?" said another. "Ugly as sin."

"Skinny as board fences," agreed the third. "Real lemons, never going to get husbands . . ."

Having captured the shocked ears of some of the other tourists, the three played it bland and innocent, studying Andrew Jackson's likeness.

"Now this portrait of Martin Van Buren, you will notice—" was the last Lillian heard as she was unceremoniously yanked back into the staff corridor by an irate Maggie.

"What you think you doin', chile?"

"Mama, you should hear the terrible things those girls sayin' 'bout the Wilson family."

"Where? What girls?" Reacting as though she had been personally insulted, Maggie pulled back the drape for Lillian to identify the three young women now covering giggles behind their pocketbooks. *"Them* the girls?" Maggie broke into a chuckle that stayed with her all the way back to the kitchen. "Why, they the President's daughters . . . always playin' their little jokes . . . My darlin' Wilson girls . . ."

A phrase to stick in Lillian's craw. She was to remember the years 1913–14 as *My darlin' Wilson girls . . . had theirselves such a pretty party, they did . . . Gone and got theirselves engaged—two of 'em and a third sure to follow . . . A weddin' in the house, oh, my, wish you could seen how pretty it was . . . Cake stood three feet across, weighed hundred and thirty pounds. Bride looked like an angel, stood on a white vicuña rug . . . Now a second weddin' goin' to be takin' place . . .*

Days when Lillian's needle wasn't called upon, Maggie brought home tales of this family . . . how the President, no matter what the problems of state, found time to clown around, to make his daughters laugh . . .

dancing a jig, putting on a tablecloth for a costume and
reading a speech he'd typed himself in Greek—imagine, *Greek*—that nobody could understand but himself. And never too tired to take his "girls" out to the
shows!

"Was *my* papa home, he'd do the same thing!"

" 'Course he would, chile. I meant in no way to be-
little your papa . . ." It was the first outburst from
Lillian in longer than Maggie could remember. Now
that she thought on it, the children rarely seemed to
say anything about their father. Both growing up;
growing away from her . . . it stayed at the top of her
mind, but the White House was all-consuming. Long
days, what with the festivities of Miss Jessie marrying
Mr. Frances Bowes Sayre (backstairs talk was, he
looked like a younger edition of the President); now all
the excitement on again for Miss Eleanor to marry
her father's Secretary of Treasury, William McAdoo
(old enough to be her father, newspapers said. If
this gave the President any concern, it was kept strictly
in the family).

With all the dressmaking going on, Lillian took to
spending almost as much time in the small, cramped
sewing room up under the eaves of the attic as she
did at home. Hardly any room to turn around, with
garment racks holding bridesmaids' dresses and matching hats. She had so many stitches invested in the
beaded bridal cap and veil, she couldn't see any reason not to try it on.

"And in this room," she said to the mirror, "Miss
Lil'yan Rogers was married—that her portrait there
on the wall. Brave lady . . . While the White House was
burnin', finished sewin' her own bridal veil . . ." Maggie, who had climbed the stairs with Maureen to bring
down the bridal attendants' finery, erupted with exasperation. "Don't you realize, chile—colored girl not
s'pose to do things like that?" *But hadn't she been
hoping all the time that Lillian would do something outlandish, to show that she was back to her old self?*
"Cain't leave you alone, always up to somethin' . . ."

Lillian removed the satin and tulle from her head.

"Well, had I my choice, that the job I'd like, Mama. Tour guidin' . . ."

"Well, you never goin' make it. Got to be a man. Secret Service, an' lily-white . . . Don't dawdle now, bring Miss Eleanor's veil . . ." Smoothing the material of the gowns as tenderly as any mother of the bride, Maggie, assisted by Maureen, took the bridesmaids' dresses below. Lillian crutched her way down the steep attic stairs after them, carrying bridal cap and veil.

Mrs. Wilson was in the center hall, doing her harassed best to orchestrate her family into some semblance of organization. Two of her daughters, the still spinster Margaret and the married Jessie, wanted to try on the gowns that Maggie and Maureen had brought down. "No, no, girls, if we don't hurry we're going to be late. Can't keep the minister and all the other people waiting . . . *Eleanor* . . ." she called back through the west sitting hall. "Are you coming? It's *your* wedding we're rehearsing for . . ."

For reply came the ragtime strains of "Ballin' the Jack."

"Oh, no . . ." Mrs. Wilson despaired. "Eleanor and her records . . . You're not playing your graphanola at a time like this?"

"Mother . . . you've got to see Daddy!" Eleanor's voice came to her.

A startled peal of laughter from Mrs. Wilson. Daughters Margaret and Jessie moved excitedly forward to have front-row seats as the President of the United States danced from his bedroom with the daughter he would, tomorrow, give away in marriage. Somewhat awkwardly, but in no wise inhibited, he struggled to master the hip swinging of the fashionable new dance. Singing the words, half a beat behind, "First you put your right foot . . . dada da . . . swing it to the right . . ."

Mrs. Wilson held her sides. "Woodrow, I swan . . ."

"Don't interrupt, dear, I'm having a lesson in modern terpsichore . . . Can't go to a wedding reception without knowing the latest," he said as he swung it to the left, and did the twist around, twist around that the dance dictated. Then they were all dancing around and laughing, the girls trying to draw their mother into it. "Oh, no, not me . . . your father's the Nijinsky in this house . . ." But she did try one experimental hip twist.

From where Maggie stood, it was a sight to behold. Maureen echoed her feelings exactly. "Ain't they a storybook family now?"

"They my babies, those girls."

Through it all, Lillian stood aloof, in the background, unnoticed. When Maggie turned, holding out her hand for the bridal headdress, Lillian thrust it at her, pivoted on the crutch, and went back up the attic. *My darlin' Wilson girls!*

Wedding excitement over, the fragile Mrs. Wilson continued to spend her days painting landscapes. After a time of taking easel and palette out onto the south grounds, she tired of the view toward the Washington Monument. The north grounds were too public; Maggie showed her the way up through an attic door onto the roof, where you could promenade all around the perimeter of the building. Sentries had stood up there warning of the charge that August day in 1814 when the British put the torch to the house. During the Civil War, interested parties had watched the sky turn black with cannon fire when the Confederates came as close as Manassas, a scant seventeen miles away. Mrs. Wilson found it a serene place to paint: the broad boulevards to the north that cut the city into civilized pie-wedged pieces; the greenery to the south and to the river. "What are all those shacks over there?" she inquired one day of Maggie, sighting the area that lay to the west and south between the White House and the Potomac.

"That Foggy Bottom, ma'am."

"Who lives there?"

"Colored folks, ma'am."

Briefly, their eyes met. "Do you live there, Maggie?" she asked gently.

"Yes, ma'am, I do."

From that point on, Mrs. Wilson put aside the genteel pastime of landscape painting.

As the White House claimed more and more of their mother, Lillian and Emmett drew closer together. It was nice when they put on the summer streetcars, with long benches that ran the full length of the car, facing out, where you could see everything. For a nickel you could take a trolley ride all the way out across the District line to Glen Echo in Maryland. Trouble was, you couldn't get off; just had to turn around and come back because "coloreds" weren't allowed in the park. "Why don't you sneak in," Emmett urged Lillian. "They likely wouldn't stop you."

"How about you?" she said. "You got the blue eyes."

"Oh, I don't know . . . my hair give me 'way . . ."

Which was just the kind of talk Maggie didn't ever want to hear. *Anyplace we not wanted, we don't go* took its place along with the other family slogan, *We got some the finest blood in Virginia in our veins.* It was darned hard, in Emmett's opinion, trying to live up to that kind of blood.

"What Miz Wilson got to come to our house for, anyway?" Emmett complained. It was a late spring day of 1914 and Maggie had rushed home early from work to prepare the house for a visit from the First Lady, stopping only long enough to make the final payment to the secondhand store on K Street for a table she'd had on layaway for months. It was small, marble-topped, and bore a nodding acquaintance with Victorian design. As she fussed with it, moving it a few inches one way, then the other, to find the perfect spot in the room for it, she tried to imbue her children with enthusiasm over Mrs. Wilson's imminent visit. "This lady does nothin' but give of herself. Goes out every day, takin' food and clothes to the poor. Drivin' herself to the bone, and her in frail health . . . Working to get rest rooms for women workers, and better housin' for all the Negroes . . . That's why she comin' here, to see how we live."

"We live poor, don't she know that?" Emmett fed pieces of firewood to the potbellied stove to take the chill out of the air. Lillian, at the window, catching the last of daylight as she rapidly sewed together a tea cozy, added her personal grievance. "You'd think *they* was your family, way you carry on about 'em."

"Don' like you children talk that way . . . don't like it 'tall . . ." She placed a single china cup and saucer (from the secondhand store) with crocheted doily on the table. Then a folded linen napkin. From the corner of her eye she caught Emmett about to toss into the fire the newspaper clippings she'd saved from the Wilson weddings, and rescued them just in time.

"What you savin' all that stuff for anyways, Mama?"

Maggie didn't exactly know, except she liked to look at them. Folding the clippings more carefully, she put them away in the chifforobe.

"An' Mr. Wilson . . ." Emmett went on. "All that big talk of his bein' the Pres'dent of all the people . . . Been in office more than a year, what's he done?"

"Emmett, don't you speak disrespectful of the Pres'-dent!"

"Cain't help it, Mama . . . that's what they sayin' on the street. Tell you one thing, soon as I can, I'm joinin' the Army."

"You do no such thing! I want you in the Post Office, or civil service. You don't like undertakin', all right, I can understand that. But you goin' have a profession. You got to remember we come from good blood, why some of our kin—"

"Mama, our kin that made it to the State House was white!" Emmett's jaundiced but accurate comment startled Maggie. Before she could recover from the dissonance of it, cynicism from Lillian made her realize how far apart she and the children had become in their thinking. "Look at you, Mama, they work you like a field hand over there . . . They so anxious to do somethin' for the Negroes, why don't they start with you? They didn't give you food to tote, half the time we'd end up hungry. Emmett's still wearin' Charlie Taft's let-out pants. Wasn't for the Wilson girls' dresses, I'd be wearin' patches on patches. An' your new table, Mama—onliest thing you bought just 'cause you wanted it . . . what'd it cost—four dollars? Took 'most a year to get out of the store . . . Emmett's right, a visit from the President's wife not goin' to change things a penny's worth 'round here . . ."

In her distress, Maggie kept dusting the same spot on the table. "You the one always *believed,* Lil'yan . . ."

"Well, I come to see things got a way of not workin' out like they s'pose to . . ." As Lillian bent again over her sewing, Maggie wondered if she was thinking about those dancing slippers again. Emmett studied his sister in the failing light. "Lil'yan don't have to wait on Mr. Wilson's promises, or anybody else's. Lil'yan light enough to pass . . ."

"Nobody in this house ever goin' to say they somethin' they not. Do you understand me? We got every reason to be proud of who we be—both sides—and don't neither of you be forgettin' it . . . And, Emmett, we won't be speakin' again 'bout you goin' in the Army . . ." You could have heard her down to the corner, except that no one in that block was listening to anything except the purr of that White House limousine rolling down the street. Curtains, at windows that had them, were pulled back. Doors were opened. People stepped out and gaped. It was the first time down Nineteenth Street, but other streets in Foggy Bottom had seen this elegant phaeton, had experienced the charity of the delicate lady who stepped from it, nodded her thanks to the driver, and walked up the path to Maggie Rogers' door.

Inside, a frantic moment while Lillian hurriedly put in her last stitches and the tea cozy and teapot were in place.

"How nice of you to call, Miz Wilson, won't you please to come in?"

The First Lady stepped into the room, as easy and comfortable as though calling on a faculty wife. Maggie was the one under tension, but needn't have worried. While her children were guarded in what they said, smiled and were pleasant, they stayed in the background, Emmett keeping the fire going, Lillian bringing small corncakes to the table. Mrs. Wilson sipped tea like it was the most natural thing in the world that there be only one teacup and saucer on the table, and she alone enjoying the beverage. Ofttimes, in years to come, Maggie was to think back: *The President's wife called on me . . .*

Though pale and visibly tired, Mrs. Wilson kept up a constant, gentle query. "And the eight dollars a month you pay for rent, Maggie, does that include heat?"

"No, ma'am, we buy our coal and wood."

"Or electricity?"

"We pay for that. too, ma'am." Mrs. Wilson wanted to see the bedroom. The pump where they drew the water. She had already seen the alleys and hungry children of this area. "Mr. Wilson was elected the President of *all the people of all races,*" she said fervently. "That was not just an election promise with him, Maggie, or slogan. He means to keep his word."

"Oh, I believe that, Miz Wilson. My children and me, we *all* believe that . . ."

Lillian was at the table pouring tea when Mrs. Wilson returned from inspecting the house to pick up her gloves. "Thank you very much, Lillian, it was delicious . . . So nice to talk with you, Emmett . . ."

"Yes, ma'am."

Maggie walked her to the door, noting that the slender shoulders sagged ever so slightly, and there was a faint blueness to her pallor. "Things will get better for your people, Maggie."

"Yes, ma'am, we all lookin' forward to that."

"So gracious of you to allow me to visit. I love your new table."

"Thank you, ma'am."

As she stood in the doorway, the First Lady assured Maggie of her intention to use her last ounce of energy to better conditions for the Negro people.

For Ellen Axson Wilson, wife of the twenty-eighth President of the United States, that last ounce ran out on August 6, 1914.

They saw her failing. The President, her daughters, doctors, nurses, and Maggie stayed near her bedside days and nights, as she slipped in and out of consciousness. That last day dawned bright and hot but inside the house, gloom pervaded. Servants went about their work, hushed, fearful, waiting for the inevitable. Maggie, who had sponged the wraithlike hands and forehead during the night, would always remember the open eyes looking at her without recognition.

The heavy doors to the sitting hall slid soundlessly apart. Ike Hoover, escorting the doctor to the elevator, paused to speak to Coates who had been standing, sentinellike, for hours, as had Mays, Mercer, Jackson, and others who waited out the night on the back stairs. Coates' eyes brimmed with tears as he informed them: "The good lady is gone." Maggie's leaden heart drew her through the open door into the sitting hall from where she could see the desolated President, kneeling beside the bed, his wife's lifeless hand in his, saying, "My God, my God, what am I going to do?"

Maggie closed the door on his heartbreak and walked back through the center hall to the chore she had abandoned. It felt right and proper to be on her knees. Her tears fell into the swirls of scrub water as she washed and rinsed, washed and rinsed.

The grieving President came from his room, walked the length of the hall, descended the grand staircase. Maggie, well past the landing, quickly pulled bucket and brush out of his path, but he seemed unaware of her presence. Melancholy carried him almost to the foot of the stairs where he hesitated, looked back, as through a fog. "Maggie?"

"Yes, Mr. Pres'dent."

"Mrs. Wilson told me of her visit to you and your family and of your warm hospitality . . ." He was unable to continue. Composing himself, he addressed Ike Hoover, who had followed him down the stairs. "Tell Mrs. Jaffray that Maggie is never to be on her knees again."

4

☒ ☒ ☒

Dateline May 7, 1915

GERMANS SINK LUSITANIA

118 Americans Aboard
British Cunard Steamship

In a speech in Philadelphia, President Wilson assures the American people that "There is such a thing as a man being too proud to fight. There is such a thing as a nation being so right that it does not need to convince others by force that it is right." Still, the country worries. For months, journalists and Capitol Hill urge caution . . .

In the summer of '16, militant pacifist women massed along the wrought iron fence of the White House, dressed in white summer dresses and straw hats, and waving palm leaf fans. They carried a long cloth banner—waist to ankle wide—proclaiming in huge red and blue letters that REAL PATRIOTS KEEP COOL. Colonel House, who was to Woodrow Wilson what Archie Butt had been to Teddy Roosevelt and Taft, came out to read the banner and carried the information in to the President. Woodrow Wilson did not comment.

A young man in the brand-new uniform of the United States Army stood and watched the ladies parading. He was understandably nervous. "Your mama be right out," Mays said to him.

"You tell her?" Emmett asked apprehensively.

"Jus' tole her you was here . . . not what you wearin'. Sure you doin' the right thing, boy?"

Mays went back to his post at the door rather than be there when Maggie came out. Totally unprepared, she had to suppress panic at sight of her son in uniform.

"I'm in the Army, Mama . . ." was all he could think to say. "Goin' to Mexico with General Pershing."

"You cain't . . . you only sixteen. Army won't take you till you eighteen . . . You have to have a letter . . ."

"Had a letter, Mama. Wrote it myself."

"An' signed my name . . . ? "

"Mama, try to understand. What else am I goin' to do? Be a waiter? Janitor? Go to Treasury, and no matter how good my work, my ratin' stay the same . . . messenger."

Way back in Keswick, his papa had said to him that he could be a general! "My God, Emmett, my God, you just a boy."

"Gov'ment thinks I'm a man."

So much to say and no way to say it as the ladies paraded back and forth. "Jus' you do like you s'pose to, chile . . . Take care of yourself . . ." He leaned down, kissed her on the cheek. They clung to each other a moment, then he backed off . . . a few steps, his eyes never leaving her face. A kind of half wave and he turned away. Ran. The ladies came between them; when their numbers had passed, Emmett was gone.

Maggie's body worked on its own, moving one foot after the other back up the walk into the White House and down the corridor. On her way to the back stairs, she was vaguely conscious of having passed Mrs. Jaffray, hatted and gloved for the day's marketing. Something beyond her will turned Maggie around. With sudden resolve she said, "Miz Jaffray, I been in the White House eight years now. I would like a raise."

Mrs. Jaffray barely paused. "I'm sorry, that's impossible."

"Now why's that, Miz Jaffray?"

Somewhat surprised at Maggie's curt tone, Mrs. Jaffray stopped and told her quite frankly, "If I gave you more money, you'd be making as much as a white girl."

The insult stung. "Didn't know you paid by color."

"We have our rules." For Mrs. Jaffray, the issue was closed. Maggie, driven by forces long held in leash, followed her resolutely to the door. "With my son goin' into the Army and Lillian only gettin' odd jobs, there's no way I can make out on what I'm gettin'. I'm worth more, Miz Jaffray."

"Times are hard for all of us, we must make adjustments."

"But Miz Wilson tole me herself that things goin' get better for us!"

"I remind you, Maggie," was Mrs. Jaffray's final word, "there's a new Mrs. Wilson now."

Indeed there was, only sixteen months after the first Mrs. Wilson had been laid to rest. And if the President hadn't been dissuaded by Colonel House and others concerned with his political future, he would have married the voluptuous, spirited widow Edith Bolling Galt, years his junior, sooner than he had. Not seven months after Ellen Wilson's death, he was taking the new lady for drives right out in public. Within nine months, he proposed. It was the talk of Washington, from the Hill to salons to the back stairs of the White House. Maggie never doubted that the man suffered gravely the loss of his angel wife; what bothered her was that he didn't suffer long enough.

"Look at 'em out there," she said to Lillian, who was helping hang a mended drape in the Red Room. "World could come to an end, they'd never know it. Why isn't he in here, doin' somethin' to stop the wars?"

"Got to take some time to hisself, Mama." From her high perch on the extension ladder Lillian could see through the tall window down to the garden where the President and his bride sat on a stone bench surrounded by rose bushes just coming into first bloom. He held one of her hands in his, while he read to her from a volume of poetry. After the fragile Ellen, the vibrant health of Edith Galt Wilson was an almost shocking contrast. The orchid on her shoulder, a daily gift from the President, was, in Maggie's opinion, a vulgar display of unseemly passion. "Look at her, moonin' over him. Don't let him out of her sight. Walks him to his office, walks him back. Wonder how she feels, settin' there with him in the rose garden Miz Wilson planted."

"She is Miz Wilson, Mama."

"Never to me. Miz Wilson, bless her angel soul, she gone." And with her, Maggie's hope for a better life. The President's concerns these days focused more on European affairs and the upcoming election than on the section of Washington called Foggy Bottom.

Maggie, standing at the foot of the ladder holding the weight of the heavy drape so that Lillian could mend an area where constant sunlight had caused it to weaken, now released it, and adjusted the heavy, rich folds of fabric. The work completed, Lillian climbed down the ladder. "Now stand up straight," Maggie cautioned her, "don't lean so much on your crutch . . . brush the threads off your dress, smooth your hair. An' let me do the talkin' . . ."

Mrs. Jaffray came into the room, as scheduled. Found the work satisfactory, and was finished with the matter.

"Miz Jaffray, before you go . . ."

"Yes, Maggie?"

"Maureen be leavin' to get married, and you not replaced her yet. I been thinkin' . . . Lil'yan here could handle her work, and sew besides." The glance Mrs. Jaffray gave Lillian foretold her answer. It was one thing to be fine with a needle, but a housemaid must be quick on her feet, able to run up and down stairs. And get down on her *knees,* if need be . . . (Mrs. Jaffray had not forgiven Mr. Wilson for his interference in ordering Maggie off hers.)

"But Lil'yan jus' walked up three flights to the

sewin' room, run a treadle machine for an hour, an' helped me carry this big drape down . . ."

"Maggie," Mrs. Jaffray reminded in genteel tones, "it's undignified to discuss this further. Much as I sympathize, Lillian is handicapped."

"But, Miz Jaffray, if you jus' give her—"

"Mama . . . don't beg for me!" Smarting under the humiliation, Lillian folded up the ladder, stuck her arm through it, hung it over her shoulder, and with positive flourish swung out of the room on her crutch.

It was a changed White House. The Wilson daughters came to dinners, or to visit with their father, but were infrequently on the second floor. Miss Margaret lived there awhile, then she too went away. Maggie picked up the Irish expression "Herself" in reference to the new First Lady. That way she didn't have to acknowledge the lady's usurpation.

Herself had found out that Maggie was a hairdresser and kept her as busy as Mrs. Taft had done. There were receptions and galas almost every night. The lights that glowed from the White House brightened up all of Washington—Maggie wondered whatever happened to "Waste not, want not." As retiring and private as the first Mrs. Wilson had been, the second seemed to thrive in the public eye.

It must be said for the President that while he was consumed with love for the new lady, the weight of office was always on him. To keep his country out of war was his duty. The lights in the Oval Room burned long after every other light in the house had been extinguished. Millions of dead Belgians and French haunted his dreams . . .

Then why . . . *why* wouldn't the ladies leave him alone?

"They're out there again, Edith," he said. From the window of the dressing room, where Maggie was curling his wife's hair, Wilson could see out to the sidewalk. See their hats, moving back and forth along the top of the shrubbery. Picket signs bobbed up and down but were too far away to be read.

"A night in jail," Edith suggested, "would do them all good—for disturbing the peace."

"No, no . . ." That was the last thing Wilson wanted. "Can't you just see tomorrow's headlines: LADIES JAILED BY PRESIDENT?" No, the White House couldn't afford to give the impression that it took the militant ladies' protest seriously.

"Then for heaven's sake, Woodrow, don't worry about it . . . just a passing thing . . ." But Wilson couldn't put it out of his mind. If only he knew what was on those signs . . .

"Send one of your aides to find out." Each time Edith spoke to him, Maggie had to wait patiently for her to turn back in the chair.

"That would be as bad as going myself. Don't dare send anyone official . . ." He turned from the window, genuinely troubled, hurt. "How can they be distrustful of me, Edith? When I ran for the office of President of all the people, I assumed they understood that did not include the franchise for women . . ."

"Their franchise is at home, raising families. Maggie . . . a little more bouffant in the front . . ."

"Yes, ma'am." Maggie teased the hair with a comb until Herself nodded approval.

"What did I do to deserve suffragettes?" The President's attitude was easier now, as though making light of the matter would dispense with it. "The ladies, bless them, if they were given the vote would probably elect John Barrymore or Francis X. Bushman to office." As he paced by her, Edith reached out and caught his hand in hers. "They're no more matinee idol than you, my darling . . ."

He smiled indulgently. "You're prejudiced, my dear . . . it's a certainty I'd never be elected on my face. Nor should any man . . . Our country is at peace in a world at war, don't they realize that? *I've kept us out of war!*"

"Don't agitate yourself, Woodrow, you've enough on your mind."

He moved back to the window, brooding, as he

watched the hats and picket signs move in and out of his view. Edith came up with the perfect solution to his problem. "Send Maggie out."

"Maggie?" It was as though he'd forgotten Maggie was present, or even who she was.

"Outside, Woodrow. She's not official. Nobody would know . . ."

"Capital, my dear, capital! Would you, Maggie—go out there and find out what the ladies are saying?"

"Yes, sir, Mr. Pres'dent, be happy to."

"Thank you. Very kind of you." He took Edith's hand in both of his, and kissed it. With just a hint of Barrymore in his manner, he said, "Then I'm excused to go back and wrestle with affairs of state?"

"You're excused, darling." It was moments like this that got under Maggie's hide; she expressed her irritation in the way she put down her curling iron. "No no, Maggie," Edith said to her, "finish my hair first . . . those harridans will still be there, they're not going anywhere." Maggie laid in another wave to create the fashionable dip over the forehead. "The poor President," Edith said to her image in the mirror. "You can't know how lucky you are, Maggie."

"Ma'am?"

"You do your work and go home. Mr. Wilson stays awake nights. The Germans . . . Congress . . . now this nasty little skirmish in Mexico with that dreadful bandit, Pancho Villa . . ."

"I know all about that, ma'am."

Edith Wilson looked at her in surprise. "You do?"

"Yes, ma'am. My son is there, fightin' . . ."

"Wilson lies . . . he denies . . . women's rights," the suffragettes chanted as they marched. Maggie could hear them before she came around the tall shrubbery and saw them. They walked in a straight line down the sidewalk, turned around and walked back, ignoring the shouted taunts of the spectators clumped along the fence and across the street: "Go home, your husband's waiting . . ." "Stay in the kitchen where you belong . . ."

and "It's a man's world, don't you know that yet, sister?"

As picket signs paraded past her, Maggie tried to memorize their messages and wondered how she could bring herself to report to the President the scurrilous things they said: WILSON PROMISES WORTHLESS . . . WOMEN ARE EQUAL . . . GIVE US THE VOTE, OR ARE YOU AFRAID OF US? . . . WOODROW, YOUR MOTHER WAS A WOMAN . . . One suffragette, tiring, stepped out of line and rested her sign against the fence. It was immediately picked up and put into motion again, bobbing along a little unevenly because of the crutch underneath the bearer's arm. When Maggie realized who the substitute was, she hoped the ground would swallow her right then and there. As her daughter moved past her, she grabbed hold of her collar, pulled her out of action, and disposed of the sign before Lillian quite knew what happened.

"What am I goin' do with you, chile? Sassin' Miz Jaffray the other day, now mockin' the President."

"Wasn't mockin' the President."

"Don't you know, sign carryin' out here could cause me to lose my job?"

"I think these ladies got the right idea, Mama."

"Sometimes you try me so . . . What's goin' to become of you?"

"Don't worry about me, Mama, I'll make my way . . ." Lillian bounded away on the crutch. Sprightly. As if the world wasn't the treacherous place Maggie knew it to be.

HE KEPT US OUT OF WAR.

The slogan was everywhere: on fences and sides of buildings, on the trolleys coming and going. Everybody wanted to believe it. Nobody wanted to believe it more than Woodrow Wilson did.

It got him reelected.

In November of '16, it was JOHNNY WON'T BE GOING OVER THERE that marked the X in the Democratic column.

January of '17 found the President making an impassioned plea to the world for "peace without victory," for freedom of the seas.

February brought hostile submarine action in the Atlantic and his announcement to Congress that the United States was severing diplomatic relations with Germany.

By the time of his second inauguration, it was clear that Mars would soon acquire a Yankee accent.

Mercer, having been upped to houseman with duties on the second floor, was the one who carried the President's breakfast up to him on the morning of April 6, 1917. Ike Hoover, standing solemnly outside the closed doors, stayed Mercer from entering with the tray. "Some members of the cabinet still in there. Been with him since dawn."

"Secretary of War?" Mercer asked anxiously.

Ike Hoover's sigh was freighted with concern. "And State, Treasury, leaders of both houses. Congress isn't sleeping much these days, either . . ."

"There's goin' be fightin' . . ." Mercer, at thirty-eight, was too old to go. But there was Jackson's boy and young fellows coming up on the staff. And, to Maggie's short-lived joy, Emmett back from Mexico . . .

The solemn group of secretaries and senators filed out of the oval study to the elevator. Some of them Mercer recognized from pictures in the paper as Newton Baker (War), Robert Lansing (State), and, of course, the President's son-in-law William Gibbs McAdoo (Treasury).

Mercer carried the tray into the study and set the dishes out. The President, in pajamas and worn bathrobe, stood at the window as though turned to stone.

"Anythin' else I can do for you, sir?"

Ignoring the food, the President turned, his haggard appearance witness to his torment. "What's a schoolteacher like me doing with a war?"

Meatless days . . . heatless days . . . petty gripes to take your mind off the casualty figures in the newspapers. Empty spaces appeared at the staff dining table; younger men, who'd come in well after Mercer, Mays, and Jackson, were called up. Hardly got to know some of them. "Lafayette, we are here . . ."

"The Yanks Are Comin' " . . . the Yanks are gone . . . the Yanks are "Over There" . . . And Emmett with them. Maggie, who now sat midway up the table, tried to remember the exact words of the last letter he'd sent. Better than a month without a word . . . Mays, who was coming to be recognized as the sage of the table, read newspaper dispatches aloud each day from strange-named places like Ypres and Cambrai, the Argonne Forest and Verdun. President Wilson continued to send back trays of barely touched food. "Don't see how the poor man keeps alive," Mercer worried; Coates added that it hurt to serve dinners, watching the President pick at his food. "War or no war, a man's got to eat."

"Well, Herself ain't lost her appetite none." Acid-tongued Annie was always quick to add agreement to Kearney's and McKenzie's daily grouse about our sending fighting men into any war to help the limeys.

Houseman Michaels' number came up in the draft fishbowl and was printed in the long list of numbers in the paper. "Uncle Sam Wants YOU." Each day lessened the time he had left. One morning he showed up at breakfast in an ill-fitting U.S. Army uniform issued by some nearsighted quartermaster.

"Uncle Sam's no tailor, and that's a fact," Mercer proclaimed as Michaels grabbed up a handful of khaki in the back to make it fit in front; then a handful in front to make it fit in back—a labored attempt at lightness which Mays tried to keep afloat: "Maybe they plannin' on fattenin' you up, Michaels."

For nine years Maggie had worked with Michaels, but she didn't feel she knew him. Looking at him, she recalled a shy, rawboned young immigrant, unused to city ways. He'd been about the same age then that Emmett was now. "Maybe I can fix that jacket so's it fits you, before you leave . . ."

"Don't you touch it, Maggie." This from Coates.

"The Germans see it, laugh theirselves to death . . ." Jackson kept the lame joke alive a little longer. "Yeh, cain't you jes' see the Kaiser, surrenderin', yellin', 'Run, boys, run, Michaels done come . . .' "

"I'll get me a few, I'll do ye proud . . ."

The laughter died. No one quite knew what to say.

"You keep yourself warm over there."

"Don't worry 'bout me, Maggie. Didn't ye hear? They got steam heat in those trenches . . . steam heat . . ." Bravado deserted him. He sat down, staring at his plate.

"Wish Emmett was still in Mexico, 'stead of some-place God knows where, over there . . ." Maggie hadn't meant to articulate her fear. But Michaels understood.

"I'll find him for ye, Maggie, and keep my protectin' arm around him . . ." She reached over and touched Michaels' arm in gratitude. The only sounds in the room were cups on saucers, forks against plates.

Lillian couldn't have chosen a better time to come bounding into the room, to liven the atmosphere. "What you doin' here, chile?" The reprimand burst automatically from Maggie. "You s'pose be out lookin' for a job . . ."

Lillian was waving an envelope. "Mama . . . letter from Emmett . . . couldn't wait, jus' had to open it . . ." With trembling hands, Maggie took the letter from her; fumbling for the spectacles in her apron pocket. Want-ing to go off to a corner by herself, but all eyes reached out as though, by touching the letter, the war would be less an unfathomable nightmare. She couldn't deny them.

"Well, cain't be too personal . . ." She sat back in her chair and read aloud; those who listened, answered back in the warm, loving way they did in her church. "Dear Mama, The birthday cake you sent me finally arrived six weeks late." ("Aw" . . . "Shoot" . . .) "Fol-lowed me through the Meuse, Ar-gonne . . . Saint . . ."

"Mihiel," Mays helped her out.

"Cha-tee-au . . ."

"Château-Thierry . . ."

"Tier . . . ry. Finally caught up with me at Ver-dun.

It was so hard, could have broke it up for bullets . . ."
("My stars" . . .) "The rats ate a good piece of it"
("Can you imagine?" . . . "For shame" . . .) ". . . but
the guys in the company weren't going to have a cake
from the White House and not eat it. So we soaked
what was left in my helmet and ate it for sweet
mush." ("Now if that ain't soldiers for you!") "Don't
you fret none about me, Mama. Give my love to Lillian,
Mays, Mercer, Jackson, all my friends." ("Ain't he
nice?") "Take care of yourself, you hear?" ("We carin'
for your mama for you" . . .) "Oh, remember I told you
General Pershing and me would get along fine? Well, I
got promoted for leadership and conduct under fire.
Don't that beat all? Your loving son, Second Lieutenant Emmett Rogers, Jr."

Second lieutenant . . . The words went around the
table, spoken with respect. "Knew it all along," Mays
said almost paternally. "Goin' be the first Negro general, that boy . . ."

Maggie beamed with pride. But there were some
other words back a ways she didn't like the sound of
. . . "conduct under fire . . ." That meant—!

They quieted her fears. Emmett was a man who
knew how to take care of himself. Hadn't General
Pershing promoted him? "He wouldn't be writing,
Mama, he wasn't okay . . ." Lillian answered. It was
Mercer who noticed the return address on the envelope. The feeling at the table was so good, he almost
hated to tell her. "Maggie . . . this letter been mailed
from a hospital."

"Hospital? I knew . . . he's hurt!"

"Mama, can't be . . . They s'pose to send you a
telegram, somebody hurt . . ."

"Could be a mix-up . . ."

"It's a war, you know . . ."

Mercer held Maggie's hands tightly in his, to help
quell the panic welling up within her. "We all here
with you, Maggie . . . goin' be all right . . . all
right . . ."

Well, Mays would darn soon hook on to what was
happenin'! Take the matter straight to Colonel House.

Anybody was to know what was goin' on over there, he was the knowin'est . . .

Soaked it in his helmet . . . ate it for sweet mush . . . One day, fighting off rats for a hard birthday cake. The next, gassed in both lungs.

Maggie reread the letter constantly . . . desperate to push time back before the enemy fouled the air with phosgene and chlorine. *Soaked it in his helmet . . . ate it for sweet mush . . .*

"Mama, you got to quit tormentin' yourself . . ." Lillian tried to interest her mother in the simple meal she had prepared, but Maggie persisted in the letter, held close to the light bulb. A wood-fed fire burned in the stove, but the walls of their little house wouldn't give up their chill. "Mama, put the letter away and eat somethin' . . . You got the word straight from Colonel House that Emmett got a chance to get better . . . We got to be grateful he's alive . . ."

"So young . . . so far 'way . . . *gassed* . . ." Maggie reached out for her. They clasped hands for mutual reassurance. "Your papa ought be told, if only I knew where to find him . . ."

Lillian withdrew her hand. "You'd know where to find him, you hadn't put him out."

For the moment, they were two women, not mother and daughter.

"That how you see it, Lil'yan? That I put him out? What you know about what he mean to me?"

"I saw Mercer holdin' your hands."

"Let me tell you somethin', chile. You put your ear to my words. If I was to be walkin' out with any man and was to see your papa across the street, I would tell that man, I am sorry but that is my husband over there and my place is with him . . . and that's how I'm goin' to feel till the day I die."

"We should of kept Papa with us."

"You goin' understand better when you a grown woman," Maggie said.

"Mama, I'm 'most twenty, workin' at a job. You got to give up treatin' me like a chile . . ."

"Not much of a job, takin' tickets at a movie show. Practically on the streets."

"I like it. Like talkin' to people . . ." There was a note of defiance in Lillian that Maggie decided not to challenge.

The Four Horsemen rampaged across Europe, adding to other horrors pandemic influenza that knew no loyalties, recognized no uniforms, no national boundaries. French, Germans, Poles, British, Yanks fell before the onslaught of the dread disease. Not content with decimating a continent, the winds of pestilence crossed the ocean. In a snap of time's finger, twenty million graves were filled.

In Washington, funeral parlors overflowed; caskets were stacked like cordwood on sidewalks and gravediggers dropped from exhaustion. Hearses were horse-drawn, their engines silent—not in tribute to the dead but to conserve gasoline. People feared to go into public places, so the Howard (along with other theaters) closed, and Lillian went to work for a doctor, the nurse whose place she took having collapsed right on the street. "You got fine hands," the doctor told Lillian. "You'd make a good nurse."

"I couldn't live with the sufferin'," she told him. "My own I can handle. Not other people's."

As if Maggie didn't have enough to worry about, Lillian, since Emmett's gassing, had taken to getting up at four in the morning to go down to Pennsylvania Station before work and wave goodbye to soldiers on their way overseas. And Lord knew how many of them already had the "influenzy" and didn't know it!

Gradually the plague ran its course and life got somewhat back to normal.

For the man in the White House the burdens, abroad and at home, doubled him over like Atlas. He sought relief in whatever laughter he could find, with Charlie Chaplin, Buster Keaton, and the cross-eyed wild man, Ben Turpin.

The word went out: "Movie show tonight, everybody

invited." They trooped up the back stairs, the old guard and the new people: kitchen helpers, laundry, gardeners, doormen, office workers. Tumulty, the President's secretary. Mrs. Jaffray. Ike Hoover. Anybody, everybody, to sit on chairs or the floor, to stand. It didn't matter. In the dark, laughter made them all the same rank.

Edith Wilson watched her husband: how thin he looked and how strangely boyish—head thrown back, teeth gleaming in the flicker of projector light, guffawing, cares forgotten. She wished she could hold on to this moment for him. But inevitably the pianist played out the last frantic bars of chase music, the last sprocket of film ran through. Lights on, and it was back to the seventeenth month of the war.

Wilson rose from his chair, nodding gravely as each one walked by with expressions of gratitude. "Thought we could all use a little cheering up," he said. "Glad you enjoyed yourselves. Good night, everyone . . ." The President was escorting his wife back to their suite when Colonel House came from the elevator with a handful of dispatches that would keep them closeted throughout the night. One concerned Maggie. The President called her to him.

"Some good news. Colonel House informs me that your son's ship landed in New York yesterday."

New York? So close? Tremulously, she asked, "He goin' to be all right?"

"He's going to need care, might have to go to another climate—Arizona, probably. But I promise you, Maggie, his country won't forget him."

"Thank you, Mr. Pres'dent. Thank you, sir . . ."

Mercer, helping dismantle the movie screen, heard the President's words, read the mixture of joy and fear on her face. "Your boy be comin' home, Maggie . . . that all you want to think on, don't you worry now, he goin' to get well . . ."

"Yes, Mercer . . . yes . . . he goin' to get well . . ."

"That's it, Maggie. You jus' keep knowin' that . . ."

They had just finished setting the room to rights, were

on their way down when they met Mays on the way
up the back stairs, two at a time. "Maggie . . . this
telegram come here for you . . ."

Telegram . . . never before in her life had she had
one, but she knew the yellow envelope to be nothing
but a harbinger of doom. The President wouldn't lie
to her, would he? Could something have happened to
her boy the President didn't know about?

They closely watched her face, her shaking hands, as
she opened the envelope: "Now be calm . . ." She read
the few words. "I got to go find Lil'yan" was all she
said.

The box office of the Howard Theater closed early.
Business was never much good, the nights of a house
hop. Lillian turned the cashbox over to the manager
and hurried on down the street as fast as she could go.
She wouldn't be getting any money watching the table
at a house hop, but pay wasn't what drew her, it was
the music. She could hear it way down the block before she even turned the corner. The battered old upright piano sure was getting a workout: "Tiger Rag" . . .
"Ja-Da" . . . "N'Orleans" . . .

"Hi there, Lil'yan."

"Hi there, Billy."

"Sure glad when you handle the table for us, Lil'yan
. . . money stay right where it belongs."

Billy's was a nice two-story house. Front and back
parlor with sliding doors open between. Rugs rolled up,
shoved against the wall, turning it into a dance hall.
The place was jammed with young congo,ened swivel
dudes and their sweet patooties. A uniform or two with
an armful of organdy. Stompin'. Movin'. Raggin' . . .
Getting sounds out of the piano that nobody else had
found was a lean, handsome young man so caught up in
his music he almost forgot to smile. When he did, fine
white teeth torchlit his dark face. It was a new sound
he brought, bridging ragtime and jazz.

Lillian stayed at the door, making certain everyone
paid or bartered their way in (with doughnuts, cake,
beer), swaying, feeling the music all the way into her

bones. A "sun-pecked jay" recently up from Georgia put down a nickel and started through. Without breaking rhythm Lillian slid her crutch across the table, denying him entrance. "Not a nickel tonight, it's a dime."

"How come?"

"Piano player gettin' five dollars, not two."

The jay peered across her at the piano player. "Don't know him. Who is he?"

"Neighborhood fella from Twenty-first Street. Name of Eddie Ellington. Calls hisself Duke."

"Sure hope he worth a dime." He dug up another nickel and went in.

"Care to dance?" The voice came from behind her. A half turn back showed her a khaki sleeve. A soldier . . . *"Emmett!"* Uniform loose on his gaunt frame, but a grin from ear to ear. "Oh, Emmett, Emmett . . ." They hugged and started swaying together in place, just moving with the rhythm; Lillian careful to throw all her weight on the crutch rather than let him carry her as they'd always done before when they danced.

"Caught me the first train . . ." It hurt in Lillian's chest to hear his tortured breathing. "Conductor asked did I want to ride white or colored—musta been the uniform—told him didn't matter damn to me, jus' wanted to get home. Manager up there to the theater told me you down here . . . How's Mama?"

"Oh, Emmett, don't talk, don't talk."

They kept the beat. Someone on the dance floor sang, "After you gone, after you gone away . . ."

Maggie hurried from the theater up the side street from Seventh. She approved of this neighborhood—T Street and U, high in the alphabet and farther from the river—but not of Lillian's hanging out with what Maggie considered street people. Her resolve to scold lessened as she began to hear the music. Made her feel good all over. Somewhat vixen, though Maggie would never admit it. That, and the telegram in her pocket.

As she stepped from the porch through the open door, a cry escaped her.

The long months of anxiety, the waiting. Now the
pain of seeing her injured son. This wasn't the boy who
went off to Mexico because the government thought
him a man. This was a hurt, hollowed man of not quite
twenty who would never be whole again . . .

"Mama . . ." He saw her, grabbed, hugged her.

"Emmett . . . my baby . . ." The three of them, in
the tightest circle, clinging to each other. Maggie
pulled her arm up through the tangled embrace, held
aloft the telegram. "My cup runneth over . . . Your
papa's comin' home . . ."

Emmett, comin' home . . . Three streetcar transfers
took them back to the little house on Nineteenth. Maggie had arrangements worked out even as she was opening the door. *Papa comin' home* . . . "Now, bein' your
papa is sick, he goin' have to be kept warm. We
bring my bed out here for him by the stove . . ." She
had the mason jar down from the kitchen shelf and was
counting out pennies, quarters, dimes. "Lil'yan can
take the daybed. We get another one for you, Emmett . . ."

"I be livin' most time at the hospital, Mama." Lillian,
lighting the fire in the stove, started urgently toward
Emmett as he lowered himself into a chair, fighting
to catch his breath. "I'm okay, okay . . . " He held off
his anxious mother and sister. "Don't you worry 'bout
me . . . let's jus' take care of Papa."

Maggie's savings, plus six singles Emmett brought
from his pocket and Lillian's paycheck coming up on
Saturday, only added to a little past thirty-two dollars. The telegram said he needed a hundred and
twenty to pay back rent and ticket home . . .

"We goin' pay every cent of it," Maggie assured
her children. "Your papa not goin' leave debts behind . . ." Her good friends Mercer and Mays had offered help. She would borrow. There was to be no
worryin'. Nothing was to mar the happy time. "Goin'
get your papa back on his feet . . . you, too, little Emmett." Hadn't called him that in a long time. It made
them all laugh. "Goin' be a whole family again . . .
I tell you, I feel so joyful . . ."

He was to be little Emmett again only for that moment in time. The late night knock disturbed Maggie. "Who is it?"

From beyond the door: "Me. Mercer. Got to see you, Maggie." *Oh, Lord, hope nothin' gone wrong at the White House, sure hate to have to go back now . . .* She admitted him.

When Mercer didn't smile, he had a kind of mournful demeanor. He was wearing that face as he stepped into the room. Then he saw Emmett and broke into a welcoming grin. Even as they pumped each other's hands and hugged, Maggie sensed a threat in his visit. All the years she'd known him, never once had he taken it on himself to call without invitation.

"What you come by for, Mercer?"

"Maggie . . . as I be leavin' the changin' room tonight . . . they give me this to bring you . . . Come after you left . . ." In his hand was another of those frightening yellow envelopes. She couldn't bring herself to reach for it. Emmett took the telegram from him, opened, read it. "Papa won't be comin' home. Died . . . this afternoon."

A cry escaped Lillian. Maggie stood rooted, fiercely willing herself not to scream. "He be comin' home," she said. "We goin' bring him . . ."

Work. It kept her in one piece, was her salvation. One day like another. Up before dawn, walk to the White House on dull fall mornings. Dust. Clean. Beds to make. Trays to carry. Hairdressing for the First Lady, manicures for Mrs. Jaffray. Tramping the back stairs forty times a day. Up to the linen room, down to the laundry. Seeking bone-aching fatigue that would drag her home too tired to mourn. She would have even welcomed the scrub brush until her arms ached, but a new, apple-cheeked maid named Bridget now had the duty of scrubbing the grand stairs. Maggie's friends, Mays, Mercer, Jackson—even the truculent Annie—waited out her grief patiently, considerately.

In self-imposed isolation Maggie sat at the breakfast table away from them. A lately hired houseman,

O'Hara, and a new girl from the laundry whose name was spoken, but which Maggie, in her preoccupation, forgot, had joined their ranks. The stringency of wartime menus, the despair of war itself, dulled conversation. Most ate in silence or, from sheer habit, muttered complaints about shortages. Haines, the new serving man, was carefully counting out spoonfuls of sugar when they first heard the shouting from the corridor.

"D'ja hear . . . D'ja hear?" The door burst open and Mays, in white barber jacket, towel over his arm, comb in pocket, scissors in hand, bellowed joyfully. "It's over . . . over . . . WAR'S OVER!"

Some pushed back chairs. Some were almost afraid to believe it.

"God's truth," Mays insisted. Newspapers didn't even have the story yet, but both sides agreed the last shot would be fired before eleven o'clock tomorrow morning, the eleventh of November. "Was cuttin' the Pres'-dent's hair," he said, "phone rang—man, he was waitin' for that call! Got tears in his eyes, he did. 'Thank God,' he said . . ."

Over . . . The impact finally hit everyone in the room. They were on their feet, shouting—men slapping each other on the back, women embracing. Mrs. Feeney, Viola, other kitchen workers rushed in to join in the excitement. Jackson ran to the window, flung it open, shouting to the world outside, "It's over . . . OVER . . ."

Mrs. Jaffray, who heard the cacophony all the way to the elevator, rushed in, ready with a stern reprimand, only to be swept into the noisy melee. "Over, Miz Jaffray . . . war's over . . ." Hugging; moving; a joyous quadrille of changing partners in which Maggie and Mrs. Jaffray, to their mutual surprise and discomfort, found themselves in embrace. Each quickly backed away, to seek other involvements. Mays, Jackson, and Mercer, hands on one another's shoulders, were doing a three-way shuffle step when Mays suddenly remembered. "Lordy . . . plumb forgot to trim the Pres'dent's other sideburn . . ."

It was a healing time for the world and for Maggie.

For the President, in search of his Holy Grail of lasting peace, it was a time of travel. And travail.

A sultry late summer night in 1919 Lillian sat in the box office of the Howard Theater, watching the utility man change the marquee to D. W. Griffith's *Broken Blossoms*. It was the last night for Lon Chaney's *Miracle Man* and the theater, despite the heat, was filled.

"Got any seats left?" a young neighborhood man inquired just as Lillian was about to close the ticket booth.

"Few on the side."

He put down his money, she gave him a ticket. "How things goin' with you, Lil'yan?"

"Copacetic . . . how you?"

He shrugged. "Know anybody want to hire an out-of-work soldier?"

"Sure wish I did."

"How's Emmett doin'?" he called back from the door.

"Back in the hospital. In, out, you know . . ." She pulled down the curtain of the booth and carried the cashbox into the theater. From the grainy screen President Wilson's lined, intense face flickered along with those of France's Clemenceau, Britain's Lloyd George, Italy's Orlando. THE BIG FOUR AT VERSAILLES, the title explained. Lillian watched. She knew President Wilson to have been back from Versailles for some time, and wondered if they were running an old newsreel by mistake—until she saw what followed: the President in a touring car covered with American flags, riding down the streets of San Francisco. The film was captioned: PRESIDENT WILSON, DISAPPOINTED OVER HIS FAILURE TO CONVINCE CONGRESS OF THE NEED FOR A LEAGUE OF NATIONS, TAKES HIS CASE TO THE PEOPLE . . . Hard to believe that the man standing up in the touring car was the same man as at Versailles. In the brief months that separated those two events, Wilson had gravely aged. Lillian thought back on the only time she'd actually seen the President—"ballin' the

Jack" with his daughters. For a fleeting moment, her own father was in her mind. Then she carried the cash-box into the manager's office.

Mrs. Jaffray being nowhere in sight, Bridget grabbed up the skirt of her stiffly starched uniform, boldly exposing her ankles, and bounded up the steep stairs to the attic. "Maggie," she called, " 'Tis Mrs. Wilson sendin' for ye, says you're after takin' too long with that dress . . ."

Maggie was in the sewing room, pressing a chiffon evening gown with the electric iron (which she didn't yet fully trust). "What does she expect? I'm workin' fast as can be . . . Her that never ironed a handkerchief in her whole life."

Bridget's innocent eyes widened in amazement. "Is that a fact now? My, my, was that in the papers?"

"The papers? 'Course not, why should it be?"

"I thought we was only free to gossip about things written of in the daily newspaper." Bridget was right, of course, but Maggie was in no frame of mind for agreement. Her bias against Edith Galt Wilson hadn't diminished. Carefully carrying the delicate gown down the attic stairs and across the center hall where some of the first Mrs. Wilson's landscapes still hung on the walls, Maggie worried about how tense and ashen the President looked since his return. During the whirlwind, tub-thumping tour of the western states, he had collapsed in Pueblo, Colorado. Exhaustion and high altitude were the reasons given to excuse the embarrassment of the President incoherently mumbling and crying during a public appearance.

It was Maggie's privately held opinion that his wife wasn't taking good enough care of him.

She knocked and was admitted to the dressing room. The President was with the First Lady, his comfortable frayed green bathrobe worn over dress shirt and evening trousers, accentuating his pallor. His long, slender hands seemed almost bloodless. He paced the small area nervously, reading off notes from a speech in preparation. "I have seen fools resist Providence before and I have seen their destruction, and it will come again. Utter destruction and contempt." Edith Wilson, at her dressing table selecting jewelry for the evening, watched his image closely in the mirror, and caught the twitch in his left cheek: it was more pronounced than it had been.

"Woodrow, I wish you'd let me cancel out for tonight . . ."

"We won the war," he went on. "We must not let the peace be lost . . ." An almost zealot fire burned in his eyes.

"Darling, did you take your medicine?"

"Yes, yes, I did, yes." He cut off his wife impatiently, and again the twitch appeared in his face. "Now the Senate must take *its* medicine . . ."

Maggie hung up the gown and moved to back from the room. Edith Wilson gestured her to remain.

"Darling, please don't upset yourself so," the First Lady urged the President.

"Hiram Johnson . . . Borah . . . Reed . . ." he went on, uttering the senatorial names with contempt, "following me across the country with their anti-League speeches . . . threatening all our good efforts at Versailles : . ." Succumbing to fatigue and frustration, he sat in the boudoir chair, removed his glasses, vigorously rubbed his face like a man assuring himself he *has* a face. Maggie busied herself by smoothing the folds of chiffon, and wished she could leave the room.

Edith Wilson reached out and held his hand, "Darling, you worry me so . . . Let me go down, Woodrow, you stay up here and rest . . ."

"No . . . the President must put on a positive appearance. They must not know that the President doubts . . . The President is in the ring till the last round . . ." The concept appealed to him. He brightened. "You know, I like that? *In the ring till the last round . . .*" Forcing a jaunty smile and step, he went back to his own room. Edith Wilson slipped out of her peignoir and waited while Maggie helped her into the chiffon gown. "Maggie . . . does he look well to you?"

"Well, ma'am, he does seem tired-like . . ." As Mag-

gie hooked her into the gown, Edith Wilson found it
disturbing to discover that her husband had left his
pince-nez behind.

"That's not like him," she worried.

"No, ma'am, that sure not . . ."

A fire burned in the marble-faced fireplace of the
President's room. Wilson stood before it to warm his
hands. The twitch in his face was more frequent now.
"Is it cold in here, Mercer? Or is it just me?"

"Just 'bout October, sir, always a little nip in the
air." Mercer helped the President out of his dressing
gown and on with the waistcoat. The President's
thoughts seemed far away. He rubbed his left arm, as
though it pained him.

"You feelin' all right, Mr. Pres'dent?" Mercer
asked with concern.

"Just a little weary."

The President made no move to button the waistcoat. Mercer did up the buttons, as if for a child. "You
don't mind my sayin' so, sir, but you pushin' yourself
very hard. You have to remember, it not more than a
week, you collapsed out there in Colorado."

"Maybe, after tonight, I can take a few days off."

"Yes, sir . . . good idea, sir. After you bein' all that
time in France, then all this speechmakin' across the
country . . . Very tirin' on you, Mr. Pres'dent . . . be
good you rest . . ."

"You know what Clemenceau said of me, Mercer?
*'Mr. Wilson's Fourteen Points bore me. Why, God
Almighty has only ten . . .'* "

Mercer clucked sympathetically and tied the President's tie, trying not to look directly at that poor
contorting face. The eye had become involved and the
muscle at the corner of his mouth. He seemed distant,
as though only his body were in the room. Then he
straightened to full height and moved to the mirror.
Studied himself. "What I should have been, Mercer . . .
an actor. You go onstage, you cry and plead and beat
your breast, and when the curtain goes down you take

off the makeup, have a good meal, and sleep the sleep of the innocent . . . I can't do that . . ."

It was good to hear him talk. It was his brooding spells of silence that had begun to worry Mercer. Now his voice took on strength. "We are such hypocrites . . . I give a dinner for my enemies, and they come and eat my food. *Republican senators . . ."* Posturing theatrically, he raised a hand—and for the moment one could recall his putting on a tablecloth and declaiming for his daughters. " 'Friends, Romans, countrymen . . . lend me your ears . . .' "

Mercer, moving off to the armoire for the evening jacket, smiled as the President's voice came to him. "I come not to praise Henry Cabot Lodge, but to . . . to . . ." The pause elongated. Too long a silence.

"I'm listenin', Mr. Pres'dent, hear you jus' fi—" Mercer turned, to see Wilson stagger backward, right hand grabbing for the support of the table. *"Mr. Pres'dent!"*

Just as Mercer reached him, Maggie came through the door with the President's eyeglasses. Together, they eased him into a straight-backed chair.

"No, no . . . it's nothing . . . nothing . . . left arm just hurts a bit . . ." His words thickened. "Don't alarm Mrs. Wilson. It will be all right . . ."

He insisted on going down to dinner, after which he played a game of billiards.

On the morning of October 2, 1919, Edith Wilson found her husband collapsed on the bathroom floor. Mercer, with Ike Hoover's help, picked up the stricken man, carried him to his bed. The left side of his face sagged, his left arm hung useless. Gently Mercer picked up the long-fingered hand, laid it beside him on the bed. The President's eyes were open in hopeless appeal. But no words came.

5

▨ ▨ ▨

Tom Mix galloped across the screen. Tony the Wonder Horse reared, whinnied. Guns were pulled from holsters, fired. The only sound in the room was the clacking of the projector as the film went through.

Woodrow Wilson, fragile, haggard, lay propped up in the twin bed, thinning hair as gray as his face. A growth of white beard gave him the look of an ancient. The crippling stroke had left the President a half-useless body. A great mind, short-circuited, caused him to utter inanities that sent him into crying tantrums. The only effective panacea was the flickering images on the movie screen, which he watched, hour after hour, giving the same solemn attention to Keystone Kops as to *The Birth of a Nation*.

The First Lady wiped his pince-nez on a linen handkerchief, then ever so gently clamped them onto the bridge of his nose. He reacted with severe anxiety, grasping anxiously with his good, right hand for hers. "Li-li'l gir . . . girrrl . . ." His speech was guttural, slurred.

"I'm here, Woodrow, I'm here."

He fumbled for his glasses, adjusted them, and thanked her with a vague, twisted smile. Then his attention strayed back to the film. Tears welled in her eyes.

From that day in October, two months back, when he collapsed, the White House had become a hospital; a cloister in which the doyen of the body politic was to be kept from hostile eyes; a battleground on which were to be waged jousts for power. Edith Galt Wilson had taken her stand between her stricken husband and the world, keeping at bay the press, the Senate, the cabinet, even, increasingly, the President's secretary, Joseph Tumulty.

Now the enemy was at the battlements.

"We *must* have the Lincoln bed," she told Ike Hoover. "Tell everyone it's imperative that it be found!"

How could you lose the Lincoln bed? Mercer, going down the back stairs with the President's tray, squeezed past Mays, still wearing his overcoat, on his way up. "Not able to keep track of a thing that big . . . Makes you wonder how the country runs . . ."

"Does for a fact," Mays said. Between himself and Ike Hoover, they'd been over the Fort Washington warehouse with a fine-tooth comb. Wasn't on any inventory. Last President to use the bed, according to what records could be found, was Benjamin Harrison. What happened to it after that, only the good Lord knew. As Mays rounded the stairs at the second floor and continued on up the narrow tunnel of steps to the attic, he could hear furniture being moved around and came on a scene that looked for all the world like a hastily assembled barricade. McKenzie, O'Hara, Annie, and Maggie dragged, pulled, pushed furniture, household goods, accumulations of leftovers from past administrations, out of the cubbyhole rooms into the hallway to facilitate the search.

"You'd think they'd be more respectful of Mr. Lincoln's bed," Maggie lamented. Mays, shoving aside a chifforobe that blocked his passage, informed them that if the bed wasn't up here, it was gone to kingdom come.

"Well, you better find it or my work goin' to be wasted," came Lillian's voice above the sound of the sewing machine. Working the treadle at top speed with her strong right foot, she pieced together two double sheets to make one huge one. "No other bed in the place big enough to take this."

Mays helped Maggie move a sofa that Chester A. Arthur had last used, and the search moved into the largest and last of the storage rooms. "If it's not in here, it's nowheres," Mays said.

"Gives me the chills, that's what it does." Annie was of the mind that the newspaper rumors were right. "The President, poor man, is dyin', that's what he is ... Why else would Herself be wantin' the Lincoln bed, if not for the poor, ailin' creature to draw his last breath on?"

As McKenzie had heard it, the bed wasn't for *him,* 'twas for *her.* The lady was just turning his study into a room for herself. "And rightly," was Mays' opinion, "the Pres'dent needin' his rest like he does." If they were merely preparing a bedroom for the First Lady's personal use, it only served to strengthen Maggie's opinion of that headstrong lady. The house was full of beds. Some had slept royalty. Wouldn't you know Herself would want the grandest bed in the house. "My angel, first Miz Wilson . . . any bed would have done for her," she said aloud.

Mays, edging in sideways between two immense pre-Civil War armoires at the far wall, reached up for a faded velvet drape. As he touched it, he felt it slide. It fell, sending years' accumulation of dust into the air and revealing a high, magnificently carved rosewood headboard.

"McKenzie, O'Hara, give me a hand . . ." he called jubilantly. "I think I found it!"

They moved the armoires out of the way. There it stood, flat against the wall; the footboard behind it. Lillian came in from the sewing room, the long sheet double-draped around her slight body, watching as the three men began to bring it out, piece by piece.

As the headboard went past her, Maggie, profoundly moved, felt impelled to touch it. "So that was his bed . . . rest his soul . . ."

They assembled it in Mr. Wilson's austere study, now to be Edith Wilson's bedroom. The filigree carved headboard soared in graceful arc midway between the height of the tall doorways and the ceiling molding. Twenty feet above the floor, a gold-leaf canopy curved out from the wall in the shape of a crown, from which lace draperies hung loosely to the floor, overswagged with tasseled velvet.

The bed brought to the room the awesome dignity of the man for whom it was first made—which, Maggie began to realize, was the effect the First Lady had in mind.

Edith Wilson's confrontation with the Senate of the United States was expertly staged from start to finish.

As Maggie and Annie made up the bed, covering it with a handmade, fringed counterpane resurrected from a trunk, and placed oversized pillows on it, Lillian worked rapidly with needle and thread, hemming the lace that hung from the canopy. O'Hara and McKenzie brought matching rosewood and velvet chairs which Mrs. Jaffray sent up from the Red Room.

Mays, pressed into service as barber, groomed the President. The First Lady stood by, approving, soothing, as Wilson was shaved, his hair trimmed. "You look splendid, darling, splendid . . ." Mercer separated him from his comforting old bathrobe, helped him into a brocade dressing gown selected by the First Lady, and tied his ascot.

"Don't . . . want . . . see anyone . . ."

Anxious and uneasy, he was placed protesting in the wheelchair and brought into the newly prepared room; his wife walking alongside, holding his trembling hand in hers.

"Just for a little while, darling . . . you can do it . . ."

Mays and Mercer lifted him from the chair and placed him on the bed, Edith Wilson covering his knees with an afghan. Annie took one look at the President, her worst fears confirmed, and was grateful she was no longer needed. Maggie remained to hold the weight of the drapery to facilitate Lillian's finishing.

As Mercer took the wheelchair back to the bedroom, Edith Wilson surveyed her setting, and had one of the rosewood chairs removed from the room.

"Mays, will you be on the door?"

"Oh, yes, ma'am."

"Please tell Mr. Hoover and the other ushers that no one is to be available to accept the gentlemen's coats and hats."

"Yes, ma'am."

Maggie wished Lillian would get the hemming finished so they too could leave. The tension in the room was of such acutely personal nature that being witness to it was painful: the President, a man of power and world-renowned stature, reduced to the role of fearful dependent; his wife, burying her own anxieties beneath a facade of almost aggressive confidence.

Edith Wilson stood at the side of the bed, sighting to the door. Yes, the way the President's body was positioned, the paralyzed side of his face would not be visible from their visitors' view. She tucked the afghan around his body, covering his paralyzed arm. His eyes filled with agitation. Her hand firmly held his, hoping to transfer some of her strength to him. "You must see them, darling . . . they won't stay long . . ."

"No. . . no . . ."

"Woodrow, they're talking impeachment on the Hill . . . If you don't see them, they'll believe you're totally incapacitated, that your holding office is invalid. We need time . . . that's all . . . time for you to get well. We can't let all your work for peace be lost . . . You want the Treaty ratified, don't you?"

"Yes . . . yes . . ." The passionate phrases he'd uttered during the long hard sessions in Paris and the grueling trip to the people were trapped in his mind, and all his recalcitrant tongue seemed to manage was "Yes, yes . . ." He burst into tears. The First Lady, pouring a glass of water for the President, threw Lillian an urgent glance. But Lillian, already putting thread and scissors back into her sewing basket, quick to her crutch, left the room. Edith Wilson deterred Maggie from following. "Maggie, please bring fresh water . . . but wait until the gentlemen have arrived. Give them about two or three minutes and then come right back in."

"Yes, ma'am." Maggie left with the pitcher, a thought occurring as she did. The First Lady had said "until the *gentlemen* have arrived." If there was to be more than one, why had she had the second chair removed?

Wilson drank from the glass his wife held for him, his outburst subsiding. Gently she urged him back against the pillow, and patted the drooped corner of his mouth where water, which he couldn't feel, dribbled. She dried his tears, picked up a small worn volume of poetry from the bedside table, and sitting beside him on the small slipper chair, began to read aloud.

" 'The year's at the spring, and day's at the morn.' "

"Rati-fied . . . must be . . ."

"Shhh . . ." She patted his hand. " 'Morning's at seven, the hill-side's dew-pearled; the lark's on the wing; the snail's on the thorn.' "

"Won't—stay—long?" It pleased her to see the gray-blue eyes had calmed; the look of anxiety had left them.

"Trust me," she said and continued reading. " 'God's in his heaven—' " A knock came at the door. "Come in," she said, without pause continuing with Robert Browning's reassuring words: " 'All's right with the world!' "

Tumulty, the President's secretary, was in the doorway. "The senators have arrived, madam."

An instant of distress in Wilson's eyes. Edith held his hand firmly, steadying him. "The President would like them to come in," she said.

Calling upon every inner resource, Wilson sat straighter, back stiffening, eyes sharpening, readying himself for the ordeal. When Tumulty next appeared at the doorway it was to usher in two gentlemen of the Senate. Republican Albert Fall of New Mexico was given to string ties and Stetsons, but only the uninitiated could mistake his open folksiness for naiveté. Underneath the bluff, hearty facade he was shrewd, penetrating, self-serving—which at this point meant playing the game on the side of Senator Henry Cabot Lodge, who unequivocally wanted Wilson removed from office. There could be no doubt that Senator Fall had come to do a hatchet job.

He strode into the room, hand extended: "Mr. President—" only to find the way blocked by a radiantly beaming First Lady.

"How nice of you to come."

Senator Gilbert Hitchcock, of dignified late middle age and a member of the President's party, had been chosen by the investigating committee to balance the invasion.

"Most kind of you to receive us," said Senator Hitchcock.

"How thoughtful of the Foreign Relations Committee to send you both," she murmured. They looked around for a place to divest themselves of their outer garments, but there was none. "And you can tell the committee when you return how improved the President is."

Giving them only his living profile, Wilson extended his right hand; in measured, determined speech, he said, "Senator . . . Hitchcock."

Hitchcock stepped to the bed to receive Wilson's firm handclasp.

"Mr. President . . . You look well, sir."

"Thank you. Senator Fall?"

Fall stepped forward, trying to see the other profile without being too obvious, but Edith Wilson thwarted the tactic by stepping past him to adjust the coverlet, limiting his area of maneuverability. "Excuse me, madam."

"That's quite all right," she said, but stayed in his path. Then Maggie was back in the room with the pitcher, creating another distraction.

With Fall's hand still in his, Wilson, forming the words thoughtfully, asked, "How are your foreign investments doing, Senator?"

Fall, momentarily thrown off base by the question, managed a sickly smile. "May I sit down, madam?"

"Of course."

He was lowering himself into the chair when he realized there was only one. In half squat, he gestured Hitchcock to take it. "Senator?"

"No, thank you."

Both, burdened with coats and hats, feeling uncomfortable, stood as Mrs. Wilson again seated herself on the small chair beside the bed, picked up notebook and pad, poised to write . . .

"Madam—you seem uncommonly occupied," observed Fall.

"Don't let it bother you, Senator." She smiled benignly. "Go right ahead, speak freely. I'll just be making notes . . . so there's no misquoting in the newspapers . . . you know how these things happen, gentlemen."

"Yes, yes, of course," agreed Hitchcock.

Fall could feel the sand pulling from under his feet as if he were standing at the water's edge. Floundering for a comment of consequence, he said, "Mr. President, I want you to know Congress is praying for you."

"Oh?" Wilson responded with avid interest. "Which way?" A hint of smile crossed his crooked face.

Edith Wilson had bought time.

Reporters swarmed outside the White House like locusts after a new crop of corn. The handful of people who worked backstairs went their stoic way, keeping inviolate what every government in the world, including their own, was desperate to learn. Only when she was at home, sharing a toted supper with Lillian and Mercer and Mays, did Maggie feel free to discuss conditions surrounding the presidency.

"The look on that senator's face when I come back in with the water pitcher." Maggie's rare laughter brought smiles to all their faces.

"Well, they sure didn't stay long," Mays added. "Hardly let 'em in the door when they come back out. I make it to a hundred, I never goin' forget that high and mighty senator standin' there, holdin' his hat, knowin' he'd jus' rolled snake eyes . . . Sorry, Maggie . . ."

"I live to be a hundred," Mercer contributed, "I likely be bent over with an ear trumpet and no hair."

"Way things are goin', Mr. Mercer, you won't have no hair time you forty-five."

"Oh, now, Mr. Mays, what you talkin' . . . I jus'. got me a tall, proud forehead."

Maggie brought the steaming pot to the table and poured chicory-rich coffee into cups that, to Maggie's pride, now matched and had their own saucers. "Lil'yan, chile, you rush through your supper so."

"Got to get to work, Mama."

"Picture show," Maggie grumbled. "Wish you find yourself somethin' more respectable."

"Oh now, Maggie . . ." Mays and Mercer both protested. "Picture show respectable. Pres'dent sees 'em all the time . . ." The wan, incapacitated President lying in his bed, day after day, staring at images on a screen, or reading from the khaki-covered soldiers' Bible as he had every day since the war began, was now in the room with them and couldn't be laughed away.

"First Lady may have got rid of those two senators for a while," Mays said grimly, "but we not heard the last from the Hill. They not too happy 'bout her, I can tell you. Heard one of 'em say to those newspaper people hangin' 'round, 'We got petticoat gov'ment . . .' "

Well Maggie sure didn't like the newspapers calling her what they did: "President Edith."

"That White House in some rut." Lillian pushed her plate away. "Duck or chicken salad . . ."

"We all should have been there, Teddy Roosevelt's time," Mays said. "Used to serve a lot of sucklin' pig then . . ."

"Mays, how you find these things out?"

"Older I get, curiouser I get . . . Mercer, you closer to the Pres'dent than the rest of us . . . What you think 'bout what the First Lady doin' for him? You think the paper' right, that she runnin' the gov'ment?"

Mercer wouldn't speculate, but did comment that the President's mind was sharp, all right. They couldn't stay away from the subject closest to their minds . . . the poor President . . . Having to face those senators had taken a lot out of him. Barely left his bed, the days following. Maggie had caught glimpses of him, on brief outings when he'd been wheeled in his chair to the window of east sitting hall to catch the rare winter morning sun. Sure broke your heart to see a man proud as that having to be cared for like he was a child. "Maggie, I've reflected on how partial you be to the first Miz Wilson," Mercer said, "but I tell you, his new lady is doin' a bang-up job."

"Doin' what she can, I know that." Maggie grudgingly admitted the First Lady was working hard. Certainly a changed woman from when she came in.

But run the country? No . . .

"What's wrong a woman runnin' the country, Mama?" In this barren room they debated the problems of state. "Mays, you a knowin' man . . . what you think? That Treaty goin' to get passed? Or is it goin' die a-bornin'?"

Lillian was putting on her coat and hat to leave for the box office when an imperative knock was heard. Maggie, who would never rid herself of anxiety about the unknown at the door, opened it to find not only a stranger, but a tall, sallow white man.

"You Maggie Rogers?"

"Yes, sir, what can I do for you?"

"Sylvester, *New York Herald*." He stepped into the room. Mays and Mercer, still at the table, eyed him suspiciously.

"What you want with me?" Maggie asked.

"Won't take much of your time, Mrs. Rogers. Understand you work in the family quarters of the White House."

"I do."

"My paper would be grateful for some information. So grateful, we'd pay, say, ten—" His ferret eyes flicked across the room, absorbed the obvious needs of this house. *"Fifteen* dollars . . . Tell me, is it true the President's helpless, can't talk or care for himself, that Mrs. Wilson's got him locked away . . . that she signs his name to bills and makes cabinet appointments?"

"You hear what this man wants?" Maggie indignantly asked of Mays and Mercer, "Wants us to sell information 'bout the White House." The two of them rose from the table and moved to the door, Mercer somewhat in the lead. "Might be better you go, Mr. Sylvester."

The reporter took the measure of the two of them, but held his ground. "How about the answer to one question, just one . . . worth . . ." He pulled a bill from his pocket, dangled it tantalizingly, "Twenty dollars. How about the bars at the window? Were they put there, like they're saying, to keep the President from jumping out?"

Mercer was poised to shove the interloper out the door, but Mays plucked the twenty from the man's hand, and undaunted by Maggie's and Mercer's shocked looks, pocketed it.

"I take that twenty," Mays said, "and you start writin', Mr. Sylvester, 'cause what I tell you is fact, right from the horse's mouth . . ." A pencil stub appeared in the reporter's hand, a notebook from his coat pocket. "Those bars at the windows . . . got that?" Sylvester eagerly nodded. "Well, they was put there by Pres'dent Teddy Roosevelt so's his young children wouldn't likely to climb out, fall—as young'uns will— or somebody to come in, kidnap 'em . . ." Mays smiled guilelessly. "What you ought to do, Mr. Sylvester, is read more history. Or at least the back issues of your own newspaper. Good night to you, sir."

The hapless reporter retreated. As he sought the quickest way out of the neighborhood, he could hear them laughing.

When they were alone, Mays took the twenty from his pocket, thoughtfully studying it. "Lil'yan, you the one with the schoolin' . . . how do twenty be divided by three?"

"Jus' hang on to it, Mays, we'll divide it by four as soon as I get through at the box office tonight." Maggie delivered her nightly admonition to come straight home from work, not to talk to just anybody on the street . . .

"Mama . . . I'm grown!"

Grown or whatever, Maggie would feel a whole lot better if Lillian was to be working at the White House every day with her . . .

"Not on your life," Lillian called back as she went down the path. "You don't catch me scrapin' and bowin' to a housekeeper . . ."

Maggie bowed to Mrs. Jaffray—tucked her foot behind her, deferentially bowed her head, and went into a deep curtsy.

"Again," said Mrs. Jaffray, like the headmistress of a school, "No, no, you don't have it right. *Deeper.* Eyes to the floor . . ."

They'd been at it all morning. Chairs and long table in the staff dining room were pushed against the wall. Maggie, Bridget, and Annie, in varying versions of the curtsy, faced Mrs. Jaffray while the male contingent— Mercer, O'Hara, McKenzie, Coates, and butler staff— bowed to Ike Hoover.

"With dignity, men," he said. "From the waist . . . Now then, raise up . . . slowly . . . fine."

Mrs. Jaffray's voice rolled over his, like a wave breaking. "Curtsy, curtsy . . . *Graceful,* Annie . . ." Annie, who had gotten down, had difficulty getting up. "Sorry, mum, don't have the joints for it."

"Now remember." Ike Hoover, who had been to Buckingham Palace with President and Mrs. Wilson during the peace talks, and who knew about these things firsthand, instructed the assemblage. "If we were to have occasion to address our visitor directly, we would never say 'Prince of Wales,' now would we?"

"No, sir . . ." A multiple reply.

"And certainly not as 'Prince' . . ." Mrs. Jaffray interjected her exasperation. "We don't want a repetition of the humiliating experience we had with one of the maids engaged to accompany the President and First Lady to England—and who is no longer with us, I might add . . ."

"Mrs. Jaffray, please . . . I'm conducting this exercise . . ." Ike Hoover was doing his level best to remain in control; a difficult thing to accomplish with a lady of Mrs. Jaffray's sensibilities. "The incident Mrs. Jaffray refers to," he explained to the staff, "occurred when Her Royal Highness inquired if the servants' quarters were satisfactory, and the maid in question replied, 'Sure, Queen, you bet.' "

The laugh released tensions in all but Mrs. Jaffray. "I certainly don't find that amusing, Mr. Hoover."

"The Queen must have found it humorous—she smiled."

"Never so disgraced in my life!"

"May I remind you, Mrs. Jaffray . . . you weren't there." (*It was well and good for him to talk,* Mrs. Jaffray thought. *How could a man who had begun life as a laborer recognize the desperate condition of the manners of the American serving class?*)

"Never turn your back on royalty." Ike Hoover illustrated the proper method of walking backward in the royal presence. Backward . . . always backward until you were out of the room.

Contracting their bodies as though in the first step of a bluegrass dance, Maggie and Annie practiced. Annie didn't approve of these pretensions one bit. "Bendin' me knee to an Englishman . . . me sainted father would turn over in his grave . . ."

The call box pulled Maggie from the endeavor, to her relief. Hairdressing case in hand, she hurried to the second floor. Months now since the First Lady had called on her—since any social event of note had been planned in the White House. Now, with a royal visitor, the lady was sure to be dolling herself up fit to kill . . .

"Come in, Maggie."

Edith Wilson lay on the chaise, surrendered to exhaustion, one arm flung across her face, the other dangling to the floor. It had been days since Maggie had seen her, closeted as she kept herself; weeks now since she'd tended her in any personal way. The strain of the President's illness had startlingly altered her appearance. Her dress was severe, dark, unadorned. Her hair, pulled tightly back into a bun, exaggerated the sag of her cheek.

"Would you like me to come back later, ma'am?"

Edith Wilson opened eyes shadowed with fatigue. "No, no . . . let's get to it." As Maggie touched match

to the Bunsen burner and set out the curling irons, the
First Lady wearily moved to the dressing table and
scrutinized herself in the mirror. "You're going to have
to be a magician, Maggie . . . I look a fright." Her
hair, as she pulled out the pins, fell well below her
shoulders, a dark silk curtain. "Here I am, due to have
tea with the man who will one day be King of England,
an ally whom we must impress, and my hair as straight
as my great-great-great . . . well, anyway—ancestor's
. . . Pocahontas . . . At least the newspapers haven't
criticized me for that. Maybe they haven't found out
I'm part Indian . . . they've taken me apart for everything else . . ." The laugh she reached for dissolved in
a hurt cry. Maggie, brushing the lady's hair, studied her
in the mirror and thought of the cruel things that had
been said. If the reporters could see her now, would
they picture her as an "iron female moth drawn to the
flame of power"? Hesitant to utter what was in her
mind, Maggie finally said, "Not meanin' to be forward,
ma'am . . . but I'm part Indian myself."

"You are, Maggie?"

"Oh, yes, ma'am. Roanoke. My mother's side."

"Well . . . I guess then, somewhere in nature, we're
blood sisters." Their eyes sought each other's in the
mirror. *Imagine* . . . her and the First Lady, bein' part
of the same blood . . . Should have known it. Look how
strong she stands beside him. "Let's get you out of that
dress, ma'am . . . put on one of your nice comfortable
negligees. You so wore out, you need some relaxin' . . ."
Giving herself over to Maggie's ministrations, Edith
closed her eyes. The strong, gentle fingers massaged her
neck and shoulders. "Now there, don't that feel better,
ma'am?"

The coil of tension unwound. "Are you married,
Maggie?" she asked in awhile.

"I was."

"Did you lose him?"

"Yes, ma'am, I lost him."

Edith Wilson reached up to clasp the hand stroking
her neck. For the moment, the chasm in their stations
was erased. Maggie couldn't pinpoint the exact moment

when her resentment ceased. It must have been awhile back. Matter of fact, near as she could recall, since just after Mercer and Mays had been over and put that reporter in his place, and shamed her somewhat about blaming Edith Wilson for marrying the President too soon.

"I took the liberty, ma'am, of bringin' you somethin' . . ." Maggie reached into her black case for a piece of lined notebook paper. "That is, if I'm not bein' too forward, ma'am . . ."

"What is it, Maggie?"

"Well . . . all the things you was referrin' to bein' said 'bout you . . . I copied down some words that Miz Taft had put on a sign for Mr. Taft's desk . . . I been keepin' 'em ever since. Mr. Taft had his problems with the newspapers, too, you know . . ."

"What are the words, Maggie?"

"They some words Mr. Lincoln wrote—Miz Taft found 'em in some old papers. If you care to read 'em, ma'am." Maggie offered the paper to her.

"Would you read them to me, Maggie?"

"If you wish, ma'am." Maggie brought the spectacles from the deep recess of her apron pocket and haltingly, but clearly, read Mr. Lincoln's words: " 'If I were to try to read, much less answer, all the attacks made on me —this shop might as well be closed to any other business. I do the best I know how, the very best I can, and I mean to keep on doing so until the end. If the end brings me out all right, then what is said against me won't amount to anything. If the end brings me out wrong, ten angels swearing I was right would make no difference.' " Maggie put her glasses back into her pocket. Edith Wilson held the lined paper with the carefully penciled words in her hands.

"Thank you, Maggie."

Edward Albert Christian George Andrew Patrick David, Prince of Wales, Earl of Chester, Knight of the Garter, emerged from the designated royal suite and walked across east sitting hall and down the two steps into center hall. At twenty-six he had newspaper writers reaching into their bag of journalistic clichés for "debonair," "boulevardier," "dazzler," "heart wrecker," "catch of the century," and that old saw, "prince charming."

Mercer, in full livery, standing at the farthest end of the room just outside the double doors to west sitting hall, watched him approach and thought, *Poor handsome young fella, carryin' a lot of freight on his back*. A bespoke back, to be sure. Bond Street day suit, pearl-gray spats, kerchief, and waistcoat—worn with ease and grace. But it was the smile that caught you: a tired boy's smile, a blend of mischief and world-weariness.

Ike Hoover backed down the hall before the Prince, passing along the way more members of the staff than were usually on duty: Dixon, O'Hara, and McKenzie (tugging on his white gloves behind his back). Everybody wanted a glimpse of the Prince—even Annie and her Irish knees, curtsying away in her formal black moiré uniform. As Ike Hoover came abreast of the First Lady's door, it opened and Edith Galt Wilson emerged, beautifully coiffed, gowned, jeweled, radiant, and every inch the image of what the President's lady should be. Maggie, appearing briefly in the doorway to adjust a trailing panel on Mrs. Wilson's gown, curtsied to the Prince and backed away.

"Your Highness," murmured Edith Wilson.

"Madam . . ." The Prince, taking her gloved hand in his, raised her from the position of obeisance, and together they continued on to the west sitting hall. Mercer and Coates, bowing and backing, slid open the heavy double doors.

Just beyond stood President Wilson; meticulously turned out, supported by a thornstick cane in his right hand, his left side braced hard against a table. But standing. As the Prince and First Lady approached, Wilson laid the cane aside and extended his right hand and a smile.

"Welcome, Your Highness . . ."

"So good of you to receive me, Mr. President."

As the door closed on them, the look that passed between Maggie and Mercer was one of deep personal satisfaction.

"My Pres'dent comin' along fine, Maggie . . . real fine . . ."

"So is my lady," Maggie said proudly.

"Lame-duck President." The term never had a more cruel application. In Wilson's last months of office, while he struggled against infirmities he would never conquer, even his supporters in Congress voted with the "irreconcilables" against the ratification of America's participation in the League of Nations. Heartbroken at the disintegration of his dream, he tended more and more to isolate himself from public view, permitting himself to be taken for drives only at his lady's insistence. The Secret Service placed him in the phaeton so that the First Lady and her large hats shielded the President's paralyzed side from the view of the gawkers, of whom there were fewer all the time.

"Hurry," the word went out. "Limousine's comin' down Pennsylvania. He be turnin' into the driveway any minute . . ." Galvanized, servants who were available scurried down stairs, through corridors, to be out there when the somber black automobile drove up the curved path to the portico.

"Have a nice ride, sir?" Mays asked, as he held the door and the Secret Service man helped the President alight. "Lookin' fine today, sir," Jackson echoed. The staff cheered and applauded, as for a returning, forgotten hero.

The last applause came on Inauguration Day, 1921. The Wilsons' possessions were packed and moved to the house on S Street where they would retire from the world. Those most closely involved with serving him— Maggie, Mercer, Coates, Jackson, Mays, McKenzie, Annie, Mrs. Jaffray, and Ike Hoover—lined up. They pulled their ranks to a taut, straight line as Wilson emerged from his room, on his cane, carrying the Inaugural top hat. His First Lady, elegant in velvet, an

orchid pinned to her furs, followed him, her eyes filled
with concern for his every move in these, his last moments in office.

"I, Warren Gamaliel Harding, do solemnly swear—"

President Wilson, leaning heavily on his cane, and
Mrs. Wilson walked past the row of servants. Ike
Hoover stepped forward, with difficulty keeping emotion out of his voice. "On behalf of the staff, Mr. President . . ."

"Please . . . just . . . Woodrow Wilson . . ."

Applause burst from the staff and reached across to
him through eight years of joy, death, war, incapacity,
defeat.

*"That I will faithfully execute the office of President
of the United States—"*

The gaunt man, aged beyond his years, straightened
a little. As he turned and looked back at them, above
the crooked smile, his eyes misted with tears.

*"And will to the best of my ability, preserve, protect,
and defend the Constitution of the United States."*

Edith Wilson thanked them with a proud but wistful smile, then took her husband's arm. Together with
Ike Hoover, they entered the elevator and disappeared
from view.

"Knockwurst and sauerkraut are always to be available to our new President," Mrs. Jaffray had informed
them all in a briefing session in her office. "And while
our new First Lady prefers that her husband smoke
cigars, chewing tobacco, by presidential request, is to
be supplied in whichever room Mr. Harding happens
to be. Which means—"

"Spittoons? In the White House?"

Mrs. Jaffray scanned her charges, uncertain whether
it was Coates, Dixon, or Mercer who had so scath-
ingly commented on the incoming President's habits.
"We'll dispense with the personal opinions, shall we?"
One thing she'd noticed about the Africans. They came
on the job meek as can be, but give them twelve, fifteen years, and didn't they take on airs to themselves.

She'd seen that look on Maggie's face at the word "spittoons." It was as if she'd smelled something bad.

"Maggie, a word with you, please." Mrs. Jaffray detained her as the others left to go about their business.

"Yes, Miz Jaffray?"

It had been on Mrs. Jaffray's mind now for nearly seven years, and she said it with some satisfaction. "Now that we have a new administration, one of your duties will be to go back to scrubbing down the grand staircase each morning."

"I'm not on my knees, by presidential order," Maggie reminded her. "You want to—how do you say, *rescind* that order—you'll have to go to President Harding to do it. Now if you excuse me, I got my work to do . . ."

Blood rushed to Mrs. Jaffray's face like a mask of fire. If ever the time was right to discharge Maggie Rogers, this was the time: between administrations. But Maggie, in Mrs. Jaffray's opinion, had cunningly created her own power bloc. If she were to go, would Mercer, Mays, Jackson—maybe others—leave in protest? Replacements could be made, of course, but Mays and Jackson were getting to be fixtures on the door. If they were to be forced out, the Senate would no doubt write a resolution. Mrs. Jaffray dabbed at her flushed face with eau de cologne. It was getting more difficult by the year to run her house the way she felt it should be run . . .

Maggie came out of Mrs. Jaffray's office, surprised to see Lillian bounding down the corridor, a touch of spring in her manner as if it wasn't cold as sin outside.

"What you doin' here, chile? You s'pose to be at work."

"I'm on my way, Mama . . ."

Maggie stepped back, scrutinizing Lillian's hem, a good six inches off the ground. "What you done? Gone and shortened your dress? Showin' your ankles way up above your shoe tops?"

Lillian let the fashion observation go by. "Tell me you like it . . ." Pulling off her hat, she shook her head.

Her hair, released, sprang out in the short, blunt cut of the new "bob." A somewhat angular shape, it gave her a slightly Egyptian look.

"Good Lord," Maggie lamented, "gone and got your hair chopped. What next?"

"Mama, everybody's doin' it . . . I can't go around lookin' tacky . . . not workin' in a classy shop up on Connecticut Avenue."

Maggie pursed her lips in disapproval. "If you such a style setter, what you askin' my opinion for?"

"Want you to like it, Mama . . ."

"Never goin' like it . . ." Softening Lillian's disappointment, she added, "Well, might get used to it . . ."

Things were changing, no doubt about it. It just wasn't the same place. Polishing cuspidors wasn't Mercer's idea of a valet's proper work, nor the brass receptacles for tobacco juice the proper accouterment for a President. They'd been up in the attic since God knows when. Some of the more badly corroded had seen service as far back as Ulysses S. Grant. Stylish people, as far as Mercer was concerned, were all smoking cigarettes these days. As he dug an ornate spittoon with Federalist eagles for handles out of the cluttered storage room, he caught a glimpse of himself in a dusty gilt-framed mirror. Mays was right. His forehead was getting higher than just proud. He touched the crown of his head. Getting thin up there, too. Twelve years on the job. Come to think of it, this was his third President coming in . . .

Maggie's too. The nexus of events was never as clear to her as at the dismantling of the second floor. How easily and quickly all evidence of occupancy was wiped out. Gone the staid oak desk, straight-backed chairs, subdued worn carpets and sofas, treasured oils and watercolors. In with art nouveau: fringed lampshades, tasseled sofa cushions, bridge lamps, and standing ashtrays everywhere. Where Wilson's umbrella rack had held his canes now stood a pseudo-Greek draped female figure holding a vessel for cigar butts on her head. "Not so fast," Maggie wanted to cry out, "Mr. Wilson and my good lady, they fadin' away too fast . . ." But Wilson, like the war, was old hat. Over. Done with. Gone.

From a carton of discards Maggie picked up a cracked pair of Mr. Wilson's pince-nez. She wiped them clean with her apron, put them back in their case, and the case in her pocket. She would keep them.

The Lincoln bed was on its way back into exile, headboard, footboard, canopy being carted across the hall to once again repose in the ignominy of the dusty attic. In its place would now stand an upright piano which the movers were at this moment rolling across from the elevator. The robust, purposeful lady walking alongside directed this activity in a strong voice rooted in the flat accent of the Middle West. "Careful with that now. Don't want it knocked out of tune."

Mrs. Florence Kling De Wolfe Harding, thirty years the childless bride of Warren G. Harding, was a lady hard to overlook under any conditions. Arriving as she did with an enormous fur piece draped around her neck, ankle to ankle, over a coat of fur, a hat heavily laden with ostrich feathers, and carrying a birdcage, her entrance into center hall prompted several glances of astonishment among the servants. Despite her elaborate overdressing, something of the pioneer woman came through: posture ramrod straight, iron-gray marceled hair, mouth set in a severe line, and rimless pince-nez, suggested the frontier teacher.

"Thank you." She dismissed Ike Hoover, who held the leash of her pet Airedale. "I'll take Laddie Boy now. No, no, you don't need to escort me any farther. I know my way from here. Mrs. Jaffray showed it all to me the other day. Which one is Maggie, the hairdresser?"

Maggie, who was straightening the lie of a rug, got to her feet. "I am, ma'am."

"Come with me," Florence Harding said.

Maggie followed the new First Lady into the room that had lately been Edith Wilson's bedroom and which now, with the introduction of the upright piano and heavy overstuffed sofas, had taken on the hard-edged look of an Ohio front parlor. Mrs. Harding hung her birdcage on its stand. She introduced the canary to Maggie: "His name is Bob." Unhooking the dog's leash, she patted the sofa. "Laddie Boy . . . new home . . ." The dog hopped up onto the sofa, tentatively sniffed it, circled three or four times, then settled into the comfort of the cushions. Only after she was satisfied that her menagerie was happily ensconced did Mrs. Harding allow herself to be divested of hat, furs, coat.

"Do you do facials?" she asked Maggie.

"Well, that not somethin' I've had a lot of experience with, ma'am."

"Learn how. I want a facial every day. By someone in the house. Don't like strangers around."

"Yes, ma'am."

Maggie started for the dressing room with Mrs. Harding's wraps. "That can wait." She sat at the piano, eyes closed, and ran her hands across the keyboard from one end to the other, not depressing the keys. After resting her hands in her lap a moment, she began to play, singing a phrase or two of the popular new song "Look for the Silver Lining." Her skill at the piano would never challenge Paderewski's, but the instrument seemed to have some special significance, as though she were communicating through it. Maggie stood by, puzzled why she had been asked to wait.

Abruptly Mrs. Harding stopped playing, gestured Maggie closer. Taking one of Maggie's hands between both of hers, she looked intently into her eyes. "Yes . . . I get good psychic vibrations from you, Maggie . . . you're someone I can trust."

"Yes, ma'am."

"You know how people are on the outside. Vicious." Maggie stayed motionless, uncertain how to respond, but Mrs. Harding didn't expect an answer. Just as abruptly, she resumed playing. Maggie accepted the dismissal. Mrs. Harding's strong voice carried out to the center hall with the song's optimistic message that somewhere the sun was shining. She played for the better part of that afternoon. It took three maids four days to set up her closets of elaborate beaded silk, satin, and tulle gowns. An entire bureau drawer was filled with decorated neckbands designed to conceal the en-croachment of age.

The First Lady was right . . . people talked. Caustic tongues took aim at the presidential target. The gossip went out like a stone skipping on water, from the halls of Congress, hotel lobbies, gentlemen's washrooms, la-dies' tea parties, the fitting rooms of exclusive shops on Connecticut Avenue.

The Celeste, catering as it did to a clientele of wives, daughters, and mistresses of those on the Hill and in diplomatic and social circles, was a whirlpool of infor-mation; sometimes last night's indiscretions being aired before the gentlemen in question could send long-stemmed roses to their wives. In this elegant little salon, where ladies could indulge their nostalgia for Paris while Lillian's expert needle fitted couture gowns to their daringly uncorseted bodies, the peccadilloes of "the sporting man from Ohio" who had attained the presidency were much discussed.

"How will he ever find time to be President, what with that 'little house on K Street' he frequents . . ." wondered the chic, overly thin client.

"And that Delilah of his, up in New York . . . think he's going to bring her down here?" added the client's friend from her horizontal perch on the satin chaise.

Lillian sat on the floor of the fitting room, carefully pinning the fashionably uneven hemline. *From the free way they're talkin', they must think of me as a piece of furniture.* The client, elevated on a plush-covered platform, watched her fitter's every move in the long mirror, and continued to dissect the new residents at 1600 Pennsylvania Avenue.

"Wonder if his wife knows about her?"

The client's friend put a third cigarette into her foot-long ivory holder and lighted it. "Well, if she doesn't, she's the only one in Washington. The child, they say, looks just like him . . ."

"Child?"

"Didn't you know? It's all over town. And he told the Republicans he had nothing to hide when they ran him, can you beat that? Oh, have you heard the latest? That a politician is known by the women he keeps?"

"That's a wow!" said the client, who was being kept herself. Lillian put in the last pin. Her leg had gone to sleep. Reaching for her crutch, she pulled herself to her feet. The client looked at her for the first time as other than an arm connected to a hand that put in pins. "How old are you?"

"Twenty-three," said Lillian.

The friend airily dismissed her. "She's old enough to know about these things . . ."

"Just hope she's wise enough not to repeat them," the client pointedly delivered into the mirror.

"Oh, no, ma'am, that would never do . . ." The client didn't catch the mockery in Lillian's tone. She and the friend had turned their attention to a critical scrutiny of the gown. "You like it?" asked the client.

"I'm absolutely dippy about that hemline . . ." said the friend. "It's the cat's meow—so new . . ."

"Why thank you, ma'am . . ." The response to the compliment came with such naturalness from Lillian that it took the client a moment to realize what it meant. "Are you telling me that you designed this gown?"

"Well—" Lillian didn't want to take all the credit. "I have seen some pictures from Paris . . ." It was hard for her to understand why the client became suddenly so agitated. "Celeste . . ." she called. *"Celeste . . ."*

"Did I do somethin' wrong, ma'am?"

Celeste, a formidably structured lady in black and pearls, appeared in the doorway. *"Oui, madame?* Something you wish, *madame?"* Indeed there was something the client wished! If the colored help was doing the designing, then Celeste's prices were way out of line. And it wouldn't take until cocktail time for the word to be all over town . . .

"Oh, mon dieu, non, madame . . ." Celeste hovered, placating. "Lillian expresses gratitude on behalf of the salon, no, Lillian?" She merely does our hand-work, *n'est-ce pas,* Lillian?"

Lillian got the message. "Yes, ma'am. Just the hand-work." The client, stepping out of the gown, posed in front of the mirror in her racy new teddy. Lillian carried the gown to the back workroom to make the adjustments. It wasn't going to be the easy road she'd hoped. That night, as job insurance, she stopped off at the new Dunbar Theater that had opened just across from the Howard, and told them she'd be available for the box office nights, and maybe even Sundays.

The Nineteenth Amendment, granting women the vote, had been ratified during the last year of Wilson's tenure. In the District of Columbia, where nobody had the vote, it wasn't worth the paper it was written on (unless, of course, it helped get you elected back home). The Eighteenth Amendment, outlawing alcoholic beverages, was taken just about as seriously. Bootleggers were recognizable by their derby hats and spats. "Private clubs" sprang up in houses like mushrooms after rain, adopting the new name "speakeasies" that had come down from New York. In the changing rooms and on the back stairs, these things were discussed, Maggie steadfastly refusing to hear them. What she didn't hear, she didn't know. And what she didn't know, just plain wasn't there. If that meant not reading the newspapers, then she wouldn't go near those scandal sheets.

Her days were full. Facials and attention to the First Lady's clothes had to be fitted into the daily bed making, dusting, and scrubbing. Annie, who still held the job as first maid, had come to accept Maggie, if still not totally comfortable with the anthropological differences between them. Mrs. Jaffray would never make such concessions. The more extra work Maggie was called on to do, the more exacting was the supervision. Maggie had learned to "Yes, ma'am, Miz Jaffray" and "No, ma'am, Miz Jaffray" her way out of confrontations—a demeaning subterfuge, but she had to admit it worked. Mercer, Mays, and Jackson, catching her feigning stupidity, kidded her unmercifully: "Yes, ma'am, Miz Rogers ... no, ma'am, Miz Rogers ..."

This day she had managed to sidestep Mrs. Jaffray's manicure by going out through the furnace room. She'd get a dressing down for it tomorrow, but meantime she had a chance to run home for a few minutes with Lillian and to see if there was a letter from Emmett at the hospital before having to come back to the White House.

"What you doin' here, Maggie? Thought you'd be long gone home ..." Jackson in uniform was alone at the staff dining table, having himself a cup of coffee. Maggie poured one and joined him. "Been home and back—no word from my baby and Miz Harding goin' be needin' me ..."

Jackson agreed on that. "Poor lady," he said. "Been on her feet since seven this mornin' . . . not stopped shakin' hands. I swear, don't know how she holds up ..." Maggie, returning through the gloom of early evening, had found her path brightly lit by illumination from every window of the White House; the public, by invitation of the First Lady, was still lined up, as it had been all day, down the street and around the corner.

"How many people been here today?"

"Not kept count. Must be thousands." Jackson glanced anxiously at his watch. Mercer hadn't come back. Mays, also in uniform, came in from the door and poured himself some coffee. "You better get out there, Mr. Jackson, and hold the door for the great American public for a while."

Jackson, buttoning his jacket, wondered if Mays had seen hide or hair of Mercer.

"He not back yet?"

Maggie, back to the coffee urn, couldn't see Mays' face, but she read the anxiety in his voice; and from the way Jackson was telegraphing with his eyebrows, it was evident they thought they were keeping something from her.

"He on one those *errands* again?" she said disap-
provingly. "He goin' to sure get himself arrested . . .
don't you all know it's against the law . . . don't he
know?"

The clank of bottles underscored Mercer's arrival.
"There's a game on tonight, Maggie . . . they run short
last time."

"That's no excuse for you to be out riskin' yourself . . ."

Mercer moved quickly to the table and divested himself of the weight of two filled shopping sacks. Removing a camouflaging bunch of bananas from the top of
each, he began to bring out bottle after bottle of rye,
bourbon, and scotch.

"We were gettin' ready to send out the Marines,"
Jackson said.

"You do that, wouldn't have any booze left for the
President . . ."

Maggie didn't find any of this funny. "Can smell your
breath clear across here, Mercer . . . That's why you
late . . ."

"Now, Maggie, how can a man say no to twelve-
year-old bonded scotch?"

"It's illegal to drink in this country, you know that,
Mercer."

"Didn't drink it in this country. Drank it on foreign
soil—in the embassy."

Mays, helping him unpack the bottles, said, "You
know, I could use some of that diplomatic immunity
. . . might ask 'em to send me next time . . ."

Maggie kept at Mercer. "But drivin' back through
Washington, that's U.S.A.—what if you got stopped
by a policeman?"

Mercer put the bottles on a serving table and
changed into his white jacket. "Not too likely—in a
White House ve-hicle. Had I been, Maggie, I'd offered
the man one of these bananas . . ."

"Wrapped in a ten-dollar bill," Jackson interjected.

"That's about the size of it. And I'd come back here
a bottle short."

Mays joined in the laughter.

"We come to a sorrowful time, breakin' the law right here in the White House . . ." Maggie said.

Mays leaned back in his chair, shook his head. "Nothin' to worry 'bout, Miz Rogers," he said with a cynicism not usual to him. "Feds not likely to bust in here and cause a ruckus . . . not with the Attorney General in the house . . ."

6

☒ ☒ ☒

The Attorney General was indeed in the house, along with the Secretaries of Interior and the Navy, and three other gentlemen of the unofficial privy council whom the newspapers were beginning to refer to as presidential cronies. Any number of cabinet meetings had convened on the second floor, command decisions had been made in these rooms, but this was the first time a cabinet agenda waited on the turn of a hole card.

The game was five-card stud.

Smoke hung in the air, heavy enough to cover an infantry advance. The green baize that dressed the large round table in the west sitting hall had, for its centerpiece, a scattered heap of paper currency. Neat stacks of tens, twenties, and fifties sat in front of each of the participants.

Attorney General Harry Daugherty pulled on his cigar and riffled his cash. Sixty years of living and lobbying had brought him to the point where he sat at the right hand of the President of the United States. His own political ambition blunted by his backroom personality, this was certainly the next best thing. Twenty some years—more than a third of his life—devoted to Harding. But it had paid off, yes, sir. First time he'd laid eyes on Warren G., he remembered thinking, *He looks like a President ought to look* . . . That, coupled with Harding's hail-fellow-well-met charm, and he knew he had a vote getter. He had patiently brought him along, like a boxer, from the preliminaries to the main event: from the State Legislature, to the Senate, to the White House. A man couldn't ask for more than that.

"Well, what are you going to do, Denby?"

Edwin Denby, Secretary of the Navy, hated that Daugherty talked down like you were some kid who'd forgotten your galoshes on a rainy day. He particularly disliked being pushed during a poker game where he felt the need to deliberate, and perhaps recoup some of his losses, although losing to the President was the unspoken outcome of the game.

"I'll see the bet," Denby replied. "What's it going to cost me?"

"Forty."

"Okay. I'm in."

Albert Fall knocked on the table twice, signaling the third card being dealt all around, he felt gratified to be at this table. Not bad for an old cowpoke: going from Senator to cabinet status. Losing to the President was a small price to pay for being inside the main corral. He glanced up from dealing, his eye falling on the entrance to the First Lady's quarters, realizing it was just through that door where Edith Galt Wilson had made a fool of him the day the Senate sent him over to evaluate the stricken President. She was a devil, that woman. Well, no matter now. Harding's in the saddle. This was an administration Fall could live with—comfortably, he decided, as he pulled off his benchmade hand-tooled boots and settled down for what he hoped would be a profitable evening.

"I'll bet my ponies . . . just need more of the same spots."

The spittoon with the Federalist eagle handles had found its vocation beside the foot of the twenty-ninth President of the United States. Studying his cards thoughtfully, Warren G. Harding chewed the tobacco, spat, and stored the wad in his cheek. A man of considerable size rather than stature, excessive good living was beginning to take its toll. His waistline expanded beyond comfort, he lowered his suspenders and opened the top button of his trousers. Daugherty was right about his looks. He had a noble head, like a Roman senator, with penetrating blue eyes, a sensual mouth, and a strong, almost hawklike nose. But these days his face was florid; tiny tributary veins in cheeks and nose were beginning to be discernible. It was the thick, fur-like eyebrows, startlingly black in contrast to his almost white hair, that demanded attention. Now concentration danced in those brows as he decided whether or not to stay in the hand.

"If every cabinet meeting was like this, it would sure take the pain out of government . . ." Daugherty downed a double scotch. "Good stock, Mr. President . . . who's your bootlegger?"

They all laughed, Jesse Smith the longest and hardest, until Daugherty silenced him with an impatient look. Jesse knew he'd better be careful. At fifty, a man didn't get many more chances at position, and lately Daugherty had been increasingly impatient with him. Being aide to the Attorney General carried penalties along with benefits. Jesse flushed and concentrated on his cards.

Harding brought the discussion back to bootleggers. "Don't blame me for Prohibition. Look at my record in the Senate. I voted wet thirty times."

"So you did, Warren, so you did." Only since he'd come to occupy the White House had Harding become aware of a slight patronizing note in Daugherty's voice. How could he not have seen it in him before? Or— give the guy a break—maybe he just imagined it. Harding held out his glass for a refill.

Before the President's arm was fully extended, Mercer was there, pouring from the cut-glass decanter, as much a part of the background as the draperies and chafing dishes on the serving table. Lighting cigars, emptying ashtrays, tidying his bar, he watched the money move across the green and thought of the courtly Taft and the scholarly Wilson.

"Can you imagine Herbert Hoover," Daugherty went on, "or Andrew Mellon, or that dry-stick Vice-President of yours—Coolidge—joining us in the pleasures of the flesh?"

"Now come on, Harry . . ." Harding took exception to his other secretaries being demeaned. He was proud that men of such stature had seen fit to serve under him; felt it a tribute to his leadership. While he called his cronies by their first names, he could never bring himself to refer to Hoover or Mellon or Henry Cantwell Wallace as anything other than Mr. Secretary. "These men are geniuses, Harry . . . look what Mr. Secretary Hoover's done about world famine; no one in the financial world can touch Secretary Mellon. Don't know much about Coolidge," Harding admitted, "haven't heard him say ten words."

"Who has?"

Even so, the Harding-Coolidge ticket with its lofty campaign mottoes—"America always first" . . . "Back to normal" . . . "Law and order"—had helped put him in the White House, and he was still a bit in awe that all this was happening to him.

Harding draped his leg over the arm of the chair. His dog Laddie Boy raised up from where he was curled underneath the table and rubbed against his master's knee.

Charlie Forbes, still in his forties, the youngest at the table, had been brought from Marion, Ohio, as adviser to the President. He still felt a foot off the ground. Imagine . . . chief of the Veterans Bureau, with invitations to all the best parties. He hadn't quite got used to his position yet and was always looking for a way to ingratiate himself. "Way you're sitting there, Mr. President," he said, taking off his steel-rimmed spectacles, moving them up and back as though to capture him in perfect focus. "Puts me in mind of you campaigning back home from your front porch."

"Common as an old shoe," Harding deprecated, but

Forbes could tell he'd pleased him. "Man of the people . . ." Studying his hole card, Harding pontificated,
"That's what the public wants . . . Tired of war shortages . . . Time for a man who touches the pulse . . ."

"No need to politick anymore, Warren, we won."
Daugherty studied the table. "Country got what it
wanted. A common man . . ." *How did he mean that?*
Harding wondered. But the Attorney General was eval-
uating Denby's open sixes.

"Well, Mr. Secretary of the Navy," Fall inquired,
"you going to bet your sixes or sink 'em?"

Denby put twenty in the pot.

Forbes turned his cards down. "Pass."

Fall put his twenty in. "Department of Interior will
see the bet," he said.

Jesse Smith studied the table with owlish eyes and
hesitated. Stay or pass?

The President chewed. Spat. "I got your note today,
Harry. Why do you keep pressing for Secretary Hughes
to preside at the Navy Disarmament Conference? No
place for a *common man?*"

"Oh, Warren . . . Mr. President . . . no offense. After
all, Charles Evans Hughes *is* your Secretary of State."

"But Wilson never sent anybody in his place . . . he
went himself."

"Fat lot of good it did him . . ." The whole table was
getting impatient with Jesse Smith's indecision. "Come
on, Jesse, bet or turn down . . ."

He finally passed.

Daugherty, who had a king on board, saw the twenty
and raised twenty. "By sending Hughes," he went on to
Harding, "you show how much smarter you are than
Wilson . . . don't you see that? Delegate authority—
always the sign of a good executive . . ."

Harding chewed hard on the tobacco, bull's-eyed
the cuspidor.

"Mr. President," Fall said, "will you make your bet,
please?"

"Oh . . . what is it—forty to me?" As he studied the
cards, he spoke to Daugherty. "Well, I'll do it your
way . . . Hughes can take the conference . . ." He

turned down his cards. "Too rich for my blood. Pass."

Denby put in twenty. "Navy stays."

"But I am appointing Taft Chief Justice," Harding said, expecting resistance from Daugherty.

"Why not?" Daugherty, studying the cards, was laconic. "You owe him . . . he exposed you to the country, letting you make the keynote speech in '12."

Fall dealt a fourth card to those still in the game. "Your sixes are still high," he told Denby.

Harding didn't want the matter to drop there. "You make it sound like a nine-year-old payoff . . . This is no bribe, Harry. Taft's a good man, educated with a sharp legal mind."

"That what you want, Warren. Fine . . ." It was like patting a child on the head.

"Damn good man, Taft," contributed Charles Cramer, on Harding's left. New to the group, he'd said very little during the game. A small man, he felt dwarfed sitting next to the President, frequently running his hand over pompadoured hair that gave him an extra half inch of height. "Damn good man," he repeated, which seemed to please Harding very much, who punched Cramer in the shoulder.

"You see?" Harding said to Daugherty. "Our California lawyer says I'm right . . ."

"Didn't say you weren't right, Warren . . ." There was a slight testiness in Daugherty's voice. He put twenty in the pot, announcing to the table that it would take twenty to stay. Cramer said he'd see it. Denby anted up two tens. The pot grew.

In sudden irritability, Harding told Mercer he was getting damned hungry. It was the first any of them had spoken directly to Mercer. He was used to that. He prepared a heaping plate of knockwurst and sauerkraut for the President. Presidential adviser Forbes left the game and went to the buffet to serve himself. Fall dealt to Daugherty, Cramer, Denby, himself. "Last card, gentlemen."

Daugherty could tell by the way Harding's jaw knotted that he would sit there pouting, unless he brought him out of it. "All right, Warren, what else is gnawing at you?"

"Unemployment . . . recession . . ." His sigh was weighted with confusion. "I listen to one side and they seem right, and then—God almighty!—I talk to the other side . . ." The subject drifted away from him. "The soldiers' bonus . . ."

"It'll pass both houses," Daugherty assured. "When it comes to your desk, sign it."

He puzzled. "But won't we have to raise taxes?"

"You've got Hays, Hoover, Mellon—and all of us. Spread the problems around . . ." Daugherty put two twenties in the pot. "Forty says you're beat," he said to Denby.

Cramer, patting his pompadour, let it be known he wasn't out yet. "Forty, hm? I'll see it."

The game held the attention of the table, but Harding still mulled, unsettled in his mind. "You two Charlies"—he spoke to Forbes and Cramer—"you're both Veterans Bureau, you're in touch—how do you boys feel about the soldiers' bonus?"

"Every soldier's a vote, Mr. President," Forbes advised.

"They love you in California, Mr. President," Cramer contributed.

"They do? They really like me?" Mercer brought the plate of food to the President, who disposed of the wad of tobacco into the cuspidor, and started to eat. "Really like me, hm?"

"You come out our way, San Francisco'll turn the town upside down for you."

"Really like me . . ."

Denby pushed in his cards. "You two fight it out." Daugherty turned up his hole card. Jacks. Cramer turned up his. Queens. Daugherty took losing in stride. All in a day's work . . . He got up, stretched, and moved to the buffet table, where Mercer filled his plate.

"Well, tell you one thing I am going to do," Harding said, out of the blue, "and that's pardon Eugene Debs." Which brought protest all around, with Daugherty, as usual the strongest voice. "Warren, you haven't been in office six months. Take it slow. You don't want people tarring you with a Socialist brush . . ."

But Harding was stubborn. He'd wait awhile, but he was going to pardon him. Norman Thomas had been Harding's newsboy out in Ohio, and he'd told him Debs was a good man. If Norman Thomas said Debs was no traitor, that was good enough.

"Just don't get carried away, Warren."

Another hand was dealt. As the game got underway again, Fall casually inquired, "Oh, Mr. President, have you signed those papers transferring the oil reserves to my department from Navy?"

Harding admitted he hadn't given it much thought. "What do you think, Harry?" he asked.

"It's all right with the Attorney General if it's okay with Navy."

"It's okay with Navy if it's okay with Interior," Denby said.

"Department of Interior votes aye." Fall made it unanimous.

"You boys seem to have it all worked out."

"That's what I've been trying to tell you, Warren, put in good men, let 'em work for you." Daugherty leaned over and patted his President on the shoulder. "Go out, do some of the things you like, Warren—play some golf, go to a ball game . . . let us have the headaches. Have we ever steered you wrong?"

"Okay, I'll sign the leasehold transfers in the morning." Daugherty was right. They were good men. Loyal. He admired that. He took a drink, savoring the smooth, aged scotch. "Just where are these federal oil reserves, anyway?"

"Out in my neck of the woods," Fall said. "One's in Elk Hills, California. Other one's in Wyoming."

"Oh? Whereabouts in Wyoming?"

"Godforsaken spot." Fall bit off the end of the cigar, Mercer lighted it for him, Fall brought it to full draw. "Place called Teapot Dome."

Harding fed a bite of knockwurst to his dog, then one to himself. "Teapot Dome . . . wonder who saddled it with that crazy name?" They all laughed. The dog suddenly lost interest in the food. "Mercer, let Laddie out, he wants to go to the Duchess." Mercer opened the door, the dog ran out. Harding finished off the knockwurst and picked up his cards, thinking how good it was to be surrounded by friends.

Maggie had been waiting on a bench near the elevator for better than an hour. Hearing the mechanism engage, which meant that Mrs. Harding was on the way up, she quickly got to her feet. Laddie Boy, who came running out of the room where the card game was going on, must have heard it too. Together, Maggie and the dog waited.

It had been a long day, but an even longer day for the First Lady. When Maggie arrived in the morning, the line of people waiting to shake her hand already extended from the entrance all the way to the street and around the corner. Mrs. Harding had doggedly stuck it out, not eating or resting. Twice during the day Maggie had brought her a fresh dress so that she could change downstairs without being away from the crowd too long. When her feet gave out, she stood shoeless on a pillow. "I want everyone to know what a friendly White House this is," she told Maggie. Everyone, that is, except those in her little red book who would never —so help her—set foot in this building while she was in residence.

The day had been carefully planned. Mrs. Harding, who laid out the cards each morning, said for a week running, "Luck's against me, I must wait until it changes." When she discovered that Mrs. Jaffray also admitted to a psychic streak, and knew of a good fortune-teller, the two ladies went several times for consultation. The Ouija board, a new craze that was sweeping the nation, was briefly introduced into the White House, but failed to give her all the answers she sought. Mrs. Harding even asked Maggie if she knew anyone.

As it happened, Maggie did know of a Foggy Bottom lady who, it seemed, had been born with a caul over her face, and made arrangements for her to come to the

White House. But the day that Mrs. Harding's cards told her was the right time to come, the caul lady's spirits warned her not to go up any stairs, so the connection was never made. The cards finally assured Mrs. Harding that the time was ripe for her open house. The invitation went out by newspaper, radio, and word of mouth.

Sixty-seven hundred and fifty-eight hands—and she shook every one of them.

Florence Harding stepped from the elevator in a stage of exhaustion bordering on hysteria, her hands—swollen, red, raw—extended in supplication. "Maggie, help me . . ." Maggie supported her to the bedroom, tenderly helped her out of the heavy, beaded dress, Laddie Boy trailing along, whining at being ignored.

"Miz Harding, let's get you to bed . . ."

"No . . ." Grimly proud of having been on her feet for fourteen hours and shaken every hand the public thrust at her, she allowed her hands to be bathed in a basin of warm water, viewing the painful, bruised appendages as badges of honor. Smiling . . . that was the worst of it . . . smiling all day long . . . "Maybe now the newspapers will say something nice about us."

"Rest, ma'am, close your eyes . . ." Maggie removed the rhinestone dog collar from her neck and prepared bottles and jars for the facial. Florence Harding leaned forward, scrutinizing herself in the mirror, lifting the aging skin on her face with the backs of her injured hands, painfully aware at this moment of looking far older than the six years she was her husband's senior.

"My father was wrong," she said.

"Ma'am?" Maggie liberally applied cold cream to the lined neck.

"Said Warren would never amount to anything, never be more than what he was—a small-town newspaper editor, without an opinion . . . Didn't want me to marry him . . . refused to speak to us for years. You see how wrong he was."

"Yes, ma'am."

"Night before I met Warren, a psychic told me I would meet a man who'd go all the way to the top and take me with him." Maggie applied cream to the tense forehead. Florence Harding began to relax under the soothing strokes. "Lot of people in this town snubbed me, when we were Senator, didn't believe we'd be in this house. I've got all their names written down . . . I won't forget . . ." Laddie Boy lay down at her feet. She petted him with her slippered foot. "And that Mrs. Wilson . . . Were you here the day she was supposed to take me around, show me how the White House works?"

"Believe I was, ma'am."

"Treated me like dirt . . . cut me cold. I said I wanted to bring my good friend, Evalyn Walsh McLean —you know, the Hope diamond?"

Maggie knew. She'd dressed the hair of Mrs. McLean, had heard tell of the legendary diamond that she wore like it was a piece of glass, knew the Du Pont Circle gossip about Mrs. McLean having been consistently snubbed at the White House. Maggie could have told her that acquired wealth wouldn't get her through that front door. You could be poor as a church mouse if you had the right pedigree.

"Told me I wasn't acceptable. Didn't come right out and say it, but I know she felt too good for Mrs. McLean. Well, I'll have Evalyn McLean in this house— knock everybody's eyes out. Really give them something to talk about . . ." She closed her eyes, celebrating her accomplishment. "Sixty-seven hundred and fifty-eight hands . . ." The canary began to sing. Mrs. Harding sat up abruptly. Alarmed. "Maggie, hurry, cover him, quick. It's a bad omen for a bird to sing at night!"

Maggie covered the bird. When she had her lady settled for the night, she went home, wondering if there were anything to Mrs. Harding's omens. Bad things that happened in Maggie's life always took her by surprise. The night Lillian was taken with the paralysis, the day the news came of Emmett's gassing, and the day of her husband's death she'd just been going along, like any other day. Hurrying down the dark street to her house, she saw a black cat ahead and crossed over to the other side. Now if that wasn't a fool thing to do. The only specters on Maggie's horizon were the price of sugar and the cost of bread. These days, her spirit was constantly being tried—what with prices going up, the rent raised. Coal going for twenty dollars or more a ton—although she only bought it by the scuttle. Lillian was working pretty steady, but Emmett was still in and out of the hospital. And the poor soldiers—those who had left jobs trying to get them back; the others, looking. What was an omen and what wasn't? Too tired to give it any more thought, she went into her house and was asleep as soon as her head touched the pillow.

That winter, the words UNEMPLOYMENT . . . PROFITEERING appeared with regularity in the newspapers. In the White House, Mrs. Harding had the silver service triple-plated with gold.

It was nearing 6:00 p.m. Lillian set the latch, pulled down the shade, and closed up the Celeste. Pausing to glance at the gowned mannequin in the display window, she reminded herself that come morning, she'd press out a wrinkle near the shoulder. Instead of boarding the streetcar that would take her directly to the White House, as time demanded, she walked, cutting across Jefferson Place, M Street, to Nineteenth. There was a rumor there that just had to be checked out. Turning the corner onto Twenty-first, she hurried down to the middle of the block and stopped. The moving van gave her the answer she'd been looking for.

The darkening sky told her she'd catch it for being late. Fortunately there was a car taking on passengers at the corner of Nineteenth and Pennsylvania that would drop her within a block of the White House. She hopped off at Seventeenth and crutched like greased lightning past Blair House, down West Executive Avenue into the staff entrance, and down the long corridor to the women's changing room.

"Where you been, chile?" Maggie was already changed into the evening uniform of black moiré with white lace apron and cap. Hurrying Lillian out of coat, hat, and dress and into the smallest moiré the White

House had to offer, Maggie brushed aside Lillian's excited "Mama, on my way here you won't believe what I saw!"

"You bring the napkins?"

"In the sack. Mama, up on Twenty-first Street—"

"Got 'em all mended nice?" Maggie had some of the contents of the shopping bag Lillian had brought in with her out on the mirror shelf, scrutinizing the mended folded linen. "And iron 'em all?"

"Did I ever bring 'em back not done proper?" Lillian set the lace cap on her bobbed head, Maggie tied the apron around her slight body. "You know I've mended some those same napkins six, seven times— put in my own secret stitches 'round where it's embroidered U.S., so I can count. And while we talkin' 'bout it, Miz Jaffray back-owes me for the last bunch."

"You'll get paid."

"I better. The Chief Justice of the Supreme Court's a friend of mine, havin' met him in a bathtub."

Maggie smiled in spite of herself, "I swan, Lil'yan, you sassy sometimes jus' like those suffragette ladies."

"They got the vote, didn't they? Mama, let me tell you what I saw . . ." But Maggie was rushing the napkins to the pantry for use in the State Dining Room. They met again in the cloakroom where receiving ermines, sables, silk top hats, chesterfields, and Inverness capes kept them too busy for private conversation. When all of the guests' wraps had been checked, the receiving line traversed, and the notables seated at dinner, Maggie finally allowed herself a deep breath. She sat on a stool at the back wall, observing Lillian, who was leaning against the counter, putting down figures in a small note pad. "What you writin' there?"

"Twenty-five dollars a month, Mama . . . in winter, twenty-seven . . ."

"What you talkin' 'bout?"

"You know that nice apartment buildin' up there on Twenty-first Street with the iron fence out in front? Well, they got a vacancy. It's got electricity, heat from a radiator in every room, its own bathroom . . ."

"Oh, no, chile, not that buildin' . . ." Her objection

was interrupted by Dixon of the butler staff arriving at the cloakroom in full livery and high dudgeon. "Maggie, you cleaned the pantry last, didn't you?"

"Why, somebody complainin'?"

"Where the toothpicks?"

"Toothpicks? At a state dinner? Who'd dare to ask for toothpicks . . ."

"The Pres'dent . . ."

"The *Pres*—oh, well, lessee . . ." She closed her eyes, visualizing the pantry. A package could be found at the back of a corner shelf in the second cabinet from the kitchen stove. "But for heaven's sake, Dixon," she called after him, "Present 'em in *sterling!*" She sat down again on the stool, offended to the core. *Toothpicks . . .*

Lillian's concentration remained on the note pad. "And the extra rent it would cost, we'll save on coal. With both of us workin', Mama, and all this overtime we pickin' up, we can afford—"

Maggie was again on her feet, shushing Lillian with a glance as Forbes and Cramer approached from the grand entry hall. The two Charlies, as the President called them, presented claim checks for their own and their ladies' wraps, and turned away, speaking in low, strained voices.

"Shouldn't be leavin' so early," Cramer said. "It'll look strange."

Forbes was furious with Cramer. His own relationship with the President went back to Ohio, and this newcomer to the inner circle from California had upset him very much. "That was some gaffe back there in in the dining room. You could have said you hadn't read today's paper . . . Damn fool columnist didn't have any facts . . ."

Cramer nervously ran his fingers through his pompadour. "I was only covering for Jesse Smith . . . I tried to signal him to shut up, but you know how he is when he gets wound up—a biddy, nervous biddy . . ."

"Oil's not our department. Now you opened it up, they'll likely start digging, asking questions about the Veterans Bureau. You leave the tip."

Cramer dropped two coins in the glass bowl. "You're

taking on too strong, Charlie . . . What I said was inconsequential . . . party talk. Be forgotten by morning . . ."

"Hell it will! With Senator Kendrick—of *Wyoming?* Didn't you see what he did when we left the room? Went right over, sat down with those two Senate bird dogs, Borah and La Follette . . ."

Lillian laid a velvet cape trimmed in stone marten and a full-length sealskin coat on the counter. Maggie added an Inverness cape, an overcoat, and two silk hats. Forbes and Cramer picked up the garments and left. Lillian was talking as though there had been no interruption in her flow of thought. "And Mama, this apartment's got a nice little room for Emmett so's he can have a place of his own any time he can come in from the hospital . . ."

Maggie sat back down on the stool. In a way, Lillian's single-mindedness was good. It eliminated the need to acknowledge that both of them had just been privy to a conversation that—although they didn't understand it—had disturbing overtones. But that building she was figuring so hard on was not for them. "Don't get your hopes up, chile. That whole neighborhood over there been lily white a long time."

"That's the point, Mama. I been keepin' my eye on that whole block, and a Negro family moved in today—I was there, saw the furniture goin' in. And there's a vacancy in that same buildin'."

"Can I help you, Mr. Attorney General?"

Lillian turned, to find Maggie's attention focused on Harry Daugherty, who was now standing near the check stand, looking around.

"Did you see two gentlemen leave?" he asked. "Friends of the President?"

"Gentlemen he plays cards with? Mr. Cramer and Mr. Forbes? Oh, yes, sir, they jus' left with their ladies."

"Thank you." Daugherty hesitated. Maggie and Lillian busied themselves with nonexistent chores, straightening hangers, adjusting hats on the shelves, but still he didn't leave. A moment later, an anxious Jesse

Smith hurried in from the main foyer. "Harry, look, I didn't mean anything . . ."

"Mr. Smith will have his coat." He snapped his fingers for the check. Smith nervously searched his pockets and finally found it. As Maggie moved to get the coat, Daugherty took him forcefully by the arm, moved him a few steps away, Lillian stepped discreetly to the back of the check stand, to allow them some privacy.

"Jesse," Daugherty said, "just go home and keep your mouth shut."

Jesse Smith kept shooting his cuffs, like a nervous tic. Apprehensive. "Aren't you coming?"

"I've got to back in there and try to cover for your big mouth."

"You're not going to spend the night here again, are you, Harry?"

"I'll be home, I'll be home . . ."

"When?"

"Keep a light in the window, all right?" Daugherty took an overcoat and a hat from Maggie and shoved them at Smith.

"Wait. I didn't leave a tip." Smith came back, opened his pocket change purse, left a coin, and went out with Daugherty.

Working the cloakroom was the guarantee of a long-drawn-out evening. After a time, there wasn't much of anything to say to each other. Just sit and wait for the hours to pass. Exchange furs, wraps, coats, hats for checks. Hope the tip bowl filled up. This particular night there were several dollar bills among the coins, but Maggie's body had gone numb and Lillian had her shoes off and was trying to rub some life back into her foot. It was well past one in the morning. In four hours, Maggie would be awakening to return—if she ever got to bed. Not a sound from the ballroom or dining room. The last strains of music had long died out. From where they sat they couldn't see into the main foyer, but judging from the lack of sound out there no one had gone through in over half an hour. So long as one garment remained, so did Maggie's obligation to the cloakroom.

And one garment did remain: an opulent floor-length ermine coat, double faced, trimmed with tails. At one point Lillian had run her hand over it and said she purely wished she could try it on, an impulse Maggie quickly laid to rest. When the coat had been checked Maggie had been impressed with it herself. But at this time of night, aching as she was to get home, it was just a left-behind coat. A white weasel . . .

"Got to be up so early," Maggie voiced.

Ike Hoover came in from the main foyer to turn off the lights and was astonished to find them still there.

"Miz McLean not picked up her wrap," Maggie explained.

"Mrs. McLean? Why, she left over an hour ago . . ."

Strange, a cold night like this, to leave behind a coat. Lillian found it particularly peculiar that anybody could forget ermine. Ike Hoover said he'd deliver the coat to the First Lady; it would be safer for Mrs. Harding to keep it until her friend Mrs. McLean called for it.

"Now you close up, Maggie, get on home. Get some rest."

" 'Night, Mr. Hoover."

" 'Night." He went upstairs with the truant coat. Maggie emptied the coins and bills into her purse, far too exhausted to count them. Lillian put on her shoes. They turned off the light and left the cloakroom.

Ten days later they moved into their first real home. Two Negro families in the block now, and some of the white tenants were beginning to read APARTMENT FOR RENT ads "farther out." Maggie didn't take offense. Her third-floor front was satisfaction enough: a cozy parlor with casement windows to the street, and lace curtains to the floor cut down from White House discards; two small bedrooms, with white porcelain bathroom between; and, for the first time, a real kitchen. With the acquisition of the new apartment, business picked up for the secondhand man on K Street. Maggie had long been a fifty-cent-down, fifty-cent-a-week customer of this shop, sometimes taking as long as a year to bring home an important purchase, like the Victorian love seat. Now the secondhand man had Lillian for a client. A splurger, impatient, she skipped lunches and paid a dollar a week. Eight payments and she brought home the floor runner, oriental design, that perfectly suited the narrow entry hall.

Emmett had come in from the hospital the day she got it out of "will call" and helped her lay it. Out of olive drab, with civvies draped on his thin frame, he couldn't seem to put on an ounce. His breathing was a continual wheeze.

"Like it?" Lillian asked, unrolling the runner from the front door, kicking it along with her crutch.

"Swell. Sure is classy." He nodded approval of the parlor, of touches of quality—a velvet over-swag, Victorian chair, crocheted antimacassars, cut-glass vase— that reminded him of the traditional furnishings of the White House. On the walls a gallery was forming: framed photographs of Presidents Taft and Wilson, Mrs. Taft, and the two Mrs. Wilsons. The apartment even boasted a telephone.

"Mama, come and see." Maggie, aproned, came out of the kitchen, cooking spoon in hand, and admired the runner. "Lil'yan, I declare that is beautiful . . . won't ask what you paid for it, I know it's too much."

"Place puts the East Room to shame, Mama," Emmett said.

"In that case, will you join me in the State Dinin' Room for a repast?" Laughing, they went into the tiny kitchen where the table and mismatched chairs from the little house on Nineteenth were still in service, but would be replaced when enough half dollars had accumulated.

"We got a surprise for you tonight, Emmett," Lillian said as they sat down. "Duck."

"Oh, no! You know that thought crossed my mind on the way over?"

"Well, put your mind to rest, son. Nothin' fancy tonight." Maggie dished up the pork chops and greens she'd cooked. Lillian brought bread and milk to the table. "Now eat, Emmett, got to put some meat on your bones."

It was a welcome change to Emmett from hospital chow. "Food over there is lousy. Slop. Cuttin' down on sugar, coffee. Not seen milk in a month . . ."

Maggie hadn't heard of that before, and it distressed her terribly. "And don't say 'lousy,' Emmett . . . that's bad as 'ain't.' "

"Sorry, Mama, but that's onliest word for it . . . They so short over to that hospital, it's a crime. Place is dirty . . . sheets wearin' out, blankets thin—rationin' bandages even . . ."

"Why, that is fierce, Emmett . . . Somebody should be told . . . the Pres'dent's friends runnin' the Veterans Bureau—they ought to be able to do somethin' . . ."

"Well, whoever's runnin' it, the money's sure not gettin' to the veterans, I can tell you that . . ."

Lillian voiced the wish that Emmett could leave the hospital and stay with them in the apartment, but Emmett couldn't give up his lifeline. Some days he felt pretty good, but some days were so bad he could hardly breathe his way through them. But he was tired, just lazing around, and he'd been talking to some guys he knew about going into business. "We can rent a boat real cheap, see . . . charter trips on the Potomac— ought to pay real good . . . take congressmen out on joy rides with their lady friends . . ."

Maggie didn't cotton to the idea. "Oh, I don't know, Emmett. Don't like the sound of that . . ."

"Don't know what else I can do. Cain't work a whole day, discharged from the Army . . . Pres'dent Harding vetoed the bonus . . . I tell you, the soldier's the forgotten man . . ."

"Pres'dent Wilson said your country would never forget you!"

Exasperation erupted from Lillian. "Oh, Mama, you know better than that!"

Maggie set her jaw. "I got to *believe*. If I don't, I die . . ."

"Mama . . ." Emmett touched her arm, gentle but

firm. "You're closin' your eyes to what's goin' on. Lil'-yan know . . . tell her, Lil'yan."

"You mean—the little house on K Street?"

Maggie was horrified. "What you know about that house, chile? You don't walk by there, do you? Not safe for a decent girl!"

"You don't have to fret 'bout me, Mama. They don't bother the young ladies at the YWCA, and that's jus' round the corner from that house. 'Sides which, they got all the recruits they want, no trouble."

"Lil'yan!"

"True, Mama . . ." Emmett said it with weary sadness. "Some of the stuff I hear goes on, I wouldn't repeat to you . . . But the money that goes through that place on K Street! You can buy anythin' over there—booze, a woman, a judge, congressmen—you name it . . . and it all goes on in broad daylight."

"Don't want to hear 'bout it. Pres'dent wouldn't let it go on, he was to know," Maggie stoutly defended.

Well, if the President knew or didn't know, Emmett wasn't about to smear him. "But it's goin' on, Mama, and all his friends are over there. They call 'em the Ohio Gang."

"Don't want hear another word about it . . ." Maggie shoved back her chair and worked off her anxiety by pulling the drip pan from underneath the icebox.

"Here, Mama, let me help you . . ."

"You let me be!" She snapped at him. Balancing the pan of water, she got it to the sink and emptied it, leaning against the wall, crying. She couldn't say why: her husband gone, the children, the destroyed inno-cence? And always the struggle to just get by . . .

In the parlor, the phone was ringing. Lillian picked up her crutch and went in to answer it. Emmett moved to Maggie, put his arms around her. "Poor Mama, sweet Mama . . . you want so hard to believe every-body's upstandin' . . . Wish it was so . . . for your sake, wish it was so . . ."

Maggie dried her eyes and went into the parlor. "That call for me?"

Lillian held out the phone to her. "The White

House." Maggie's words into the phone were few. "This is Maggie. Yes. All right."

"They want you back, don't they?" The way Lillian said it was an indictment.

"Got to go, Miz Harding took sick, needs me."

"Mama . . . you're givin' up your life to those folks at the White House!"

"It's my job." Taking off her apron, she turned back to the kitchen, talking as she moved. "Emmett, I prob'ly won't get home till sometime tomorrow, hope you still here . . . Oh my God!"

The panic in her mother's voice drew Lillian to her. They found Emmett leaning against the sink. His hands tore at his shirt, ripping it open. His bony chest heaved in a desperate attempt to take in air. Each hard-fought breath carried on it a light wailing sound that was a cry for help, yet when they ran to him, he held them off with a wry smile. "Nothin' . . . nothin' at all . . . jus' the humidity . . ."

Armistice Day 1921—three years after the Allies and the Germans climbed out of their trenches and embraced each other—the anonymous bones of the Unknown Soldier were interred at Arlington Cemetery. President Harding presided and later made a speech on the radio. People crowded sidewalks for the exciting new experience of standing outside a music store to hear the President's own voice coming out of a loudspeaker. Praise came to him from all quarters. His Attorney General was ecstatic ("The people love you, Warren") and began laying plans for a Harding second term. Maggie heard the speech over the radio in the White House where they took turns listening through the earphones. Lillian heard it on a crystal set in the back room of the Celeste. Emmett didn't hear it. He was on the river, joyriding some members of Congress and their sweeties. Some of Papa's charm in serving had rubbed off on Emmett. That and his ability to look the other way brought word-of-mouth recommendations from one legislator to another. Emmett and his partners ran a quality operation serving only the best booze. They didn't patronize the house on K Street, but got their stock the "legal" way, through embassy connections, and sold it at a nice profit. Business, even with a three-way split, was coming along pretty well, but the rotten weather was always a threat. Washington's humidity, as Emmett had said, was as much his enemy as the Huns had been.

Whether or not Mrs. Harding's mystics or cards foretold her illness, Maggie, without any psychic instincts, could see it coming. Mrs. Harding's piano could be heard far into the night while she waited for her husband to come home. Mornings, Maggie would find the First Lady haggard, having barely slept, laying out the cards. She would study them, shake her head, murmur "I've got to be careful today" or "Oh, my, it looks so bad for Warren . . ." It was not Maggie's place to inquire what she meant, but you had to be blind not to see that tension had taken up residence in the White House and wasn't about to move out. The newspapers were beginning to take broad swipes at the administration, with none too subtle hints of corruption surfacing. One night, having worked late, Mercer found the President out on the south lawn, crying. "A man must be loyal to his friends, Mercer," he said.

Maggie's new apartment rarely saw her these days. A cot in the First Lady's dressing room became her sometime bed as the second floor again took on the hushed atmosphere of a hospital. The whisper went out and down the back stairs that, with the First Lady having only one kidney, and that badly infected, another funeral could be expected at any time. But as Florence Harding rallied, her fears intensified, and a Secret Service man was stationed outside her bedroom door from dusk to dawn. When even that assurance failed to bring her a sense of peace, the only thing that quieted her was Maggie's presence. While this brought some calm to Mrs. Harding, it only roiled the waters of Maggie's own household. On those rare occasions when she got home, Lillian kept up the refrain, "Mama, why cain't you see those people over there jus' usin' you up?" But Maggie held stubbornly to principle. "My lady won't eat less'n I'm there to feed her, and I'm not goin' let her starve to death, no way . . ."

Some days it was all Maggie could do to cajole tea and toast into the First Lady. Sitting by her bedside, waiting for her to rouse, Maggie sorrowed at the sight of her: worn, ashen, cords standing out in her neck; a loose jowliness to her jaw; hands as thin as claws, jerking in agitated sleep.

Maggie was ready with spoon and broth as her patient opened her eyes. But Florence Harding's demons wouldn't give her respite or allow her to eat.

"I saw it over Warren's head this morning—an aura . . ." Describing a mystic arc with her hands, she shuddered. "And a word written there, plain as can be: 'Tragedy.' "

"Ma'am, you had yourself a bad dream."

"No, no, I saw it . . ." Abruptly another fear surfaced as she looked around for her dog. "Where's Laddie Boy?"

"Right here, ma'am. Lyin' right here beside you . . ."

"Oh . . ." Her sigh was a small explosion of relief. The dog, hearing his name, raised up, stretched, and put his wet nose against her cheek. Her thin arms encircled his body. "Hand me the newspaper, Maggie . . ." Maggie got it from a table, Mrs. Harding folded it neatly and held it out to the dog. "Take this to Warren, Laddie . . . Take it to Warren." She *had* seen the aura. What's more, she'd lately been aware of a strange deterioration in her husband; felt he, too, had an impending sense of doom. Back in Ohio when she ran the newspaper for him, and when he was in the Legislature and the Senate, he'd always confided his worries to her. In those days he had few things to trouble his mind. He'd be out in the streets, shaking hands with people, swapping stories, playing golf, and going to ball games. Rumors of other women had come to her, but she'd always turned a deaf ear. They were on their way, in those days. Going places. Now there was that awful feeling that they'd traveled as far as they were ever to go . . .

Mrs. Harding swallowed without tasting the spoonful of broth Maggie fed her. "Do you read the newspapers, Maggie?"

"Afraid I don't have much time for that, ma'am."

"They say awful things. Awful things . . ."

"You got to quit worryin' so, ma'am, and get yourself better . . ."

Mrs. Harding accepted another spoonful and a bit of toast.

"He didn't come back."

"Who, ma'am?"

"Laddie Boy . . . When I send Warren the paper that way, he always sends Laddie back with something for me. Go find out, Maggie. I've got this terrible feeling . . ." She grabbed Maggie's hand in fear. Maggie eased her back against the pillows.

"I'll go, Miz Harding, but you got to promise me to rest . . ."

"Maggie, please . . . *go* . . ."

The President stood at the fireplace of his sitting room, vehemently ripping a book apart and throwing pages into a blazing fire. The dog stood beside his master, the newspaper in his mouth, waiting for approbation. When none came, he dropped the paper and lay down. As Maggie stepped into the room, she immediately sensed something badly awry. Mercer was there, just inside the door, holding a tray with a glass of whiskey on it, his manner one of quiet anguish, like being at a deathbed.

"Oh, 'scuse me, sir . . . Miz Harding, told me to come find Laddie . . ." The President, appearing not to hear her, hurled the rest of the book into the flames. He downed the drink from the tray, then picked up the poker, stirring the hard spine of the book's cover deeper into the fire. Unsure whether to go or stay, Maggie looked to Mercer for guidance, but his eyes, strangely clouded, were on the President. There was a moment when Harding seemed mesmerized by the fire; then he turned to them. His cheeks shone with tears. His voice was barely audible. "You're a credit to your race, Mercer. I apologize to you. To you too, Maggie." He handed the poker to Mercer and left the room. The dog picked up the newspaper in its mouth and followed him.

Something in the way it all happened made Maggie fearful of asking the question. "Don't understand, Mercer . . . what'd he mean—credit to our race?"

Mercer stirred the fire. His eyes never left the flame. "Pres'dent rang for me . . . brought him his drink . . . found him standin' here, tearin' up that book. Didn't once look at me."

"Why in heaven's name would he burn a book?"

"Couldn't help readin' the cover . . . Mays told me 'bout that book—bein' bootlegged all over town . . . all about the Pres'dent bein' part Negro, way back, and hidin' it . . . Contaminated blood, book writer calls it. Say all our people low, shiftless, no good, won't work—lazy do-nothin's . . ." The pain in his voice went back to slave ships. Maggie took the poker from him and struck the book's cover. It broke in half; a shower of sparks chewed at it from all sides. They stood together and watched it being consumed.

7

☒ ☒ ☒

The Vice-President sat on a straight chair just outside the west sitting hall, hands clasped in his lap, feet
crossed, one shoe on top of the other, waiting. An
office boy summoned by the boss. He was fifty years
old, pale, thin, sandy where once he'd been red-haired,
with lips set in a severe line, and in desperate need of
a good tailor. He sat motionless, completely ignoring
the housekeeping activity going on all around him. Mc-
Kenzie, Bridget, and Annie mopped and polished,
almost (but not quite) lifting his feet to dust around
him.

Maggie, who had run down to the kitchen for a fast
bit of noonday sustenance, hurried back to join the
cleaning crew, expressing surprise. "What's Mr. Coolidge doin' here?"

"Waitin' to see Himself, I guess," Annie told her.
"Ike Hoover brought him up, set him down there, he
ain't moved a muscle." Drawing Maggie aside to the
supply closet, Annie suggested that she try to get more
cleaning hours in, since Mrs. Jaffray had been making
inquiries about Maggie neglecting that part of her
work.

"What am I s'posed to do? Miz Harding calls me,

205

needs me . . . I hardly ever get home. She won't touch a bite if I don't feed her . . ."

"Maybe our esteemed housekeeper's nose is out of joint. She was feelin' in favor, goin' to the fortune-tellers with Herself, now you're the one close to the throne. Tell you what . . . you carry all the dirty linens down —go right by her office to the laundry—that'll keep her happy . . ." It puzzled Maggie to find Annie on her side. "Well, wouldn't want you to lose your rank as second maid, me gettin' close to retirement and you next in line . . ."

That Annie was full of surprises.

"Maggie, you look 'bout ready to fall down," Coates said to her when they passed on the back stairs, she with the armload of linen, he with a tray of finger sandwiches and a pitcher of lemonade.

"Don't fall down that easy," she said. "What you got there, Coates?"

"For the Pres'dent—*lemonade!* Now don't that beat all? Who's his visitor anyways, that he's servin' this tame stuff?"

Maggie chuckled. "You'll see."

Vice-Presidents didn't usually call at the White House. Except for an occasional social function when they were admitted, like any other guest, through the front door, they were seldom in the house and almost never on the second floor; cabinet meetings were seldom graced by their presence. Harding was different from other Presidents in that respect: every official cabinet meeting, he tendered an invitation to Mr. Coolidge, who came, sat, remained silent, and left. Everyone in the White House knew of this pattern, and all wondered what the Vice-President was doing here today.

"So nice of you to come, Mr. Vice-President . . ." Harding came out of his sitting room in the manner of a candidate, smile ready and hand extended. Calvin Coolidge allowed himself to be reluctant party to a handshake and grunted a response that Harding interpreted to mean "Nice of you to ask me." Together they went into west sitting hall, closing the doors. The room had been completely transformed for the occasion. The poker table was graced with a lace tablecloth; the side table, where booze had been openly displayed, contained a basket of fruit and bouquet of flowers. The President indicated a chair. "Sit down, Mr. Vice-President . . ." Assuming the same uncomfortable stance as when he waited in center hall, Coolidge perched on the edge of the chair, laced his fingers together in his lap, and crossed his feet.

"And I appreciate your attending cabinet meetings, Mr. Vice-President."

In his high voice, with a dry Vermont edge, Coolidge replied, "Try to oblige." It was all he said and it looked like all he intended to say. Coates, at the side table, put out the finger sandwiches and poured two glasses of lemonade.

Harding sat back in his chair, elbows resting comfortably on the arms, and hoped he looked confident. "A matter is coming up in the Senate," he said, with elaborate casualness, "that disturbs me . . . Thank you, Coates. No . . . serve the Vice-President first . . . There's a faction, Mr. Vice-President, that wants me to get rid of my Attorney General . . . but Harry Daugherty's a very good, loyal party man, I depend on him . . ." Coolidge ate three of the finger sandwiches and reached for a fourth, and Harding wondered if he was really listening to him. "I thought, Mr. Vice-President, if it comes to a tight vote, that you—as President of the Senate—"

"Would vote my conscience, Mr. President."

"Of course, of course." Harding backed off a little. "Exactly what I would expect of you. But, you know, there are always some senators who abuse their power —go to any lengths to destroy a man . . ." Coolidge sipped the lemonade, letting his taste buds render their verdict. "Could use a mite more sugar . . ." He took the last of the tiny sandwiches off the tray, turning it over in his hand, examining its lilliputian dimensions. "Must say I admire your economy in the White House . . ."

Harding couldn't tell for certain if he'd been rebuffed,

ignored, or belittled. Of one thing he was certain:
the Vice-President had just terminated the interview.

Winter gave in to spring. The year was 1923. Maggie
redoubled her efforts, cleaning, scrubbing, making beds,
and traversing the back stairs—creating a truce between herself and Mrs. Jaffray, who never relaxed her
scrutiny. Sometimes Maggie began to feel that she was
getting old, then rationalized that sixteen–twenty hours
of labor could even wear out young bones. The time
she spent at Mrs. Harding's bedside, massaging and
caring for her, was relaxation in a way. Often she
hoped for her number to show up in the call box, if
only for the chance to sit down at her lady's bedside.
Sometimes it was just plain impossible not to drop off
to sleep in that shuttered, shadowy room.

Maggie had drifted away on a warm cloud when a
hand grabbed her. For the moment she'd forgotten
where she was; Mrs. Harding's voice oriented her.
"Maggie . . ." she said in anxiety, "where's the President?" Night had fallen in the room. Maggie's hand
fumbled, found the light switch. A dull amber glow
warmed the room. Mrs. Harding was sitting up in bed,
trembling and breathing rapidly.

"The President . . ."

Maggie had to fight through the woolliness in her
mind. "It's all right, ma'am. He gone down to dinner,
said he'd be back and look in on you."

Mrs. Harding, pulse racing, sat up on the edge of the
bed, holding her head, blocking out her thoughts. Maggie slipped a light robe around her. "I've brought you
some tea, ma'am. Then, if you like, I'll give you a
nice rubdown." She was helping Mrs. Harding move to
the chaise when they heard men's muffled voices.

"Shhh . . ." Mrs. Harding quickly switched off the lamp
and silently urged Maggie forward to open the door.

If there was anything Maggie wanted to avoid, it was
eavesdropping. One of the cardinal rules of the house
was "Hear nothing, see nothing, tell nothing," but the
moment for caution was past. Mrs. Harding was at the
hinges as Maggie gingerly released the latch. A sliver

Olivia Cole, eighty-year-old Lillian Rogers Parks, and Leslie Uggams on the set of the mini-series production of "Backstairs at the White House." Olivia Cole plays the part of Maggie Rogers, a White House maid who began service during the Taft family's residence at the White House. Lillian Rogers Parks, Maggie's daughter, also became a White House maid, engaged by Mrs. Herbert Hoover, and collected her mother's notes, and her own, into a bestselling book, *My Thirty Years Backstairs at the White House*, which was one of the sources of this book, and of the Ed Friendly Productions mini-series. Mrs. Parks, often called "Little Lillian," had polio as a child, and did her White House work for thirty years even though she had to use a crutch as an aid in walking. Lillian as an adult is played by Leslie Uggams in the series. (Ed Friendly Productions, Inc.)

President William Howard Taft and his wife, Mrs. Helen "Nellie" Taft, as played by Victor Buono and Julie Harris. (Ed Friendly Productions, Inc.)

"Little Lillian," as a child, was brought to the White House by her mother, Maggie Rogers, and discovered the new extra-large bathtub just delivered to be installed for the corpulent President William Howard Taft, who had got stuck in the old, regular-size tub. She was playing in the large tub when President Taft came in and was amused to discover her. "Little Lillian," as a child, is played by Tania Johnson, and President Taft is played by Victor Buono. (Ed Friendly Productions, Inc.)

Mrs. Florence Harding, played by Celeste Holm, confronts President Warren G.Harding, played by George Kennedy. Maggie Rogers, White House maid played by Olivia Cole, is in the background unnoticed. (Ed Friendly Productions, Inc.)

Maggie Rogers and Mrs. Harding in a happier moment. (Olivia Cole and Celeste Holm) (Ed Friendly Productions, Inc.)

Maggie Rogers, first maid of the White House, with Levi Mercer, serving man, and later houseman. (Olivia Cole and Louis Gossett, Jr.) (Ed Friendly Productions, Inc.)

Leslie Uggams playing Lillian Rogers Parks, White House maid. (Ed Friendly Productions, Inc.)

Maggie Rogers, first maid, Mrs. Jaffray, head housekeeper, and Coates, head butler, in a backstairs setting at the White House. (Olivia Cole, Cloris Leachman, and Hari Rhodes) (Ed Friendly Productions, Inc.)

John Mays, Maggie Rogers, Lillian Rogers (Parks), and Levi Mercer share a letter with good news that Maggie has just received, as all sit at the servants' dining table at the White House. (Robert Hooks, Olivia Cole, Leslie Uggams, and Louis Gossett, Jr.) (Ed Friendly Productions, Inc.)

President Franklin D. Roosevelt and Mrs. Eleanor Roosevelt as played by John Anderson and Eileen Heckart. (Ed Friendly Productions, Inc.)

Two polio victims compare their experiences: Lillian Rogers Parks, White House maid and seamstress, and President Franklin D. Roosevelt. (Leslie Uggams and John Anderson) (Ed Friendly Productions, Inc.)

President Harry Truman talking to Levi Mercer in the White House. (Harry Morgan and Louis Gossett, Jr.) (Ed Friendly Productions, Inc.)

Ed Friendly, producer of "Backstairs at the White House," and Michael O'Herlihy, director of the series, in front of portraits of U.S. presidents as used in the series—Harry Truman (Harry Morgan) and Woodrow Wilson (Robert Vaughn). (Ed Friendly Productions, Inc.)

Two aspects of President Dwight Eisenhower and Mrs. Mamie Eisenhower—
ready to face the world in formal dress, and caught during an intimate moment—
as played by Andrew Duggan and Barbara Barrie. (Ed Friendly Productions,
Inc.)

Paul Dubov and Gwen Bagni, who wrote this book and script-writers of the series, "Backstairs at the White House." (Ed Friendly Productions, Inc.)

Lillian Rogers Parks, after her retirement as a White House maid, showing dresses of First Ladies that had been given to her and to her mother, Maggie Rogers, when they were working as maids in the White House. Mrs. Parks and her mother carefully preserved the dresses, and Mrs. Parks gave this collection to the Smithsonian Institution in Washington, D.C., together with other mementoes of White House service. (Collection of Lillian Rogers Parks)

Maggie Rogers, as a young woman, as shown in a portrait owned and treasured by her daughter, Lillian Rogers Parks. (Collection of Lillian Rogers Parks)

of light cut into the bedroom, along with Harding's anguished voice. "My God, Harry—*you're* the Attorney General . . . *Why?*" Mrs. Harding's eye at the tiny opening showed her the President in smoking jacket, Daugherty and Jesse Smith in overcoats. It hurt to see the despair in her husband as he clasped his head and asked, *"Why,* Harry, *why.* Why did Charlie Cramer have to kill himself?" The suicide had haunted her dreams for days. Warren's, too. She knew he hadn't slept. Anxiety and confusion were written in the clumsy way he groped for understanding. Jesse Smith just stood there in mute panic. But Daugherty maintained a deliberate, forced calm.

"Charlie was a good friend of all of us, Warren. Jess and I are as upset as you are . . ."

"Didn't you have any inkling? Did you know he was in that state of mind?"

"Who knows what's in another man's mind?"

Desperate for answers, Harding turned to Smith. "Jess?" But all Smith could do was turn his hat around and around in his hands, muttering, "Oh, God, oh, God, oh, God . . ." In the darkness, Maggie felt her flesh crawl at the anguish she was forced to observe as Harding paced the room, grasping for something to cling to. "He said I was well liked in California . . ."

"He left a suicide note, Warren . . ."

"You read it?"

Daugherty extended it to the President. "It was addressed to you." Harding pulled back from the sealed envelope as from a precipice. "Don't want it . . . don't want to see it . . . Why . . . *Why?* Cramer kills himself . . . Forbes sends his resignation back from Europe . . . Both of them in the Veterans Bureau —now all the accusations from the Senate about funds misused . . ."

Daugherty poured himself a shot of whiskey that overflowed the glass. "Just because a man gets despondent, Warren, and goes off the deep end doesn't mean there's any wrongdoing . . ."

"Fraud . . . that's the word the committee kept using. *Fraud . . ."*

"We'll weather it, we can handle it, Warren."

"What do you mean 'we'? And what about those oil leases in that place in Wyoming—what's it called —Teapot Dome? All seems to be piling up . . ."

"Warren," Daugherty placated, "don't you recognize this for what it is—just a little political backbiting from the Democrats?"

Harding, emotionally exhausted, sat down at the table, absently toying with a deck of cards. "It's not my enemies I'm worried about . . . it's my friends that keep me awake nights . . ."

"You surely don't include me in that statement, Warren."

"Don't know, Harry . . . just don't know . . . I wanted to be a good President—knew I couldn't be the best—was hoping to be the best loved . . . Guess now the only thing I can do is go before the Senate and have it out . . ."

"You'll have nothing out. I put every cent I have in the world in your campaign. I made you, Warren. Why, I could have taken any two-bit stock company leading man and made him President . . . You'll keep your mouth shut as you did during the campaign . . . And quit taking yourself so seriously . . ."

Harding looked at Daugherty as though he had never seen him before. "If you wanted to run the country, why pick me?"

"You were available. Fifteen ballots in a deadlocked convention. Some day you'll look good on a stamp."

Harding seemed to stagger, as though he had been struck. It took moments for him to recover, then he moved to Jesse Smith, touched him kindly on the shoulder, thinking back to Ohio when it had all been simpler. "Jesse, you can't come here anymore . . . can't have the committee assuming you're my mouthpiece. Anything you say is a brush that tars me, you understand that, don't you, Jesse?" Smith stood up, but lacked the capacity to speak. "You're to prepare a statement, Jesse . . . come clean . . . everything you know . . ." Harding turned to Daugherty, from somewhere finding a special strength within himself. "You, too," he said. "I want it all out in the open. *Available* or not, I am the President. I want answers on my desk, first thing in the morning. That's an executive order. Now get out."

Daugherty walked to the door. Jesse Smith was so dissolved in despair that he had to be tapped on the shoulder. Eyes downcast, stumbling, he followed his mentor from the room. Harding threw a stiff shot of bourbon down his throat.

These last moments of activity afforded the First Lady the opportunity to scurry back to the chaise, where she motioned Maggie to turn on the lamp and roll the food table to her. Maggie was just handing her a cup of tea as Harding came into the room, his turmoil masked with his most disarming smile.

"Well, you are looking better, Duchess," he said to his wife. "Maggie taking good care of you, hm?"

"Some day, Warren, you'll realize I'm the best friend you've got."

He looked penetratingly at his wife, then moved to the bedside table and picked up the telephone. "This is the President. Please have my car ready for me."

"I want to know what's going on, Warren . . ."

"Nothing to worry your head about, Duchess."

Mrs. Harding jumped to her feet and followed him into the dressing alcove. "And stand up straight! You're the President of the United States."

"What else do you want of me?" he asked wearily as he hung his smoking jacket in the armoire and changed into suit jacket. "You wanted the state house, the White House, you got it . . . Newspapers today say the Episcopal ministers are taking the word 'obey' out of the marriage ceremony . . . Little late for us, isn't it, Duchess . . ."

"I helped get you the presidency. What are you doing with it?"

"I'll tell you who got me the presidency—the ladies, bless 'em. They filed into the voting booths and pulled the lever for good old Warren G. . . ." He checked himself in the mirror. Finding nothing wanting, he put on topcoat and hat and left the room.

"I know about that house on K Street . . . and that woman up in New York . . ." She bombarded him as he strode the length of the center hall. *"Warren . . . you are not to leave this house tonight!"* Her voice ricocheted off the walls as he went down the grand staircase and out the front door.

Maggie, an unwilling witness, tried unobtrusively to make her escape to the back stairs. She was just short of her objective when Mrs. Harding, turning back in tears, cried out to her, "I need you. Maggie . . . don't . . . don't go . . . please, please, don't leave me . . ."

Throughout the hours that followed, Maggie sat on a chair, blanket around her shoulders, fighting off sleep, while Mrs. Harding poured her distress into the piano; her fingers searching out the melancholy chords of "When You Come to the End of a Perfect Day." Florence Harding felt abandoned on an ocean of debris with no safe harbor in sight. In a futile attempt to assuage the pain she had enveloped herself in Mrs. McLean's ermine coat. A vestment of reassurance, it fell to the floor in folds, surrounding her and the piano stool. Like the song, she sat alone with her dreams. The room got cold. Maggie wrapped the blanket tighter, shivered some, but didn't move. And still the poor lady played. It was near dawn when the President returned. The door opened slowly. He stood in the arch, large, blocking most of the light from the center hall. Just stood there. Shattered. The walking wounded. In his hand was an extra of a newspaper. Unsteadily he made his way to the piano.

His wife looked up at his tear-scalded face. "My God, Warren, what is it?"

The words rasped from his soul. "Jesse Smith . . . just shot himself . . ." A lost child, he handed her the newspaper in a gesture that pleaded for her to put it all back together again.

No one on the staff spoke of Jesse Smith's suicide, as they hadn't of Cramer's. The staff had developed its own unspoken rules. While extras were being shouted up and down the streets, sensationalizing the dark mood of the White House, no newspapers were brought to the table. It was as though the press had ceased to function. Even Mays ate in silence, the President's distress his own.

Maggie was in the pantry when she felt the blood drain from her head and saw the walls closing in.

"Maggie ... Maggie?"

She opened her eyes and studied the faces looking down at her. "Why, Maggie, you burnin' up ..." *What was she doing on the pantry floor?* Last she remembered was reaching into the shelf. In her hand was the President's toothpick holder. The faces swam in and out of her vision: Mercer . . . Coates, Dixon, Annie . . . they wore aprons, as did she. Must have all been polishing silver—no, not silver. Gold, since Mrs. Harding. Gold ...

The First Lady needed her ...

"No, no, Maggie, you jus' lay there." Now she remembered. The President and Mrs. Harding were away . . . gone someplace . . . a trip . . . across the country on a train . . . get-away-from-all-the-bad-things . . .

Somebody summoned the White House doctor. Someone else called for a car. Maggie didn't remember much of anything. For a week she thrashed about on her bed at home, alternately urging Mrs. Harding to eat a little something and protesting to Dixon the presidential use of toothpicks at a state dinner—*and tell the Pres'dent careful where he spits!*—until finally the crisis passed; the fever that engulfed her was gone.

When her eyes opened, Lillian and Mercer were looking down at her. Mays had just been there, they told her, and Jackson was coming by later.

"You give us a bad scare, Maggie," Mercer said.

Lillian held her from rising up. "Oh, no, Mama, you not gettin' up. Doctor say you to lay flat, another whole week. That right, Mercer?"

"That is for sure right, Maggie. That what he say."

"*Pneumonia,* Mama . . . you know you could have died? All from overworkin'. You goin' to listen to me now?"

"You listen to Lil'yan, Maggie."

She let them scold and fuss over her. It was too much effort to protest, and it felt so good just to be quiet in the dimness of her own room, to look at the lace curtain fluttering gently in the warm, summer air, creating patterns of light on the ceiling. A week later, she sat up, and even read a newspaper that told about the President and the First Lady enjoying a successful trip across country, gathering enthusiastic crowds wherever they went. That was good news to Maggie. In her opinion, they'd suffered enough.

But the big news, with which she was to regale Lillian when she came home from work, was her caller. When the knock came on the door, her first thought was, *Now that can't be Mercer or Mays, they rap harder. Besides, they'd both be on duty at this hour. And not Annie. Her knock has a shillelagh in it. Such a refined, dignified tap on the door . . .*

"Come in, it's unlocked." From her bed she couldn't see the front door. Precise footsteps came down Lillian's floor runner. Mrs. Jaffray appeared, in her go-to-market costume of veiled hat, white gloves, and beaded reticule. Bearing a gift.

"I brought you a little calf's-foot jelly, Maggie. From *McGruders.*" She emphasized its value.

Maggie barely found her voice. "Why, thank you, ma'am." Habit motivated her attempted rise from the bed. "No, no, Maggie, you're not to move." Mrs. Jaffray sat beside the bed in the stiff-backed chair, explaining that she couldn't stay long, but Maggie was to understand she had nothing to be concerned about in terms of her job. It would be waiting for her. Everyone at the White House wished her well. "We must all take care of our health," she said. "After all, it is a very important responsibility given into our hands, to take care of the First Family of the land." Through the open window, Maggie could hear the children in the street, wonderment in their voices at the elegance of the White House horse and carriage. What few horses remained on the streets these days hauled junk or ice wagons.

"I must be going. You know I have my marketing to

complete. Even though the First Family is away, there are still a great many people to feed." And Mrs. Jaffray was gone. Maggie slept awhile, awakening to wonder if she'd dreamed it. But no, the calf's-foot jelly was on the chifforobe. *Now didn't that just beat all . . . Think you know someone, then they turn around and you see 'em different.*

Maggie was back at work days sooner than the doctor or Lillian wanted. But with the President due to return, a lot of work was piling up. Only time you could really house-clean was when the place wasn't occupied, and she wasn't about to put her share off on somebody else.

It was pleasant on the second floor. Felt good to be back. Everybody working hard, but kind of easygoing, at your own pace. Different from when the President and First Lady were in the house and doors would open unexpectedly, and you had to always be on your good behavior. The staff even used the elevator to bring up some of the cleaning equipment. Furniture was sheet-covered. Beds were stripped, mattresses aired. Drapes that held an accumulation of dust were out on the clothesline that had been strung up under the trees on the south lawn. The place smelled clean and fresh.

Mercer elected himself her watchdog. "Don't you do too much now, Maggie. Anythin' too hard for you, you call me."

"Don't need to mother-hen me, Mercer. I'm feelin' jus' fine."

"Well, I got my eye on you, remember that . . ."

"You as bad as Lil'yan."

Mercer wrapped a clean rag around a soft broom and joined McKenzie in sweeping down the walls. Maggie, working a bit slower than usual but no less meticulously, washed and dried all of the glassware on the President's bar, dipping each glass carefully into a suds bucket and then into hot, clear water.

"Pres'dent and Mrs. Harding sure looking a lot better than when they were at home," McKenzie volunteered to Mercer.

"How you know that? Picture of 'em in the paper this mornin'?"

"Saw 'em in the movie show news last night. On a boat, smilin' away, goin' up to Alaska, havin' a high time. Imagine, middle of summer and all bundled up in furs."

"What else playin' at the picture show, besides the Pres'dent?" Bridget asked as she passed through, lugging a bucket of used scrub water to the back stairs.

"Lon Chaney—*Hunchback of Notre Dame.*"

"Ooh," Bridget shuddered. "Don't want to see that . . . scare me outa ten years' growth."

Maggie laughed, calling after Bridget as she disappeared around into the corridor, "You got the years to spare, Bridget." Yes . . . pleasant working in such easygoing atmosphere. Annie breezed across center hall with mop and pail, humming to herself.

As Mercer moved his ladder to another wall, he paused beside Maggie. "How about you and me takin' in a vaudeville show tonight? Foraker Theater got Butter Beans and Susie on the bill. And The Wags."

"Thought you jus' told me to be takin' it easy."

"Depends on what we're talking about, Maggie."

"Mercer, you always tryin' to come 'round the back door . . ." It was good to joke a bit, and to hear McKenzie whistling—last thing in the world she would have expected of him. But then everybody was surprising her these days.

Maggie gave some thought to going to the vaudeville show, but by the time she'd finished work, she'd run out of steam. At home she had supper and went off to sleep, barely conscious of Lillian stopping in to change from her day's work at the Celeste before going off to her second job at the box office.

Pounding awakened Maggie just before midnight. It took moments to realize it was coming from her own door. When Mercer's voice replied to her "Who is it?" she at first thought it some more of his foolishness carried over from the afternoon. Quickly fastening her bathrobe, she admitted him. "Mercer, they better be some good excuse . . ."

His clothes had been hastily thrown on. Shirt buttoned wrong, no tie. "We got to go back, Maggie, they need us. Word just come . . . Pres'dent Harding died this evenin' . . ."

She lowered herself into a chair, numbed. "When they go out of that house you jus' never know how they comin' back . . ."

Warren G. Harding came back to rest in the East Room in a flag-draped casket on a black catafalque. Four young servicemen, rifles at rest, stood solemn guard over their fallen leader. The pungent scent of floral tributes permeated the vast room, pushed out into the main corridor and up the stairs, to hang in the trapped August air. A continuous stream of mourners and curious filed by. At night, when the populace was locked out, Maggie found Mrs. Harding standing in the gloom beside her husband's coffin. "They can't hurt you anymore, Warren."

8

🏺 🏺 🏺

Maggie stepped behind the cover of her open locker door for a modicum of privacy and pulled off her skirt and shirtwaist. As Annie put it, everything was plumb out of kilter, what with the widow Harding refusing to leave the White House and the new President living in the Willard Hotel like some itinerant drummer.

"But I'd think you'd be more feelin', Annie, after all the poor lady's gone through—you bein' a widow yourself."

Annie, equally modest, was behind the door of her locker. Stocky body corseleted, one forearm decorously masking an ample bosom, she reached around the door into the locker for her uniform. Pulling it over her head, she replied, "Oh, I'm not unfeelin', Maggie . . . but havin' a President's body layin' in state right here in the house gives me the creeps. I lived through Mr. McKinley's passin', don't forget. Went up there to Buffalo, healthy as you please and bullet found him while he was shakin' hands. Wasted away up there in hospital, just never come back . . ." Properly clothed, Annie stepped from behind the cover of the door. "Makes you wonder . . ."

"For a fact it does . . ." Maggie joined her at the mirror, both doing up their final buttons and setting on their starched caps. The feeling of gloom in the White House was almost more than Maggie could bear. She had stood on the south grounds, off to the side, as the military escort placed Mr. Harding's coffin on an artillery caisson and, to the beat of a drum, it was drawn away to the train station for its final homeward journey to Marion, Ohio. Put her in mind of poor Mr. Lincoln. Not being scholarly, she didn't know how many Presidents had died in office. Mays took the trouble to look it up and told her that besides Lincoln, Garfield, and McKinley, assassinated, there was William Henry Harrison, Zachary Taylor.

And now Warren G. Harding.

Eighteen days had passed since the night of August 2 when Harding's body and spirit gave up the struggle in a San Francisco hotel room, and still the scandal-mongers picked his bones. Rumors proliferated: he'd killed himself; his enemies had him done away with; his wife murdered him. Some wordsmith came up with "He did the only politic thing left to do—die." The epitaph got bent, twisted, and word-of-mouthed across the land. Only one thing was certain: a new administration had been ushered in.

During the four hours it took for the telegraph wires to bring Harding's death to the East Coast, and for an automobile to chug up a Vermont country road to a telephoneless farmhouse where the Vice-President was vacationing at the home of his father, the country was without a President. At 2:45 A.M. on August 3, 1923, Calvin Coolidge raised his right hand and swore to execute the office and to preserve, defend, and protect the Constitution. The senior Coolidge, a notary, administered the oath by lamplight, after which the new President, in his unflappable way, went back to bed and to sleep.

Now, almost three weeks later, that swearing-in was being challenged as illegal, and according to the newspapers President Coolidge was going to have to raise his hand all over again. "Out of kilter" was right.

"Somebody ought to be tellin' Mrs. Harding she's outstayed her time," Annie said as she and Maggie ascended the back stairs to their duties.

"Well, it's not goin' to be me."

The prevailing mood of the second floor was of a last-ditch stand. Mrs. Harding, having buried her husband, had esconced herself into the White House and didn't show any inclination of accepting eviction. Whoever occupied the First Lady's bedroom, in Maggie's opinion, it was her obligation to serve. If that meant listening to the same piece being played on the piano with deadening repetition, she would listen. If it meant just standing by with a tray of food in her hands while the bedeviled lady poured out her hurts—real or fancied—that she would do, too.

"They're trying to push me out, you know that, Maggie. Those Coolidges, in the funeral cortege, tried to get their auto in ahead of mine. Newspapers say it was a mix-up, not their fault, but I know better. Trying to outdo us all along. There was a bill before Congress—my husband told me about it—for an official residence for the Vice-President. I had him squelch it, couldn't have them living finer than us. And the Wilsons—they were at the funeral, too. And the Tafts . . . all of them trying to usurp Mr. Harding's position . . ." She played the wistful tune "When You Come to the End of a Perfect Day" endlessly. "Three million people," she said as she played.

"Beg your pardon, ma'am?"

"Three million . . ." It seemed at first to be a reverie, then it became evident that Florence Harding was talking to the silver-framed photograph of her husband that smiled down on her from the piano top. "They came from everywhere—all along the track . . . to see the casket—beautiful casket, so many flowers . . . Children sang 'Nearer My God to Thee' . . . Train could hardly get through them . . . They cried. Warren . . . all across the country people cried . . ."

Later that day, Mrs. Harding had Maggie help her dress in black silk with rhinestoned black velvet at her neck. She called for her hat, furs, and gloves and requested an audience with Ike Hoover. When he came into the room, she announced she was leaving.

"Have my things packed and sent to me at Mrs. Mc-Lean's until I decide where to go."

"Yes, madam. And if there is ever anything else we can do for you . . ."

Mrs. Harding swept away Ike Hoover's concern. "Maggie, I want you to have my bird."

"Thank you, ma'am, I'll take good care of him."

"Mr. Hoover, find a home for Laddie."

"Yes, madam."

Mrs. Harding walked out of the room and across center hall, her dog tagging at her heels. Ike Hoover followed her into the elevator, quickly closing the door. The elevator descended. Laddie Boy stood on his hind legs, clawing at the cage, whining. Florence Harding never once looked back.

A week to the day after the Coolidges moved into the White House, Annie Gilhooley retired. It was a real *do*. The new third cook dished up the oxtail soup, Viola brought the glazed ham from the oven and placed it on a silver platter, surrounding it with *pommes frites*. Mrs. Feeney personally squeezed frosting roses onto the cake. The Eighteenth Amendment was now being strictly observed in the White House, but something better than water had to be used for toasting, so Mercer had come up with a stock of near beer that was closer to the real thing than most. A green tablecloth couldn't be gotten for love nor money, but from the recesses of a storage trunk Maggie had found a lot of green napkins. The centerpiece was a good-luck horseshoe (Mays' contribution) and a clay pipe (McKenzie's).

Throughout the luncheon and the toasts ("For she's a jolly good fellow" . . . "There's none like her, and ain't that a blessing" . . . "Who'll search out the dust now?") Annie sat at the head of the table in her "going to mass" dress, slightly at odds with the clump of orchids pinned to her shoulder. Her age (known only to herself) was sixty-seven. Time had thickened her waist, made a road map of her face. but it hadn't grayed her nutmeg hair or taken the wasp sting out of her tongue.

"All this bloomin' fuss . . . you'd think it was for the faerie queen . . ." But she was pleasuring in every minute as she looked down the long table where she'd taken so many meals. All the faces she knew so well turned to her as she was presented with the official gift —a silver tray—by Mrs. Jaffray; her eyeglasses steaming up as she read the inscription: "To Annie Gilhooley in recognition of twenty-five years' faithful service to the White House." Only Ike Hoover had served longer than her. *I'll not be forgettin' a one of ye, not likely.*

Aloud, she spoke to the young new maid who sat at the foot of the table: "Well, Moira, me young flower, now that Bridget's second, and Maggie's moved up to first maid, ye can see what ye got to look forward to . . ."

Maggie, quietly relishing the honor of being the first Negro lady to "sit high," smiled benignly down at the novice. "Took me fourteen years to make my way up this table."

"Fourteen? Saints alive, I'll be an old lady then . . ." Realizing the faux pas, Moira clapped a hand over her mouth. Ike Hoover, in light vein, informed the table that as senior member, having come in with Benjamin Harrison, he expected the respect due him. "What year was it you came in, Mrs. Jaffray? Was it before or after me?"

Mrs. Jaffray chose to ignore the napkin-covered smiles. "You know as well as I do, Mr. Hoover, when it was I came in. I've more important things on my mind than keeping track of years." Ike Hoover, solemn as an owl, winked at Maggie.

There was a lull in the conversation as the silver tray passed around the table and those with many years of service envisioned their own names inscribed there.

"What you goin' to do now, Annie?" Mercer asked.

"Well, I won't be after sittin' on a front porch, rockin' me life away, that's for sure."

"No, Annie's goin' to be out, dancin' a jig," Mays proposed. "Isn't that so, Annie?"

"You bet your boots I can still do it with the best of 'em."

"Now that'll be the day." McKenzie discredited the idea.

"Think so, do ye now?" And Annie was on her broad feet, fists planted on her hips, head swinging like the pendulum of a metronome, vigorously jigging to her own vocal accompaniment. Then the whole group was smiling, laughing, and clapping along with her like a tribe of Eire.

The call box buzzed. Merriment stopped. Almost in unison, each head turned to see who was being summoned.

Responding to his number, Ike Hoover shoved back his chair. Before he'd gone two steps, another buzz— and Mrs. Jaffray's number appeared. Then, in rapid succession, Mercer's. Mays'. Maggie's. Coates'. Mrs. Feeney's. . . . Until every square was filled. Either an emergency of enormous proportions had taken place on the second floor, or the call box was having a nervous breakdown. Chairs were pushed back so violently some fell over. Goodbyes were shouted to Annie as everyone tried to get to the door at the same time: "Sorry, Annie" . . . "Goodbye" . . . "Come see us" . . . Maggie, partway to the exit, ran back to her.

"I'm goin' to miss you, Annie."

"Goin' to miss you, too, Maggie." For a faltering second they faced one another, uncertain what to do. Annie broke the barrier, hugged Maggie to her. In their embrace was all the labor and living they'd shared. Then Maggie too fled the room. Annie stood alone. Feeling foolish for having danced. Feeling the jig in her knees. Feeling old. Her eyes grew wet, and she moved back to the table and rewrapped the silver tray.

It was a veritable stampede up the back stairs. The narrow, turning staircase had not been designed by its original architects for more than a few servants ascending at a time, and then at well-spaced intervals. And here was almost the entire staff clambering up like passengers on a gangway seeking escape from a sinking ship.

Ike Hoover in the vanguard, they arrived in center hall almost in a dead heat. There stood the President of the United States, hands clasped behind him, the corners of his thin mouth turned down in severity.

"You rang, Mr. President?"

In a brittle tone, Calvin Coolidge informed them, "Just wanted to see if you were all on your toes." Putting both index fingers into his mouth, his shrill whistle pierced the walls. The staff quickly pulled out of the way as, from several directions, five dogs came racing pell-mell. The three white collies, the Airedale, and the mongrel joyously joined their master, frolicking around his feet. "Come, doggies," the President said. They raced noisily alongside as he walked the length of center hall and descended the grand staircase.

As the staff began to disperse to their duties, they could still hear the dogs on the floor below. It was in all their minds: Was this new President a hawk who would monitor their every move? Or was it possible that this unsmiling, laconic man had just pulled their collective leg?

Several mornings later, the question still hung in midair. Maggie, on her way in to work, hurried up the path to the servants' entrance. concentrating on the dozens of obligations that now rested on her shoulders as head maid. Some distance from the little iron gate, she glanced ahead to see Jackson—trailed a few steps by Bridget, then Dixon, and Viola—all on their way in; each startled to discover the President standing to the side of the door, his pocket watch in hand. Clocking them in.

"Mornin', Mr. Pres'dent" . . . "Mornin', sir" . . .

For reply, his eye went from watch to person to watch, causing all to guiltily move a little quicker. Maggie was the last one down the three steps to the door.

"Mornin', Mr. Pres'dent."

He peered at her from under knit brows. "Just under the wire . . ." Returning the watch to his vest pocket, he strode away, leaving a somewhat intimidated Maggie.

Backstairs there was subdued conversation about what had taken place; confusion, and some concern.

Transition from one administration to another always brought startling changes, but in the months between election and Inauguration, the newspapers could be counted on to fill in the personality and habits of the newcomer. Assuming office as abruptly as he had, even the newspapers were scrambling to determine what manner of man Calvin Coolidge was.

That same afternoon the telephone rang in the usher's office just off the main entrance, the President's voice informing Ike Hoover to make immediate preparations for the imminent arrival of a most important government personage. "You have less than ten minutes," he said, and hung up. Ushers, who a moment before had their feet up on the desk, were quick to move, checking shirts, ties, jackets. The Secret Service men, stationed at the front door, had to be rounded up from the pantry where they were having cake and coffee. Mays and Jackson inspected each other's uniforms, and quickly polished the toes of their shoes on the backs of their trouser legs. All was in readiness in the ten minutes allotted. And they waited. Glanced anxiously down the driveway, but no limousine drove in.

Instead, Mr. Coolidge appeared on foot from the path to the Oval Office. Having sent his own Secret Service man away for "seegars," he had made his way unhampered through the west exit, and now ascended the steps to the portico of the White House.

"By cracky," he mused, "what's all the fuss about?"

"Mr. President," Ike Hoover reminded, "you called and said one of the most important government personages was about to arrive."

"Well, by heck, I'm here. You know a more important government personage than the President of the United States?" As he reached the door, Mays and Jackson were there in unison to hold it open. The President walked inside, went upstairs, and took a nap.

There could be no doubt about it now. There was a "kidder" in the White House.

And there was something else: the almost forgotten sound of laughter on the second floor.

Doors were seldom closed anymore. Rooms were filled with light: birds singing, dogs barking, radio blaring. You could work without being under a blanket of silence.

As the President and the First Lady ate their breakfast in west sitting hall, the President tried to teach a myna bird the word "veto." "Oh, Calvin!" Grace Goodhue Coolidge's laugh was a spontaneous arpeggio of delight, beginning in the throaty alto range of her speaking voice and ascending to coloratura. "You and your tricks . . . what will the servants think?" At forty-four, a vibrant personality; she was olive skinned with lyric eyes and the slightest veiling of gray on raven's wing hair. There was something so youthful and unfettered about her that Maggie found it hard to think of her as the mother of two almost grown boys. The First Lady couldn't have been more different from her frozen-faced, sly-tongued husband, which may have accounted for those at work on the second floor trying to keep within earshot while the Coolidges breakfasted.

The President gave the myna bird up as hopeless and concentrated on his newspaper. The First Lady tried to peer around it.

"Can I talk to you about tonight, Papa?"

Silence, as Coolidge ate his oatmeal and scanned the front page.

"Will there be a reception line, or are we going straight in to dinner?"

Coolidge turned to the want ads. "Well, what do you know. Here's a find—Buick, one owner, good condition, forty-two dollars."

"Mr. Coolidge, please give me your ear . . ."

Without turning from his paper, he made a gesture of unscrewing his ear and handing it to her.

"If it's a receiving line, Papa, I can't wear a gown with a train—they always get in my way."

He turned to the editorial page. "Well, I see they quoted me right for a change: 'The business of America is business.' " Holding the paper up to screen his words, he leaned across the table to her. "There's a fly in my cereal . . ." As intended, it was heard by the butler,

Roach. Newest to the staff, he envisioned his month-old job evaporating, and turned from the serving table, appalled. "Oh, my, Mr. Pres'dent, sir, don't know how that could've . . ." As Roach reached for the offending bowl. Coolidge drew it away in mock reproach.

"Mammy, I thought butlers weren't supposed to eavesdrop."

"Yes, sir, I mean, no, sir . . ." Realizing he was being ragged, Roach retreated to the serving table. From the far end of the room, screened off as an aviary, tropical birds gave forth with song that put Roach in mind of the back Florida country he came from. For a while there he saw himself catching the next freight home, but Mrs. Coolidge's apologetic smile put his mind at ease. The President was again isolated behind his newspaper as Roach filled his plate with eggs, bacon, steak, sweet rolls, and buttered toast (*My, how that man can eat!*).

"Tonight," Mrs. Coolidge reminded her husband, "I don't know whether to wear my beige lace, or what."

"Wager you don't know the date of William Shakespeare's birth, either."

"Shakespeare? How would I know that? You're the classical scholar. But I know Rogers Hornsby's batting average so far this season . . ."

"Never heard of him."

"Four twenty-four. Now can we get back to the plans for the evening, like who's coming to dinner and what's on the menu?"

"My dear Grace, confidential White House information like that is never given out indiscriminately."

Mercer was in the open doorway. "Excuse me, sir, madam . . . didn't realize you still at breakfast . . . we be comin' back later."

Coolidge motioned him in. "Go right on with your business. Time wasted is lost forever."

"It's the Lincoln bed, sir."

"I can see that. Bring it in." Mercer and McKenzie guided the huge headboard through west sitting hall and into the First Lady's bedroom. Having lived a hotel existence throughout their vice-presidential years, the

Coolidges had very few personal effects, so once again, the underside of the White House furnishings bore the legend U.S. GOVERNMENT PROPERTY. A collection of oddments was hastily pulled together to provide the New England atmosphere with which the Coolidges were comfortable—all rather undistinguished except for the peripatetic Lincoln bed, requested by the First Lady. Mercer and McKenzie had made two trips back for the footboard, slats, and mattress. Maggie, assisted by Moira, had collected the oversized bedding and canopy. She also hesitated to enter when she saw the President and First Lady still at breakfast.

"No, no, Maggie, it's all right," Mrs. Coolidge called out. "Come on through . . . the more the merrier . . ." adding that she wouldn't be needing the canopy. "Nine feet long, I'll get lost in that bed as it is." Her uninhibited laughter lifted Coolidge's head from his paper. "Oh?" He finished his statement in sign language.

In the First Lady's bedroom, Moira, who had observed the hand gestures, whispered to Maggie, "Is she hard of hearin'?"

"Said in the papers she used to teach school for the deaf."

"Did she now?" Maggie lent a hand to McKenzie and Mercer, connecting the parts of the bed, but Moira, curious about the silence in the next room, couldn't resist a peek back.

The First Lady's fingers were rapidly spelling out another message. The President followed each sign avidly, then cleared his throat. "Madam, I shall regard that as top secret information." Grace Coolidge's contagious laugh made everyone within earshot smile.

Coolidge folded his napkin. "Good supper, 'Bug,'" he said to Roach, who pulled back his chair. The President's parting words were "Don't wear your beige lace, Mammy. People have seen it. Can't have people saying the President's a tightwad." Winding the stem of his pocket watch, he left the room.

"Veto," the myna bird shrilled.

As Coolidge waited for the elevator to ascend, he watched Mercer cross the center hall with one of the twin headboards that would be used for the Coolidge sons when they came down from school.

"Aren't you the fella who went out and got me the morning newspapers?"

"Yes, sir, Mr. Pres'dent."

"What's your name again?"

"Mercer, sir."

"Well, 'Mercy Me,' you owe me seven cents."

"Oh, sorry, sir . . . of course, sir." Mercer leaned the headboard against the wall and dug for the coins. Coolidge put them into his change purse, then into his pocket, calling out, "Rebecca!" From the far end of the hall came a fat raccoon, waddling as fast as her legs could carry her.

"Morning, Mr. President," Ike Hoover said from the elevator.

"Morning." Coolidge waited for the raccoon. "Morning, Rebecca." They entered the elevator and were taken below. While his Secret Service man took Rebecca to the Oval Office, the President made a detour to the kitchen to instruct the cooks in the Yankee art of saving money.

Mrs. Feeney silently fumed. Viola and the other cooks and helpers kept to the background. Coolidge moved from stove to stove, pot to pot, uncovering, sniffing, stirring, tasting. "Chowder . . ." he smacked his lips, "can always be stretched with more potatoes, and a little water in the milk won't hurt the taste—my mother did it and she was a fine, thrifty cook . . ." He squatted to peer into the oven. "Heat's too high, shrinks the meat. Can lose three, four ounces that way." Of stale loaves of bread in the bread box, he said, "Weren't fixin' to throw this out, I hope . . . makes excellent puddin' . . . I'll bring you my mother's recipe. Grew up on it."

Mrs. Jaffray had been on the telephone to a tradesman when she saw the President enter the kitchen. She did her best to disengage from the conversation, but it took three to four minutes before she could free herself and rush across the hall to protest the usurpation of her territory.

"Mr. President. with all due respect, sir, I can take care of anything that needs to be done, with reference to the kitchen, or the help . . ."

The President was occupied with a clipboard that hung on the wall. "This your shopping list, Mrs. Jaffray?"

"Yes, sir, it is that."

"Too much butter. *Margareen's* just as good. Strawberries? Too dear this time of year, buy only what's in season." He opened the refrigerator and stood there cataloging its contents. "We had roast beef last night. Mrs. Coolidge had a slice, I had a slice . . . where's the rest of it?"

Mrs. Jaffray threw a castigating look at the help, who looked at their shoes. Mrs. Jaffray turned back to the President, who, having just breakfasted, was now making himself a sandwich from a huge wedge of cheese. *Slicing the bread himself* . . . To help correct this unpardonable offense, she hurried to him with a plate on which to put the sandwich. Which he ignored.

"Where's the mustard?" he asked.

"Bottom shelf of the refrigerator," Mrs. Feeney said through tight. disapproving lips. He found the jar and spread the mustard liberally.

"Mr. President . . ."

"Yes, Mrs. Jaffray?"

"In all the time I've been in the White House I've dealt only with the First Ladies . . ."

"Well, then, this should be a nice change for you, 'cause you're going to be dealing with me. Kitchen's not one of Mrs. Coolidge's favorite spots, happens to be mine. We'll be having twenty-six for dinner tonight." He handed her a folded note from his pocket. "The guest list. Now . . . in future, I want to see all bills— want waste cut down . . . nothing to be thrown out, leftovers always better, second day. I like crackers and preserves always available in my bedroom and bowls of peanuts all over the house. I'm sure you'll make the adjustment, Mrs. Jaffray. Incidentally, I understand you insist on going to market by horse and carriage. Automobile's here to stay, Mrs. Jaffray . . . not all of us can lay claim to that kind of permanence." He walked out of the room, eating his sandwich.

Mrs. Jaffray had run into a granite wall. "And they call him Silent Cal . . ."

Mrs. Feeney added water to the chowder.

In no time Coolidge found a nickname for everyone, including Mrs. Jaffray, whom he dubbed "the Queen." The staff returned in kind and secretly taught the myna bird the name they'd given him, "Smiley." The President thought it a cracking good joke. The First Lady earned her own title, "Sunshine."

At the last gasp of summer the Coolidge boys came home, their arrival heralded by shouts—"Mother" . . . "Dad" . . . even as they were getting out of the car that had picked them up at the station. They burst through the front door, Mays barely getting it open in time. Three steps at a time and they were up the grand staircase well in advance of Roach and Coates, who futilely tried to take their suitcases and tennis rackets. "If you wait up, sirs, we take your things . . ."

Long-legged, tanned, sinewy, John and Calvin Junior paused at the head of the stairs, looking around at this unfamiliar place. At seventeen and fifteen, already taller than their father and favored with their mother's good looks, they brought with them youth, vitality, and such a sense of well-being that Maggie, and others at house-keeping chores, couldn't help but grin right back at them.

"Rob Roy . . ." brought out the lead collie and the welcoming committee of dogs. Mrs. Coolidge, crochet hook and ball of yarn still in hand, came joyfully out of her room to be caught up in embrace. Then, from the elevator, the President—moving at a pace the staff had never seen—melded into the four-way family hug fest, holding and kissing his sons with a warmth none of them would have expected from this reserved man.

Rebecca the raccoon, attracted by the commotion, stuck her head out of a door. Both boys let out a whoop. "Where'd you get that?" As they made a move to grab her, she ducked back out of sight. "Got to approach her cautiously," the President advised. "I think she's a Democrat."

Arms linked, laughing. the Coolidge family squeezed through the door into the bedroom the boys would occupy. "Dad, I brought you one those new puzzles—everybody's doin 'em, you'll be a whiz—they call 'em crosswords."

"Dad," Calvin Junior overlapped his brother, "you know when you were sworn in, one of my friends said if his father was President, he wouldn't be pitching hay."

"What'd you say?"

"I said if my father was his father, he sure would be."

Maggie, already in the room, helping Coates unpack the boys' suitcases, heard in their joy the echo of Cape May when she, her children, and their papa were once as bound together as this family. Determined not to let her own feelings intrude, she clamped her jaws and hung up an item she'd never expected to see on the second floor of the White House: a pair of much laundered, well-worn overalls.

"Oh, boy, doesn't this knock the cover off." John Coolidge expressed his enthusiasm for the room.

Calvin Junior did a running belly flop onto one of the beds. "Swell . . . dan-dan-dandy . . ."

Coolidge, the eternal realist, smiling from the doorway, advised his sons not to get too comfortable. "Remember . . . we weren't invited here, we're just in on a sublease."

Time turned the page to 1924.

President Coolidge, sublease or not, vetoed the soldiers' bonus in the interests of fiscal responsibility. The bill passed anyway, but the veterans weren't cheering: the bonds wouldn't mature until 1945.

Woodrow Wilson died, and with him, his dream of a world without war.

"Day by day in every way I'm getting better and better" was on the tip of the national tongue: a philosophy devised by a man named Émile Coué; it claimed to cure whatever ailed you, mental or physical. What it didn't cure was the abscess of Teapot Dome that was beginning to ooze, or the burgeoning new industry known as organized crime, with gangsters in pin-striped suits and tommy guns carried in violin cases. And it didn't alter the fact that there were a thousand times more speakeasies than hospitals for the victims of rotgut alcohol.

The Coué approach had little effect on those still trapped in Foggy Bottom. And none on Emmett's lungs.

Maggie *didn't* feel better and better about seeing Lillian less and less. She left notes in the kitchen, in the bedroom: "Get in touch with your mother." Lillian read them late at night when she came in after work or dates that took her car riding around Rock Creek Park, or out to Suburban Gardens to shows and dances at the new amusement park for Negroes. "I'm fine, Mama," Lillian replied in writing to the notes, and "Please take this sack of napkins back to Mrs. Jaffray." Mornings, when Maggie usually beat the sun out, the exchange between mother and daughter consisted of proddings from Maggie that they find some time for each other—and muffled groans from Lillian's pillow to just let her sleep another minute.

In Cleveland the Republicans unanimously nominated the incumbent President on the first ballot for a term of his own. "KEEP COOL WITH COOLIDGE."

Maggie had a birthday: her forty-fifth.

She realized the minute she came back from church and found Lillian moving the furniture around and clearing off the top of her little marble-topped table that something unusual was afoot.

"I know you got somethin' up your sleeve for me, Lil'yan, and I appreciate that . . . but that little china cup and saucer not to be moved."

"Mama, we goin' need the tabletop . . ."

"Jus' Mays and Mercer comin', we can eat in the kitchen. That cup and saucer very precious to me. You know the first Miz Wilson drank tea from that, and it goin' stay right where I always keep it."

Lillian was bursting with the secret. "When you see your birthday present, you goin' change your mind.

Now why don't you go in your room and take off your things . . ."

"You jus' be tryin' to get rid of me . . ."

From out in the hall, "Sugar Blues" sweetened the air. Maggie opened the door to find Mays and Mercer in their summer suits, straw skimmers tilted over their eyes, leaning against the wall—like it was the most natural thing in the world to have a Victrola on the floor, needle picking up syncopation fit to make a corpse move.

"Gets to you, don't it?" Mays grinned.

The two men, enjoying her astonishment, picked up and brought the bulky music machine into the room and put it down, at Lillian's direction, on the marble-topped table.

"Happy birthday, Mama . . ."

"Well I never . . . you three in on this . . ." They stood there, grinning at her delight and amazement, watching the record spin round and round, and sweet accelerated jazz came out of the tulip-shaped horn. Maggie couldn't get it straight in her mind at first. "Who'd you borrow it from?"

"Didn't borrow it, Mama. Bought it."

"Mays and Mercer?"

"No no, we jus' the delivery men . . ." But the phonograph records *were* their gifts to her, and they were anxious to play them.

"You mean, Lil'yan, you spent—? Where'd you get the money? Lil'yan, chile, we can't afford—"

"Jus' enjoy it, Mama." "Sugar Blues" gave way to "Yes, We Have No Bananas" and "You Gotta See Mama Every Night or You Can't See Mama at All." Maggie did a little two-step with Mays and stretched her toes to a strut with Mercer, while Lillian brought in the cake and coffee. Maggie paused in her joy to find a soft cloth and carefully wipe the horn of a few specks of dust. Her own Victrola . . . soon as she could manage, she'd get some records of hymns. "But, Lil'yan, I know you paid too much for it."

"Mama, don't fret about the cost . . ."

"But forty-three dollars and fifty cents . . ."

"How you know what I paid?"

"You think I'm blind? I see the signs in the windows—buy this, buy that—I know what things are goin' for . . . Lil'yan, you don't have that kind of money to spare . . ."

"Easy time payments, Mama."

Maggie jawed Mays and Mercer for knowing about it and letting Lillian take on such an obligation, but Mays, who read the newspapers carefully, assured her that the country was booming. "Everythin' goin' on credit, Maggie. Mr. Secretary Andrew Mellon says that's progress."

"Not surprised he say that, he's rich, don't need credit. Easy payments . . . never saw an easy payment in my life . . . every one of 'em come hard. Forty-three dollars and fifty cents, Lord almighty . . ." But as she went into the kitchen to put on another pot of coffee, she was singing along with the machine.

Sounded good, having their own music in the house. Lillian smiled to herself. She picked up the frayed American flag she'd been mending and settled down to work, tapping her foot.

"Lil'yan, don't drop any threads," Maggie admonished from the kitchen; calling Mercer's attention to the small oval rug of colonial design she'd just gotten out of "will call." "That's what you should have done with the Victrola, Lil'yan." Mercer agreed with Maggie that the rug did indeed put him in mind of the one in the little back guest room at the White House.

The Victrola ran down. Mays gave it a quick winding and brought it up to speed. Mercer ate a second piece of cake and observed that Mays wasn't wearing his campaign button.

"Wear it on the job, makes the boss happy." Mays took the circle of tin from his pocket, studying Mr. Coolidge's face and the ubiquitous slogan on keeping cool. "What's the use wearin' one, anyway, when nobody got the vote here in the District. Probably never will."

Lillian stuck the needle with the red thread into the

sofa arm, and began to work with the blue. "Sure would like to be livin' over in Virginia now. Go in a pollin' booth like all the other ladies, shut that curtain and put my vote down."

"An' pay your poll tax," Mays reminded her.

"You'd vote for Mr. Coolidge, I hope," Maggie prodded from the kitchen.

"S'pose so, Mama. Most folks seem to like him."

"Think he's goin' to get elected?" Mercer asked Mays.

"Shoo-in."

Mercer and Mays exchanged a conspiratorial look that said the time was right. Mercer stepped out into the hall. When Maggie came back into the parlor with the coffeepot, he reappeared with a bottle. "Now, Maggie, don't be sayin' no—it's your birthday—have a little embassy wine. Wouldn't want to offend the ambassador, after his houseman went to all the trouble to get it for us . . ."

Lillian had the glasses from the kitchen. "Come on, Mama, one little sip won't hurt . . ."

"Sure, Maggie, you don't want to be jeopardizin' our relations with Great Britain."

Maggie's protestations bore no conviction. She lifted the wineglass. "First, I got to say the good Lord's been very kind, everythin' goin' so fine these days. One thing I would like to do, though—take a moment to remember our good Mr. Wilson, lost to us this year."

They raised their glasses. "To Mr. Wilson."

"And to Emmett, couldn't be with us today—workin' out there on the river, so bad for him . . . and his friends, not carryin' their load, like they promised."

"*Mama,* you jus' told the good Lord everythin's fine . . . let it be."

They laughed together, sipped their wine. Mercer made a move for a refill, but Maggie was quick with the cork. Lillian folded the flag, set it aside, announcing it was time for her to go to her Sunday evening job. "Got to hurry, they be standin' in line for tickets, waitin' for me to open the box office."

"When you goin' finish the flag, chile? Got to get it

back to the White House, only got two and they fray
somethin' terrible in the wind."

"I'll get to it, Mama—so ragged, needs lot of
work . . ." It seemed to Lillian that the President
could buy a new flag. But she didn't know him like
they did: one penny-pinching man, except where his
lady was concerned—which endeared him to Maggie:
"My, yes, Miz Coolidge put on the same dress twice,
that man has a fit . . . Now you get home early, Lil'-
yan, finish your sewin'."

"Not tonight, Mama. Got a date after work."

"Who? Who you goin' out with?"

"New fella, you don't know him," which brought
forth a maternal barrage from Maggie: Does he drink?
Go to speakeasies? Play the numbers?

"Maggie, Maggie, leave the girl be."

Lillian smiled gratefully at Mays and Mercer, ran a
comb through her hair, put on a slash of lipstick. And
that was another thing! Lipstick, short skirts, rollin'
stockings . . . If there was one thing Maggie didn't
want, it was Lillian turning into a flaming youth . . .

"Mama, it's goin' come as a big surprise to you, but
I'm twenty-seven years old."

Twenty-seven or no, Lillian was still her baby. At
the door, she thanked her for the birthday. "Love the
present, chile, love it. But how we ever goin' pay for
it?"

"Not we, Mama. *Me.* Love you."

Maggie watched her swing cheerfully down the corridor on the crutch, and on down the stairs. When
she went back into the parlor, Mercer put on the
phonograph record he'd saved for last, "I'll See You in
My Dreams," but her mind stayed with the niggling
worry that buying on time was a bad thing. Mays
retrieved the campaign button from the table, musing
over it: "Pres'dent fine man, decent and all. Takin'
the country's mind away from poor dead Mr.
Harding's scandals, but papers sayin' Mr. Coolidge
don't seem to be doin' much else. Papers say Wall
Street is runnin' the country."

Mercer's mind didn't go to such concerns. "Beauti-

ful summer evenin', Maggie, shame to waste it. Let's
you and me walk out to the band concert. Mays here
such a Gloomy Gus, he can stay behind and play hisself the blues."

"Don't mind," Mays said; so agreeably, Maggie suspected a put-up job. "I walk out with one of you,"
she said, "I walk out with both."

"Cain't blame me for tryin'," Mercer laughed. "I'm
like Mr. Coolidge, I see me a lovely woman, I don't
look past her."

The three of them went for a walk to Lafayette
Park and sat on a bench facing the White House, listening to the band. When darkness fell, Mays and
Mercer walked her back home. Mays went on. Mercer
and Maggie sat out in front of the apartment building
in the pleasant summer air. Down to the boulevard
could be seen the headlights and taillights of all the
auto cars making a design in the night. Maggie said it
was the nicest Sunday she'd spent in a long, long time.

Grace Coolidge stood at the window, anxious, her
hand tightly clasping the high-collared neckline of her
dressing gown. *Of all times for him to get his hair cut.*
*His weekly trim was traditionally late afternoon, after
his nap. Why—after breakfast—today of all days?*
She turned, listening intently. "Did you hear anything?"

Maggie, spreading up the Lincoln bed, answered
with the same almost whispered urgency, "No, ma'am,
not a sound." The First Lady tiptoed to the barely
open door that separated her bedroom from her husband's, and peeked in. He was still in the chair, reading his newspaper while Mays, respecting the President's silence, snipped and combed.

Maggie was moving the collection of dolls onto the
bed from the sofa where they'd rested during the night
when Mrs. Coolidge, turning back from the door,
quickly rescued a Victorian doll with a china face
from underneath a porcelain-headed baby.

"Oh, sorry, ma'am, didn't mean to pile 'em careless
like that."

"That's all right, no harm." Observing the care with which she smoothed the doll's clothing, Maggie wondered if it had been the First Lady's when she was a child, or if she had acquired this enormous collection later. Wondered what they meant to her. Often, she'd seen her spending long afternoons in their company, trimming hats while she listened to the ball game on the radio; sorting her collection of feather fans; waiting for her husband to inform and instruct her about their plans for the evening: who was coming, what to say, and what to wear. In these months of service Maggie had come to see the shadowed side of Mrs. Coolidge's laughter and joy.

"Before we came here," Grace Coolidge mused aloud, "I used to get out and about so much . . . played ball with my boys . . . went on hikes and picnics."

"Why don't you take a nice lunch sometime out on the south lawn, ma'am? No pleasanter spot in Washington."

"My idea of a picnic is not to have one Secret Service man hand me the pepper, and another one the salt . . ." They heard a door close in the other room. *"He's going* . . . Maggie, make certain." But it wasn't necessary to look into center hall as the President's shrill whistle, the barking of dogs, and the diminishing ruckus as man and animals descended in the elevator informed them that the President had departed for the Oval Office and his day's work.

With the barely contained excitement of a schoolgirl about to play hooky, Mrs. Coolidge quickly unfastened her dressing gown, revealing a riding habit. Dropping to her knees, she brought out a pair of jodhpur boots from under the bed and sat, amid all her dolls, extending her foot for Maggie's help.

Together they slipped down the back stairs, Maggie in the lead, hiding Mrs. Coolidge's derby under her apron, the First Lady wearing a long coat that concealed her riding habit.

"Now if the President should come back early for

any reason and ask where I am, just say I'm out. That won't be a lie, Maggie, that's where I'll be. Out."

"Yes, ma'am . . . but will you be all right by your-self?"

"If I don't get away from the Secret Service once in a while, I'll go mad. The President sneaks away from them all the time . . . I used to be able to walk out by myself and look in windows, try on hats in stores. Now everywhere I turn, somebody's trailing me . . . Oh, and make certain there are peanuts upstairs, will you? You know the President, always nibbling, hates to put his hand into an empty bowl." As they came out into the ground-floor corridor. the First Lady's enthusiasm sagged perceptibly. The Secret Service man assigned to her was standing there, waiting.

"I was trying to lose you."

"I had that feeling, madam. But you know the President's orders."

"Do I ever." Mrs. Coolidge accepted defeat tolerant-ly. "Very well . . . do you know how to ride a horse?"

"No, madam."

"Then I hope you can run . . . just give me the horse and a little breathing room."

Maggie removed the derby from under her apron. The First Lady set it squarely on her head and off she went, trailed. Maggie spent the rest of the day in Mrs. Coolidge's suite, laundering, ironing, and refreshing the dolls' wardrobe. Her cloistered hours kept her from being witness to any of the events in the house which Moira excitedly recounted in the changing room as both prepared to go home.

"Big blowup in the kitchen . . . oh, my, yes. The President come in, started weighin' all the hams, mind you. I thought for certain Mrs. Feeney was goin' to have a heart attack. Then her highness, Mrs. Jaffray, threatened to quit—of course, she waited till the Presi-dent was out of earshot . . . And then you heard about McKenzie and Mercer, didn't you?"

"No, what 'bout 'em?"

"Why, McKenzie's movin' to Canada to work on a

farm. That means Mercer's stepped up to head house-man."

Maggie felt herself strangely disturbed. "Yes, it does, don't it?"

Moira, hanging up her uniform, found peanuts in a pocket, and offered some to Maggie. "D'ye fancy some?"

Peanuts . . . "Oh, my goodness, I forgot . . ."

On her way up the stairs with the bowl of presidential peanuts, Maggie ran into Mercer. He was beaming.

"You hear about me?"

"I heard. 'Scuse me, I have a duty to perform."

Her aloofness took him aback. "Thought you'd be glad."

"Be gladder, somebody'd notice I been workin' upstairs longer than you. But 'cause you a man, you goin' be gettin' more pay."

"Maggie, I don't make these rules."

"Lil'yan's suffragette ladies would have somethin' to say on that. *'Scuse* me." She edged past him.

"Maggie, wait . . . I got a raise, that's a fact. Got McKenzie's job, all right, but I am the wrong color to get his pay."

His words took hold at the landing, stopped her. She looked down at him, at the face asking for understanding, and noticed the lines that were etching their way around his eyes. And the gray in his hair. Up to now, she'd only been aware of her own. Her resentment dissipated. "We both paddlin' upstream, Mercer . . . you know I'm real glad you got the job."

She made the last turn in the stairs, distressed with herself at having diminished his moment of joy. Selfish of her: she had no right. Did you get crotchety at forty-five, she wondered? She'd have to watch that, and be more understanding with Lillian. too, now that she was thinking on it. True, the child was twenty-seven, not right to direct her every move. Still, had to admit she was a pretty impulsive child, and these were times when a mother couldn't be too careful . . .

She was about to take the extra few steps that

would bring her up to the second floor when she heard voices through the wall that separated the back stairs from the elevator. Clutching the bowl of peanuts to her, she stepped back down the stairwell so as not to be observed. Never had she heard President Coolidge so angry.

"Don't I have enough on my mind without worrying where you'll be when I get back?"

And Mrs. Coolidge's voice, penitent. "But Papa, just a little horseback riding . . ."

The elevator came to a jolting stop, evidence of the irritability of the presidential hand on the lever.

"Papa, you can't know what it did for me, to canter down by the river. I never get out of the house alone . . ." As the elevator disgorged them, Maggie caught a glimpse of the First Lady in her habit, derby in hand, and the President, carrying the long coat she'd worn as concealment.

"Sneaking out . . ."

"Papa, you sneak out."

"How is a Secret Service man going to protect you on a galloping horse . . . who does he think he is, Hoot Gibson?"

"Papa, I'm a prisoner of this house . . ."

"Madam, there are things you just cannot do on this job." Moving his wife rapidly along to their suite, he gave her jodhpurs a scathing look. "And wearing pants in public . . ." Mrs. Coolidge hurried inside; the President paused briefly at the table just outside the door to reach into a bowl for peanuts, but it was empty.

When Maggie heard west sitting hall doors close, and their muffled voices reached her from the inner sanctum, she emerged from the stairwell, hurried out into center hall with the bowl of peanuts, exchanged it for the empty bowl and scurried back to the stairs, barely rounding the corridor when she heard the door open again and the President come out. Propelled by irritation, his body was in forward thrust when, out of the corner of his eye, he saw the filled peanut bowl and braked, as though jerked back by a halter. Puzzled, he looked around, but there was no one in the hall. With a shrug, he took a handful of the nuts and munched away his disturbance as he got into the elevator and went below.

The following morning Maggie, ascending to the second floor, met Coates, descending with a serving tray of used breakfast dishes.

"Mornin', Coates."

"Mornin', Maggie. 'Sunshine' just rang for you."

"Oh, my goodness, I'm not late, am I?"

"You not late, she's early. And 'Smiley' . . . the cold shoulder. You never got the silent treatment till you get it from Mr. Coolidge . . ."

"Why, what happened?"

"Don't know . . . They had breakfast. I served 'em. Didn't speak a word. She tried, but not him. I tell you, that man can be silent louder than anybody I ever run into. But he eats . . . nothin' stop that man from eatin', don't know where he puts it."

Maggie's knock at Mrs. Coolidge's door brought an almost inaudible "Come in." She entered, shocked to find the First Lady making her own bed.

"Oh, Miz Coolidge, you not s'pose to do that . . . that's what I'm here for."

"So used to doing my own housework, hard to break the habit." Together, they tautened sheets, plumped pillows, put on the counterpane, and moved the collection of dolls from sofa to their accustomed place on the bed, without another word from Mrs. Coolidge. Her usual ebullience gone; manner solemn, dark eyes hooded . . . from tears? a sleepless night? The simple domestic task seemed to bring her comfort. As she carried the last doll across the room and paused at the foot of the massive Lincoln bed, Maggie sensed more peace in her than when she'd entered the room.

"Maggie, are you the one who put peanuts on the table last night?"

"Yes, ma'am."

"Then you must have heard?"

Maggie bit her lip. "Well, I . . . was . . . yes, ma'am . . . that is, a little, ma'am."

"It's all right, Maggie. Fear makes the President like that sometimes. He lost his mother when he was just a boy . . . it disturbs him when things don't remain the same . . . If he doesn't know where I am every minute of the time, he just can't seem to function. Feels the same way about our sons, but he tries not to show it with them . . . I just wanted you to understand, Maggie. Mr. Coolidge is a good man, a good man . . ." She held the doll in her arms, unconsciously cradling it. Long after Maggie left the room, she stayed, rearranging her dolls on the bed.

Clarence Fraser had come to the White House to work just about the time Annie retired and Mr. Coolidge assumed the presidency. A dark-skinned, loose-limbed Georgia boy who'd wandered north, he'd run from a few railroad yard bulls, held some odd jobs, and somehow ended up as alternate doorman at the White House. A free spirit, it was just a stopgap and it even surprised him that he'd stayed put a whole year. Maggie once asked him, didn't he have anything at all on his mind. "Time not come for me to worry, Maggie . . ." She'd known the answer would be something like that, even before she asked. He somehow brought to mind Emmett Senior in his younger days, when she first met him. Not that he looked all that much like him; just a kind of natural, easygoing charm he had. Two or three times, coming off duty, Fraser had tap-danced his way from the front door to the changing room, leaving Mrs. Jaffray aghast at this breach of decorum. If she'd had her way, he'd been given his notice. But Mays and Jackson had established autonomy over the door and they liked having the boy around. Joked him about his appetite—same as the President's, they said. Any time you wanted to find Fraser, just look in the dining room . . .

That's where Maggie found him, happily consuming well-done beef ends and day-old bread.

"Hope you got your dancin' shoes on. Girls in the kitchen say you one fine dancer."

"Me and Bojangles." He grinned and did a few flashy steps around a chair. "Why? You got me a bookin'?"

"Might say that. The Coolidge boys lookin' for someone to teach 'em how do the new dances."

"Well, you have come to the right man . . ."

Lillian, returning the mended flag during her lunch hour, heard the snappy music almost as soon as she came into the building. By the time she got halfway up the back stairs, she was swinging along on her crutch, and singing along with it, "Cha'leston, Cha'leston." Her destination was the attic, but the flag delivery would have to wait. The lure of the music pulled her into center hall.

There, shirt-sleeved, was an exhilarated Fraser, legs swinging in abandon, crisscrossing his knees in the uninhibited new dance movement, while his pupils, John and Calvin Junior, in tennis clothes, their rackets tossed onto chairs, attempted to imitate their graceful, limber instructor.

Captivated by the music, and using her crutch as a second, sound leg, Lillian swung along with several pretty good swipes at the dance herself.

The record ran out. Fraser rewound the machine and lifted the needle to start over. "Let's try it again, boys, okay?" John was game. "How about you, Cal?" But Calvin Junior, who had found the going painful, wincing slightly through the last few steps, limped to a chair and sat down.

"What's the matter?" asked his brother.

"Don't know . . . think I got a blister on my heel that last set of tennis we played. You go ahead, I'll wait awhile."

The record spun. Fraser Charlestoned. John Coolidge bit his lip in concentration and rendered a too literal translation of the free-swinging dance. Calvin Junior took off his shoe to ease his hurting heel and laughed at his brother's stilted rendition.

Lillian stood a distance off, smiling, thinking how wonderful it was that such pleasure should be in the White House; not knowing that she was witnessing the last few grains of Coolidge family happiness running through the hourglass.

That evening Mercer was turning down the President's bed. "Will you be needin' anythin' else, Mr. Pres'dent?" He approached him cautiously, the President still being in a bit of a rage over Will Rogers imitating him over the radio. (*"That cowboy is never to be invited here to this house."*)

"No, thank you, Mercer. Good night." The President didn't glance up from his newspaper. Not then, or a moment later when Mrs. Coolidge stepped into the room.

"Calvin, dear . . ."

"I'm reading."

Grace Coolidge couldn't control the urgency and fear she felt. "Papa . . . Calvin Junior is sick . . . running a high fever . . ." His face flooding with anxiety, the President threw down his paper and bolted across the hall to his son's room.

After four days of blood-poisoned delirium, Calvin Junior slipped into the coma from which he would never awaken.

A blister . . . how could it take him away . . . only a blister . . . Unable to grasp or accept the finality of his son's death, President Coolidge stood for hours at the window of his boys' bedroom, aching to go to his remaining son, whose tortured sobs burdened the air. He couldn't take the steps. If he touched, if he showed any affection—if he crossed center hall into the darkened room in which his wife had entombed herself—if he offered comfort, would he tempt fate? *Would he lose them, too?* For an instant, the years dropped away and he was a child in a cemetery and they were lowering his mother into the ground. "He was just a boy," he said to his tear-blurred image in the windowpane, "just a boy."

Mercer, Mays, and Roach, tasting the salt of their own tears, carried the disassembled parts of the sickbed from the room. Fraser assisted, stunned that this boy, only six years younger than himself, with whom he had danced just days ago, could be gone. A grieving

Maggie walked alongside them to the attic stairs, carrying the unsheathed pillows. It was not in her to question her good Lord's intentions, but the anger she felt emboldened her. "Miz Taft lost her power of speech in that bed," she railed. "The first Miz Wilson died in it —now this poor boy! We got to break up the pieces of that bed so nobody can ever put it together again . . ."

"We do that for you, Maggie," Mercer promised. "We do that." The four men carried the bed up to the storage room and destroyed it.

For a very long time days ran into each other. Maggie rose each morning, performed her duties, filled the hours with work, and went home to bed. She was unable to find any answer within herself, or any way to bring comfort to the desperately bereaved First Lady, who sat in her room day after day in heavy mourning. Many times Maggie found her, a small pathetic heap on the bed, surrounded by her dolls, a photograph of her son in her hands.

With the heavy drapes perpetually drawn, it was sometimes hard to see her in the gloom.

"You rang for me, ma'am?"

A voice diminished by heartbreak came from the bed. "Maggie, take them away."

"Take what away, ma'am?"

A vague gesture to the dressing table bench made Maggie aware of a mélange of discarded, gaily colored and beaded gowns, ostrich plume fans, evening shawls. "Oh, no, ma'am . . . couldn't take these . . . you be wearin' 'em again some day."

"No . . . you and your daughter have them. I never want to see them again . . . never again . . . ever . . ." Maggie obediently removed the party clothes, so filled with remembered laughter, from the room.

The grief of the White House touched the country. Calvin Junior became everyone's lost son. A comment the President was heard to make was picked up by journalists and reprinted across the country: "Now he will eternally be sixteen years old." Whether or not these poignant elements affected the election is debatable; but in November of '24, Calvin Coolidge won at the ballot box; the frugal man in the White House became, on his own, the thirtieth President of a nation that was on a wanton spending spree.

"Recession" was a word the newspapers were using more and more; and they wrote about the failure of certain sections of the economy to recover from the downturn of '20 and '21. In Washington, the last horse-drawn fire engine was retired from service and made the front page; Sacco and Vanzetti were relegated to the tenth. Lillian, in the vanguard of fashion, powdered her knees. Maggie worried about the jazz age and the lost generation.

From time to time, Negro refugees from the slavish sharecropping life in the deep South found their way north; some applied at the White House for jobs. Most were refused, but it served to keep those who were employed on their toes and made them hesitant about asking for raises.

The Ku Klux Klan, its ranks swollen to over 4 million, marched down Pennsylvania Avenue from the Capitol. Mays and Jackson stood rigid at the door as they passed by—forty thousand strong—in their white robes and tall white cone hats, carrying towering American flags, leaving in their wake the memory of night riders, burning crosses, lynchings.

Maggie watched with Mercer from a window on the second floor. Coates, Roach, and Dixon pulled back the velvet drape in the East Room and watched. Fraser stepped out of the service door and watched from just inside the little iron gate—one of the rare times he wasn't smiling.

Ike Hoover, discovering the cause of the commotion in the street, stepped out onto the north portico and stood, dour-faced, between Mays and Jackson for the entire time of the parade.

9

墨 墨 墨

It was a rare summer day. Mays felt that if he just
listened to the birds' songs and felt the warmth of sun
on his hands and face it ought to wipe away the
thoughts that held his spirits down. The memory of the
KKK had lingered with him. But it was the date on the
calendar that troubled him most this morning, and he
couldn't shake loose the melancholy memory that it
evoked.

The President, on awakening, felt the dread of this
anniversary day. He breakfasted alone, hoping that his
wife would put on one of her bright smiles and sum-
mery negligees; that she and her ebullient laughter
would join him at the breakfast table. But she took her
tray in her room.

Everyone in the White House knew what day it was.
On the back stairs and in the kitchen, they wondered
when the President would abandon the black armband;
if he would ever resume his practical jokes. Kitchen
workers who had found his interference a nuisance began to wish he would lift lids and poke his nose into
pots. But when he came into the kitchen this morning
it was, as of late, merely to get his little cloth sack of
chicken feed.

"Morning, Mr. Pres'dent," Maggie said to him as they passed in the ground-floor corridor. "Nice day, sir." He merely nodded and went on out the door. Yes, she noticed sadly, he still wore the black armband.

Mays was at the side door. He held it open for him. "Mornin', Mr. Pres'dent."

The President stood in the bright sunlight, almost as though he'd forgotten why he'd come out. "No joy being President, no glory . . ."

"I understand, sir."

President Coolidge sighed heavily and moved a slight distance to where his flock of a dozen chickens were penned by a low wire fence. He cast a handful of feed and the chickens came running.

"Mays, do you realize that today it's . . ." His voice trailed off.

"Oh, yes, sir, I do, sir. A year today . . . Everybody aware of that, sir, and mighty sympathetic."

"If ever any young boy comes to the White House door, wanting to see the President, he's to be brought right in."

"Yes, Mr. Pres'dent, I'll sure to remember that. I'll tell all the other doormen."

Coolidge absently fed his chickens. "Why is it, Mays, my chickens always taste of mint?"

"I'm not surprised, sir. They always eatin' out of that mint bed Pres'dent Teddy Roosevelt planted for his juleps."

Coolidge's sorrow-filled eyes met Mays'. "A year," he said, "a year . . ." He finished feeding his flock and then went into the Oval Office where he closeted himself. He removed the black armband from his sleeve, smoothed it carefully, and put it away.

Lillian, occupied with double jobs at the Celeste and the box office of the Dunbar, was somewhat removed from the daily events of the White House, except for those that Maggie brought home. But, being one of the last people to have seen Calvin Junior enjoying life, she'd been tugged into the tragedy, and was aware of the anniversary. She was stocking-footed in the display window of the dress salon, adjusting a vivid, gypsy-hued georgette dance dress onto a mannequin's unyielding form. The sleeve not fitting properly, she unscrewed the mannequin's arm and was just in the process of slipping it back through the folds of fabric when she heard the tap on the window and looked up into the eyes of the President of the United States.

He stood close to the plate glass, his Secret Service men a polite distance behind him, examining the dress. Before the loss of his son, Calvin Coolidge had been an almost daily figure on Connecticut Avenue, enjoying his constitutional on this haut monde street where he could size up the fashionable gowns, often buying them, without asking the prices, for his wife.

The gown Lillian was adjusting, he scrutinized from hem to neckline, mentally calculating its size. Solemnly, he nodded his head. "I'll take it," he mouthed through the glass. "Wrap it up."

Grace Coolidge had been listless all day. She'd almost forgotten what it was like to have a full night's sleep. Drab gray mourning clothes accentuated her pallor. Maggie tried, as she did every morning, to perk up her spirits. "What shall we do with your hair today, Miz Coolidge?"

"Doesn't matter, Maggie."

"What do you say we give it that nice big dip on the forehead that's so stylish. That look wonderful on you, ma'am."

"Any which way, Maggie." Grace Coolidge reached forward to the dressing table, adjusting the single rose in the vase beside the photograph of Calvin Junior. Even the roses she chose in memoriam, Maggie noticed, were pallid. Pale yellow, palest pink, white. It was hard to detect, in this disinterested, colorless setting, the lady who'd always loved red; who had the capacity to bring the sun into a room with her.

As Maggie put in the tortoiseshell pins to hold the chignon, she noticed more than a dusting of gray now in the First Lady's thick black hair, and deep shadows under her eyes. A glance into the mirror showed Maggie shadows under her own eyes, put there by sleepless nights. A sigh escaped her and drew Mrs. Coolidge from her reverie.

"Maggie, forgive me for being so thoughtless. I haven't even asked about your boy . . . How is Emmett doing?"

"Doin' pretty well, ma'am. In the hospital right now." Normally Maggie minimized her problems, but this particular morning the weight of worry was so heavy it needed only the slightest nudge to break her dam of restraint. Once she began, she couldn't hold back. "Truth is, ma'am, he's in the hospital more often these days than out. Had himself a disabled-officer job, escort at the War Department, but even that got to be too much. Was workin' the river for a while, but the weather so bad for him, thought he'd die . . ."

Not visible from the dressing room, Calvin Coolidge stepped through the bedroom door from the hall, a ribbon-tied box under his arm. Maggie's emotion-laden voice came to him. "When my boy got his medal and was decorated right out here on the Ellipse, everythin' looked so promisin' . . . Wanted so to stay in the service, but bein' wounded so bad, Army put him out, and climate here is killin' him. Mr. Wilson said his country would never forget him—and I know he meant it—but a Pres'dent's got so many things on his mind . . ."

Coolidge stepped into the doorway. "Should have come to me sooner, Maggie gal. His country owes him. You're right about Mr. Wilson, he did have a lot on his mind. So I'll just take it on myself to see that the promises made your son are kept." Before Maggie could respond, Coolidge put the dressmaker box on the bed. "For you," he said firmly to his wife.

"Papa, no . . ."

"Mammy," he said gently, "it's time." He walked from the room and closed the door. Grace Coolidge rose from the dressing table and stood looking at the ribbon-tied box.

"Shall I open it for you, ma'am?"

"No, Maggie." Approaching it as would Pandora, she

slowly pulled the ribbon ends, removed the lid, and from the tissue bed lifted the fragile, colorful gown. The First Lady held it in her arms, crying over it as if it were a living thing. Dredging up a long unused smile, she moved to the mirror, holding the gown in front of her. It was a painful acceptance. It meant letting that fatal day recede into the past, distancing herself from the silver-framed photograph on the dressing table.

The words came hard. "I'll need my hair done after all, Maggie. The President and I will be dressing for dinner."

Faithful to his word, President Coolidge had Emmett sent to a military medical facility in Arizona. With him went his bride, a full-blooded Inca (which pleased the Roanoke side of Maggie) whom Emmett had met in one of his forays to the Peruvian embassy. Judging from the letters and snapshots postmarked Arizona that came to Maggie and Lillian, Emmett's health was no longer deteriorating. The dry air had given him back the gift of breath. They had to be grateful for that.

The last spring snow of 1927 fell with a vengeance throughout the night and by morning drifts covered automobiles and the only way you could get to work was to dig your own path. And still it came down—not in delicate, lacy crystals but like a weighted cloud bank plummeting to earth.

The irrepressible Fraser, part of the shovel brigade clearing walks, broke into a tap dance in his heavy, wet boots as he came into the ground-floor corridor from outside. Every step, his boots squished and he left a dirty puddle. "Lucky Lindy"—he sang accompaniment to his muddy ballet—"up in the sky, Lucky Lindy, flyin' so high . . ."

"Fraser . . . anybody . . . Hurry . . ." Coates came running from the back stairs, a veritable Paul Revere— shouting down the corridor, flinging open the door to the staff dining room where he caught Mays and Roach, still in wet clothes from snow shoveling, having a shot of hot coffee. "Hurry . . . Mercer and Jackson up in the attic, need all the help they can get. *Roof's cavin' in . . .*"

The rescue squad, four strong, bolted past Mrs. Jaffray's office and up the stairs, bringing her out into the corridor to protest their muddy footprints. "Careful. Can't you see what you're doing . . . dirtying up my floor?" But they were out of earshot.

It was snowing in the attic. The steep slanting roof, carrying more weight than it could handle, sagged dangerously inward. Wet, packed snow oozed through the cracks. Mercer, on a ladder, used the force of his shoulder to hold the roof in place while Jackson, below, hoisted a two-by-four into place to take over the load.

"Hurry up with that, my back's breakin' . . ."

The two-by-four buckled. A chunk of snow fell into Jackson's face. Coates, Frazer, Roach, and Mays, charging up the stairs, were implored by Mercer to get some bed slats to add to the support. A bureau was hastily pushed under the threatening roof to extend the length of the shorter slats.

Coolidge, in the middle of his afternoon nap, had felt the thudding footsteps running through, heard the muffled shouts. He opened one eye to see the chandelier swinging from the clumping of boots overhead. Quickly pulling on his shoes, he hurried across center hall and ascended the attic stairs. He'd never had occasion to go up them before.

"What's all the commotion?"

Mercer, manning the operation from the ladder, saw the President's head as it came up out of the stairwell. "Roof's fixin' to collapse."

"Happens every time it snows," Coates added as Mercer came down the ladder, grabbed two more slats, and wedged them in, and the others put their muscle behind bracing the roof. "Usually get men up on the roof with shovels, but this time, storm so bad, hit us by surprise."

"Let me give you a hand." Coolidge picked up a blanket and started up the ladder.

"Mr. Pres'dent," Mays protested.

"I'd be pretty much of a fool just to stand here, wouldn't I?" Coolidge stuffed the blanket into the gaping hole the roof had developed, and for the moment the snow was kept out. While Fraser and Roach piled tables, dressers, chairs into a makeshift support system and shoved them under the most threatened section of roof, and Mays went off for hammer and nails, the President peered around the attic. "Never been up here before, what are these rooms used for anyway?"

Storing, sewing, they told him. Sometimes sleeping, when there was round-the-clock duty.

Still forcing the blanket, now wet and freezing to his hand, into the hole, the President took in the clutter and confusion of the cramped attic. "Shameful . . . totally inadequate. Congress has got to appropriate some money immediately. And those steep stairs—surprised nobody's broken their necks . . ."

Mrs. Jaffray, raising her out-of-fashion floor-length skirt ankle high, negotiated the offending stairs like a battleship at full throttle. It was not proper conduct for servants to ignore their betters, which was exactly what Coates and the others had done when they muddied up her floor and walked off, ignoring her remonstrations. She had considered waiting to dress them down, but the longer she thought about it, the more heinous the offense became. And the back stairs—mud from bottom to top!

Her voice preceded her as she sailed up into the attic. "Now pay attention, *all of you*. I will not countenance this kind of insubordination." Ignoring the crucial operation going on, she continued to berate them. "When you come down, it's shoes *off*, is that clear? I am not going to have any of you tracking up my fine car-car . . . pet." The word was half in, half out of her mouth when she focused on the man on the ladder and realized it was the President of the United States.

"Mrs. Jaffray," he asked, "wouldn't you be more comfortable in Buckingham Palace?"

"Are you asking for my resignation, Mr. President?"

"Are you tendering it, Mrs. Jaffray?"

Only one could back away from this impasse. "I will

be gone in the morning," she said. Valiantly retrieving
her ego, she turned and haughtily descended the
stairs. When she came to the second floor she could
have continued on down by foot. But it was a matter
of principle. She rang for the elevator. It was a long
time in coming.

The signal for the elevator was received at the ushers'
desk, but at that moment Ike Hoover and his staff, in
galoshes and mufflers, were occupied with shovels and
brooms, trying to keep the north portico free of snow
that blew in endless gusts and piled up against the door.
He paused to catch his breath and caught a glimpse
through the blowing snow of a bright red hat. It moved
toward them from the street, then disappeared. *Good
Lord* . . . the First Lady had left wearing a red hat!

Ike Hoover in the lead, the ushers plowed through
the drifts, sinking in up to their waists; the red hat
bobbed in and out of view as Grace Coolidge threw
her slight body against the wind, only to be driven
back, knocked off her feet. It was a bedraggled First
Lady whom they pulled out of the snowbank. As they
helped her up the steps, across the slippery portico,
and into the elevator, she was laughing. "Isn't snow
fun?"

Later, when Ike Hoover had a chance to think
back on it, he realized it was the first time she'd
laughed in over a year, and felt some good had come
out of the storm after all.

Maggie, quickly summoned to her aid, got the First
Lady to her bedroom, out of her soaking clothes, and
into a warm bathrobe. Her eyes sparkled and her cheeks
glowed. "Maggie, I loved it . . . it was just like Vermont
out there . . ."

"The Pres'dent goin' be mighty upset with you,
ma'am, bein' out in weather like this . . ." Maggie
snugged her into a chair, wrapped a blanket around
her, and was toweling her hair dry when the President
—the roof temporarily secured—came into the room.
His chuckle preceded him. "Well, Mammy, Queen
Jaffray and I have come to the parting of the ways . . ."

Mrs. Coolidge smiled at him from her blankets, like the heroines of *Orphans of the Storm.*

"Good grief! Pshaw!" was as near as he could come to profanity as he took in her crumpled wet garments, picked up her drenched hat, castigating, "You were out in this weather?" Maggie, an expert at marital warning signs, quickly removed Mrs. Coolidge's garments to the bathroom where she hung them to dry; then regretted her destination, since there was no way out except back through the room where the President and First Lady were poised on the brink of discord.

"It's all right, Papa," Mrs. Coolidge placated. "I won't melt." But he wasn't satisfied. Where had she gone? Why hadn't she told him of her plans to go out? And her Secret Service man—what had become of him?

"Poor fellow got stuck in a snowdrift, Papa. The car just froze up on him. I only walked from the other side of Lafayette Park—only a block, Papa, it was fun . . ."

"You could catch your death. What took you out on such a day, anyway?"

"Campaign rally. You're always telling me to go out and meet some new ladies—well, I went out and met some. Wasn't snowing badly at all when we left. Mrs. Taft was there, you approve of Mrs. Taft . . ."

"Campaign rally? You don't know a hoot about politics."

"Nothing profound. Mrs. Taft invited me and some other women, that's all. They just want to get things started for you—for '28, and a second term. Chief Justice Taft favors you above anyone else . . ."

Their voices occasionally penetrated the closed bathroom door. Mention of the Tafts took Maggie's mind back to a similar time when she'd been trapped in a dressing room and chided herself—as she was doing now—for being a clumsy fool. The tense, high voice of the President was no longer audible. Either the anger had gone out of him or he'd left the room. Maggie silently slid the door open a fraction of an inch, venturing a peek. All she could see of him was one of his hands which Mrs. Coolidge held in both of hers, pressed to her cheek. His voice was low, troubled.

"Don't get involved, Mammy. I'm not certain of my plans."

"But you are going to run . . ."

"If they draft me, that's one thing—but to impose myself, as things are . . . no no, can't do that."

"But people like you, Papa. You should have heard the women. They're saying you healed the country, made everyone forget the scandals . . . Teapot Dome . . . What do you mean, *as things are?*"

Maggie closed the door, feeling embarrassed at having heard even as little as she had. She knew how to keep her place. What was said between a President and a First Lady was not for her ears. And yet—while she didn't understand it—the President's words, "as things are," had made her feel uneasy.

Coolidge moved to the window, wiped condensation from the pane, and watched a small wren trying to find shelter behind the drift on the sill. "The economy is overheated," he said—more to himself than to his wife. "Those optimistic statements I've made to the public . . . window dressing . . . Never felt I could impose my own frugal attitudes I hold as a private citizen. Been up to me, nobody would gamble a cent in the market . . . Beginning to feel I was wrong, let too many things happen of themselves . . . should have spoken out . . ." On the wall next to the window was a framed photograph of himself in wading boots, in a stream, holding aloft a string of fat trout. "The trappings of office," he said to the picture, "the silly poses you put on, to prove you're a regular guy . . . Catching fish for the camera from a pond stocked with ten-inchers any child could grab with his bare hands . . . And all the while the country's in jeopardy . . ."

"What do you mean, Papa—*in jeopardy?*"

"Too much money being borrowed . . . too easily . . ." And again he was talking to himself. "And the stock market . . . frightens me . . ." The hollowness in his voice, the slump of his shoulders, chilled her more than the snowbank had. "Mammy . . . inside me I feel there's going to be a depression. It's got to come to that, and there's no way I know to head it off . . ."

While the roof was being replaced and the attic re-built, the Coolidges moved out of the White House and into the Patterson mansion on Dupont Circle. In the interests of economy, several new members of the staff were let go. By some stroke of luck, Fraser remained. A new housekeeper, Mrs. Ava Long, took over from Mrs. Jaffray, and things went on as usual. When the President and First Lady went out to summer in Rapid City, South Dakota, photographs of the President— in Indian warbonnet, being initiated into the Sioux tribe; and wearing full cowboy regalia, chaps, ten-gallon hat, boots, and self-conscious smile—were printed in all the newspapers.

"If that man isn't runnin' for office—gettin' himself up in those funny outfits—I will eat that newspaper," Mays offered to the table at breakfast.

A few weeks later, Mercer came into the dining room with an extra just off the street. "Get yourself set for printers' ink indigestion," he told Mays, as the morning newspaper passed from hand to hand. The headline, dated August 3, 1927, read: "I DO NOT CHOOSE TO RUN," SAYS COOLIDGE.

When everyone had finished reading and puzzling over this unpredictable man, Maggie tore off the front page and took it home with her to add to her box of clippings, photos, and mementos she'd kept from almost her first days in the White House.

Hopelessly behind in putting them together, she sat in her kitchen into the early hours of the morning sorting, scissor-trimming a front-page story from 1924— EX-FIRST LADY FLORENCE HARDING DIES—dipping the brush into the library paste, and carefully placing the obit in her scrapbook on a page facing the account of Warren G. Harding's death. She paused for a moment, reliving the pain of those days, and discovered her coffee had gotten cold and so had her feet. Tightening the bandanna she wore so as to cover the tops of her ears, she pulled the bulky beacon bathrobe around her and turned on the gas jets to heat the coffeepot and warm the room. *Almost three o'clock in the morning, and that child not home yet . . .*

The old Model T came chugging up the street. She heard it stop out in front, but couldn't tell whether or not the engine was still running. Crossing the unlighted parlor, she slid the window open and leaned out. Below, the arc of an electric streetlamp cast a dull yellow circle onto the sidewalk. The spare tire in back of the Model T was in the light; the rest of the black car blended into darkness. A flash of glitter and red stepped from the car, aided by a crutch. *About time, young lady . . .* Lillian, fancied up in Mrs. Coolidge's red chiffon, an ostrich plume extending like a cockade from a beaded headband, had a moment's difference with her escort, a young man who got out of the car and tried to convince her he should accompany her inside. Lillian let him know, with a brief kiss, that the evening had come to an end. Maggie looked down on the top of Lillian's bobbed head as it disappeared into the apartment building.

She was back at her pasting in the kitchen when Lillian, on an inhalation, turned the key, held her breath, and silently oozed the door wide enough to squeeze through.

"I hear you, chile."

Lillian moved through the dark parlor into the lighted doorway of the kitchen. "Mama, what you doin' up so late? Should be in bed . . ."

"My words exactly, took 'em out of my mouth. Lil'yan, this is no time for a respectable girl to be comin' home."

"You still cuttin' and pastin' after workin' all day? What you goin' to do with all that stuff, anyway?"

"I don't know . . . might write me a book some day."

"Write a book? Oh, Mama . . ." Lillian leaned over and kissed her on the cheek.

"Been to one them speakeasies, I can tell."

But the euphoria in Lillian was deeper than the slight bit of liquor she'd consumed. "Don't go there for the drinkin', Mama . . . go for the music, the show . . ." She leaned on the crutch, both she and the ostrich plume drooping with fatigue, reminding Maggie of a tired little circus pony after a parade. "That line of girls, dancin', wearin' long silk stockings and feathers . . . I danced every step right along with 'em, in my head."

"What's to become of you? Worry 'bout you every minute of the day."

Lillian opened the recently acquired refrigerator and poured herself a glass of milk. "I'm takin' care of myself."

"Out with a new fella again tonight?"

"Nice fella, you'd like him. Tall, good-lookin', put me some in mind of Emmett."

Maggie carefully trimmed another newspaper item, and as carefully asked the question. "You thinkin' of marryin'? You're old enough . . ."

Lillian sat at the table with her glass of milk. "Not him or anybody else. Marriage, far as I see it, is carin' and waitin' and worryin'. I've come to see what you went through, Mama."

It was the first that Lillian had ever seen her side of it, yet she couldn't let anyone speak down of her Emmett, even now. "Your papa couldn't help the way things worked out for him . . ."

"I know that, Mama . . . but I will have you to understand, I got to feel free."

"I worry so 'bout you, you're all I got—you and your brother, and him so far away out there in Arizona. Wonder if I'm ever goin' to see my boy again . . ."

"'Course you are. Why, one these days I'll jus' put you on a train, send you out, with nothin' on your mind but havin' a good time . . ."

"Chile, that costs money. Still so much to pay for—the refrig'rator . . ."

"I paid for the Victrola, didn't I? Now you let me

worry 'bout things for a change." Lillian took the empty
milk glass to the sink, washed, dried it, and put it
away. Again Maggie was cautious in approach. "With
Miz Jaffray gone, Lil'yan, I know I could get you a
job in the White House—permanent."

"Not me. Never goin' to go to the White House. Got
no life of your own over there. Look at you, Mama,
at their beck and call. Phone ring right this minute,
you'd go runnin' back, not even ask why. Workin' in
the White House, might as well be in a convent. It's
like takin' the veil . . ." She helped Maggie tidy up
the table, put the clippings, scrapbooks, and scissors
back in the box. "You quit worryin', Mama, I'll work
things out for both of us. Now, let's get to bed." As
Lillian leaned down to kiss her mother good night she
inadvertently knocked the bandanna askew. Maggie
quickly tugged it into place, but not before Lillian had
seen underneath it. She pulled the bandanna off, and
Maggie's hair sprang out into a wiry triangle.

"Why, Mama, you bobbed your hair!"

Calvin Coolidge often said that he and radio came
in at the same time. Radio certainly ushered him out.

"The—Republicans—nominate—for—the—next—
President of—the—United States . . ." All over the
second floor you could hear the voice, out there in
Kansas City, shouting above the din of the convention.
". . . The—Honorable—Herbert—Clark—Hoover . . ."
Maggie was glad that President Coolidge was spared
the tumultuous shouts, cheers, bells, and whistles. Having removed himself from radio's reach, he and the
First Lady were at that moment on a train bound for
their Maine summer home. When they returned to
the White House in September, there were no practical
jokes—and very little laughter. From then until the end
of his term, the President spent a large portion of his
days watching the third floor being rebuilt into twenty-
two proper rooms.

That's where he was, the day before the Inauguration,
like a sidewalk foreman—supervising, critiquing. Get-

ting under foot. (*"Missed a spot there, near the base-board . . . Got to cut the paint in proper-like, with a brush . . . Nail isn't covered, needs putty . . . Don't think that board's in plumb . . ."*) To the reviewing stand being hammered together right out in front of the White House on Pennsylvania Avenue for Herbert Hoover, he never once gave a glance. When the time came for the President and First Lady to leave, and the staff lined up for the ritual of farewell, all Calvin Coolidge permitted himself was a guttural sound deep in his throat. Looking intently at the floor, he walked briskly by everyone and into the elevator. Grace Coolidge stayed a moment, her eyes imploring them to understand him.

"Happy days are here again . . ."

You heard the peppy anthem everywhere in 1930. Anyone rich enough to own his own radio caught it on every turn of the dial. Maggie and Lillian, by putting their ears to the wall, could enjoy Amos 'n Andy from the apartment next door. Warm nights, if you sat on the steps out in front, neighbors, by grace of open windows, shared their radios with you. Music stores, unasked, broadcast to the world through public-address systems.

There was one such store next to the Celeste: a place utterly without class, in Lillian's opinion. Any store that had signs in the window: RADIOS, $2 DOWN, $1 A WEEK was like an acne scar on the patrician face of Connecticut Avenue. But a lot of quality establishments had pulled down their window shades for the last time, taken down their fine awnings to sell for what they could get. The auctioneer's voice was heard up and down the street, putting the gavel to fixtures and furnishings.

The Celeste had hung on to the very last gasp, sending polite dunning letters ("Your balance with us has undoubtedly been overlooked"). Many of the gentlemen who paid the bills had margined out in the stockmarket crash. One lavish spender had terminated his account by jumping out of a fourteenth-story window, joining the swelling ranks of investors who had no recourse left except the final plunge.

The Celeste was now nothing but raw walls, uncarpeted floor, the plate glass to the street Bon Ami'd over to mask its nakedness. Everything that hadn't been sold or carted away was in boxes of trash in the alley. Lillian found the mannequin's arm in one of them, shook its hand: "Good luck . . ." picked up her sewing basket and came out the front door, carefully closing it. Two men were taking down the sign.

March had blown in like a lion. Wind whipped around the corner, stung Lillian's knees, and blew her coat open. Tucking the sewing basket into the crook of the arm that held the crutch, she tugged the cloche hat with the other one, pulling it down like a helmet. To save the carfare she walked all the way to Seventh and T, where the Dunbar Theater advertised BINGO EVERY NIGHT and FREE DISHES on its marquee. The box office wore a new sign, CLOSED UNTIL FURTHER NOTICE.

It seemed everywhere she turned, the word "depression" was illustrated in graphic detail—especially on street corners, with World War vets and other unemployed selling apples. She hadn't meant to stop. Head bent into the wind, it would have been easy to walk by and avoid his eyes. But there was something about the way he stood that made her think of Emmett. About the same age and build. The vet, wearing partial uniform of overseas cap and blouse with two medals, had a fire going in a bucket. His apples, in a neat pyramid, were polished and shining. Lillian paused beside the fire.

"My brother was with the three hundred seventy-second."

"That so?" The whites of his eyes, which completely surrounded the pupils, highlighted his dark face. "They pulled some hard duty. He sellin' apples, too?"

"No, he's in Arizona. Was gassed."

"Tough," he said. But it was clear he understood.

"Things'll get better." She repeated the rote of the day, which the vet couldn't buy. "Mr. Hoover been in more than a year—I'm still waitin' for the chicken in my pot, the car in my garage. Arizona, huh? Hear it stays warm there."

"That's what he writes." From her purse she found a nickel, took an apple. The vet nodded his thanks. A block farther on a newsboy was shouting "Ex-try—ex-try—William Howard Taft dies . . ." She bought a paper and stepped into the entrance of a shuttered store to let the tears flow in private requiem for the big man who'd shared a sumptuous meal with her and told her not to let anybody stop her from doing the best she could with her life.

Then she walked home. As she reached the top of the stairs, the repossessors were waiting at the door of the apartment.

"Come on in, it's in the kitchen."

"You want us to empty it, or do you want to do it?" one of them asked her.

"I'll do it." The half-filled bottle of milk, the saucer-covered plates of leftovers she placed on the table. One of the men pulled the plug. Never once did he look at her. The other one was the talker.

"Sorry, miss, just doin' my job. I got family . . ."

"Don't understand why they couldn't wait. I been payin' regular, only back-owe a couple payments."

"Don't hold me to blame, got to take what work I can get." Together the two men set and tied the refrigerator on a dolly. Lillian opened the newspaper and scanned the want ads.

"What kind of work you out of?" the family man asked.

"I sew. Make stylish dresses."

"Not a whole lot of call for that these days."

"You're tellin' me."

"When my wife looks in a window, sees one of them dresses, and we can't afford to keep shoes on our kids' feet . . ." His voice cracked. Lillian noticed that the soles of his own shoes were held on with twine.

She signed the manifest for him.

"Best put that milk in some cold water," he cautioned, "before it turns sour."

The two men dollied the refrigerator out of the apartment and down the stairs. Lillian watched them out of sight, closed the door, went back into the kitchen and did as he suggested, refrigerating the food in the sink. The veteran's apple was on the table with the want ads, but she'd read enough these past days to know practically nobody was advertising for "Energetic Young Woman with Crutch." Idly, she scanned SITUATIONS WANTED:

EXEC VICE PRES OF CORP—Drives car, willing accept labor, exclnt refs . . .
REG NURSE—20 yrs expr, take any offer, waitress, you name it

The inevitable had been staring her in the face for some time; she'd just been pushing it away. "Lil'yan," she said aloud, "you have come to the end of the line. Don't you have sense enough to know when to get off?"

Setting her hat firmly on her head, she wrapped her coat around her, picked up her crutch, and set out on the path her mother trod every morning of her life. It brought her to the sidewalk in front of the White House. She paused for some minutes, looking through the iron grilled fence where Maggie had stood that day back in 1909 when she made her first pilgrimage into the building . . . where Emmett had said goodbye and gone off to war, where Lillian had helped carry a suffragette banner; where she'd stood so many times, knowing that she could go in and come out almost at will.

Well . . . those days were over.

She started up the walk, reluctantly. The crutch, which usually served her, now forced her along. But as she rounded the corner and went through the little gate and down the steps to the staff entrance, some of her natural optimism began to come through. By the time she came down the corridor, she was moving briskly.

Maggie, Mercer, Coates, Dixon, Mays, Jackson, O'Hara, Roach, Fraser, Bridget, and Mrs. Feeney were at lunch as she came through the door.

"Mornin', everybody."

They all looked up at her.

"I have come to take the veil," she announced.

10

☒ ☒ ☒

The uniform, smallest in the house, hung like a sack on Lillian's slight frame and required multiple safety pins from inside to give it some semblance of fit. As Maggie accompanied her down the corridor from the changing room to the housekeeper's office, it was in Lillian's mind that they looked for all the world like a prison matron and an inmate. It was in Maggie's mind that her prayers had been answered: her child was now under her wing.

"Now mind your tongue, don't say anythin' fresh, don't speak unless spoken to, remember to say 'Ma'am,' stand up straight, and don't lean on your crutch."

"Mama, I have you to remember I am past thirty." But Maggie was as nervous as a hen with a single chick as she presented Lillian to Ava Long, the housekeeper who had come in as replacement for Mrs. Jaffray during the Coolidge administration. They found her poring over ledgers, harried. "Never get caught up in this place—luncheons, teas, dinners . . ." Between notations, she glanced up. "So you want to work with us, Lillian."

"Well, ma'am, I have given it some thought."

Maggie threw Lillian a warning glance to watch what

she said. "Lil'yan very anxious to work here, Miz Long.
She'll alter her uniform. She fine with a needle."

"Indeed you are, Lillian, I've seen some of your
work."

"Thank you, ma'am. I am *well acquainted* with the
White House linen."

Maggie quickly amended: "What Lil'yan means is
that she always willin' to mend anything needs mendin',
you jus' ask her."

"I understand what she means, Maggie. I've often
wondered what foreign dignitaries who dine here
would think if they knew they were eating off patched
linen. But then none of their countries have paid
back on the war debt, so I guess that makes us even."

The laugh that began on Lillian's face was nudged
out of existence by Maggie's elbow to the ribs before
it became audible. Mrs. Long leaned wearily back in
the chair, shoved her eyeglasses onto her head, and
tucked up a stray strand of hair. Her harassed manner
and disregard for face powder or coiffure spoke of her
having been at the desk hours before the day began
for anyone else, and she would be there hours after
everyone else left. "All right, Lillian, we'll give it a try.
You understand, every administration is unique. President and Mrs. Hoover have their own ways, we try
at all times to respect them. There are a lot of new
rules . . . yes, indeed, lot of new rules."

Mrs. Long's burdened sigh was only the tip of the
iceberg. As Lillian traversed the back stairs to the
second floor, she was bombarded by Maggie with new
commandments of conduct: Work quickly, quietly, go
in, do your work, come out, no talking. *Quietly,* you
understand, QUIETLY.

The staff practically tiptoed the last turn in the stairs,
to the service closet and their work in center halls
and bedrooms. Buckets were handled gingerly, so as
not to inadvertently clink and make a sound. There
was a perpetual sense of breath being held, as though,
on exhalation, a word might escape. Those few words
deemed absolutely essential were muted, barely above
a whisper.

Lillian, who hadn't been on the floor since the day the Coolidge boys learned to dance the Charleston, was fascinated by the changes in decor. Gone was New England austerity. The new furnishings were splendid, and spoke of wealth, objets d'art reflecting the eclectic taste of the world-traveled Hoovers: brass samovar, Persian rugs, antique Chinese vases, tapestries that had graced castles, carved teakwood tables reminded you of the Tafts. The complexion of the staff was also changing. Where once Maggie had been the only dark face on the second floor, there were now three. The two Irish maids, Bridget and Moira, and houseman O'Hara, now took orders from Maggie and Mercer. None had ever spoken openly of it, neither worker nor supervisor, but the subtle difference was felt. O'Hara, in a private aside to McKenzie just before that gentleman left, said he'd never stay on if it meant having a "colored" tell him when he could and couldn't spit, but a greater force than injured pride kept him at his post. *Depression.* Jobs were as scarce as a flock of sheep on Pennsylvania Avenue, and too many of his relatives back in Boston were without work and needed his help. So he kept his feelings to himself and went about his business. And this new administration, with its rules of silence! If he'd known he'd end up in this monastic setting, he might as well have taken the vocation his mother wanted for him and gone into the priesthood.

Maggie and Mercer handled their positions with great care, always prefacing any order with "If you would please," and working right along just as hard. In fact, as Mercer and McKenzie carried the headboard of the Lincoln bed on its way back to anonymity, Mercer realized he'd obligated himself for the heavy end.

Maggie tiptoed across the hall to head them off, wondering, in a whisper, why they were taking the Lincoln bed to the attic when it had just been brought down the week before.

"First Lady changed her mind."

She turned at the slight sound of Lillian's crutch tip

on the floor. Lillian was coming out of the bedrooms, crossing the hall, arms full of used linen, which she stuffed into the laundry bag. Chief Usher Ike Hoover (now dubbed "Mr. Usher," since there couldn't be two Hoovers in the White House) slid the double doors open and President Herbert Hoover emerged from the suite.

Fifty-six, tall, full-faced with practically no gray in his straight, center-parted hair, his ubiquitous high starched collar seeming to hold his head even more erect, he moved briskly, purposefully, unsmiling. If he saw anything on the periphery of his vision, he gave no indication. As one, at sight of the President, the staff immobilized, to blend into the woodwork.

Lillian's buoyant voice reverberated in the hushed atmosphere. "Mornin', Mr. Pres'dent."

Shocked at this flagrant breach, Mercer, Maggie, Usher Ike Hoover turned and stared at her. The President, giving no indication of having heard, entered the elevator and was taken below.

Maggie grabbed Lillian by the arm. "When you goin' learn, Lil'yan? You were given the rules. Servants not to be noticed."

"How could I not be noticed—pushin' a big old laundry cart like that?"

"Shhh . . . keep your voice down. The Pres'dent's got a lot on his mind, don't like servants in the way."

"Well, sure don't seem friendly, not sayin' 'Good mornin',' him right there."

"Jobs hard to come by, young lady. You want keep this one, you got to learn things way *they* want 'em . . ."

Lillian learned that Maggie was part of the "they." She made a bed. Maggie gave it a quick look of inspection, then yanked the bedding off. "Again . . ."

"Mama, why'd you wait till I got through if you didn't like what I was doin'?"

"Hush . . . You might talk back to your mama at home, but not to First Maid Maggie Rogers, not if you want to work here. Now—make the bed again, right this time . . ."

Lillian was on a ladder, meticulously washing off each individual teardrop crystal of the wall sconce, Maggie scrutinizing her work from below. Maggie found a speck of dust at the very top.

"You need your glasses to read, how can you see dust way up here?"

For days it went that way, Maggie riding her. On her fourth morning in the White House, it rained. Maggie set her to work scrubbing the ground-floor corridor. *A thankless job if there ever was one*, Lillian thought. *Just get it cleaned, someone comes along, muddies it up.* Mays came in from the outside, pulling off his raincoat, and started to remove his rubbers before he saw her, on hands and knees, scrubbing with a brush. "Sorry, Lil'yan, didn't mean to track up your floor."

She dipped the rinse rag in the bucket, wrung it out, and wiped up his footprints. "That's all right, Mays. Jus' give me more practice, make the first maid happy . . ." this last was meant for Maggie's ears, who was hurrying down the corridor with a bucket of clean hot water. May drew Maggie aside: "You pushin' her a little hard there, Maggie . . ."

"Got to learn to do her share." Maggie put the bucket of water down beside Lillian. "*Clean* water. You jus' putting dirt on from that bucket."

Lillian slammed down the brush, glared at Maggie, anger rising. Maggie, ignoring it, picked up the pail of dirty water. "Oh, and when you get through with that . . ."

Oh, and when you get through with that . . . Lillian heard it so often, it was popping up in her dreams. One place she could work off her resentment was in the new sewing room on the third floor.

She finished the hem of a long, vivid orange linen table runner, was folding it as Maggie came up the stairs with a half-dozen other outsized pieces of linen fabric of various bright hues over her arm.

"Well, now that you got that done, Miz Hoover likes different-colored table runners for each day's luncheon. Needs five more for this week . . ."

Without reply, Lillian took the fabric and began to measure. It bothered Maggie to have this rising resentment between them, but she wasn't about to dignify it by acknowledging it existed. Instead, she sat down in the wicker chair facing the large window. "Nice to work up here now. Can thank Mr. Coolidge for that . . . that old slantin' roof and the snow cavin' it in? Remember I told you about that, Lil'yan?"

Lillian ignored the ameliorating attempts. "When you want these runners done, *Miz Rogers?*"

All right, young lady, it's goin' be that way—two can play that game. "You do the best you can, young woman. I'm sure you'll have 'em all done well before they needed . . ."

Later that day, Lillian was summoned by telephone to the second floor. She came down the stairs that were no longer steep and narrow, to find Maggie waiting at the foot. "What you want of me to do now, Miz Rogers? Clean the furnace?"

"Hold your horses, miss. First Lady wants to meet you." Crossing center hall, Maggie spoke in hushed tones. "Now remember, she don't like talkin' to servants any more than has to be. She's got a lot of little hand signals—you got to watch for 'em—if she does like this"—raising her index finger—"that means come to her. If she does like this"—Maggie lightly brushed her lip with her index finger—"that means don't talk, she thinkin' . . . If she turns the back of her hand, that means you stop whatever you doin' till you get further orders. But if she walks, that means—you go. Now knock."

"Wait a minute, Mama, I didn't get any of that straight—"

Maggie knocked for her. From within, a voice, which Lillian took to be Mrs. Hoover's, bade her enter. A moment of terrible uncertainty, while Lillian smoothed uniform, hair, then opened the door.

Barely into the room, she stopped, awed. Lillian had read some of Somerset Maugham's stories in magazines, but she'd never expected to step into one. West sitting hall was now a setting straight out of the South

Seas, overflowing with potted palm trees, caged exotic birds. Woven straw furniture. Totally out of context with the look of tropical ease which the room projected was the industry of its occupant. Mrs. Lou Henry Hoover, a tall, elegant, white-haired woman, sat at the large wicker table which she used as a desk, providing work for three secretaries. Two stood by, arms filled with papers up to their chins, while a third made rapid notes on a shorthand pad. The First Lady didn't glance up, but continued dictating: "The President and I heartily endorse the *Buy Now* movement, and urge your organization to join in the effort to keep money in circulation. Thank you for your cooperation, et cetera . . ." To a second secretary: "Check the Smithsonian, see what they have on the Monroe furniture, if we can't locate the originals, let's see what we can do about duplicating them from photographs." To the third: "Oh, and the Girl Scouts, thank them for the honor they've paid me, et cetera."

The secretaries, taking stacks of papers and books, left the room for their offices on the third floor. Lillian stepped aside as the secretaries walked past her, and still Mrs. Hoover's attention remained on her desk. Finally she removed gold-rimmed glasses, revealing thoughtful brown eyes. Raising her right hand midway from table to chin, she extended an index finger and waited. Lillian, frantically trying to recall the meaning of the gesture, stood, rooted. Mrs. Hoover repeated it, slightly beckoning with the finger.

"Oh . . ."

Lillian took a few steps forward, stopping a distance from the desk. Mrs. Hoover smiled. "So you are Maggie's little girl."

Lillian cleared her throat, whispered, "Uh, yes . . . ma'am."

"Do you have a cold?" Mrs. Hoover asked in concern.

"Oh, no, ma'am." Lillian regained her normal voice. *"Madam . . ."*

Mrs. Hoover leaned back against the tall fan-shaped wicker chair. "Fine woman, Maggie. Dependable. With a mother like that, you must have some of the same attributes."

"Well, ma'am—madam, I . . ." Mrs. Hoover lightly brushed her lip with her finger, and Lillian stopped speaking. "We only expect light work of you, and, of course, sewing, which you do so well. You look a bit thin, we'll have to see that you fatten up. I presume you like desserts . . ."

Unsure whether to reply or not until Mrs. Hoover raised a hand, palm upward, Lillian answered.

"Oh, yes, madam, I like ice cream, especially chocolate. And I . . ." But Mrs. Hoover was on her feet, moving to a broad-leafed plant, systematically examining the leaves. Lillian stammered, then, realizing what was expected of her, backed out of the room.

Maggie, waiting midway between west sitting hall and the back stairs, fell into step with Lillian on the way back to the sewing room. "Well, you get along all right?"

"You bet. Saw eye to eye. She only wants me to do *light* work."

"That so?"

"This light enough for you?" Maggie asked as she set Lillian to polishing state silver in the staff dining room. Hours later, surrounded by stacks of flatware and dozens of pieces of hollowware, some polished, some not, Lillian paused for respite. The muscles in her arms continued to scream. She rubbed them, then dipped the cloth in the polish, and bracing an ornate punch bowl almost the size of a washtub between the table and her knee, began to wipe tarnish away.

The door opened and a tall, swarthily handsome, graying man who looked like a diplomat came in the room, carrying a covered silver serving tureen.

"You are Maggie's little girl?"

"Yes, who are you?"

He introduced himself as Boris, the President's valet. Lillian quickly got to her feet. He put the tureen on the table. "The First Lady sent this to you."

"Yes, sir, I'll get it polished right away."

"Not polish. Ice cream, for you to eat . . ." Removing the cover, he revealed a gargantuan portion that for a moment took her back to the clandestine feast with President Taft. "You are to eat now. All of it," and stood sentinel.

With resignation, she wiped her hands on the apron, picked up the spoon, and dug in. After that, Mrs. Hoover took to sending her bowls of ice cream with regularity.

Maggie never let up. Under her critical eye, Lillian worked. The adversary relationship followed them home. Meals were taken in silence. Maggie passed her evenings working on her scrapbook, waiting for Lillian to relent and say she understood why she was being driven so hard. *You my daughter, all right,* Maggie thought. *You jus' as stubborn and prideful as your mother . . .*

"This the way it's goin' stay with us, chile? You not sayin' two words to me after we get home, day after day?"

Lillian tightened the belt on her bathrobe, poured herself a glass of milk. "I'm tired—that's two words . . . And this milk's warm—that's four. Darned old icebox don't keep anythin' cold enough . . ."

"Well, we goin' stay with it. No more time payments for us. Every last cent we got's goin' in the bank till we can pay cash for things . . . I was thinkin' maybe we could save all your salary and—"

"You want words, Mama—I'll give you a whole bunch. Put 'em down for that book you're always fixin' to write 'bout the White House . . . Maggie Rogers, First Maid, is a Simon Legree. All that's missin' is the whip . . ."

"That how you see me, chile?"

"Makin' me do twice what you ask anybody else to do—"

"You think I like you on your knees? Come home, too tired to eat? It aches me, chile. But a lot of people out of work, hungry . . . Not a servant over to the White House don't have some friend or family they'd like to bring in for a job. I go easy on you one tiny bit, they all goin' be down my neck, even if they don't mean to be . . . it's the times, child . . . hard times . . ."

Hard times. Strange times. Worrying about keeping your own job. All around, the depression deepening; relatives, friends, neighbors going hungry—while in the White House, a continual round of lavish entertainment acquainted even the lowliest scullery helper with a diet of leftover truffles and sturgeon. As unsettling as the outside world was, so was the atmosphere of the White House, with rooms being eternally redecorated, restructured, furniture in a constant state of flux, no decision having been reached on which were to be sitting rooms, and which bedrooms. And—crucial problem of the day—whether Mrs. Dolly Gann, sister and hostess of Vice-President Curtis, or Mrs. Alice Roosevelt Longworth, daughter of a former President and wife of the Speaker of the House, should sit higher at the table. "Some times I think White House protocol is worse than the French court," Mrs. Hoover was heard to say.

And the President. When Mr. Hoover came into office, the staff knew more about him (through the newspapers) than they'd known about Mr. Harding, and infinitely more than about Mr. Coolidge. After more than a year in residence, he was still an enigma. A mining engineer of international reputation, a cabinet member in both the Harding and Coolidge administrations, a philanthropist who'd loaned his own money —$1.5 million—to stranded Americans, strangers to him, in London at the outbreak of the Great War, he'd never spoken a word to any of the staff. Mays, who cut his hair, and Mercer, Roach, and Coates, who served his meals, had a wager going on who could get him to speak. But not a "Good morning," "Yes," "No," or "Thank you" out of him. An isolated man in a tower. Mays wondered, when the President read the papers (and he surely did), what he thought of the cartoon showing a pocket turned inside out, called a "Hoover flag."

And the thousand-dollar bill on the First Lady's

dressing table. That was a mystery none of the staff wanted to unravel. The first time Lillian came in to make Mrs. Hoover's bed and saw it lying right out in the open, she became fearful, and called Maggie. "No, the First Lady didn't forget it, it's jus' there. Don't touch it, jus' dust carefully around it like we been doin' every day since she come into the White House." So they did. Every day. Dusted around it.

Lillian, splurging $2.95, bought herself a Eugenia hat, all the rage, with red feathers. It was her badge of courage against the tension of the times.

The hope of spring wilted in a blanket of muggy, moist air that settled over the city and refused to budge. Summer dragged on interminably. The only good thing was the few less dollars paid out in rent for heatless months. The apple sellers on the corners had long since doused their bucket fires and now stood under makeshift overhangs of elusive shade. Soup kitchens ladled food onto tin plates for a constantly moving parade of the hungry. Almost nowhere did you hear the sound of laughter.

The dismal mood of the country intruded into the staff dining room.

"Goin' be another scorcher," Coates observed. No one responded. A new servingman, name of Morgan, passed the tray of Nova Scotia salmon for the second time. Lillian took some, and noted that several at the table were setting aside seconds and thirds, to tote to less fortunate family and friends. Roach, she noticed, looked especially bad this morning, like he hadn't slept.

He hadn't. Hadn't slept and couldn't eat, the fear that he would lose his job was so great, and him with a family. He could kick himself for having been such a lummox, serving at dinner last night. Forgetting the First Lady's hand signals—mixed up as to whether touching her forehead meant to serve the dessert or come around again with the meat platter—he'd started to remove the plates for dessert. Wrong choice. Coates, who was in charge, hadn't sacked him yet, but that didn't mean he wouldn't. Roach gulped some coffee, and got heartburn.

Mays mopped his sweating face with a handkerchief and folded his newspaper. "Says prosperity jus' around the corner."

Jackson held the cold water glass against his forehead. "Around the corner, huh? So that's where it went."

"Guess those fellas in the breadlines don't read the papers."

An assenting grunt from Jackson, and again quiet fell over the table. Maggie hadn't found it necessary to speak. Wasn't much to say, actually. Never one to utter what was deep within her, she couldn't bring up a worry that was just a-borning. Hardly there, but a worry. Walking to work this morning with Lillian, she'd got a kind of stitch in her chest, and felt out of breath there for a minute. She blamed it on the heat, but the back stairs were getting a little longer every time she climbed them. Twenty-two years service to the White House had brought her—along with Mays, Mercer, and Jackson—into her fifties. She'd get some rest, she promised herself, and focused her mind on a fresh concern. Mercer's chair was empty. Wasn't like him to be late . . .

The call box dropped a number summoning Dixon from the table. He pulled on his butler's alpaca jacket and left. Coates spoke of the big luncheon coming up today, and said they'd better cool off the dining room. Dig up some extra electric fans from somewhere, and bring in some potted palms to hide them.

"Luncheons, dinners every day." Coates sighed. "So many parties—those dinin'-room chairs never get a chance to cool off."

Lillian saw the bright side. "Well, one thing, they don't need much dustin' that way." No one even smiled.

Maggie finally voiced her concern. "Not like Mercer to be late."

Mays, checking his pocket watch, agreed. "Think

he could be sick?" He got up, put on his uniform jacket. "Maggie, you mother hen to the world. I'll go ask Miz Long can I use her phone." Before he reached the door, Mrs. Long came in. She appeared nervous. With her was a Negro man in his forties, short—five-six at the most—shabby-neat, his hat in his hand in the apologetic manner of a man who'd heard "No" too many times. She introduced him to the table. "Everybody, this is Luke Henry . . . Mays, don't leave, I want everyone here."

There were "How do"s, nods, and perfunctory smiles for the stranger. "I thought, Coates," Mrs. Long went on, "that with all the entertaining going on, you could use a new man on your staff."

Roach, in inner panic, thought: *He's come to take my job.*

"Yes, ma'am," Coates said, "sure can use an extra man."

"He comes well recommended."

The small man eagerly pulled envelopes from his pocket. "Got letters from the finest resorts . . ."

Mrs. Long deterred him. "That can wait." It was obvious something heavier pressed on her mind. Consulting her clipboard, she said, "Coates, last night one of your part-time waiters wore a black tie."

"Yes, Miz Long, sorry 'bout that . . . jus' didn't catch it in time."

"I remind you of the First Lady's orders. Tuxedo and black tie while serving luncheon, white tie and tailcoat for serving dinner. And one of your staff spoke out loud last night—I'm not going to ask which one . . ."

"Won't happen again, Miz Long . . ."

"Now, a matter of importance to every one of us . . ." She took a deep breath and plunged into the dire message that had brought her into the room. "We're all going to have to take a cut in salary . . ."

Those who'd been eating stopped. Roach couldn't believe his luck: only a salary cut, no mention of the faux pas with the hand signals—that meant he still had his job. But he'd be careful . . . Mrs. Long went on: "Myself included. A hardship, I know, on all of us . . . every department in government is facing the same problem. Don't know that it'll make you feel any better, but the President himself isn't taking any salary from the country. He pays all of his own entertaining out of private funds. Not a pleasant way to start the day, but let's try to remember, a lot of people are out of work. We all have jobs." She left them. For an instant everyone remained stunned, then overlapping protest poured forth: "I got family" . . . "Can barely make it now" . . . "Kinfolk back home dependin' on me" . . .

The new man, Luke Henry, remained standing, holding his hat. Lillian, aware of his discomfort, patted the seat next to her. "Mr. Henry, you come sit with me. We both low at the table."

"Thank you, miss." Gratefully he took the chair she offered. Morgan was at his elbow with a serving dish. "Crepes suzette?" Luke Henry asked in astonishment.

"Leftovers, last night's dinner party."

Luke Henry spooned a generous portion onto his plate, then returned part of it to the serving dish rather than betray how long it had been since he'd eaten. And became aware everyone in the room was staring at him, the interloper.

He pushed his plate away, a denial that he was taking food from their mouths. "I had put in for a job here, long time ago," he apologized to the room. "Didn't mean to cut into anybody's money . . . sorry, it's just I need a job . . . bad . . ."

O'Hara, Bridget, Moira, and some kitchen people got up and left. In a minute, Jackson and Roach followed. Coates stood by, waiting to read Luke Henry's references.

"Not your fault, our takin' a cut in salary, Mr. Henry." Maggie rose from her chair and moved to Mays, who stood just inside the door. "Please, Mays, try to find Mercer . . ."

Lillian and Maggie ascended the back stairs, Maggie huffing a little, which Lillian mistook for a sigh. "It'll be all right, Mama, we work it out."

"Wasn't worryin' 'bout that."

Dixon was descending with the President's tray. Maggie paused to speak with him. "He finished with breakfast already? Tray jus' went up to him, poor man goin' get sick, not takin' proper time to eat."

Dixon nodded agreement. "Caught a glimpse of him. Looks terrible, like he not been to bed for a week. Secretary Treasury don't look much better."

"How you know Mr. Mellon up there?"

"Oh, he up there all right—lookin' as plagued as the Pres'dent. Things must be bad . . . bad . . ."

On the second floor O'Hara was taking cleaning equipment out of the service closet, passing carpet sweeper, dustrags, and feather dusters on to Lillian, Moira, and Bridget when "Mr. Usher," waiting at the elevator, urgently signaled that the President was coming. The staff quickly stepped down into the stairwell, out of sight.

The President and Secretary Andrew Mellon strode across center hall. Little better than two years in office had considerably altered Mr. Hoover: his shoulders drooped, hands trembled slightly as he rubbed forehead and eyes to relieve the ache from lack of sleep. He moved quickly, as though time was the Philistine. "It's imperative that you talk to the bankers again, Mr. Mellon. Convince them to hold the line, not call in their mortgages—give the people a breathing spell . . ."

Mellon, thin, ascetic, his white hair, brows, and mustache intensifying his aristocratic mien, listened politely. "Mr. President, there are those who will survive and those who won't. It has been so since the beginning of time."

They stepped into the elevator. "We have an obligation, Mr. Mellon. The intervention of government in everything is anathema to me, as it is to you, but we must take steps—raise taxes, cut government spending. Prime the economy with private money."

Mellon admitted that the market was recovering

to some degree. Over the whir of the elevator mechanism the President was heard to say, "We must diminish the fear that is blanketing the country. Fear, Mr.
Mellon . . . that is the enemy. Fear . . ." The word
stayed in the air after the elevator was gone.

The staff proceeded out of the stairwell to their
work. Maggie, a bit slow in joining the others, was
alone at the service closet when Mercer came racing
up, still in street clothes, controlled desperation in his
voice. "Maggie . . ."

"Oh, we worried 'bout you, Mercer. Mays went—"

"Saw him, Maggie." He drew her quickly aside.
"You got any money in a bank?"

" 'Course, Mercer. You need some?"

"You better get it out right away."

"What you talkin' 'bout?"

"On my way to work this mornin'—come by my
bank—a mob there, Maggie—shovin', breaking windows. They closed—"

"What you mean?"

"What I said. Bank closed. I had me over five
hundred dollars . . . all gone . . ."

Maggie ran down the stairs and all the way to her
bank, pausing several times to cool the red heat in her
chest. Before turning the corner she could hear the angry voices. The mob spilled out into the street, the
alley. Men in shirt sleeves, some women in their kitch-
en aprons, still wearing ruffled dust caps—clawing, yell-
ing. Policemen, pressed flat against the door by the
pressure of the crowd, tried to hold them off: "Get
back" . . . "Stay away" . . . "Can't get in there." And
the panicked chorus of depositors: "Want my money"
. . . "It's my money . . . "Gangsters, thieves" . . .
"That Hoover and his bunch" . . . Caught in the crush
of hot, steaming bodies, Maggie tried to forge a way
through to the door, but there was no independent
movement, only that of a surging mob. She waved her
bankbook futilely at a policeman, who shoved her back.
Ducking under one unfriendly elbow after another,
there remained only a glass door between herself and
the banker, whom she could see on the other side, so

close she could read the terror in his eyes. The sign on the door read: 8 TO 5. The last glimpse she had of the banker was of his tortured face; a fox with hounds at his heels, he pulled down the curtain between them. CLOSED. A brick was hurled. There was a crash of glass breaking, and the hard wood of a billy club was heard against a skull. Someone screamed.

The scream stayed in Maggie's ears (had it been she who voiced such anguish?). The rest of the day she went through the motions of working. At home, Lillian made the simple meal. They took their coffee out on the fire escape to catch what breezes there were. Maggie couldn't rouse from her despair.

"No use mournin', Mama, it's done . . . over. We didn't have all that much in the bank anyway."

"Yes, we did."

Puzzled, Lillian took the bankbook that Maggie held out to her, squinting to read it in the light from the streetlamp. "Five hundred and eighty-four dollars!"

"More than twenty years of nickels and dimes, come to nothin'. Been squirrelin' away that money for when anythin' happen to me, to take care of you, chile, or to help your brother, should he come to need it . . ."

"Oh, Mama, Mama . . ."

The weight of failure sat hard on Maggie.

"Back where I started . . . What am I goin' do . . ."

"Tell you what you're goin' do, Maggie Rogers First Maid. You are goin' let Lil'yan Rogers Fourth Maid do the worryin' from now on, you hear?" Caught in the lamplight, Lillian's bright face took Maggie back to a time when she'd feared her child would never believe again. If she could smile, after the burdens she'd carried on her young shoulders, Maggie could find the courage to start over again. (*Forgive me, Jesus, for doubtin'*.) "Chile, you are a pleasure to me and I am proud of you."

"I have you to bear in mind, I'm to do *light work* —by orders of the First Lady."

Maggie's laugh gladdened Lillian, even gladdened the people on the next fire escape, who didn't know what the joke was. "Lil'yan, I think you got more devil in you than you can cast out."

Some days later the housekeeping staff were at their chores, Maggie and the maids cleaning and dusting, Mercer and the housemen in their perpetual act of rearranging furniture. Although the President and the First Lady were elsewhere in the building, no one spoke. Lillian, cross-legged on the floor, polishing the carved legs of a teakwood table, was the first to hear the running footsteps. The Secret Service man came charging up the grand staircase, gun drawn.

"Everybody . . . out of the way!"

It shocked them. They'd seen Murdoch before. He'd seemed mild enough out on the south lawn when the President played medicine ball, or accompanying the First Family in their automobile. Now, waving the gun, he was a lighted fuse.

"Back, get back!"

Maggie, Mercer, and the others scurried out of the way into the T-corridor. From the back stairs a second Secret Service man, his gun at ready, reached center hall. Finding it empty except for Murdoch, he called down the shaft: "Clear. Bring them up." For the next moments, all that was heard was the sound of the elevator bringing up a tense, distressed President and First Lady, buttressed by two more Secret Service men. The four guards formed a cordon and escort to the privacy of west sitting hall. Two of the men entered with them and closed the door. Murdoch and the other man—Peters—remained outside on guard at the presidential suite.

Lillian cautiously peered around the corner. "Now what was that all about?"

Minutes later, Chief Usher Ike Hoover summoned housemen, maids, doormen, gardeners, chauffeurs, laundry workers, kitchen help—everyone within sound of voice or buzzer. He faced them, stiff-backed, informing them that the President had been endangered.

"A man—a stranger—walked into the State Dining Room during the formal luncheon and threatened the President. How he got in—whether through a momentarily unguarded door, with tradesmen, workmen, tourists—it doesn't matter. He got in." Nothing like this had ever happened before during Ike Hoover's tenure, and he was determined it would never happen again. "Security is being tightened. Get used to seeing the Secret Service around. The tours are indefinitely canceled. Everyone, including the servants, must be identified before entering the building. As further protection, whenever the President and the First Lady move to or from their rooms, there will be a signal: three bells for the President, two for the First Lady. At the sound of the bells, drop whatever you're doing, no matter what it is, and disappear from view. *Disappear.*"

The day following the intruder incident the Lincoln bed was on the move again. "Poor Mr. Lincoln," Mercer said, as he, O'Hara, and Fraser guided the unwieldy headboard around the sharp bend from the attic stairs to the second floor. "No wonder his ghost gets restless—cain't find a place to rest his poor head." They passed Secret Service men Murdoch and Peters at their posts outside the President's and First Lady's bedrooms. Mercer and his crew had the headboard exactly in the middle of center hall when the bells rang out.

Murdoch and Peters were instantly on their feet. *"Move."*

Unused to the new discipline, Lillian at the cart, getting an armload of linen—Bridget, coming out of a guest bathroom, with bucket and brush—Moira, dusting furniture—Maggie, running a carpet sweeper—all froze in their tracks.

"Get out of sight."

A second bell. An instant's confusion, then Maggie, Moira, Bridget, buckets and all, making a beeline for the backstairs corridor, suddenly decided to duck into the service closet. Lillian, starting after them, realized she had an armload of linen. Habit ran her back to put the linen on the cart.

There was no way or time to hide, disguise, or jettison the Lincoln headboard. Standing it upright, Mercer,

Fraser, and O'Hara backed it to the wall and sand-wiched themselves behind it, invisible except for their hands on the sides and their feet below.

On the third bell, Lillian hop-skipped on her crutch to the closet. In this jammed, dark space of buckets, mops, and brooms the four women clumped together. Maggie's hand extended upward through the tangle of arms, trying to find the light switch.

President Hoover came out of his room, head down, in deep, troubled thought. Murdoch followed him to the elevator, where Ike Hoover waited. About to enter, the President looked around, momentarily uncertain. "My papers . . . I had a file folder . . ."

"Would it be the one in your hand, sir?"

"Oh . . . thank you . . . yes . . ."

Peters followed him into the elevator. Usher Ike Hoover took them below. Murdoch watched their descent. "All right, everybody." The captives slipped out of the closet. "Somebody ought to tell 'em we're on the same side," Lillian complained.

Before going back to his post Murdoch had a sharp word with Mercer. This being the first time, he wouldn't take exception. But in the future: "No matter what you're carrying—put it down and *evaporate.*"

"Yes, sir."

As they placed the Lincoln headboard in the Treaty Room and went back to the attic for the footboard and slats, Mercer wondered how Fraser liked his new job of houseman.

"Sure different. On the door, I never had to hide behind a bed."

Now, added to the frustration of maintaining silence was the unnatural state of being under constant scrutiny. Even "at ease," sitting on a chair reading his newspaper, Murdoch's eyes caught every move that went on around him. Lillian was convinced she'd never get used to seeing Secret Service around, in spite of what the usher had told them.

During a lull in the morning's work, Fraser had a moment with Maggie at the service closet. "Wonder, could I talk with you some?"

"Sure, Fraser, but keep your voice down . . . what's the problem?"

"Well, with my cut in pay and the money I send home to my kin, I can't make out. Been thinkin'— you got Emmett's old room and it's empty. Might be, you could take me in to board."

Fraser moved in the following Sunday. It felt good to Maggie, almost like having a son around, not the same as had it been Emmett, but close. Fraser was good company, always pleasant, never asked for much.

And he brought a radio. Now Joe Penner's "Wanna buy a duck?" and Red Skelton's Clem Kadiddlehopper livened up the place with laughter. There had to be a state dinner to keep Maggie away from "The Lone Ranger." Lillian, working as hard as she did, only went out once, maybe twice, a week—but not Fraser. He was conversant with the beat of every jazz joint up on U Street. Coming home late, he'd more often than not find Maggie asleep on the sofa, the radio still on, buzzing empty air, having long since signed off with "The Star-Spangled Banner." She'd come awake, no matter how quietly he closed the door.

"Fraser," she'd greet him, shaking her head, "when you goin' to grow up, start thinkin' what you goin' to be? You got potential. You cain't jus' dance your life away . . ."

Invariably the answer was the same. "Time not come yet for me to worry, Maggie."

1932

They called themselves the Bonus Expeditionary Force. A veteran by the name of Waters who'd been in Mexico with Pershing was their leader. At first a small group, they started out from Portland, Oregon, but during the months it took them to cross the country by boxcar, walking, and rattletrap auto—sometimes being denied the right to cross state lines, other times being aided into a bordering state by one that wanted to be rid of them—this ragged army's ranks mushroomed. By the time they reached Washington, there were close to twenty thousand of them.

They'd come to the nation's capital for their bonus money. "NOW," they shouted. They wanted the soldiers' bonus paid while the need was great, instead of waiting for the bonds to mature in 1945, by which time, as they saw it, most of them would have starved to death.

The administration, fearing what a disastrous rush on the Treasury would do to the sick economy, was dead set against payoff. A brigade-sized group of Bonus marchers, in threadbare vestiges of uniform, medals tarnished but still shining in the sun, marched past the White House. President Hoover didn't come out. The marchers lobbied Congress, and were hustled away.

Feelings ran high. Makeshift signs appeared: HEROES IN FRANCE, BUMS IN U.S. In the newspapers, the words "Bolshevik" and "anarchist" were commonplace. Headlines informed that the Bonus Army was rampant with Communists.

Whatever their politics, they camped in vacant government buildings, parks, alleys. Their main body dug in across the river at Anacostia Flats, existing in tents, lean-tos, carcasses of old atuomobiles, anything that would put a roof over their heads. For a brief time, while the weather was favorable, some residents drove across the bridge on weekends just to get a look at them, in the same way that Washingtonians, during the early days of the Civil War, had carriaged out to enjoy a picnic while observing the distant battle.

Once the novelty wore off, people went back and forgot about the Bonus Army. Or tried to.

Capitol Hill wore blinders, hoping they would go away.

June came in, stinking hot, humid. Electrical storms lighted Anacostia Flats by night. Rain turned it into a bog with flies, mosquitoes, rotting garbage, and flooded latrines. And still the Bonus Marchers kept coming; those who were already there stayed.

The heat spell seemed as if was never going to break. Fraser sat in front of the open window in his undershirt, barefoot, mending his socks and listening to the radio. Static erased the music. He turned the dial in search of some comedy, but an authority-charged voice caught, held him:

> The ragged and hungry men massed for hours in front of the Capitol waiting to learn their fate . . .

Fraser put the darning egg in the toe of the sock and leaned closer to the lamp, carefully threading the yarn in and out, forming a basket weave to fill the hole.

> The mood of the more than seven thousand veterans had been somewhat hopeful, since the House had voted in favor of paying the bonus immediately . . .

Maggie and Lillian heard the same words from radios as they came down the street, dead tired from a long arduous day. "Evenin'," they nodded to neighbors in windows; "Evenin'," to those who sat out in front.

> When the tally was announced—that the Senate had voted by a better than three to one majority against the measure—

Fraser, hearing them ascend the stairs, opened the door. "Expected you two'd get home before me. We got through in the pantry early. Been worryin' 'bout you."

Maggie sat down to catch her breath. "That checkroom's a godsend—though rich folks must be havin' a tryin' time, too—tips keep gettin' smaller."

"Made some iced tea," Fraser said. "You set, I'll get it."

"Chile, do me a kindness, take off my shoes."

Lillian eased off the heavy black shoes. "Mama, you workin' too hard. You got to remember you not as young as you used to be." Maggie shushed her and leaned closer, intent on catching the words from the radio.

> The crowd of desolate men who had come across the country by boxcar seemed stunned that the Senate of the United States had voted against them . . .

Fraser stepped in from the kitchen with the iced tea and listened solemnly.

> Then slowly, as though lost, they began to disperse back to the makeshift shantytowns that have been their homes since they ar-rived at the capital—where conditions under which they exist are deplorable . . . These people are eating out of garbage cans—

"Oh, Lord, keep an eye on those poor folks . . ." Maggie's eyes were closed, her face a mask of ex-haustion.
"Come on, Mama, let's get you to bed."
"I can manage, chile."
"You sure you not gettin' sick?"
"Jus' tired, chile, tired." Lillian led Maggie to the bedroom. Fraser went back to his darning.

> It is expected that there will be few takers of the government's rumored offer of a free railroad ticket back home. In the next few weeks, more and more men are likely to converge on the city of Washington . . . homeless, hungry, angry . . . The word heard mostly on Capitol Hill these days is "siege" . . .

Fraser turned off the radio. He no longer felt in the mood for comedy.

The colors broke into whirling chunks, a kaleido-
scope, then bled off like rain washing a palette of oil
paints. Maggie grabbed hold of the dividing pole in the
armoire until the dizziness lessened and the colors came
back to what they were: dresses, a hundred or more
evening and afternoon gowns: brocades, silks, satins,
with matching shoes for each one that filled the massive
cabinet built to house the overflow of Mrs. Hoover's
wardrobe.

Maggie looked quickly across the room, afraid that
someone might have observed her momentary weak-
ness, but the activity that had been going on for an
hour was still in progress. The First Lady stood before a
full-length mirror having a gown altered, while Lillian,
pincushion at her wrist, moved, set pins, adjusting
seams. Two secretaries had chairs pulled to the double
bed, which, of late, served as a desk; it was completely covered with papers, photographs, correspon-
dence, all relating to the restoration of the Monroe
Room. Mrs. Long stood by with her clipboard and
pencil, correlating menus; Mrs. Hoover orchestrated
this multiple activity with ease. "And for Thursday
night?"

Mrs. Long consulted her list. "Caviar in artichoke à
la Russe, mock turtle soup—then I thought garnished
saddle of mutton with currant jelly, potatoes Anna,
buttered beans . . ." She waited for approval or disapproval. Mrs. Hoover waved Lillian away, reset two of
the pins, then hand-signaled her to resume the job.

"Saddle of mutton will be fine. Let's add mushrooms
à la Périgord. We haven't served that before to the
diplomatic corps, have we?"

Mrs. Long flipped back through the pages of her
notebook. "No, madam, we haven't."

In deliberate succession the First Lady dealt with the
fabric for the Monroe chairs not having arrived, directed one of the secretaries to telephone the mill in
the morning, had the other read the guest list for an
upcoming tea, and reset another of Lillian's pins.

Three bells sounded. The President was on the move.

The First Lady frowned, puzzled that he would return to his room at only four in the afternoon. But perhaps he would rest; he desperately needed it. Yes, that must be why he'd come back so early . . . to rest before dinner. He remained on her mind, but she had obligations to fulfill. "Kentucky string beans, mushrooms, what else?"

"Cutlet of sweetbreads à la Theodoria, lettuce salad, and for dessert, frozen almond soufflé with meringue."

Maggie moved the blue cut velvet evening gown trimmed in sable on the rod, and made a note on her clipboard. The dizziness had left her a trifle apprehensive. She took several deep breaths, felt better, and told herself it was just a momentary thing.

"Fourteen dinners and receptions scheduled for the rest of the month," Mrs. Long was saying, to which the First Lady replied, "Well, at least tonight I'm going to be comfortable, I'll be wearing my gray lace."

Maggie quickly turned to the back pages of her clipboard. "Excuse me, madam, but you wore the gray lace when the ambassador from Argentina came to dinner, and he's one of your guests this evenin' . . ." Mrs. Hoover sighed wearily. "All right, Maggie, you tell me what I can wear."

Maggie brought a flowered chiffon gown on its hanger to Mrs. Hoover. "You not had this on since the King of Siam, early this year. None of the people on your guest list tonight ever saw you in it." Mrs. Hoover studied the gown, dissatisfied.

"Men are luckier. One tailcoat and white tie looks the same as another. But I suppose if the President can stand all the aggravation he has to put up with, I can certainly wear a dress I dislike." Three bells again echoed in the hall. "Oh, dear . . . he's going back to the office . . . It's the Bonus Army, that's all he can think of . . . walks the floor nights . . . the election coming up, the hateful things in the press, the economy . . ." Somewhat impatiently she gestured Lillian that the dress-fitting session was over. Maggie helped Mrs. Hoover out of the pinned gown into a comfortable negligee. "Bonus Marchers . . . if any of you ever see them on the street, don't go near them. General MacArthur has warned the President that they're not veterans at all, but Communists fomenting revolution."

One of the secretaries, sorting through papers, let out a startled gasp. "Oh, madam . . . a dreadful thing has happened . . ." She held out two engraved invitations. "I just noticed the invitation for tonight's dinner and the one for Thursday have the same date. Instead of two hundred guests tonight, there will be *five hundred!*"

Laundresses, maids, housemen, doormen, even gardeners were pressed into emergency service. Servants came pouring out of the White House and moved off in every direction, by foot, auto, trolley, each with a shopping list and money. It was an organized assault on every grocery store, meat market, and pastry shop in the area. In preparation for the expected deluge of food, every pot and pan in the kitchen was out, ready. Water boiled. Ovens heated up. Every piece of silver was checked and polished. Mercer set up an ironing board in the staff dining room. Lillian, pressing and stacking napkins, recognized some she'd mended six, seven years back.

Butlers set up extra tables extending beyond the State Dining Room out into the grand foyer. Ushers were pressed into writing and rearranging place cards. For a while, moving the party out of doors was considered, it being a hot night. But Usher Ike Hoover diplomatically suggested to the First Lady this might not be wise, with the Bonus Army out there.

The menu of beef Wellington had to be scrapped. Instead, the improvised menu was dinner all-American: fried chicken, ham, potato salad, coleslaw, and pie à la mode (all kinds of pie, since they soon exhausted the District of apple pies).

"Looks like we goin' get old Wellington's beef for lunch tomorrow," Jackson commented as he and Luke Henry (whom everybody now called Li'l Henry because of his size) returned with sacks full of freshly butchered kosher chickens. "And tomorrow and tomorrow," Mays added, putting his hams to the growing pile on the staff dining table and turning his talents to the paring knife and washtubs full of potatoes.

Within the hour the staff table was loaded with bags of food, efficiently opened and on the move. "Henry Ford sure be proud of us, the assembly line we got here."

"Except they all laid off, up there in Detroit."

No one noticed Coates when he first came back. He put his packages down and sat on a chair near the wall. It was Fraser, just come in from the kitchen to pick up another bagful of cabbages for shredding, who noticed the blood on Coates' forehead, and his torn sleeve.

"You hurt, Coates . . . what happened?" Maggie quickly brought a wet compress from the kitchen. They helped him out of his jacket. He kept shaking his head, trying to wipe away the memory.

"They was hungry . . . two, three fellas on the corner there. I come out the store, asked me could I give 'em some. I said, yes, but not much—wasn't mine. We hungry, that's all they said. Grabbed at it, I tried to hold on, got one sack away from me, knocked me down . . . They was jus' hungry, plain hungry . . . My God . . ."

Very late that same night, Maggie, Lillian, and Fraser dragged home. For the first time, negotiating the apartment stairs was too taxing for Maggie and she allowed herself to lean on Fraser. "Workin' the kitchen . . . pantry . . . checkroom, same night—too much."

The evening had taught Fraser one thing. "I'm for sure no waiter."

At the upper landing Maggie stopped to catch her breath. "You been doin' that a lot lately, Mama. I worry 'bout you."

"Frank to admit it, chile, I'm feelin' my years." As they came down the dimly lighted corridor they saw a man sitting on the floor, leaning against their door, asleep. He looked like a bag of old clothes, a derelict. Fraser cautioned Maggie and Lillian back and approached the man, touched him with the toe of his shoe.

"Hey, fella."

The bag of clothes stirred, the man opened his eyes and was immediately awake. "Gee, hope I didn't scare you." His speech bore the flat accent of the Middle West that Maggie had come to know during the Harding period. He got to his feet, pulled off his cap, revealing sandy hair, smiled apologetically. "Evenin'."

Fraser sniffed. "Evenin'? It's past three in the mornin'."

"Oh, sorry . . . name's Roy. Roy Clayton." He dug into the pocket of his worn jacket for a scrap of paper. "Been waitin' here, hopin' to find an old Army buddy—was in a hospital in France with him. Been three places, they told me he moved here. Emmett Rogers, know him?"

Maggie nudged Fraser out of the way. "I'm his mama, you come right on in, son."

The four of them had coffee together in the kitchen. Tired as she was, Maggie insisted on staying at the table to hear firsthand of the friendship between this young man and her son. Roy Clayton told them he'd come to town with the Bonus Army. Too bad he wouldn't get to see Emmett, but he felt he knew Maggie and Lillian from all the snapshots Emmett had shared with him in the hospital.

"How long you been over to that Bonus camp across the river?" Fraser asked him.

" 'Bout a week now."

Maggie, who could no longer keep her eyes open, insisted that he stay the night with them, what was left of it.

"Don't want to put you out, ma'am."

"Emmett would want you to stay. Lil'yan, get a pillow and blanket for the sofa."

Fraser said he would get it.

Lillian poured another cup of coffee for their guest and brought out bread, milk, and meat from the icebox. They talked some about Emmett; Clayton was of the opinion he was lucky to be out in Arizona, way things were in this city.

"Not always like this," Lillian defended.

"Maybe it's just us," he conceded, "but town sure don't seem too friendly. Except for you folks . . . Talk is, they're planning to run us out, now that Congress killed the bonus . . . but I just can't believe they'd call out soldiers against us, not after us fightin' the war and all . . ."

"You hardly touched your food . . ."

"Oh, yeah . . ." He took a careful forkful, smiled a bit sheepishly, then dug in with the eagerness of a man whose stomach hadn't been appeased in days.

Lillian leaned on her elbows and watched him. "Where you from?"

He smiled at her. "You know, those pictures Emmett showed me never did tell you was so pretty."

She flushed. "You didn't answer my question."

"Southwest corner Nebraska . . . farm . . . been in our family more than a hundred years, belongs to the bank now. My brothers, father, and me tenant-farmin' our own land. Had to shoot our milk cows, couldn't raise enough grain to feed 'em. Land's goin' back to dust, that's what."

Fraser was in the doorway. "Bed's ready, Clayton."

"Call me Roy."

It wasn't in Fraser's nature to be resistant to people, and he had to get it out in the open. "Mind if I ask you somethin' personal, Roy?"

"Shoot, no."

"You one those Bolshevik reds General MacArthur talks 'bout in the papers?"

"Me? Hell—excuse me, ma'am—I don't know nothin' 'bout politics . . . just know I served in the Army, brothers, too. Train carryin' the Bonus Army come through, I went down, talked to some of the guys— served with a couple of 'em—need that bonus money somethin' fierce . . . If there's Communists around— heard there was, but I don't know one from the other— they haven't bothered me none, I haven't bothered them. All I know, there's guys out there at the camp got their families with 'em—livin' in tents—crates—chicken coops . . . Starvin' . . ."

Lillian turned urgently to Fraser. "We got to get some food to those people."

"Oh, no." Roy Clayton wouldn't hear of it. "Can't let you folks share what little you got."

"How does beef Wellington and almond soufflé sound to you? 'Course, it's all leftovers."

"You mean—from the White House?"

Fraser knew he should have tried to deter her. And he wasn't sure himself why he was going along with it. But the next day, when four o'clock came around and Lillian covered her sewing machine and came down the back stairs, Fraser was waiting for her with the rattletrap he'd borrowed from a friend. They filled the trunk with food from a raid on the White House refrigerator. Then they and Roy Clayton drove across the river to the Bonus Army.

Not more than five minutes after Lillian left the White House, Maggie ascended the attic stairs to the sewing room, talking as she climbed each wearisome step. "Lil'yan, after I finish straightenin' Miz Hoover's dressin' room, we can go home, get a little rest before we have to come back . . ." She came into the room, surprised to find it empty. Way it was tidied told her Lillian had gone for the day, which didn't set at all right with Maggie. Not to have been told Lillian was leaving gave Maggie the empty feeling of being left out. Like this morning: getting up without being coaxed, after only two-three hours sleep, making breakfast for Emmett's friend Roy. Him, all combed and shaved, thanks to Fraser giving him a brush and what have you. The two of them high-tailing it off, him walking her to the White House. *What could Lillian be thinkin' 'bout, him bein' a white body; troubles they'd be askin' for* . . . Completing the errand that had brought her up, she removed from the dress form the evening gown that Lillian had altered for Mrs. Hoover and carried it below.

She had just stepped out of the backstairs corridor, heading for west sitting hall, when two bells rang out, bringing the Secret Service men on duty to attention. Maggie scurried back to the service closet and

waited out the all clear, as Mrs. Hoover, accompanied
by Secret Service man Peters and Mrs. Long with her
clipboard, took the elevator downstairs.

Secret Service man Murdoch went back to his chair
and newspaper, barely glancing up as Maggie came out
of the closet and again started across the center hall.
Neither one of them was prepared for what happened
next.

Without warning, the door to the oval study opened
and the President came out. He was in shirt sleeves, a
packet of official papers in his hand. Caught out in
the open, undecided which way to turn, Maggie froze
in her tracks. Murdoch was instantly on his feet, but it
was directly to Maggie that the President walked. She
hadn't laid eyes on him in weeks; he was at his office
when she came on the floor mornings, and with his
cabinet and other advisers far into the night. She was
shocked to see how stooped, lined, he'd become. He
was looking right at her, yet he seemed not to see her.

"There . . . were no bells, Mr. Pres'dent . . ." she
stammered in apology.

"Mrs. Hoover . . . where is she?"

Petrified, almost tongue-tied, she managed to reply,
"I think, sir—down to the State Dinin' Room—to check
on arrangements, sir . . . for dinner . . ."

He turned and went back to his study. She hung the
evening gown in Mrs. Hoover's dressing room, and as
quickly as she could, went down the back stairs.

Mercer was in the State Dining Room sitting alone at
the table, scissoring a piece of cardboard into the shape
of a shoe sole. When Maggie told him of the encounter,
he couldn't get over it.

"*Spoke* to you? Pres'dent actually *said* somethin' to
you?"

Maggie poured herself a cup of coffee from the urn
and sat down with him. "I was caught right out there,
couldn't get back to the closet, didn't know what on
earth to do . . ."

"My stars and body, *spoke* to you . . . 'Most four
years, you the onliest one of us he's said a blessed
thing to . . ." Mercer fit the cardboard insole into his

worn-through shoe. It was still a shade too big. He trimmed it some more.

"You seen Lil'yan?" Maggie asked.

He answered cautiously. "Seems I did, while ago. Finished her work, left with Fraser, I believe."

"You sure? Wasn't with a young white fella?"

"Believe he was with 'em too."

"Mercer . . . were they carryin' food . . . for that Bonus Army?"

He shrugged, noncommittal. "Well, you know . . . everybody always totes sometimes, Maggie."

"Don't lie to me, Mercer."

"Maggie, those people are hungry."

"Lord, Lord, I know . . . but the way the Pres'dent so against 'em . . . Was he to find out, Lil'yan would lose her job. Fraser, too."

"Well, he won't find out—unless you tell him, since you the one talks to him." This time the cardboard fit fine. Mercer left it in and tied his shoe. Maggie leaned on her hand and thought how hard it was to know what was the right thing to do, and what was the wrong. "Jus' pray nobody gets hurt . . ."

Lillian, Fraser, and Roy Clayton weren't the only ones on their way to Anacostia Flats.

Earlier that same afternoon, Major General Douglas MacArthur, with his aide Major Dwight D. Eisenhower at his side and leading a contingent of cavalry and infantry equipped with tanks and machine guns, conducted a mop-up operation along Pennsylvania Avenue, routing out small pockets of Bonus Army squatters from unoccupied government buildings.

Then they turned their attention to the larger problem and crossed the river into Anacostia.

11

The sky was on fire. Smoke rose in ugly black belches and cut off the moon. When the rapacious tongue of flame reached another tin lizzie's gas tank, its explosion and the cries of anguish from those who'd hoped to drive that rusted metal home were straight out of the *Inferno*.

Fraser stood at the window of the apartment he shared with Maggie and Lillian and watched the horizon burn. His torn, scorched, and soot-filled clothing, the crude arm bandage where blood had already dried, were his *croix de combat*. The wound would heal, the clothes be discarded, but never, as long as he lived, would he forget the cacophony of screams as cavalry and tanks rode in, knocking over lean-tos, putting the torch to the possessions of the dispossessed.

Roy Clayton had had the worst of it. Attempting to protect Lillian, he'd come in direct contact with a cavalry boot, been knocked to the ground and almost trampled by a horse. He sat slumped in a chair, dabbing at his cheek with a compress where a purple bruise was spreading. Lillian hurried in from the kitchen with a pan of water and soft cloth in which she'd wrapped a piece of ice. Gently she bathed the gash

305

above his eyebrow. "That hurt you? I'm sorry . . ."

His wound was deeper; to the soul. "The stompin',
the beatin'," he said in disbelief. "People runnin' like
rats . . . My God, those children . . ." He started to
cry but regained control. Lillian wiped the dried blood
from his face.

Fraser turned away from the window. "Lil'yan,
there's a dinner tonight, don't forget. We gotta go
back, we workin' the pantry."

"I be there."

Fraser went in to clean up.

"You go ahead," Roy Clayton urged Lillian, "don't
let me hold you up."

"You sure you goin' to be all right?"

"Likely to have a powerful headache, I guess. Right
now, don't feel too much of anything." He touched her
ripped, dangling sleeve. "Too bad your dress got tore
. . . sure you ain't hurt?"

"I'm all right . . . scared for a while." The control
she'd maintained threatened to desert her. "Sorry it
worked out this way, nobody even gettin' to eat anythin' we brought."

"You're a fine soldier." It was the nearest he could
come to the personal statement he wanted to make.

"You stay here and rest now, Roy. I'm obliged to go,
but I won't be late . . ." Lillian and Fraser changed
their clothes and went back to the White House. For a
long time Roy Clayton stood at the window watching
the sky burn.

Mercer's conscience had troubled him from the moment Lillian and Fraser rode away with that Roy Clayton. Even if he'd tried to stop them, they wouldn't
have listened. And it wasn't that he disagreed with
what they were doing: hungry people have to be fed.
It was the soldiers he saw on Pennsylvania Avenue,
heading in the same direction of the camp, that worried him sick.

Every time the door of the changing room opened
he hoped it would be Fraser. This time it was Roach.

Before that, Coates and Dixon. And then Mays, limping in. It was common routine now to come back to the White House evenings and change into livery. As he put on the formal trousers and boiled shirt, Mercer admitted to himself that he was getting a little old for these long hours.

Mays, already changed, sat on a bench near his locker, shoes off, rubbing his feet. "These corns a visitation of the devil. I sure must have sinned."

"You still cuttin' your own calluses, Mays? You oughta go see a doctor." But Mercer knew it was useless to try to convince Mays. Always got the same answer out of him, "What I need a doctor for, to trim corns?"

Dixon put studs in his shirt. "You hear what happened to Tent City?"

"Didn't have to hear. Jus' look down toward the river, see it burnin'."

Mercer put his foot on the bench, leaned down to tie his shoe, and heard the door open. This time, much to his relief, it was Fraser. Never seen him wear such a dismal face before. And the way he carried his arm Mercer knew, without being told, that under the sleeve was an injury. He followed him over to his locker, leaning in close so that the others wouldn't hear. "Everythin' turn out all right?"

"Considerin' the circumstances, all parties are okay."

"You goin' be able to work?"

"I'll do all right."

The others hadn't paid him any attention. Coates and Dixon were at the mirror, tying their white ties. Roach, who had hurried into his uniform, took a pair of shoes out of the paper sack he'd brought in with him. Putting one shoe on and carrying the other, he walked lopsided over to Coates and Dixon.

"Now," he said, "let's see." Putting his weight on the shoeless foot, he was shorter than the other two men. Stepping onto the shod foot gave him two added inches. He grinned: he was now exactly as tall as they.

"Say, shoemaker did a fine job there," Coates complimented. Fraser turned from his locker. "What'd you do, Roach? Have somethin' put inside?"

"Had 'em built up."

"How come?"

"You not heard the latest order? You guys in the pantry are lucky. New order from on high—all butlers got to be the same height."

Mays rubbed his feet. "While Rome burns."

"Huh?"

"Somethin' I read in the papers."

Roach finished tying his shoes and moved to the mirror, where his eye level was now the same as Coates' and Dixon's. He couldn't stop grinning. When he first heard the order, he'd run like a scared rabbit down the street till he found a shoemaker who'd do it for him right then. Now everything was hunky-dory. He wouldn't be losing his job.

The three butlers were still tying their ties when the door opened and Li'l Henry's face joined them in the mirror. A good five, six inches shorter than the rest of them, no shoe could build him up. From the smile on his face he was blissfully ignorant of what was in store for him.

"Evenin', everybody . . ."

"Evenin', Henry."

He went to his locker, took out his liveried outfit, and began to change. "Boy, I tell you, sure is great to be workin' . . . Told my wife, you go to the grocery store and tell 'em we goin' be able to pay the bill . . . You know, I have me a little life-insurance policy, thought before I come to work here I'd have to do what some those Wall Street men been doin'—you know, go up to the roof of a tall buildin', you know, so my family'd have something to eat on . . . I tell you, I do enjoy this job." He felt the silence, turned to see their grim faces. Foreboding gripped him. "What's the matter? Somethin' the matter . . ."

Coates found it hard to look at him. "Henry . . . want you to know we all sorry . . . anythin' we can do . . ."

Henry looked from one to the other, trying to search out the meaning, panic building in him. "Somethin' wrong . . . I don't have the job . . . I lost the job . . . didn't I?"

Nobody wanted to be the one to cut him down. Mercer appointed himself to the task, "There's rules, Henry . . . always changin'. 'Fore you come back on this evenin', we got a new rule passed down to us . . ."

"Don't want to hear it . . . don't tell me nothin', don't tell me . . . don't want to hear it . . ." He hung his liveried outfit back in the locker. Carefully put on his suit jacket that was shiny at the elbow and fraying at the lapels. Meticulously put each button through the proper hole, keeping the lid on his inner scream.

"Wait, Henry, you got somethin' on your coat." Mercer caught him at the door, made a pretense of picking a thread off his jacket, while stuffing a dollar bill into his pocket. Li'l Henry walked away. They could hear his footsteps fading down the corridor.

Mays put his shoes on. "These feet goin' be the death of me."

The apartment was dark when Maggie and Lillian returned from the evening's work in the pantry. Maggie thought, as they stepped quietly in from the corridor, that Roy Clayton had probably gone to sleep. No question he needed the rest after his ordeal. But Lillian sensed, as she tentatively called out, "Clayton . . . Roy . . ." that he was gone.

The blanket was neatly folded on the sofa, pillow on top. And there was a lined piece of paper with careful handwriting. Lillian carried it to the lamp.

"He leave? Go back home?"

Lillian's voice was strained. "Said to thank you, Mama, for bein' so kind to him."

"That's nice."

"Said please tell Emmett he hopes he sees him some day. Said . . ." She turned away to read the remaining words to herself: *I'm proud we met. I'm leaving my address, as you can see, should you ever choose to write. Or come out our way. Wish we could be in the*

*same town, like to see you. Don't know how you feel,
but I knew right off I liked you. A lot. Like I said,
pictures Emmett showed me weren't no way as pretty
as you. Your friend, Roy Clayton."*

"He was a fine young man," Maggie ventured, then
thought with relief, *What was I worryin' about* . . .
Conscious of Lillian's need to be left alone, Maggie
went into the kitchen and put on the coffee.

Lillian stood at the window. The fire from Anacostia
Flats was now a dull red glow in the distant sky. Like
Roy Clayton, it would disappear.

The results of the election of '32 surprised no one.
Herbert Hoover's stumping tour, asking the country for
more time to implement his Reconstruction Finance
Corporation and other remedial programs, failed. Newspapers wrote that he was worn out and so were his
ideas. His voice went out on the air, but few listened.
A meteor had shot across the political skies by the
name of Franklin Delano Roosevelt.

With Inauguration Day nipping at their heels, the
staff was once again run ragged. Trunks, crates, boxes
crowded center hall. Rugs were rolled up, paintings
removed from walls, carefully prepared for shipping.
Precious objets d'art, handled like eggshells, were
wrapped in cotton batting and placed in excelsior-lined
containers. As soon as Mercer and Fraser, in constant
action with the dolly, took a trunk or crate below,
another trunk or crate grew in its place. Maggie, the
only one Mrs. Hoover would trust with her personal
wardrobe, had been at it for two weeks straight. With
Lillian's aid each gown, each purse, each shoe was
separately wrapped and labeled. By Thursday of the
second week—with only Saturday to go to the Inauguration—they were still at it.

The First Lady's bedroom was an obstacle course:
wardrobe and steamer trunks open, the bed and chairs
covered with items yet to be packed. Lillian brought
an evening wrap and two gowns from the armoire.
Maggie was carefully cushioning the folds of a gown
with tissue paper and laying it, gently as a newborn in-

fant, into the trunk when a sudden rush of blood to her head threatened to topple her in after it. She held on to the lid until the moment passed. Straightening up, she let a slight moan escape her.

"Mama, when you goin' sit down? More than nine hours today, all this walkin' and foldin', not good for you."

"Got to get the job done, chile."

It seemed to Maggie (although she didn't utter it to anyone else) that Mrs. Hoover was dragging her heels, taking her husband's defeat hard. Like Mrs. Harding, she was reluctant to leave. During the electioneering months Maggie had seen the First Lady, like the President, reach the point of exhaustion, had listened to Mr. Hoover's voice on the radio as he struggled to be heard over dissenters who tried to shout him down. He'd sounded old and—long before the votes were cast— vanquished.

"My husband will live to do great things for his country, you'll see," Mrs. Hoover said vehemently to Maggie the day she and the President returned from casting their futile votes out in Palo Alto, California.

"I'm sure he will, ma'am," Maggie had assured her. But nothing seemed to bring comfort to the First Lady.

Mrs. Hoover moved restlessly throughout the White House, observing the packing activity that meant going back to California where they had begun. On the third floor, secretaries were working practically around the clock, cataloging and preparing files for shipment. The second floor was almost stripped bare of a lifetime of collected items that had turned the many unfamiliar places her husband's profession had taken them, into homes. She watched some eighteenth-century Peking glass being carried out. Before she returned to her bedroom she walked the length of center hall, indelibly imprinting images on her memory: the graceful arches, the room where Lincoln had slept, the grand stairs. The oval room where her husband had labored throughout so many nights, attempting to use his organizing genius to save the country, all to no avail. Then she went into the room that had been hers for almost four years.

Lillian was handing Maggie a magnificently ornate silk Chinese jacket. "No, don't pack that . . . not yet . . ." Mrs. Hoover took it from her, studying it, running her hand with affection over the ultrafine stitches of the embroidered dragon. "I'd forgotten I had this . . ." But she was no longer talking to them. Something about this handful of silk impelled her to her husband's quarters.

Mays was cutting the President's hair. As usual, Mr. Hoover sat straight-backed, silent. It crossed Mays' mind that this was his last chance to try to engage the President in conversation and pick up the money wagered on who would get him to speak. (Actually Maggie had already accomplished this, but she'd never put money in the pot.) Mays was mulling a possible opening comment when the First Lady came in and his chance was gone. (Guess now they'd have to split the pot, or jointly have a high old time on the seven dollars.) He ran the clippers across the President's neck. Chin to his chest, Hoover raised his eyes, nodded a greeting to his wife. She held the jacket out to him.

"Remember this, Bert?"

As he studied the mellow silk a slow smile grew on his face. "I do indeed . . ."

"Know how old it is, don't you? I bought it in China."

"Our honeymoon . . . got to be thirty years."

"Thirty-two. I wore it in Tientsin the day they started shelling the compound. I remember thinking, *If I get shot, I'll get blood on it* . . . and I didn't want that to happen."

"Some way to start a marriage, eh, Lou?"

She sat on the bed, ran her fingers over the rosewood of the Lincoln footboard. "Never thought I'd get nostalgic about the Boxer Rebellion."

Mays brushed off loose hairs, powdered the President's neck, and moved away to prepare the shaving mug. They seemed unaware of his presence. The jacket had taken them out of this room and back through time.

"Dodging bullets . . . In a way, my dear, easier to

cope with than trying to hold a country together against depression and panic."

"They were good years, weren't they, Bert?"

"The mining years? Great years . . . Things were simple. You go where the minerals are, find them, dig them out of the ground. In government, it's not enough to know the way . . ."

She felt his pain. "People will recognize your contribution . . ."

"Doesn't matter, as long as things get better."

"You've done great things, Bert. Why, half the children of the world would be dead today, if you hadn't gone where you were needed, fighting famine . . ."

"There were children with the Bonus Army, Lou . . ." He closed his eyes against the image. "MacArthur . . ." His voice faded for a moment, then he resumed. "When men regard themselves as men of destiny, they are hard to restrain . . . Burning men and their families out . . . I never wanted that." He slowly shook his head. "I have no talent for persuasion. Not the fervor of a Wilson, nor the spellbinding tongue of a Roosevelt. He's a Pied Piper, that man . . . the people will follow him anywhere." He reached out, took her hand. "Thou hast been a good companion, Lou."

Her smile trembled. "You haven't said 'thee' and 'thou' in years, Bert."

"Did I say that?"

"Yes, thou did . . . just now. Did thee not mean it?"

"The Quaker in me . . ." he said ruefully, "Urging me, as in my youth, to sit silent, unsmiling, until the spirit moved me to speak. Not very good training for the President of the United States, I'm afraid . . . not in this day of radio and movie news . . ."

The intimacy of the moment was pierced by a frightening shriek. *"Mama!"* Out in center hall, they heard the desperate call for help. *"Mercer . . . Mays . . . somebody, please . . ."* Mrs. Hoover ran back into her room just a step ahead of Mays. Mercer anxiously flung open the door from the hall.

Maggie had collapsed on the floor, an evening gown still clutched to her chest. Lillian was on her knees, trying to rouse her mother, her eyes frantic with worry as she looked up at them. "Please . . . help her . . ."

It had been long in coming. Maggie had known it, Lillian had feared it. The White House doctor put words to it: hardening of the arteries, elevated blood pressure. But as Maggie stubbornly insisted after a day's rest at home in bed, "My heart did a little flip, my blood pressure got up there someplace. Notwithstandin', I am not ready to lay down. Not yet . . . Got no time now to be sick. We got an Inauguration."

In spite of all efforts to restrain her, Maggie was at the White House that last frantic hour when not only the presidency was changing hands up on the Hill with the oath of office, but the second floor was already taking on the complexion of the incoming family. The furniture being hastily shoved into place didn't seem particularly distinguished, in Mercer's view, just good and functional; most of it scarred from long years of family living.

Maggie and Lillian and some of the housemen were still up on the third floor, converting Mrs. Hoover's offices back into bedrooms, when the motorcade came down Pennsylvania Avenue through the gates to the south portico.

Mercer called up the stairs, "They be comin', Maggie." She and Lillian barely got down to the second floor into the reception line when the elevator stopped, stuffed to the gills with Roosevelts, chatter, and laughter. Usher Ike Hoover pulled back the door, and the tall, angular lady with the toothy smile strode out, and without waiting to be presented, greeted the staff in her high, somewhat reedy voice, "How do you do, everyone, I am Mrs. Franklin Roosevelt." The elevator spilled a half a dozen other people—all, it seemed, tall, toothy, and smiling. Some, it developed, were her children—son Elliott, daughter Anna—friends. Others of her brood came bounding up the grand staircase, bursting with youth and vitality; Franklin Junior and John, the youngest at eighteen and sixteen, pulling along two breathless young women, melding with the rest of the family, opening doors, crisscrossing the hall, exclaiming at each discovery—"Wow, nice digs" . . . "So this is what the great white whale looks like inside" . . . "Where do I sleep?" . . . "Hey, looks bigger from the outside." Eventually they all went downstairs. Mrs. Roosevelt only took time to drop off her coat and hat, then she followed them, calling back to the staff, "I'm afraid you'll find us a very noisy family."

Didn't it sound good, though, doors banging open instead of silently closing shut. If you dropped something, heads didn't turn; heads didn't roll. All you got was a shouted "Pick it up." One thing to be said about this new White House—it moved. And you moved with it.

The Inaugural luncheon, throwing tradition to the winds, was a buffet. There was new energy in the White House, permeating every corner, and the staff responded to it immediately. Waiters, moving in and out with their trays, found themselves smiling at each other. Every time the door to the pantry opened and a butler backed in, the swell of animated conversation and free and open laughter came in with him. The sound of life.

Aches and pains forogtten, Maggie, moving at less than normal speed, but keeping up, set paper doilies on silver trays, passed them along to Lillian, who filled them with pastries. Fraser snitched a petit four or two as he moved the tray along to Mercer, who checked it out to the butlers. Lillian kept an anxious eye on her mother.

"Mama, you take it easy now, don't overdo."

"Jus' hearin' voices again perks me up."

"You goin' do like you're told," Mercer called down the line to her, "take some time off, Maggie? Or we goin' have to tie you down?"

"Now Mercer, don't take on so . . ."

Coates backed in from the dining room with his tray of empty dishes, muttering to himself. "Never heard such a thing in my life . . ."

"What, Coates?"

"The Pres'dent of the United States—he's out there, in that chair—having to wait in line for his food like everybody else . . ."

"Is he complainin'?"

"Complainin'? No, he is laughin' . . ."

"Well, what you complainin' about? Sounds like he havin' fun."

When had a President had fun last? As she worked, Maggie thought back over the years. Seems they'd all had some unhappiness shadowing them a good part of the time they were in this house. *Jesus Lord, if you could, let it stay like it is today . . . like breathin' fresh air.*

What came up from the kitchen was more like a brisk wind: Mrs. Roosevelt, with a coffee cup in her hand. "Oh, my, you are busy here, you can use some help." She set down the cup, picked up a tray and pastries, and started for the dining room. The staff, unused to seeing a First Lady in these surroundings, didn't have time to react. Fraser, who'd just shoved a petit four into his mouth, stopped chewing, cheeks bulging. Mercer quickly reached out to relieve the First Lady of the tray. "I'll take that in, ma'am." But she waved him off. "I raised a family of five children, I've served a lot of meals . . ." She paused briefly, scanning the pantry. "My, my, this pantry's as dreary as that old kitchen. We must do something about it. As I was telling Franklin, it's not right to ask people to work with antiquated tools." Holding the swinging door open with her elbow, she nodded pleasantly to Fraser, indicating the pastry tray. "Try the marzipan . . . they're delicious." And she was gone.

They stared after her, dumbfounded. Mercer put it into words. "That is one fast-movin' lady."

That she was. One of her first moves was to get rid of all the Monroe furniture that Mrs. Hoover had spent her time researching and duplicating. The Lincoln bed was swiftly dismantled and trundled directly to the room that Louie Howe would occupy. "We want Mr. Howe to be comfortable," she said as she picked up an armload of books and carried them along.

Thousands of books . . . to be unpacked, dusted, put

away. Bookshelves to be dug out of storage; extra
ones built. "This has got to be the readin'est family,"
was Mercer's comment. He was grateful that there were
no longer priceless porcelains that gave you heart
failure every time you had to move and dust one of
them. But there were ships' models and scrimshaw, and
the President's huge collection of miniature glass,
wooden, and ceramic dogs and pigs. Mrs. Roosevelt,
moving swiftly by as they were placed on the President's mantel, recognized an interloper among the
group and took it out. "How did that donkey get in
there? Franklin hates donkeys, get rid of it."

On their way to the back stairs, each with a repro-
duction of the gilded chairs President Monroe had ordered from France, Fraser asked Mercer, "Who's Louie
Howe?"

"You gotta read the papers more, boy." Mays, bound
for the same destination, carrying to storage an unwanted rococo nightstand from the Harding days that
had somehow gone unnoticed in a guest bedroom,
joined them. "Mr. Howe's been with Mr. Roosevelt
from 'bout the time the Pres'dent started politickin' . . ."

"Oh, I been readin' the papers," Fraser said as the
trio went up the stairs. "Listenin' to the talk on the
radio, too. That Bonus Army's back. You know what
the papers say—Mr. Hoover, he sent the Army, Mr.
Roosevelt, he sent his wife. That's goin' to set well,
come reelection."

"Fraser, you comin' along, yes, sir, you comin'
along." Mays paused at the landing to shift the weight
of his burden and let them go ahead of him. His feet
hurt, and the less he moved around, the better. Yes,
sir, that Fraser was comin' to be a thinkin' young
man . . .

Lillian had been at the sewing machine from early
morning, stitching together sheets to the size of the
Lincoln bed. A burst of speed, and yards of fabric
went under the needle. The Monroe chairs, borne by
Fraser and Mercer, went by the open door. Mercer,
pausing briefly, stuck his head in. "How's your mama?
Doin' what she's told?"

"Well, stayin' home, like the doctor wants, but for doin' what she's told, don't count on it."

Mercer chuckled: "Don't I know . . . that's your mama." He called back as he disappeared, "Tell her I be comin' by." Lillian ran the last hem through the machine. She could hear Fraser and Mercer in the storage room at the end of the hall, shifting furniture around. Mays reached the head of the stairs and paused, looking around as at a strange place. Lillian, biting off the thread, called, "Come on in, Mays." He came into her room, limping slightly. "Not been up here in years, since Mr. Coolidge had it all fixed up. Hardly know the place." He put the Harding table down against the wall.

"You not leavin' that ugly thing here?"

"Why not? You can always use another little table. You not goin' ask me to carry it all the way down to the storage room, are you?" He sat down, removed his shoe and began to rub his foot. "Hard to believe it's the same old attic . . . hear there's a new room up here, Miz Roosevelt fixed up for a person to lay down and rest."

"Cross the hall. Why, your feet botherin' you again? Bet you not gone to a doctor like you s'posed to."

"Don't need one."

"Still usin' a razor blade to cut your corns, aren't you?"

"Nothin' to worry 'bout, Lil'yan, you beginnin' to sound jus' like your mama." He took a newspaper from his pocket, cracked it open. "You hear 'bout Miz Roosevelt and the Secret Service?"

"No, what?"

"She told 'em right off she didn't want to be bothered with 'em tailin' her everyplace. They said she had to carry a gun, so she's doin' that."

"You're kiddin' me."

"No . . . carries it right along with her in her pocketbook. Learned how to use it, too. Things are sure different." He gave his attention to the newspaper. "Country's commencin' to sound like alphabet soup— CCC . . . NRA . . . TVA . . . WPA . . . PWA . . ."

Lillian gathered the large sheets in her arms and left the room. "Have fun, Mays." Halfway down the stairs she heard the double-time clacking of high heels coming up. They reached the landing at the same time.

"Hi, I'm Marguerite LeHand." The woman was prematurely gray, but Lillian recognized her to be about the same age as herself, thirty-four or -five. Open, outgoing, she smiled easily and was possessed of boundless energy and enthusiasm. "You must be Lillian."

"Yes, ma'am, Miss LeHand."

"Everybody calls me Missy. I'm the President's secretary. My bedroom's right next to your sewing room, stop in sometime, anytime—to gab, have a cup of coffee. Can't offer you a drink. Prohibition, you know . . . Sorry to rush, if I don't grab a shower now, I'll never get one." With a broad smile, she hurried past.

Well, Lillian thought, *I'll take you up on that . . .* She grinned all the rest of the way down the stairs, thinking things in the White House were improving. The signal of three bells rang out as she reached the second floor. Murdoch, on duty at the elevator, was on his feet.

"Don't rush me, Mr. Murdoch, I'm disappearin' . . ." She carefully opened the door to the service closet and went inside. She couldn't reach the darn light pull. Being shorter than everybody else, whenever she got trapped in the closet by the bells she depended on her companions to turn on the light. Being alone, she'd have to wait it out in the dark. A mop fell against her. "Don't get fresh now," she said.

President Franklin Roosevelt, just being wheeled to the elevator by his personal valet, McDuffie, thought he caught something out of the corner of his eye. Matter of fact, he was sure he'd seen something. A door didn't open and close of itself, and no one was standing outside the closet. It stood to reason the person who'd manipulated the door had to be standing inside.

Lillian, arms full of sheets, waited for the sound of the elevator. It puzzled her why it didn't come . . .

The President, acting on impulse, waved McDuffie away. Strong hands on the wheels, he manipulated the armless converted kitchen chair that, from first rising until the heavy braces were removed from his useless legs and he was lifted into bed at night, was his means of conveyance. He opened the door. They were face to face, he in his chair having to look up at her. Lillian forced her eyes to stay in contact with his, not to stray to the wheelchair, the heavy steel and iron on his legs; and for an instant she was in a doctor's office up on Pennsylvania Avenue, steel and iron on her own leg, and the doctor was telling her to walk.

"What's this all about, little girl?" the President demanded.

Her shock at the encounter and his stern voice made her barely able to get the words out. "Bells, sir . . . it's the rule . . . when the Pres'dent's comin', get out of the way."

He threw back his leonine head and laughed. "Who thought up that idiocy? Come on out . . . don't go around playing hide-and-seek." She stepped out of the closet, pivoting on her crutch to close the door. Seeing her in the recesses of the closet, with brooms and mops, he hadn't noticed the crutch. Now that he did, laughter disappeared from his eyes.

"What's your name?" he asked gently.

"Lil'yan, sir."

"Well, Lillian, you and I, we know what it's all about, don't we?"

Their eyes met in mutual understanding.

"Yes, sir, Mr. Pres'dent . . . guess we do."

He wheeled back to the elevator. She started for the stairs to take the sheets below to the laundry room and run them through the mangle. "Going down?" he asked.

"Yes, sir."

"Well, come along."

She hesitated.

"That another idiotic rule?"

"Well, sir . . ." Unconsciously, she looked to Murdoch, but Murdoch was staring at his shoe tips.

The President spoke to Lillian, but his look was directed at Murdoch. "From now on, little girl, you ride—with or without me." McDuffie backed the wheelchair into the elevator. Murdoch stepped aside for Lillian to enter; then they followed. As the elevator descended, the President stuck a fresh cigarette into his long holder and grinned at her. "Much more fun this way, isn't it?"

Was it ever!

"The Pres'dent and me," Lillian recounted to Maggie at home that evening, "ridin' down together—jus' couldn't believe it . . ." She came out of the kitchen with a plate and fork, eating a quick, light meal as she talked.

"Cain't you at least take your hat off?"

Lillian recognized a testiness in Maggie. "Sorry, Mama." She removed the red plumed hat and tossed it on a chair.

"If you'd got home earlier, we could have had supper together . . ."

"Mama, you know how they do . . . they want you, they want you."

"I know that better than you."

"Yes, Mama." Feeling out of things, that's what it was. Lillian tried to placate. "How's your book comin'? Bein' home, give you a good chance to get caught up with it."

"Don't know if I'll ever get caught up. Three-four years behind in my pastin' and my notes. I don't write 'em out clear, I'm goin' to forget what they mean." She sat down, without real enthusiasm, at her box of mementos and idly moved them around, but there was little satisfaction in it. "So you rode down with the Pres'dent . . . what else happened today?"

"Well, you know, Mr. Ike Hoover retired, had a goodbye party for him."

"I should have been there, didn't even put in my money for his present."

"I took care of that for both of us, Mama. Mr. Howell Crim, he's head usher now."

Ike Hoover gone. So many others gone. Mrs.

Feeney, Viola, retired. And Mr. Coolidge, gone back home to Vermont and died. Maggie glanced at his framed picture on her wall on which she'd draped black crepe paper. *"Sincerely yours, Calvin Coolidge."* She got up and straightened the photographs, touching the faces. "Poor Miz Coolidge," she said aloud. "he loved her for true. My lady's goin' be so alone . . ."

Lillian made another attempt to lift Maggie's mood: "Oh, you know what Eleanor did today?"

Maggie turned from the photos, aghast. *"Eleanor?"*

Lillian backed off. "Well, that's what everybody calls her—behind her back: 'Where's Eleanor goin' now?' 'What's Eleanor up to next?' "

"Well, might everybody call her that . . . but not you."

Lillian quietly took the rebuff. "Anyway, the *First Lady* cooked up breakfast herself on a chafin' dish in west sittin' hall, and then opened the door and yelled out, 'Come and get it' . . . and they come from everyplace . . . Oh, and she's sleepin' in a little single bed in her dressin' room, says it's all she needs."

"That so?"

"And the Pres'dent's mother? Said to the First Lady what did she let all that nice white help go and only keep colored and Miz Roosevelt answered, 'Mama, you run your house, I'll run mine.' Then the Pres'dent's mother said the White House had no style, it was bein' run jus' like a hotel . . ."

"I take it the First Lady confided all this in you?"

"No, I jus' heard it."

"Was it in the papers?" Maggie asked pointedly.

"No, Mama."

"Then you didn't hear it and you won't go repeatin' it . . ."

"Yes, Mama . . . Oh . . . tell you what else happened. We got a new housekeeper—Miz Nesbitt from the Hyde Park—nice lady . . . And Miz Roosevelt's own personal maid, Lizzie . . . Oh, and we hired on two new maids . . ."

"All this happened today?"

"Well, no, Lizzie's been there right along. House-keeper's been on 'most a week now."

"And you didn't bother tellin' me. Suppose you thought it was none of my affair . . ."

"*Mama* . . . So busy, you know how it is—breakin' in new maids."

"*You* been breakin' 'em in?"

"Miz Nesbitt says I'm doin' a lovely job." Lillian took her plate back to the kitchen, picked up her purse, and put on her coat and hat as she moved to the door. "Gotta run, workin' the powder room tonight, the young Roosevelts givin' a dance."

Maggie and her hurt pride followed Lillian to the door. "Well, so's you don't get yourself all overworked, you tell everybody over there I be comin' back tomorrow."

"Oh, Mama, you know what the doctor said, that's too soon . . ." Maggie's answer came through pursed lips. "I know best what my arteries are doin' . . . and I have you to remember, I am still first maid at the White House."

Lillian came out into the corridor, closed the door, listening to the latch set in place, and had a fleeting remembrance of her grandmother sitting in her chair, straight-backed, proud, and life-tired. Hadn't thought of her in years; Gran'mama'd been gone a long time. Why now? What had brought her so vividly to mind? Was the way Mama sat at her memento box a mirrored image? If that was so, if Mama was turning into Gran'mama, then what did that make Lillian? Unfulfilled dreams were sometimes like a dull toothache, not close enough to the surface to mar your day, but there. And like a cavity, you could fill the hole with another substance, but the tooth was never the same. She wondered what dreams Mama had left, if any. Papa's picture was on the bureau, but they never talked about it; funny how you could see something like that every day, not really look at it; then when you did, the years were held in one suspended, distant moment on a white beach at Cape May. Was that what the picture did for Mama? Maybe one day she'd ask her. But not now.

Lillian came out of the apartment, stood in the recessed shelterway buttoning her coat against the nip in the air. The sky was the color of pewter. Some days it took a lot more than a red plume in your hat . . .

The black Oakland parked at the curb still had some miles left in the tires, but the paint job was worn through in places to the metal. What good paint remained wore a high shine, witness to its owner's affection.

"Hi, Lil'yan, what's goin' on?"

"Oh, hi, George. You off on a trip?"

She paused briefly at the open trunk of the car where a neighbor, a square block of an ebony man with a lot of work muscle, set two rope-tied suitcases next to a bald spare tire and carton of blankets and bedding.

"New York," he said. "Give up my apartment."

"Well," she said, "have a good time."

"No good time. Work . . . I hope."

Through the rear window, her eyes briefly made contact with another young man placing a suit of clothes on a hanger in the already crowded backseat of the car. Lean, with inquisitive mocking eyes fringed all around with thick black lashes, she noticed. His warm face lighted with a smile.

"How things goin' over to the White House?" George inquired.

"I got everythin' under control." She started away. The young man inside the car jackknifed himself out and nudged his friend. "Oh, before you go, Lil'yan," George called.

She paused. "Got some message you want me to give the Pres'dent?"

"Meet my friend, Wheatley Parks . . . my neighbor, Lil'yan Rogers."

"How do, Miss Rogers."

A quick survey told her he was probably a little younger than she and darned good-looking. Put her in mind some of Cab Calloway. "How do, Mr. Wheatley."

"Parks."

"Oh . . . Well, see you 'round, Mr. Parks. Cain't keep the Pres'dent waitin' . . ." She smiled pleasantly and was on her way, wondering why she always had to be quick with a quip. Was it because people had come to expect that of her? Maybe that was another red plume . . .

Wheatley Parks was a Georgian with a restless spirit and an agreeable nature. Come up from Americus where work was scarce as free lunch or a pair of new shoes, he liked the city; felt he belonged in it and expected it to like him back.

"Well, come on, Wheatley, we goin' to New York, let's get started."

Without a moment's hesitation, Wheatley Parks reached back into the car, brought out his own good suit and a scarred valise.

"What you doin' there?"

"Not goin' to New York, that's what I'm doin'."

"Not goin'? You got to be crazy, we got a good chance of jobs up to New York . . . you know how hard it is to find work here."

"Not goin'," he said, his eyes still on Lillian, who was nearing the corner. "I'm stayin' . . . I'll find me somethin' hereabouts, but I am stayin'."

George followed his gaze. "You don't even know her . . ."

"My intention is jus' that, get to know her."

Shaking his head, George waited for Wheatley to take his few remaining possessions out of the car trunk. They shook hands, wished each other good luck. George got in and drove off. Wheatley stood a moment, watching his friend out of sight, then walked up the street, hoping his landlady hadn't rented out his room.

Three bells sounded. Murdoch got to his feet, quickly moved to the elevator. Waiting.

A moment, then the President, wearing an overcoat, a favorite gray felt hat slammed onto his head, was wheeled out of his room. Prettyman, the valet who alternated with McDuffie in his around-the-clock care, was pushing the chair.

"Morning," the President said pleasantly to servants he passed.

"Mornin', Mr. Pres'dent," answered Maggie, for herself and the other maids. Prettyman pushed the President's chair the length of center hall and up the carpeted ramp that blended the higher-level east sitting hall with the rest of the floor.

"Louie," the President called, "we're ready." He pushed open the door to the Lincoln bedroom, but didn't enter. "Come on, Louie, shake a leg, let's get going . . ."

Louie Howe's cough preceded him. He came out of the room in a cloud of smoke from a cigarette which was down to its last drag and threatened to singe his nicotine-stained fingers. He was a small, wizened man, wearing the mantle of the chronically ill and an overcoat that fit him in earlier, healthier days but now sagged on his shrunken frame. His breathing impaired by a racking cough which he tried to smother, he walked painfully, slowly, irritably waving off assistance from Mercer, who had helped him dress and now accompanied him as attendant.

"Well, Louie." Roosevelt's hearty voice masked concern, "You're looking great."

"I'm looking lousy, Franklin, and you know it." Prettyman pushed the chair slowly to accommodate Howe's shambling gait. Mercer, following slightly behind, extended an anxious hand to steady him. "Will you tell this man to leave me alone?" Louie Howe growled. Roosevelt chose to ignore the gripe.

"Now you see, Louie, wasn't so bad, was it . . . to get up, put on your clothes? A little drive, do you good. Fresh air . . ."

"Fresh air's poison."

Roosevelt's laugh was a prod. "Attaboy, Louie. A pleasure to hear you talk back, wish more people did."

"They did, you'd chop 'em to pieces."

Again the President laughed. Too hearty, too long; he wasn't fooling Howe and he knew it. "Get your strength back, get well, I'm going to need you in fighting form, Louie . . . couldn't seek a second term without you." Prettyman backed the wheelchair into the elevator. As they started down, Howe was in the throes of a convulsive coughing spell; the President's anxious look betrayed his awareness of how fragile was the mortality of this brilliant, street-wise gnome.

The instant the elevator disappeared, Mercer signaled Maggie. She and the new maids, Sevilla and Velma, galvanized into action. Pushing linen cart, rushing cleaning ordnance down center hall and up the ramp, they made a foray on Louie Howe's room.

It was an unholy mess, drapes drawn, lamps burning. The Lincoln bed looked like it had been slept in nonstop for a month. It had, Howe having refused to allow anyone into his inner sanctum. Ashtrays on every surface, even the floor; one ashtray, near the piled pillows on the bed, overflowed with more cigarette butts than Mr. Harding had had spittoons. Newspapers, magazines, scattered everywhere; shirts and socks were tossed over chairs and on the floor. How could the poor man ever expect to get well, Maggie worried, when he wouldn't let anyone take care of him, and lived in a pigsty like this?

She pulled back the drapes, threw open the window, savoring the sharp cold air as relief from the musty staleness. "Sevilla, empty those ashtrays—just dump 'em in the pail, get 'em out of this room . . ." Velma helped Maggie strip the bed, tying the used linen into a bundle to be taken below to the laundry. Then the three of them scrubbed and disinfected the bathroom. The maids worked well. In the month Maggie had been back (her heart had been behaving, but she'd been careful), she'd drilled them, inculcating them with her own high standards of cleanliness, decorum, and punctuality.

Punctuality . . . Louie Howe's leather traveling clock showed the time to be almost ten in the morn-

ing—middle of the day for a White House worker,
for Maggie, Mercer, Mays, and the others. But evi-
dently not for Miss Lillian Rogers . . .

Lillian at that moment was hurrying up the back
stairs, setting her cap on her head, tying her apron.
"Oh, you are goin' to catch what-for, girl," Mercer
told her as her crutch sped her around the corridor
corner and down center hall. Sevilla and Velma, on
their way downstairs with the Louie Howe flotsam,
gave her a warning look and hurried on, thankful to
be out of the path of the approaching storm.

Maggie was cracking the basic sheet across the Lincoln bed when Lillian came into the Howe room.

"Sorry, Mama."

Maggie went about her business, tight-lipped, brows
drawn together, stifling anger. Lilliam moved quickly
to the other side of the bed. "Meant to get right up
after you woke me, Mama . . ." Together they made
the bed, Lillian knowing the longer her mother stayed
silent the worse the blow would be. "Jus' closed my
eyes for another minute . . . didn't that ever happen
to you? Mama, I am sorry . . ."

"Bankers' hours . . . who you claim to be, Mr. Andrew Mellon?"

"Mama, never been late once in the five years I
worked here."

"Well, you not likely to be here five more years—or
five days, for that matter, you keep this up . . . stayin'
out all hours with that Park Wheatley."

"It's Wheatley Parks, Mama, and you know it."

Maggie sniffed.

"He's a very nice fella, Mama."

"Way you two been occupyin' each other's time,
next you'll be sayin' he wants to marry you."

Lillian, tentative in her answer, closely watched
Maggie for her reaction. "I told him 'No' in July, and
'No' again in September."

"Well, you seem to remember every time you say
'No' . . . what's goin' happen if you say 'Yes'?"

"Don't know, Mama, not thought about that . . ."
Lillian was a very poor liar; she had thought about it,

and the truth was on her face. Maggie, fearful of the possibility, fought against it. "He's got no steady job."

"He'll get one. He works when he can—he's out there, tryin' every day, you know how hard it is to get work, Mama . . ."

"You the one always sayin' you not goin' support a man that don't work. I loved your papa, but look what I went through . . ."

"Wheatley's not Papa. He don't drink."

Maggie turned on her. Fiercely. "Your Papa loved you 'most more than he loved anybody, and you callin' up his memory in a bad way . . ."

"I meant no such thing . . ." Not only Wheatley stood between them; there was also Papa. Lillian hated herself for having called up the memory of his lurching down the street, of the sour stench of him, of the desperate, frightened eyes, and she wanted to strike it all down, hold firm only to the good times. *Had she spoiled the memory for Mama, too?* "Now, I don't know why we fightin' like this, Mama . . . but you won't give Wheatley a chance."

"I got nothin' more to say about it, now or again . . ."

They finished the bed making in strained silence. Always before, when they'd had differences, it was just the two of them. But now with Wheatley Parks in the middle, the breach grew wider every day. One thing to be said for Lillian, though: there was no bone to pick with her work. Late that one time, and that was it. They didn't speak again about Lillian continuing to see Wheatley, but Maggie was aware of the lingering good-nights out in the hall while she lay in brooding darkness, unable to sleep until Lillian slipped into the apartment, undressed, and crept into bed without a word. Maggie likened it in her mind to how Mr. Taft must have felt when his friend Teddy Roosevelt turned against him.

12

The bell ringers populated the corners again: the
Salvation Army street bands with their bass drums,
cornets, tambourines, and black kettles, underfed San-
ta Clauses in snaggled beards beside their cardboard
chimneys, ringing for aid to the needy. It seemed you
felt the depression worse at Christmastime—even if
you had a job. Store windows full of tempting articles,
but you with near-empty pockets. There were still some
exclusive shops where chauffeur-driven limousines
waited for ladies blessed with secure "old" money, but
they were never crowded. This new administration that
brought such hope in its first months had now leveled off
for the long, hard pull to recovery. But there were no
miracles. The President gave heartening messages to the
people in Fireside Chats. His strong, rallying voice
sent encouragement and optimism out over the airways,
asking you to believe with him that there was a bend in
the road somewhere ahead. But those in the White
House who saw him after these broadcasts felt the
full weight of his worries, knew his anxiety and misgivings. Prettyman or McDuffie, sometimes both,
sometimes Mercer, would take him to his room, lift

him onto the bed, and try to massage away the burden of life bound to a chair.

"God rest ye merry, gentlemen . . ."

Lillian's sewing room was jammed with bushel baskets stacked with gaily wrapped gifts that the First Lady had spent months gathering for everyone on the staff from the head usher to those who tended the furnaces. Her sewing machine had little chance to cool off, what with stitching Christmas stockings for everyone's children. Carols from the radio kept her company. If it weren't for the curtain drawn between herself and Maggie—depression or no—Lillian felt she could work herself into a real yuletide spirit. Absorbed in her sewing, humming along with "O Come, All Ye Faithful," she was unaware of Missy LeHand ascending the stairs until she stood in the doorway.

"Hi, neighbor, can you spare a little of that hot tea?"

"Why, Miss LeHand, you are soakin' wet. You're shiverin' . . ."

Wrapped in an ample terry-cloth robe that covered her wet bathing suit, a bathing cap perched on the top of her drenched hair, Missy LeHand went directly to Lillian's hot plate and poured boiling water over a tea bag. "The pool is warm enough, it's just by the time I get up here I'm an icicle . . ."

"You set and warm yourself." Lillian brought out a large woolen shawl from a cabinet which she tucked around Missy's shoulders, urging her into a chair. Missy, enjoying the attention, pushed aside a heaping basket of gifts with her foot. "Looks like a big Christmas."

"Yes, ma'am . . . for policemen, doormen, their families, cooks, gardeners . . . Miz Roosevelt, she buys for everybody."

Missy nodded emphatically. "Don't I know it. She once bought a pair of shoes for me—saw them in a store, thought they were my style."

"Were they?"

Missy smiled. "Almost." Lillian reached to turn down the radio. "No, no, I love the carols, leave them on. Gives you the feeling the whole world cares about each other. At least for the month of December."

Lillian smiled at her as she ran the two pieces of a Christmas stocking through the machine. She liked this spirited woman; on the rare occasions they were together, she felt a sense of kinship. "Swimmin' so much, Miss LeHand, you must love the water."

Missy shuddered. "Hate it. Terrified of it. Never got beyond water wings . . . but when there's nobody else to swim with the President, I worry about him in that pool alone . . ."

"Yes, ma'am, I understand."

"Seeing him in that chair—bossing everybody around—he's a tower. But in the pool . . ." Her face clouded. "I realize how completely helpless he is . . . so I just close my eyes and jump in."

Lillian carried a stack of completed red and green felt stockings to a box. "He does make you forget he can't stand up and move around . . . the way I do."

Missy watched her maneuver around on the crutch. "He thinks you're brave."

"The Pres'dent does? He say so?" Missy nodded. "Well, I am flattered . . . Don't much think 'bout myself that way anymore . . ." She leaned the crutch against the worktable and again sat at the machine. "Anyway, it fits in with the season. I'm Tiny Tim."

Missy sipped her tea and watched Lillian paste green sequins on red felt. "It dawns on me, Lillian, that you're here when I start my day, and more often than not when I finish—and that can be Lord knows when . . ."

"I get away sometimes, Miss LeHand. Seems to me you never do."

"Hard to find time for a personal life on this job . . . but I never really missed it." Lillian looked at her and thought, *Everybody takes their own veil* . . . Missy poured another cup of boiling water into the cup, dousing the used tea bag. "You have a gentleman friend?"

"Yes, ma'am, I do."

"Going to get married?"

"Well ..."

Missy was sensitive to Lillian's hesitancy. "None of my business, shouldn't have asked . . . Oh, boy, it's cold today—mind if I take this cup along, bring it back after I dress, got to join the boss for cocktails . . ."

"No, ma'am, you go right ahead."

"Merry Christmas to all and to all a good-night," Missy called from the doorway.

Do you have a gentleman friend? Are you going to marry him? Wheatley asked the second question (in his own words), most every night. Last night Lillian had the feeling he was asking it for the final time. "You are the one I want, Lil'yan. I have made my intentions clear, seems I'm not askin' too much for you to declare yourself one way or the other. If you not goin' marry me, Lil'yan, I got to tell you . . . I am goin' marry somebody's daughter." *Oh, Mama, why is it all so hard?*

There was only one person she felt she could turn to. She picked up the phone.

It rang three times in the staff dining room before Mercer could get to it. "Yes, Lil'yan . . . well, could you tell me what the problem is?" No, she couldn't. "Well, you jus' be patient, I get up there to you."

"How soon, Mercer?"

"Well, give me five, ten minutes, got some work to finish here."

He turned from the phone and studied the oil painting Fraser was hanging on the wall. "Little more to the right, boy. That's better." Mercer's eye wandered from painting to painting. The walls that for so long had been empty, dingy, were now freshly painted, brightened by framed canvasses that brought vibrant color to an otherwise unadorned room. Mercer found the paintings pleasing. He didn't know about art, couldn't see any point in painting a picture of an apple on a table. But these he liked: working people doing their jobs, standing on a street corner of a Saturday night. These pictures talked to him. Too bad there weren't any colored folks in them, but they were still nice. "You know those WPA fellas pretty good painters. Miz Roosevelt got the right idea, sure perks the place up," he said.

"Well, is it straight?" Fraser seemed impatient to be done with the job. Mercer viewed the row, of paintings with one eye closed. "They straight, you can come down now."

As Fraser descended the ladder, he took a small book out of his pocket and began to read before he even sat down. Mercer watched him, already deep in concentration.

"What's that book you got?"

"Silas Marner."

"Never did hear of that one. You gettin' be quite a reader. See you with a book every chance you get."

"I thought you knew I was back in school nights, tryin' to get my high-school diploma."

"Oh, yeah, Maggie was tellin' me 'bout you puttin' away your dancin' shoes."

Fraser nodded, barely glancing up. "For a while anyway."

Mercer drew up a chair near him. "Now what made you go back to school, boy?"

"Got tired askin' other people what things mean. When I saw that Bonus Army, the sky burnin', people runnin' . . ." He paused, his face reflecting the horror of that day. "Set me thinkin' . . . never could get it out my mind, decided I better find out where a lot of things are comin' from . . . how a thing like that comes to happen . . ."

Mercer's face brightened with almost paternal pride. "Then you goin' get you that high-school diploma . . ."

"Yeah. Might even go on, if I can . . . try to get to be a teacher."

Mercer studied him with respect. "My schoolin' time kind of went by me, but I learned a lot from Mays' newspaper readin', years I been here." He picked up two remaining paintings, for which there was no wall space.

"Just give me a few minutes, Mercer, I'll take those up to storage for you."

"No, I might as well, I'm goin' up, Lil'yan got some-

thin' on her mind, wants to talk to me about . . ."
From the doorway he said, "You stick to that schoolin',
boy. Good idea, you come to be somebody."

Fraser smiled warmly. "I'm sure as hell goin' try,
Mercer."

Mercer went up the back stairs carrying the two
paintings under his arm, thinking what a proud day it
would be, Fraser to turn into a teacher.

The instant he appeared at the head of the stairs,
Lillian grabbed his arm, drew him into the sewing
room.

"Can you borrow a car someplace, Mercer? Take me
over to Virginia?"

Her urgency gave him pause. "Guess so . . . What's
in Virginia?"

"Wheatley and I can get married over there, and nobody know . . ."

"Ho, now . . . you mean—not even your mama?"

Lillian looked away from the demands of his direct
gaze. "Well, not till it's over and done."

"I don't know, don't know . . . I get a worried
feelin' your mama goin' be real upset with me, I do that
for you . . . Tell you what, chile, you get your mama to
go along, I'll get you the car . . ."

"Mercer, you're not helpin' me . . . Jus' take us over
there—once it's done, Mama'll come around . . . she
wants me to be happy . . ."

He wasn't that easily convinced. He walked up and
back muttering, "I don't know, don't know . . ."
One thing he did know, Lillian was trusting him like
she would her papa, and from what he'd come to know
about Emmett Senior, he must have been some fine fella for Maggie never to be able to let go of him and open
her eyes to somebody else.

"All right, Lil'yan, I take a chance your mama's
not goin' to turn on me."

He got the auto, an Essex touring car that coughed
and sputtered its way into Virginia. The steaming radiator told them what the newspapers had already said,
that it was the coldest day of the year. The celluloid
curtains on the sides of the car crackled with the icy

wind and their breath steamed up the windshield.
Wheatley kept wiping it clear with a woolen glove so
Mercer could see. It had begun to snow just as they
got to the justice of the peace, who wore a coat and scarf
throughout the service, his furnace having just given
out. The wedding was brief, everyone moving, slapping
arms, blowing on their hands. The gardenia Wheatley
brought along had frozen in the box. Lillian wore it anyway.

"I do, I do . . ."

They drove back to the District. Lillian, Mercer noticed, had surprisingly little to say; he wondered if she
was having second thoughts. Wheatley, arm around his
bride, waxed enthusiastic all the way about what a lucky
dude he was, getting such a lovely wife, and the rosy
future ahead of them. Mercer found himself warming
up to this young man and was prepared to tell
Maggie so when he dropped them off at the apartment.

"We not goin' home," Lillian said, which came as a
surprise all around. Wheatley only had a room with the
convenience down the hall, hardly a place to take a
bride. Besides, he'd told his landlady he wouldn't be
back. They had discussed spending just a night or two
at Lillian's place, until they could look for something
of their own. Wheatley wasn't flush with money, but
that was just temporary, he assured Lillian, just temporary.

"Drop us off at the Dunbar," Lillian requested.

"The movie show? What's the matter? Afraid to go
home and face your mama?"

Mercer hit it squarely on the head.

The newlyweds sat through two-and-a-half showings
of *Lives of a Bengal Lancer.* In this warm setting
the gardenia unfroze, then quickly wilted, its heavy
scent permeating the theater two rows deep; still, Lillian wore it. Wheatley, who'd been brought up to respect that ladies got emotional certain times in their
lives, was being as patient as he could, but three times
around with the Bengal Lancers, and Adolf Hitler
screaming during the newsreel, was as much as a
husband should be asked to tolerate.

"Honey, we can't keep sittin' here . . . we got to go home, face your mama."

"Jus' a little more time, Wheatley." She twisted the slim, simple wedding band until it was off her finger. Wheatley slumped in his seat and stared at the screen. Hitler was ranting at a sea of Germans. The band played *"Deutschland über Alles,"* and Lowell Thomas' voice reported that this Chancellor of the Third Reich, come to power less than two years back, had purged his political opponents and executed dissidents within his own party.

Wheatley firmly put the wedding ring back on Lillian's finger. "Lil'yan, we are married . . . for better or worse." Taking her by the elbow, he guided her out of the seat. As they went up the aisle, Lowell Thomas' deep, resonant, doomsday voice followed them out of the theater: "The implication inherent in Hitler's rebuilding of German military might is the cause of grave concern throughout Europe . . ." Their minds were on a conflict closer to home.

The snow was blowing in angry gusts, packing solid, turning to ice underfoot as they got off the trolley. They burrowed in their collars, Wheatley keeping a protective arm around her. She wanted to tell him that she could handle the crutch better alone, but she knew it would hurt his feelings. Most of the apartments in the block were dark. A welcoming glow came from the window of hers. *Hello, Mama, guess what . . .*

Maggie had gone to the window several times during the evening. She hadn't felt easy at all, knowing that Lillian had left early without a by-your-please. Mercer, too. Fraser said he'd heard him on the phone, getting a car from somebody. Going on midnight, and not a word from either of them. Didn't like the feel of it, didn't like the feel at all . . .

When Lillian and Wheatley walked through the door, their faces asking for approval, she knew. "Don't need a ton of bricks fallin' on me. You married . . ."

Lillian dusted snow from her coat, using the time to gain control. "That all you got to say, Mama?" Wheatley smiled nervously. "Congratulate me, Miz

Rogers, I am the happiest man in the world today." But Maggie couldn't bring herself to hang out the flag. "Know what's goin' happen, don't you, Lil'yan? You goin' lose your job, cain't be married and work at the White House."

There was a touch of defiance in Lillian's tone. "Well, I won't tell 'em . . . and I'm sure you won't either, Mama." She moved closer to Wheatley, put her hand in his; the gesture as conclusive as the slim band of gold on her finger and the long expired gardenia. Wheatley drew her to him, but facing Maggie Rogers when her mood cried out that the world had come to an end was like walking cinders barefoot. "I'll find me a steady job, Miz Rogers. I love your daughter, I'm goin' take care of her, be a good husband to her. And I'd be proud to be a son to you . . ."

Maggie shook her head dolefully. "Well, it's done, it's done. You can both take my room, I'll sleep out here."

"Mama, we can't do that to you . . ."

"Well, Fraser's asleep in his room, tired out from night school. I cain't jus' wake him and put him out . . ."

They'd planned badly. Wheatley felt himself losing ground with every word that was uttered. "Miz Rogers, I don't mean to cause any problems. I can sleep out here, I don't mind."

For the first time Maggie nodded approval. "Very kind of you, Mr. Parks, you do that. I'll get the covers." Lillian, near tears, followed Maggie into the bedroom, leaving Wheatley feeling alien. The snow, melting from his overcoat, formed a puddle on the rug. He stepped quickly onto the wood floor, not knowing whether to sit or remain standing, and found himself staring at a photograph of Herbert Hoover.

"Mama," Lillian cried out to Maggie as she pulled blanket and pillow from the closet shelf, "he meant what he said, he loves me, Mama. Don't you want me to be happy?"

"Chile, you bite your tongue. You bein' happy's the most thing in the world to me. You think I'm jus' bein' contrary? Gettin' old, I don't remember what it's like to love a man? I know too well what it means . . . Lost your papa . . . then your brother havin' to go so far away so's he can stay alive. Now I'm losin' you . . ." Her voice broke, she leaned against the wall, swallowing the sob that threatened to engulf her. Lillian felt a pang at how old Maggie was beginning to look: the sag to her shoulders, the hint of gray overlay to the skin that brought Gran'mama to mind. Whatever her own hurt, she couldn't hold back. "Oh, Mama, that's what it is? You think you lost me? You got no worry about that, ever . . . I'm never goin' leave you." Drawing her mother into her arms, she felt the tense muscles relax.

"Then you're not fixin' to go away?"

"No, Mama, no . . . never . . . never leave you . . ." Twice today she had taken vows: *"Till death do us part"* . . . *"Mama, I will never leave you"* . . . But hadn't that been the conflict that had tormented her all these months, the bond between herself and her mother? A silken cord, with steel at its core. It had been forged way back, so far back she couldn't mark the time it hadn't connected them. She could see herself, a growing child being wheeled in a baby buggy up Pennsylvania Avenue to the doctor, and sensed that it was way back then she'd taken the pledge: *"Mama, I will never leave you."*

Lillian carried the bedding into the parlor. Wheatley had removed his overcoat, but still held it over his arm in the manner of a man poised to say "Lovely evening, let's do it again some time," and take off.

"It's goin' be all right, Wheatley . . . you'll see . . . we goin' work it out . . ." She took his coat from him, hung it up in the hall closet.

"You talk to her?"

"I talked to her." Lillian placed a fresh sheet on the sofa, and tucked in the blanket. "Everythin' goin' be fine."

"We stay here a few days, then get our own place?"

"Wheatley, darlin', I am so tired . . . we talk 'bout that tomorrow, hm?"

"Sure, baby, whatever you say." He held her in his arms. Kissed her delicately, almost tentatively. "Good night, Miz Parks."

For an instant, her arms claimed him. "Oh, Wheatley, I didn't plan it this way . . ."

"We make it work, baby, we make it work."

With a wistful smile she went back into the bedroom. He sat on the edge of the sofa, feeling abandoned and a bit foolish. When Lillian finally fell asleep in the twin bed opposite her mother's, she was repeating Wheatley's words, "We make it work . . ."

The next morning Maggie asked Fraser to find himself another place to live. She moved into the smaller bedroom and Lillian and Wheatley took the room with the two beds. Wheatley mentioned finding a place of their own a couple of times, then dropped the subject. It was never brought up again.

The morning following the wedding, Lillian was at the White House as usual, wearing her wedding ring on a long cord around her neck. Often during the day she reached in the top of her uniform to touch it, to assure herself she was actually married. Ironically, the White House gave her a wedding gift, albeit a depressing one: a salary cut. The entire staff received the blow at breakfast when the housekeeper came into the staff dining room carrying her clipboard and wearing the glum look they'd come to associate with bad news. A different housekeeper—Mrs. Nesbitt instead of Mrs. Long. A different President—Mr. Roosevelt instead of Mr. Hoover. But almost the identical message: "Sorry, but every department in government is having to take a cut. The entire country is struggling to get back on its feet. Being the White House, we have to show the way . . ."

"*But twenty-five percent,* Miz Nesbitt," Maggie protested for the entire table. "How any of us goin' to manage?"

"I'm sorry . . . just nothing I can do."

There were mutterings at the table about having to hold two jobs to make ends meet . . . some were already moonlighting and barely making a go of it. Lillian sat, thinking what a big change a few hours could bring. Just yesterday, in her sewing room, she'd fretted about what to do. Well, she'd done it. Didn't feel any different. Nothing seemed changed. But the hard reality was, if the White House found out she was married, she'd lose her job. In the severe light of day the threat carried more bite than it had last night. She'd be careful. No one knew, except her mother and Mercer.

She looked to the head of the table where the seniors all sat and thought how hard the salary cut was going to be on them. All getting up in years, and harder every year to lay something by. Coates and Dixon were past sixty now. Mays, Jackson were well into their fifties, like Maggie. Lillian's gaze stayed with Mercer, and she felt a rush of affection for him. He'd stuck by her yesterday, and he was paying dearly for it. Maggie refused to talk to him. Trying hard to win her forgiveness, he passed the sugar to her, asked didn't she think it was going to be a nicer day than yesterday. He even got to his feet, hoping to evoke the memory of their first meeting by presenting her with a napkin-covered tray and a smile: "Would Miz Rogers care for a popover?"

On their way up the back stairs, he put a hand under her elbow, but she pulled loose from him. "I can still get up the stairs by myself . . ."

"Wasn't meanin' it that way, Maggie, jus' want you to know you can count on me."

"Oh, I can count on you." He winced at the reprimand in her voice. "Count on you to go behind my back with my own chile . . ."

"Maggie," he pleaded, "let me tell you how it was, let me explain about Virginia . . ."

"Nothin' to explain. Virginia's across the river, that's all I care to know about it."

According to the President's instructions, Lillian rode up in the elevator while the others walked. For a brief moment Maggie, Lillian, and Mercer met in the corridor at the service closet before Lillian continued on up to the sewing room. The severe set of Maggie's jaw told her that Mercer was taking the worst of it.

"Have a good day, Mama . . . Mercer . . ." Lillian called. He threw her a grateful glance, but Maggie remained aloof to him.

No, sir, it was not going to be a good day, Mercer thought.

Apparently the President was of the same mind. As he was wheeled out of his bedroom by Prettyman, his irritation was evident in the thrust of his head, in the way he jammed a cigarette into the holder, and especially in his voice. Dictating to Missy LeHand, who took it all down on a shorthand pad, he bit each word off the way a bear tears bark from a tree. "A note to Eleanor—wherever she is—'Dear Eleanor. You have got to keep this house on a budget. How can I ask everybody to cut back if we don't? And please, I beg of you, the steady diet of sweetbreads is making me very unsweet—caused me to bite two diplomats. Not ours, theirs' . . ." Mercer stepped out of his path. "Mornin', Mr. President."

"Morning," the President barked, continuing the dictation without pause as his chair was backed into the elevator. " 'And one more thing, Eleanor. After we have turkey, I want the carcass brought to me the next day . . . You know I like to pick on it . . . you're throwing away a lot of perfectly good meat with the bones' . . ."

"Shades of Calvin Coolidge," Mercer said to Maggie. She ignored him. As she walked away, his eyes stayed on her back. He saw her shoulders shake. *You're laughin', Maggie, I know you are . . . Cain't nobody laugh and stay mad, leastwise nobody I know.* He felt better. She'd come around, forgive him.

1936

The New Deal and the Good Neighbor Policy gained in momentum. Labor was making itself felt with an innovative weapon, the sit-down strike. Suffragette Susan B. Anthony was finally being recognized with her picture on a three-cent stamp. A "sports and social" organization came into being—the German-American Bund (*Amerika-deutscher Volksbund*); members wore uniforms decorated with swastikas and had parades. Vox populi was the new craze: the man on the street let his opinions be known. Get involved with European affairs? Hell, no, let them fight their own battles. Newspaper and radio stations took polls: isolationism came out on top. On March 6, Hitler's Wehrmacht marched into the Rhineland.

In the White House the Secret Service was pulling its hair. So many people around all the time, they couldn't keep track of who was who. They'd finally been able to convince Mrs. Roosevelt not to hand out her personal card to just anyone and tell them to "come visit"; down-and-outers were showing up at the door with these personal invitations, and housemen, valets, maids expected to give them practically the same class A treatment as that accorded visiting heads of state. The house was Grand Central Station, in Murdoch's view. He hadn't forgotten the havoc wreaked during the Hoover administration when an angry man came in off the street and threatened the President. Fearful that it could happen again, and needing all the help he could get, he turned to Mercer.

"You're head houseman, you must know who these people are . . . It's impossible for us to protect the President when we don't know who belongs here and who doesn't."

Mercer thought a moment, and admitted the house was for sure full to capacity. Certainly did make for a lot of extra work. "Lessee, now," he said, "on the third floor, we got those people from the youth congress. Got to admit some of them do look a little raggedy, but they guests of Miz Roosevelt . . . And"—he gestured to the corridor off center hall—"those young people down that way, they friends of the Roosevelt boys. They be gone by the weekend. But then we goin' get some movie stars—Robert Taylor, and some others, I think . . ."

"What about the fat man in the Rose Room, keeps calling for room service?"

"Oh, yeah . . . that's the writer fella, Mr. Alexander Woollcott—comes off and on, been here quite a spell this time, seems like."

Murdoch thanked him and said he'd appreciate it if Mercer would keep him informed who came and went. Mercer said he'd sure be glad to do that.

It was a beautiful spring day. Nature, Lillian thought, was trying to make amends for the bad winter. On her way in she'd stopped off in the florist's room and gotten a bowl of jonquils for her worktable. The florist, a Mr. Parker who'd taken Mr. Kearney's place when that gentleman retired, commented, "Way you wear that big smile every day, Lillian, you must be in love."

"Spring, Mr. Parker," she said. If her feelings were that transparent, she'd have to be careful. Her job was at stake. Things had eased off at home. Maggie had settled down with the arrangement and seemed almost content. She no longer called Wheatley "Mr. Parks," but once she'd slipped and called him "Emmett." Lillian wondered if that meant she was accepting him as a son, or if she saw him as a counterpart of Papa. No matter, things were easier; she and Wheatley went out dancing and to park concerts. Best of all, Wheatley was working as a part-time waiter, and getting fair tips (which may have accounted for the "Emmett").

As they ate breakfast in the staff dining room, Lillian studied Maggie and thought, *So many things about my mother I don't know.* Worked so hard (did she ever resent it?), but you could tell she thoroughly enjoyed being served: the way she sat at table, relishing the fine china, the cut crystal; the way she held her fork, her napkin . . . Mama had style. Yet she never talked about what her life might have been, had things been different.

Lillian accepted coddled eggs and Canadian bacon from the silver tureen extended to her by the serving-man, Morgan, and admitted to herself it was the only way to live. She was only vaguely aware of Jackson's comments on the day's headlines.

"This man Hitler, don't know what to make of him, struttin' into the Rhineland like that . . ."

Coates puzzled, "Rhineland? Ain't that part of his own country?"

"He think so."

"French sure not happy 'bout what he's doin'," Fraser contributed.

"The French? What they got to do with the Rhineland?"

"Somethin' to do with the Versailles Treaty and disarmament." Fraser apologized for not being more knowledgeable about it than that; he was just beginning to study about the Treaty at night school. "If Mays was here, he could explain it."

"Yeah . . . Where is Mays, anyway?" The empty seat claimed their attention. Not like him to be late, or to miss a day's work.

"Left early yesterday," Jackson reported. "Sat out most the day in the usher's office, with his shoe off— in a grouchy mood. Not like Mays to be like that."

Mercer's attempt to disguise worry was transparent. "You think that darn fool cut hisself with a razor again?"

"You know Mays, stubborn as a mule. Try to tell that fool man anythin' . . . he be all right, don't you worry 'bout him."

"Me? I'm not worryin'."

Both were lying through their teeth, both knew it. Maggie felt it. An undercurrent of fear as strong as the tie of friendship ran through the three of them. "His landlady don't have a phone," Maggie said. Jackson, pulling on his uniform jacket to go to his post, said he would check on Mays as soon as he could.

Lillian's day was spent at the sewing machine making pillowcases out of worn-out sheets. So many beds to dress and nobody putting out a nickel for linen replacements. The President's mother had been right in her observation, Lillian thought; the place was turning into a hotel! *My day,* she said aloud, in a reasonable facsimile of Mrs. Roosevelt's radio voice, and looked up to see Fraser and Mercer moving a rollaway bed into her room.

"Now jus' hold it," she said, quickly getting to her feet. "What's this all about? I didn't order a bed, I work here, I don't sleep here—though that probably be the next order of the day, what with all the work piled on me . . ." Mercer and Fraser were both frantically trying to high-sign her, but Lillian was wound up. "I'd like to know whose idea this was anyway, to—"

Mrs. Roosevelt came through the door, carrying an armful of her clothing, which she proceeded to hang on available wall hooks. "Hope you don't mind, Lillian, but the house is just so full of company . . . no place for me to sleep tonight. I won't be in your way, I promise . . ."

Lillian swallowed her protest, and hoped her voice hadn't carried down the stairs: if it had, Mrs. Roosevelt chose to overlook it.

"Here, let me help you, ma'am . . ." She provided the First Lady with a little more hanging space, and emptied a drawer for her.

"Oh, and, Lillian, I am going to need your assistance."

"Yes, ma'am."

"We must get Mr. Woollcott out of the house—this is his third visit and he seems disinclined to leave. We desperately need his room . . ." The First Lady dropped stockings and underthings into the drawer, which Lillian quickly put into order. Mrs. Roosevelt went on, "Now it is going to require diplomacy . . . strategy . . . singularity of purpose and unswerving determination . . ."

An understatement.

Alexander Woollcott had ensconced himself in the royal suite (the Rose Room), accepting its regal implications as his due, his tenancy having all the earmarks of permanence. His personal books overflowed the shelves; photographs of theater and film greats, autographed to him, were installed on the walls. He had sent for and now luxuriated on his own down pillows. "The fat man," Murdoch had called him. He was more than that. He was a sybarite, an epicurean constantly complaining about the quality of service and food from the kitchen—and of the White House switchboard as being a nuisance and an invasion of privacy. Reclining on the chaise, a groaning breakfast tray at hand, he was a Nero. And about as immovable as Gibraltar.

"Don't let the Secret Service buffalo you," he advised a friend over the telephone between bites of finnan haddie. "Just tell them you're a friend of mine, and come right up, old chap . . ." The first knock at the door he ignored. "What do you mean, they intimidate you? This is your government, old boy. The White House belongs to the people, you know . . ."

The second knock brought Mrs. Roosevelt's voice with it. "Mr. Woollcott . . . it's Mrs. Roosevelt . . ."

"Come in, come in, dear lady," he called out. To his friend on the phone, he continued: "Tell them you're a taxpayer, and that it is my instruction . . ." He didn't get any further. Mrs. Roosevelt marched into the room, followed by her troops. Before Woollcott could utter a word or swallow the forkful of food, the First Lady took over. Talking nonstop from the instant she entered the room, Mrs. Roosevelt moved immediately to the closet and brought out Woollcott's suitcases. "So nice to have had you here, Mr. Woollcott —isn't it thrilling, Princess Juliana of the Netherlands is coming to visit with us . . . do hope you'll come see us again sometime . . ." Woollcott watched, overwhelmed, as Lillian and Maggie stripped his bed of linen and Mercer emptied the dresser drawers of his clothing. Mrs. Roosevelt, now bringing his suits from the closet, continued without a pause for breath: "I hear it's a wonderful theater season in New York this year . . . We're so looking forward to reading your reviews." She set one suit aside. "This should be lovely for travel. Dark gray with pinstripes is always correct."

"Talk to you again, old man," Woollcott managed to croak into the phone. He hung up and sat, nonplussed, witness to his own eviction.

"That was the quickest stampede I've ever seen," was Murdoch's official evaluation. He'd been chuckling to himself ever since Woollcott (in gray pinstripe) came out of east sitting hall and was literally swept along by the entourage of luggage bearers, Mrs. Roosevelt moving briskly along with him until he was securely in the elevator and on his way out. "Goodbye, Mr. Woollcott," she called in her high, clear voice, waving until the doors closed on him. "Now, let's fix the room for Juliana," she said, and went on about her business.

"Our First Lady's a tornado . . . I don't think the fat man knew what hit him," said Murdoch.

"Guarantee you one thing," Mercer added. "Food bill's goin' to drop, now he's gone."

The Woollcott hustle, as it came to be known, temporarily took Maggie's and Mercer's mind away from their concern over Mays' absence. Late afternoon, and they were still laughing over it as they went downstairs for a coffee break before finishing up the day's chores. "That Miz Roosevelt," Mercer chuckled as he opened the door and they went into the empty staff dining room. "That lady is full of surprises." They poured coffee at the urn, carried their cups to the table. In this familiar setting, where their lives had mingled for so many years, Mays' empty chair sharply reawakened their concern.

"You see Jackson? He know anything about Mays?"

"No. Been upstairs all day." Mercer shoved his cup away, untouched. "I'm goin' out to the usher's office, see what I can find out . . ."

"You come right back, won't you? Tell me?"

Hospitals, with their hushed corridors and pungent, medicinal odors, had never ceased to distress Maggie. Even the months when Lillian had lain in one hadn't help dispel her angst. They were alien places, as the convent had been alien to her. People came in, looking anxious, went to the desk to be gestured on the labyrinthine way. Ambulances arrived, sirens screaming. The desperate were rushed in; now and again, a hearse drove silently away.

For three days they had sat on this bench. Before work in the morning. After work far into the night. The word remained unchanged: "critical." John Mays had pared his corns with a razor blade once too often. His blood poisoning brought to mind the Coolidge boy, who would have been twenty-eight if he'd lived. Delirious, John Mays, strapped to the bed as he flailed against the bonds, cried for release, and seemed to be in some strange dimension of his own, insisting he was being hung upside down on a meathook. Then the worst day, when he didn't move at all. Their only glimpse of him had been through the partly opened door. But they sat, Maggie with her eyes closed in prayer. If Mercer and Jackson prayed, she didn't know; it didn't matter—just being there was devotion enough.

The doctor, with the first smile they'd seen on his face, came out of the room and gestured Jackson to him. A brief quiet communication, then Jackson nodded for Maggie and Mercer to follow. They were being permitted five minutes with Mays, who lay in the bed, eyes closed, breathing shallow, looking drawn and weak. And old. Maggie and Mercer held back slightly. Jackson approached the bed.

"Mays . . ." he said softly. "Mays?"

The wrinkled eyelids fluttered and gradually opened. Mays' voice was a strained whisper. "This place . . ." Jackson leaned closer, waited anxiously for his next words.

"No class . . . Let jus' anybody in . . ."

Jackson smiled in relief and affection. "You gettin' better."

"Wondered, you'd come see me."

"Was here yesterday, every day this week . . . you didn't know me." Maggie and Mercer moved to the bed, on either side of Mays. "They been here, too," Jackson said. "Didn't know them either."

Maggie took Mays' hand, "We been so worried . . . You scared us."

"Really scared us," Mercer echoed.

Mays focused on Maggie's face, studying her, puzzling. "You the new maid?"

"You know me, Mays. *Maggie* . . ." She exchanged a look of concern with Mercer, but Mays was focusing on Jackson. "And you—oh, yeah . . . Goin' put you on the back door, 'cause you got no style . . ." Now it was Mercer who received his scrutiny, "And you— I know you—you the fella servin' that fine fancy breakfast . . ."

"Now come on, Mays," Mercer said, "I know you're not delirious now . . . what you after, hm?"

A weak smile appeared on Mays' face. "You all know what day it is, don't you?"

Maggie stroked his forehead. "Knew from the first minute I opened my eyes this morning, Mays. Twenty-seven years ago I took my first step into the White House."

"Yes, sir." Jackson nodded assent. "Twenty-seven years to the day."

Mercer grinned and reminded them that he was the old-timer, having arrived three weeks before they had.

Mays shook his head. "Don't understand . . . you folks all gettin' older, how come I stay so young?"

" 'Cause you ornery, born lazy and raised shiftless," Jackson said, harking back to the days when they were funnin' all the time.

"Workin' up a sweat not for us quality folks." Mays' eyes closed. Maggie touched his hand to her cheek, then gently put it under the blanket. The three of them stood a moment, looking at him with great, abiding affection, a sense of relief that their ranks had not been diminished; that they had been granted a reprieve; that there was time ahead for all of them. Mercer gave Mays a gentle pat, Jackson touched the top of his head lightly. Mays didn't open his eyes again, but the smile stayed on his face. They left him.

Mays was back on duty within the week. Sadly, one of the first persons through the door was Louie Howe being carried out to a waiting ambulance. The President, in his wheelchair, had followed the stretcher out of the building. "You'll get better, Louie," he called, and watched until the ambulance turned into the flow of traffic on Pennsylvania Avenue, his face drained of joy. Prettyman wheeled him to the Oval Office.

Maggie, with the help of the maids, cleaned the Lincoln Room, which to her was now the Louie Howe room. With everything immaculate and in its place, it seemed so devoid of his presence that she washed and wiped the ashtrays and placed them around the room for him to use when he came back. Sevilla and Velma went below with the linens. The work was actually finished, but Maggie remained behind, wanting to assure herself that the room was being prepared rather than abandoned. She was straightening his clothes in the armoire, reaching up from tiptoe to the topmost drawer, when she heard the leg crack, felt it give way, and caught the weight of the massive piece of furniture on her shoulder. Straining desperately to keep it from crashing down on her, every ounce of strength went into bracing herself with nothing left over even to form a scream. Fraser chose that moment to walk by the door. "My God, Maggie . . ." He bolted into the room, threw the weight of his back against the armoire, releasing her.

"Go call for Jackson, or somebody."

"Nobody else on the floor." In spite of the pain in her upper body, she managed to put several books under the fractured leg of the armoire. Fraser tilted it backward, temporarily securing it. "Come on, let me get you to the doctor."

"No . . ."

"Let me call Lillian then."

"No, don't tell anybody. I'm all right . . . my shoulder . . . jus' a bruise . . ."

The bruise was deep and painful, but so was the thought of possible forced retirement, which Maggie feared would happen if a doctor were called in. Instinctively she knew the accident hadn't done her heart any good, but kept her own counsel and extracted a promise from Fraser to do the same. From time to time during a workday she'd catch him looking anxiously at her. "Fraser, you are turnin' into a worrywort." He answered with what had come to be his byword: "Time not come for me to worry yet, Maggie." But he kept close tabs on her.

It was several weeks before she was able to use the arm without pain. She felt some satisfaction in having managed to keep her disability from everyone's notice, especially Lillian's.

With spring at hand, could the summer layoffs be far behind? Lillian and Maggie were long accustomed to the tradition that once Congress recessed and the wretched humid weather settled in, those who could, fled the city. It was new to Wheatley: hotels laying off all but a skeleton crew, some dining rooms closing altogether. With the depression on, layoffs came earlier, swifter, more devastatingly.

Wheatley was one such casualty. He searched the want ads, ran down every lead he could, but the job market, such as it was in these lean days, offered little hope.

Lillian picked up extra money sewing, after her day's work was finished, for the ladies on the President's office staff, especially Missy LeHand. "I swear, Lillian, I'd look like Apple Annie if it weren't for you," Missy would say appreciatively when Lillian remodeled and updated her dresses. Missy never had time to go near a store, but she did grab time on the run to stop in Lillian's sewing room. "The potbellied stove room," she called it, and always brought an atmosphere of camaraderie with her, tired as she might be. It seemed to Lillian that Missy was running herself down with overwork, and she said as much.

"Look who's talking. Every time I come past the door you're at that sewing machine. Don't you ever go home?"

"I'll be leavin' in a few minutes, soon as I get this hem turned."

"Appreciate you worrying about me, Lillian, but if the President can carry the load he does, I can certainly manage. Now go home, Lillian."

"In a while, Miss LeHand."

Missy planted herself in a chair. "I'm not going

to leave until you pack up and go. You don't want to get in Dutch with the President, do you? He expects me for dinner—I'll have to tell him it's your fault I didn't show up, because you wouldn't go home."

Lillian covered her machine, laughing. And carried a sack of handwork home with her.

Maggie was already in bed asleep when she got there. Wheatley had prepared dinner, but it was cold and tasteless, warmed over. "Jus' fine, Wheatley . . . good," she said, sensing his depressed mood.

"Tastes rotten, tell the truth." It was all wrong, backward, her to be the one coming home late from work, him feeling left out and useless because he couldn't provide properly. "Come on, Lil'yan, let's get out of here, walk out a bit."

"I'd like to, honey, but I can't . . . brought some collars and cuffs I'm fixin' to make for Miss LeHand." Collars and cuffs for Miss LeHand weren't Wheatley's idea of exciting evening conversation. Lillian could feel his tension and changed the subject.

"How'd Mama seem to be when she got home?"

"All right, far as I could tell."

Lillian frowned. "I don't know. I been havin' the feelin' things not right with her, seems to me she's got some kind of pain. Like to get her to the doctor."

"You two worry too much 'bout each other."

"We are all we got . . ." She caught herself, quickly amending it. "I mean—Mama, me and you."

"Meanin's clear, Lil'yan." He got up, paced the room. Finally he said, "I've got to have a car . . ."

"A car?"

"I have tried everythin' and every way here, there's no job to be had. Had I a car, I could sell things—I'm a good salesman—cross over into Virginia, Maryland, maybe get myself a territory . . . somethin' like that . . ."

"Oh, I don't know, Wheatley—car's expensive. We don't have the money."

"Don't have to do it all at once. Get it on payments."

The memory of the refrigerator being repossessed sprang clear in her mind. She sewed until her eyes rebelled, then went to bed. Wheatley, who had gone out for a newspaper, hadn't come back. He was at the newsstand, waiting for the early morning edition. Jobs in the want ads, the few that appeared, got snapped up almost as fast as they were printed. If there was anything to be had, he was determined to be first in line. He came back to the apartment and sat in the kitchen, reading:

JANITOR, 1 day a week, $2 . . .
WAITER, 5:00 p.m. till closing plus cleanup, no salary, tips only

He turned to the used-car ads.

It was a few days later that Mrs. Nesbitt sent for Lillian. Heading for her office, Lillian thought if the housekeeper needed sewing, she'd just have to fit her in.

"Come in, Lillian. Please . . . close the door." Something about her manner told Lillian the subject was more critical than sewing. "You're married, aren't you, Lillian?"

The wedding ring on the cord around her neck suddenly weighed a ton. "How'd you find out, Miz Nesbitt?"

"Your husband made application to buy a car. They checked here to see if you were employed."

"Oh, my, my . . ." Her knees felt weak; she was grateful for the support of the crutch.

"You know the rules. A married woman is not allowed to work in the White House—only widows or single. Nor is a married couple allowed to work in any government agency."

"Yes, ma'am. Shall I draw my pay and go?"

"No, no, Lillian, I didn't say that. I merely gave you the rules, which I am obligated to do. You see, Lillian, I have a son. And he has a wife. And they are both employed in a government agency . . . so we'll all keep our little secrets, shall we?"

"Oh, yes, ma'am, the devil would have to tear my tongue out . . . Good day, ma'am."

"But Lillian . . . you must be careful. Don't use the

White House as a reference point. If it should come out that you're married, there's nothing more I could do to help you."

"Yes, ma'am. Thank you, Miz Nesbitt . . ." Lillian's relief was so great, her spirit so high, she didn't bother to wait for the elevator, as ordered by the President, but practically bounded up the back stairs.

She reached second floor only to have her joyful mood broken by the sight of the President's tragic posture, slumped in his chair, slack, unseeing, as he was wheeled out of the elevator by Prettyman.

"What's wrong?" Lillian whispered to Mercer, who stood nearby. Mercer shook his head, puzzled. "Don't know . . ."

As Prettyman reached the door to the President's suite, he turned and signaled Mercer, who followed them into the room. Prettyman wheeled the chair to the bed. Together they gently removed the President's coat. "Would you like to rest a bit, sir?" Prettyman asked.

The large head nodded almost imperceptibly.

Mercer and Prettyman, on either side of the powerful but helpless man, lifted him out of the chair and onto the narrow hospital bed, propping him against the pillows. He sat there, staring off into some far distance that only he could see. Prettyman put a lap robe across his legs, and gestured Mercer to the door.

"I think he could use a drink. Stiff one . . ."

"I get him one." He drew Prettyman aside. "What happened?"

"Guess you didn't hear . . . Mr. Louie Howe died."

Mercer looked back at the desolate President who sat alone, head bowed, sobbing.

In Philadelphia, the Democrats nominated Franklin Delano Roosevelt by acclamation for a second term. It was as hard to find anyone in the country who was neutral in his feelings about FDR as it had been for Diogenes to find his honest man. The voters were divided into those who wanted to get "that man" out of the White House and those who thought he could part the waters. There were more of the latter. He was reelected by a thundering majority, carrying every state except Maine and Vermont. But the President's satisfaction at the mandate was diminished, with Louie Howe gone.

How many springs had gone into summer into fall into winter . . . It seemed to Maggie that months were fluttering off the calendar the way they did at the moving-picture shows. She noticed aging in others almost more than she did in herself. Jackson had put on bifocals. Mays had a slight permanent limp, after that bout with blood poisoning, but he was being careful with his feet. Mercer's high forehead had extended itself over the top of his head. The bald spot in back hadn't been noticeable when his hair and skin were the same color. Now that his fringe was white, the bald spot had taken on the appearance of a monk's cap. They all of them moved slower than they once did.

But the world moved fast. Civil war raged in Spain, Mussolini's troops seared the land of Ethiopia, Edward VIII reigned for a scant eleven months, abdicating for "the woman I love." In "incidents" on the Yangtze River, Japanese gunfire sank American oil tankers. Hitler's panzer divisions rolled into Austria. The French sat in their impregnable Maginot Line.

Retirement began to loom as a certainty for Maggie. Lillian, concerned about her mother's recurrent weak spells, finally forced an admission about the armoire accident, and got her to the White House doctor. Finding no immediate cause for alarm, he said if she were careful she ought to be able to serve out her full thirty years.

Her retirement date was set for March 1939. When Mrs. Roosevelt heard of it, she asked Maggie as a personal favor to stay on until after the royal visit from the King and Queen of England—a request which Maggie felt proud and honored to fulfill.

"You can mark my words," Mays said at the breakfast table as he read the morning newspaper, "it's no social visit. With all that's goin' on in Europe, the King of England wouldn't be leavin' the job jus' to come here for a holiday, if he wasn't after somethin'."

"What do you think he's after?" Coates asked.

"Money. Airplanes . . ."

"Or to get us into the war," Fraser commented.

Everybody at the table protested. World War I had been enough. There wasn't a voter in the country would keep Mr. Roosevelt in for a third term (and from what the papers were beginning to say, that was a possibility) if he was to send one American boy overseas.

"You might be right," Fraser said, without conviction. The table was beginning to respect Fraser's opinions now that he had his high-school diploma and was going nights to Howard University, and it made some of them uneasy that he'd brought up the subject of American involvement in war. But preparations for the royal visit were too time- and energy-consuming for anyone to dwell on it for long.

The royal suite (the Rose Room) for Their Majesties, and quarters for the corps of servants they would bring with them, were thoroughly gone over to make them ready. Mr. Crim, who didn't have Ike Hoover's expertise with royalty, turned to Maggie and Mercer for help in reintroducing the staff to the rules for proper behavior in the royal presence. There were curtsying and bowing classes again and the realization that a lot of knees had gotten stiff. Pantries were stocked, menus planned. Every electric fan in the place was rounded up, cleaned, and oiled; it was going to be hot, might as well be prepared for it. Draperies and bed linens had to be repaired or replaced, and again Lillian gave long hours to the sewing machine.

Wheatley often found himself in limbo these days. They'd bought an automobile, a clean, used Studebaker, and he'd scoured the city, talking to every firm that was known to have a salesman on the road. Most of them drew the color line. Where they didn't, he had to buy the merchandise in advance, and ultimately found himself selling it cut-rate to get part of the money back. He was willing to work and determined not to let the depression beat him, no matter what. But it was the wrong time and the wrong place. Back to taking part-time jobs, he'd been laid off again.

The phone was ringing as he started up the stairs to the apartment. Juggling a shopping bag delayed his finding the key. By the time he got inside and picked up the receiver, the line was dead. He took his purchases, a fat hen, a quart of ice cream, and a pint of wine, into the kitchen. Job or no job, there was going to be a meal for Lillian tonight she'd be glad to come home to. Then he was going to take his wife out for a drive along Rock Creek Park and listen to a band concert. Those were his intentions.

The phone rang again. "Wheatley?" All he had to hear was the tone of her voice to know what the rest of her statement would be: don't wait for her, she'd be late getting home, they needed her at the White House, go ahead and eat without her.

"Exactly what I plan to do," he said.

"Wheatley, I am sorry . . ."

"Honey, I didn't mean that like it sounded . . . it's jus' I'd like to see you once a while without you bein' dead asleep . . . I know you're workin' . . . You think I asked to be laid off?"

"Wheatley, I wasn't criticizin' you for not workin'—I know you try, darlin' . . ." What good was it?—two voices on the telephone, reaching out but not connecting. Wheatley put Lillian's frustration into words. "Sometimes I feel you and me are two trains, on different tracks."

"No, Wheatley," she protested. "Two trains, maybe . . . but we goin' the same way."

His sigh came across the wire to her. For a moment she didn't speak. "You understand, don't you, Wheatley? I got no control over things, I have an obligation here, Their Majesties goin' arrive tomorrow . . ."

"I understand. Don't you work too hard. Yes, I be here when you get here." He hung up and went into the kitchen. The hen and the wine were on the table where he'd left them. The ice cream had begun to melt. *Their Majesties* . . .

It was the kind of day that made you wonder why they ever picked Washington for the nation's capital. Stifling, sultry, muggy. Inside, the kitchen was a purgatory; the back stairs, a steaming chimney. But none of these discomforts compared to the "heat under the collar" the servants were experiencing—the White House servants, that is. The British were very cool indeed, casting down-the-nose aspersions on the inconsequence of the White House. ("No tradition a-tall, barely the size of a hunting lodge.")

Their Highnesses had been in residence for several days. King George VI and Queen Elizabeth, according to Maggie and Mercer, who worked the second floor and had seen them firsthand, were gracious and easy to please. It was their servants who were a royal pain in the neck. "I don't think they even sweat," Roach said resentfully, after returning one of their breakfast trays to the kitchen.

"You know why, don't you?" Fraser said, "It's all those years the British spent in the Congo."

"Well now, we from the Congo too," Mays said with a wry twinkle. "How come we doin' all this sweatin'?"

"Got to remember," said Jackson, "in the Congo we didn't wear all these clothes . . ." That got a big laugh from some in the staff dining room. But those who had to wait on "the royals" failed to see any humor in it.

"Tell you one thing," Dixon said to Roach as they balanced loaded luncheon trays around the sharp turns in the stairwell, "I am not goin' to serve 'em again."

"Somebody got to carry food to 'em."

"They got legs, don't they? Why cain't they walk downstairs to *our* dining room?"

"You know the order."

"Who they think they be, anyway? They jus' like us, hired help."

"Luggin' their food's bad enough, but you are goin'

to have to serve 'em." The grousing carried both men as far as the second floor. They made the final flight in silence. British voices, steeped in hauteur, floated down to them.

"How anyone can live in this beastly climate is beyond me." It was the head valet speaking, a man of thin face and voice.

"India's hot," reminded the second valet in a Kensington accent.

"I s'pose. Empire, you know."

The two valets and three personal maids sat about an oval table set up for their use in the third-floor corridor. It was perfectly appointed, with full silver service, Royal Doulton china, and small union jacks at each place setting. Dixon put his tray down on the server and stood by, eyes elevated, hands folded behind his back, removing himself. Roach, painfully slow, lifted the silver dome and presented the platter. The King's personal valet scrutinized the poached salmon before nodding his approval. "Only one servingman? At home we always have a full staff in waiting on the royal servants."

"And printed menus for each meal," added the ladies' maid.

Roach, deftly handling fork and spoon, added parslied potatoes to the valet's plate. "We jus' doin' the best we can . . . got to realize, we folks jus' the poor Colonies . . ."

Maggie refused to take exception to anything the visiting servants said or did. This was the final phase of her long tenure at the White House, and nothing was going to spoil it: not snobbery, not anger, and certainly not the heat. There'd been worse summers. As she came out of west sitting hall she paused a moment and looked down the length of center hall, for the moment recalling the hot summer of Mr. Taft, the big bathtub, the tropical plants, and Lil'yan—what a scamp, dining with the President. These last months she'd been storing up memories . . . fortifying herself against the day when she could no longer be here. Thirty years, half her life, had been spent in these halls, on these stairs. Walking away would be the hardest steps she'd ever taken. But she wouldn't dwell on that now. Not yet.

She took the stairs to the third floor slowly, holding on to the banister that Mr. Coolidge had so thoughtfully provided. Once she reached the head of the stairs she moved quicker, skirting the royal servants' table, nodding to Dixon and Coates, and on into the sewing room.

"Dress ready yet? Miz Roosevelt waitin' for it."

Lillian pulled a basting thread from the just completed hem. "It's done, Mama, but Miz Roosevelt jus' goin' to suffocate in the heat, wearin' wool this kind of a day."

"She wants this dress, now come along . . ." Maggie put the long-sleeved, high-necked woolen dress over her arm, Lillian followed with her sewing basket. As they passed the British servants' table, the royal chambermaid was commenting on the newspaper describing the monarch's visit to Hyde Park: "A *picnic*," she said, offended. "Can you imagine . . . the President of the United States serving hot dogs to Their Majesties . . . *hot dogs?*"

"You taste one," Lillian advised her in passing, "with all the fixin's on it—you might jus' find out why you lost the Revolution . . ." As they went on down the stairs Maggie shook her head in despair. "I was hopin' as you got older, Lil'yan, you'd outgrow bein' fresh . . . I might as well give up, it's never goin' to happen . . ."

The electric fan stirred the air of the small dressing room that served as bedroom for the First Lady. But even in the main stream of the fan there was little relief for Mrs. Roosevelt, who was already discomforted by the woolen garment. "Not meanin' to be forward, Miz Roosevelt," Maggie said as she zipped her into it, "but you goin' to be so uncomfortable, wearin' this heavy dress out in the sun . . ."

Mrs. Roosevelt tucked a strand of hair up off her perspiration-beaded neck. "Maggie, Her Majesty and I agreed that wearing wool would be symbolic of support for the wool industry in England, New Zealand, and Australia . . ."

"But ma'am, the Queen's personal maid confided in me that due to the bloody hot weather—the maid's words, ma'am—Her Majesty has changed her mind and will be wearin' somethin' airy."

"That's Her Majesty's prerogative. I gave my word." Mrs. Roosevelt waited while Lillian removed a basting thread from the shoulder, then picked up a brimmed straw hat and started for the door. Lillian moved quickly after her.

"Miz Roosevelt, the hem's not quite even . . ."

"Good enough, nobody will be looking at my hemline." On a sudden decision, she turned back to her dressing table for a handful of facial tissues. Tucking two or three into the neckline of the dress, and under her arms, she advised, "Just don't ever give your word until you've checked the weatherman."

She left, to spend the afternoon in an open car, touring the city with the royal visitors.

"That's my lady," said Lillian admiringly.

Maggie looked at Lillian, mindful of how many times she had used that same phrase. "Not quite yet, don't rush it, chile. Not your lady yet . . . I still got four more days to go."

There were times in Maggie's life when she would have liked days to go faster, but these, she would have held back. It was a strange thing: the more she slowed up, the faster the days went. She thought on that, on her streetcar ride home the night before the last day. That evening, preferring to be alone, she urged Lillian and Wheatley to walk out by themselves. When they were gone she took out her memento box and for hours mused over scrapbooks, clippings, bits of faded ribbon, feathers, Mr. Wilson's pince-nez, her own scribbled notes . . . and realized she was holding thirty years in her lap.

That last day, in her best Sunday dress and the new hat Lillian had made her for the occasion, she went to the White House, cleaned out her locker, took her uniforms to the laundry, turned in her key, and took

her place at the head of the table, wearing the traditional orchid, while they feted her. The engraved silver
tray. The gold watch from the President and First Lady.
The autographed photographs. It went by so fast. She
heard it all, responded at the proper times, yet it all
seemed to be happening to someone else. *"To Margaret
Rogers, in recognition of thirty years' faithful service
to the White House . . ."* She got to her feet. "Thank
you, everybody . . . old friends, and you new people
I barely know. I thank you, all of you . . . Now . . . I
guess I been head maid too long not to remind you
it's time to get back to work."

They pushed back their chairs, they wished her good
luck, they hoped she'd come back and see them again.
In a moment the room was empty except for herself,
Mercer, Mays, Jackson, and Lillian, who busied themselves putting her presents back in their boxes, tying
the ribbons, and wondering, what do you say when
part of you is going?

"Lil'yan," Maggie said brusquely, "whether I'm
retirin' or not, you still got your work to do, so don't be
wastin' time here."

"Yes, Miz Rogers, I'm on my way." She gave her
mother a light kiss on the cheek and left quickly, as
she knew Maggie wanted her to.

"We'll walk you, Maggie," Mercer said. "Walk you
out."

"No. Want to go out the way I come in. By myself."
She set her hat on firmly, gathered her packages, and
left the room in the same businesslike way she'd done
hundreds of times before, as though she were merely
on her way upstairs to her chores. The door closed
on her. Mays, Mercer, and Jackson stood alone. None
of them spoke. They headed out to their posts.

Maggie came out of the staff entrance into the brilliant sunlight. Putting her packages down on the step
for a moment, she adjusted the brim of her hat against
the glare. Then she picked up the farewell gifts and
walked down the long, familiar path to the street. As
she came out of the gate onto the sidewalk at Pennsylvania Avenue, a car with an Indiana license plate

paused briefly near where she stood. "There it is," the driver pointed out to a carful of children. "That's the White House . . ." The car behind honked him on. The children were still looking out the back window as he followed the bend of the avenue. For a moment Maggie felt herself rooted to the spot, unable to go forward; yet she couldn't go back. She turned and looked at the long white building. *Thirty years* . . . Then she set her shoulders, and walked away.

At about the same time Maggie reached the street, Lillian arrived on second floor to assume her new obligations in the changeover. Fraser, who took his houseman duties seriously, had preceded her and was already instructing the new maids in the proper technique of dusting. When they first heard the siren, they only gave it peripheral attention. Sirens in the street were not unusual. They would come up, a whine from the distance, grow in intensity, and diminish. This one grew to a full banshee wail, ominously closer, until its dread signal was right up to the door of the White House.

"Mama!" Lillian dropped the duster and bolted in panic for the elevator. "Somethin's happened to Mama . . ." Fraser ran after her, to help her gain control. Mercer, hurrying up the back stairs, grabbed her by the shoulders, stopped her. "No, Lil'yan, no . . . Not your mama . . ."

"Who is it, then?" Fraser worried. "The Pres'dent? Miz Roosevelt?"

Mercer eased Lillian into a chair. "Now you just stay calm. It's Miss LeHand . . . took sick, they come to take her off to the hospital."

Lillian cried out, "Miss LeHand? But I saw her this mornin', she was fine, gettin' all dressed for that office party . . ."

"Don't take more than a minute to have a stroke, Lil'yan."

"Stroke? She's no older than I am."

"Trouble's no stranger to this house, Lil'yan. Been so from the beginnin', people give their lives to it . . ." His eyes clouded. "In our time, Maggie and me, we

seen a lot . . . Miz Taft's stroke . . . the first Miz
Wilson dyin' . . . Mr. Wilson, Miz Harding so sick
. . . Mr. Harding . . . that poor Coolidge boy . . . And
you were here when they took Mr. Howe . . ."

"Mercer," she protested, "that's enough, you bringin'
me way down . . ."

"Not meanin' to do that, Lil'yan. Jus' tellin' the plain
truth. Life seems to go along nice for a bit in this
house, then sudden, unexpected-like, comes trouble . . .
Big trouble . . ."

13

☒ ☒ ☒

War. The radio, newsreels, newspapers were glutted with it. The whole world seemed to be one giant, growing conflagration. Hitler now controlled most of Europe, the Balkans, Greece, Denmark, and Norway. A new word came into being: "blitzkrieg." A collaborator gave his name to the language: "quisling." The British had been driven into the sea at Dunkirk, gallantly rescued, and the tight little island was practically defenseless. When Maggie heard that, she prayed for all those people, for the pleasant, matronly Queen and the shy, stammering King who'd smiled at her.

Italy had declared war on Great Britain and France, FDR denouncing Mussolini in a speech: "The hand that held the dagger has struck it into the back of its neighbor." The roads leading out of Paris were clogged with fleeing refugees as the Germans marched in, to parade down the Champs-Élysées. Hitler, reversing Germany's humiliation of World War I, demanded the same railroad car at Compiègne to trumpet France's ignominious surrender. Jews throughout occupied Europe were forced to wear yellow stars.

In the United States, President Roosevelt was reelected for a third term. Americans got their draft num-

367

bers, and tried to reassure each other that they wouldn't be going to war. The Four Freedoms were articulated: of speech and expression, of worship, from want, and fear. "Don't see how they goin' negotiate that last one," Mays commented laconically.

In the staff dining room while the newspapers were passed up and down the table until they were worn ragged, nobody seemed to talk much. The memory of World War I was still acrid in their nostrils, and for the older ones, even the Spanish-American, with relatives and friends lost in the Tenth Cavalry's charge up San Juan Hill; many a black family remembered having paid in blood for that victory.

President Roosevelt made a personal appeal to Emperor Hirohito to use his power to help avert war between Japan and the United States . . .

The year 1941 was in its last month. It was Sunday. Lillian and Wheatley had a suitcase packed. Wheatley's jobs had been off and on, temporary at the War Department, Finance Department; but together they'd set aside a few dollars for a run up to Atlantic City. Winter in that resort, despite the weather, had its rewards: rooms were cheaper, hardly any people around. He would push her in a boardwalk chair like she was some society lady. A time for fun, for dreaming . . .

They walked home from church—a bit ahead of Maggie and Mercer—came into the apartment, packed a little lunch for the train ride, and were just going out into the hall, ready to close the door, meeting Maggie and Mercer on their way up, when the phone rang.

"I'll get it," Maggie said, "You two go on . . ." But Lillian hesitated. "Could be the White House, maybe some word about Miss LeHand." Wheatley had a feeling he ought to get her out of there fast, before something happened to spoil their chance of getting away: if it was the White House wanting her back, and she didn't know it, she couldn't be faulted for not being there . . .

"No, we don't have the radio on . . ." they heard Maggie say into the phone. "Put the radio on, Mercer," adding to the person calling, "Why? What happened? *The Japanese?* What you mean? We not at war with the Japanese . . ."

". . . the United States Navy crippled," the radio voice intoned. "This morning at 7:55, while Pearl Harbor slept . . ." Lillian stood with Maggie and Mercer, all immobilized as the words assailed them: "Devastated . . . decimated . . . Six American battleships, destroyed . . . sunk . . . Over three hundred planes on the ground . . . Toll in American lives well over two thousand . . ."

They didn't need to be told what was expected of them. Lillian and Mercer went directly to the White House in the clothes they'd worn to church. Wheatley came back into the apartment and unpacked the suitcase.

The White House geared up for war. There was a feeling of a fortress: gates chained, padlocked; military brass from the Pentagon rushing in and out all hours of the day and night; some cabinet members taking up residence, sleeping when and where they could; soldiers and guards everywhere. No extra guests, no tourists. The staff was fingerprinted, badged, identified, and challenged every time one of them went in or out.

The elevator was the subject of one of the first orders of the day. It was to be kept locked; no one was to use it except the President, those immediately involved with his care, the First Lady, the cabinet, the brass. This order set Lillian back on the stairs.

Mrs. Roosevelt put on the uniform of civil defense. Summoning the White House staff to west sitting hall, which she'd set up as an ancillary office, she sat on the edge of the desk and issued the dictum that rationing was in effect, everyone was to bring his own sugar and coffee from home. Meals were to be cut down. Only one egg, one piece of toast for breakfast; luncheon was to be equally spartan.

Lillian wasn't bothered by the rationing, or having to climb the stairs. It was the gas mask she minded. The grotesque thing hung on the inside of her sewing-room door, to be grabbed when the warning sounded for drills in the use of the bomb shelter. She'd been handed the mask that first Monday, when the staff grouped in the dining room around the radio to hear the President's voice: "Yesterday, December 7, 1941, a day which will live in infamy . . ." A sergeant and two privates had come into the room, each carrying a large box filled with the khaki snoutlike war apparel which they passed out to those assembled. Lillian accepted the mask with trembling hands, having the awful image of Emmett, in France, in that other war, smothered with poison gases, almost choking his life away . . . "I ask that the Congress declare that since the unprovoked and dastardly attack by Japan . . . a state of war . . . has existed between the United States and the Japanese Empire . . ."

These days had been especially trying for Maggie. All around her she felt the urgency of the time, yet here she was, stuck in an apartment with H. V. Kaltenborn and "The Lone Ranger" to fill her days. When Lillian's uneven step was heard on the stairs, she threw open the door, eager for companionship, for news . . .

"You didn't tell me you be comin' home . . ."

"Didn't know myself." Lillian gave her a kiss that missed its mark and went into the bathroom, turning on the shower . . .

"Wheatley's goin' be very disappointed, wouldn't have gone out, I'm sure, had he known you comin' back here . . ."

From under the suds of a shampoo, Lillian called to her, "Just decided I had to grab a minute to clean myself up and get some fresh clothes . . ."

"Don't you want some supper? I got pork chops."

"No, Mama, no time . . ." Lillian toweled her body and hair, pulled an overnight bag from the closet, and packed it with fresh underthings, a bathrobe, nightgown, and slippers.

"You not goin' spend the night there?"

"Got to, Mama, makin' blackout curtains—big job— only time I can get enough space to lay 'em out, when nobody's around . . ."

Lillian drew a slash of lipstick across her mouth and crutched to the kitchen, where she filled two small glass jars with sugar and coffee, labeling them with her name. Maggie complained from the doorway, "Hardly see you anymore."

"There's a war on . . ."

"And you so close-mouthed."

"Mama, everythin's top secret—house under military orders . . . Everybody briefed on how to evacuate the Pres'dent, should anythin' happen . . . Now that's all I'm allowed to tell you . . ."

"I have you to know I was thirty years over to the White House . . . Was I to give away any secrets, would have done it long ago . . ."

"Mama, you got to understand . . ."

"Don't you see, I got nothin' here alone, chile? Wheatley off on his own business, you not comin' home days on end . . ."

"You got your radio, Mama."

"You ever try to spend a whole day with that box talkin' at you?"

"Work on your book."

Maggie sniffed. *Who'd read it?* she thought. *World so busy, racing to destruction, who has time, who even cares, to look back with me?* "How's Miss LeHand?" she asked. "You can at least tell me about her. Or is that secret too?"

It wasn't secret, and it wasn't good. Missy LeHand had gone from the hospital to Warm Springs, Georgia, and then, at her own request, been brought back to the White House. Frail, aged far beyond her years, the effects of the stroke permanently with her, she spent her days in bed or in a wheelchair in the small room next to Lillian's sewing room. "Don't know why she come back to the White House, Mama, unless maybe it's the onliest place she feels she belongs . . . Won't eat, unless I'm right there to scold her, cain't sleep . . ."

Maggie nodded. How well she remembered what that was like, being needed that way. "Like my lady, Miz Harding," she said.

"I got to go, Mama." Lillian put the small jars into her purse, slipped into her coat, and picked up the overnight bag. "Tell Wheatley I am sorry I missed him, I'll try to call . . ."

As Lillian came out of the apartment she heard the entrance door downstairs close and footsteps she recognized ascending. "Wheatley," she called as she started down. The footsteps accelerated. He ran the rest of the way up to her. They met on the landing. The color of his suit, she saw even before he reached her, was one he'd never worn before, one she'd hoped never to see on him: the olive drab of the U.S. Army. In place of the gray felt hat he favored, an overseas cap was tilted over one eye. Panic welled up in her, and with it a dozen things she wanted to say. "It doesn't fit," was all she could manage to get out.

There was urgency in him, but here on the landing, caught midway between their life together and the unknown, time was against them. "Been tryin' to talk to you for days now, Lil'yan, but haven't seen you."

"You could have called me . . ."

"Not somethin' you want to say on the phone . . ."

"When did you sign up?"

"Last week . . ." He made a stab at a smile. "Got to admit, I got a steady job now."

"Oh, Wheatley, I don't want anything to happen to you . . ." She leaned against the wall, hiding her face. He turned her gently around to him. "I know that."

"You got to come back."

"Oh, I be comin' back, don't you worry 'bout that. Bullet not made, got my name on it."

"Wheatley, this is no good . . . I got to get back to the White House . . . tell you what, you wait here at the apartment, I'll try to get some time off tomorrow mornin'."

"Won't be around. I'm reportin' five in the mornin' to a bus for camp down in North Carolina."

He held her close to him, then he walked with her to the streetcar stop. They said their goodbyes on the corner as the trolley clanged its way to them.

"I been seein' things clear for quite some time now,

Lil'yan. When I get back, I'm goin' get a place of my own . . ."

"Our own . . ."

"No. Way you feel about your mama, I can handle that—nobody's fault, you a fine woman, I like to think I'm a pretty nice fella . . ." He smiled sadly. "But you not married to me. You married to the White House . . ." He kissed her tenderly on the forehead. For an instant, she clung to him. "Take care of yourself . . ." The motorman delayed starting up. It was a common sight these days, partings. Lillian got onto the streetcar and it started away. She looked back through the window that held Wheatley's image until the car, bound to the tracks, turned the corner.

The material was inky black: the color of night, the color of mourning. Lillian crawled around the floor on hands and knees, pinning the huge panels together. The tedious, meticulous work kept her from thinking about herself. From time to time, as she reversed her direction and crawled toward the President's door, Murdoch, on duty, glanced up from the magazine he was reading, but they didn't speak.

She came to the end of a panel, reversed herself, and began pinning another length of material to the massive drape.

The door opened and the President wheeled himself out. The dull gray sweater he wore over an open-throated shirt accented his pallor. Dark circles under his eyes and age blotches on his skin informed of the toll the war and pressures of office were taking. Murdoch moved quickly to him. "Can I help you, Mr. President? Get anything for you?"

"No, just want to wheel around. Tired of reading dispatches . . . Lillian, what are you doing here so late?"

"Making blackout curtains, sir."

"Waste of time, Lillian. Government inefficiency. Why, this building's a great white sitting duck, can be seen a hundred miles away. Anybody wanting to bomb it from on high couldn't miss it . . . Save your energy," he advised.

"I had orders, sir, from civil defense."

"Oh, well . . . they supersede me . . ." He wheeled over to her, right across the black material.

"You're trackin' it up, sir."

He laughed heartily, but didn't wheel off it. His features arranged themselves in a severe frown. "Little girl, I've a bone to pick with you."

"Sir?"

"I'm very displeased. You disobeyed my orders, just don't know what I'm going to do about it . . ."

"Beggin' the Pres'dent's pardon, but you didn't give me any orders, sir."

"Prettyman tells me you've been walking up and down the back stairs."

"Elevator's locked, sir. Orders are, no one uses it but you . . ."

"That's what happens in a democracy. Turn your back, orders get countermanded." He called over his shoulder to Murdoch. "Whenever the little girl needs the elevator up or down, it is to be unlocked."

"Yes, sir."

The President turned back to Lillian, spoke with mock severity, "Now, do as you're told . . . or you'll get a lot of flak from me."

"Flak, sir?"

The smile disappeared from his face. "It's a new word, little girl . . . German word, war word . . . we'll be hearing it a lot . . ." Oppressively burdened, he turned and wheeled back into his room. She paused in her work, watching him go. As he disappeared behind the door, for an instant Wheatley took his place. Then he too was gone. She finished pinning the material, rolled it up. Murdoch helped her lift it, hung it over and around her shoulders. She took it up to the sewing room and stitched away most of the night.

As the war escalated, tensions great and small developed. "What's this sign say?" Mays put his face close to the handwritten message on the wall of the staff dining room but couldn't make it out. Fraser read it to him. "Says, 'If you feel attached to your hand, keep it out of my sugar ration.' "

"Who wrote it?"

"Beats me. Could be anybody."

"Seems pretty drastic, but I get the point." Mays put on his glasses and squinted down the row of individual sugar jars until he came to the one bearing his name. He spooned sugar into his coffee, sat down at the table, and started to turn the pages of the newspaper lying there.

"Don't lose my place," Fraser called from the hot table. "I'm readin' somethin' there. *Rommel . . .*" he said in stressful tones as he sat back down and resumed the article on the inside page. "If the British don't get some help soon . . ." He let the worry dangle, but no one wanted to talk about the war.

"How you doin' over to the Howard University?" Jackson asked him.

"Painful. Comin' along. College no cinch, I tell you, especially when you wait as old as I am before you go."

"You a boy," Mercer protested. "What are you anyway, Fraser, thirty-nine, forty?"

"Jus' a striplin'," Jackson echoed. But Fraser had gone back to his newspaper and the war news, face furrowed in concern.

The timid knock and "Excuse me" came at the same time. The young man who stepped into the room wasn't more than twenty. He seemed to be made of circles, with round eyes that always wore a look of astonishment, round head—and while he wasn't actually fat, his body had a roundness to it.

"What can we do for you?" Mercer asked.

The young man shifted his hat from one hand to the other. "I'm lookin' for Mr. Morgan."

"Morgan got drafted. Left yesterday to be with his folks before gettin' his orders."

"Oh . . ." He tugged at the jacket that didn't match his pants, seemingly momentarily lost. "Who do I talk to then? I was jus' hired, he's supposed to break me in. I'm the new servin'man."

"Well, I'm the old servin'man." Mercer finished his coffee. "How come you not in the army, boy?"

"I got flat feet, I'm sure I'm goin' to get my 4-F any day."

"You got any trainin', waitin' table?"

"No, sir."

"Then you got the right credentials. Flat feet and no experience . . ." He shoved back his chair. "Fraser, I'm goin' clean up the map room. You get a few minutes to spare, start trainin' this boy."

Mercer detoured to the door, pausing to put up a blue star on the bulletin board for Morgan. It made an even dozen.

"What's your name?" Fraser asked the new man as he showed him how to clear the table.

"R. Gus Handy."

"That *A-r-g-u-s?*" Fraser asked.

"No, sir, that's *R* period Gus Handy."

"What's the *R* stand for?"

"Bible name my mother give me. Reuben."

"Well, 'round here you'll be Handy, that suit you?"

"Fine, sir."

"No need to call me 'sir,' my name's Fraser. Gentleman just went out, he's Mercer. These two gentlemen sittin', readin', they're Mays and Jackson, both on the door, hinges don't work without 'em."

On his way to the map room Mercer was thinking how nice it was to have someone young around. Morgan leaving yesterday sorrowed him. All the young ones called up. Going to have a war, they ought to take the old ones, like himself. He chuckled at the thought. All get tuckered and lay down, that'd sure get the war over and done with fast. *Praise Jesus, let it be over . . .*

The young corporal guarding the door let him into the map room. The other soldier, a sergeant, followed him and stood guard while he did his cleaning. He dusted, but didn't go near the maps with all those colored pins standing for ships at sea. When the room was clean, he gathered up the bits and pieces of paper that had fallen to the floor and stuffed them into wastebaskets. Accompanied by the soldiers, he carried them to the furnace room to be burned.

Lillian was performing what had come to be her wartime chore. Flanked by two soldiers, she stood outside the White House, waiting for the laundry truck to appear. When it did, the soldiers lifted the padlocked baskets and carried them to the laundry room—at which time, Lillian often noticed, the room seemed to empty while she inserted the padlock key, opened the basket, and took out the linens. "You can all come back in," she called. "No bomb today." Arms filled with linens, she took the elevator to second floor. The sheets and pillowcases, which seemed always to need mending, she took upstairs with her.

The door to Missy LeHand's room was open. Lillian paused at the doorway, called her name. Missy, sitting in her wheelchair near the window, turned her head at the sound of Lillian's voice. The deteriorating illness had turned her hair white; her eyes were dimmed, perpetually anxious. Her one useful hand stayed in motion, like a frightened butterfly. "Come—come in . . ."

Lillian took a step into the room. "You're lookin' sprightly, Miss LeHand." It was getting more difficult all the time to pretend, and what hurt the most, Missy was aware of the pretense.

"Don't—go . . . How's—the—Pres-ident . . ."

"Oh, he's holdin' up fine . . ."

"What—will he—do—without my—help . . ."

"You think about gettin' well, that's your job. I got to get to my work, now, Miss LeHand."

Missy reached out, fearful, fingers trembling, "You'll —be back?"

Lillian held the frail hand. "You know me, always available for a quick game of cards, a bet on the horses —I'm pretty good at that . . ."

Missy tried a smile that only made the drooping side of her face look all the more distressing.

Lillian gave her a hearty wink and left. In a while, Missy could hear the steady hum of the sewing machine. She felt secure, knowing Lillian was near.

Missy LeHand's room was like Maggie's memento box, but where Maggie had six Presidents, Missy had one. A snapshot album open on the table was filled with pictures of the Roosevelt family, scrapbooks bulging with clippings on her President all the way back to when she was twenty and had come to him, barely out of school, inexperienced, bringing with her nothing but stamina, a willingness to work, and devotion. Every wall of the small room was covered with framed photographs—of FDR and the family at Campobello, before the polio . . . at Albany, in the governor's chair . . . on sailboats, in open cars, on the campaign trail; the brim of his hat pushed up, the big toothy grin, the hand raised in a wave.

Missy sat by herself, looking at the pictures that were all she had left. The nurse, one of the two who were her constant companions, came back with a refill of medicine. Missy took a spoonful, unprotesting. Through the window she could see the antiaircraft gun on the roof.

Lillian could see it, too. There were several on this side of the building, and on the other. Every four hours around the clock, two artillerymen came up the stairs for each gun emplacement, relieved the men on duty, and two artillerymen from each gun emplacement went down the stairs. Something like ships' bells, telling you the time. She'd gotten used to the sound of them, didn't even turn her head anymore as they went by her door.

But this frantic thudding of boots wasn't any routine change of personnel. The sound began at the foot of the stairs and grew like a groundswell of disaster, rolling over her, as the two young soldiers from the map room took the steps four at a time and charged past her room down the corridor, flinging open the door, banging it against the wall. And out onto the roof.

"Lillian!" Missy shrieked.

Lillian dropped what she was doing and hurried out of the room to go calm Miss LeHand's fears. Mercer was coming up the stairs, at his fastest clip (far slower than the soldiers). Lillian paused to ask him, "What's goin' on, Mercer?" Out of breath and harried, he shook his head, and went out onto the roof the same way the soldiers had. While she soothed away Miss LeHand's terror, Lillian could see the soldiers and Mercer frantically searching for something.

A short while later they came back in and went downstairs—Mercer, relieved, pausing to explain to Lillian that when they were burning the trash from the map room, one very important piece of paper had gone up the flue, only half charred. Thank God it hadn't left the roof. From now on they'd have to burn sensitive papers in a mesh basket.

When Miss LeHand was quieted, Lillian took the mended linen down to the second floor. "Never goin' get used to antiaircraft guns on the roof," she said to Fraser, who was at the service closet, taking out cleaning equipment.

"Has to be, Lil'yan," he answered. "War's goin' get worse. We goin' be fightin' in Europe too. Soon. Mark my words . . ."

"Oh, I hope you are wrong, Fraser."

"Hope I am too, but don't appear that way to me from what I read."

She watched Fraser walk away and thought, such a long time since she'd seem him smile. Or do a quick unexpected, spontaneous dance step. He had no one in the war that she knew of, yet it seemed to be on his mind all the time.

Roach and Coates rolled the luncheon cart out of the elevator. Only eleven o'clock in the morning, but it was four hours since the President and his advisers had eaten. They'd begun arriving at 4:00 a.m.—General Marshall, Secretary of War Stimson, Admiral Leahy—and had been closeted in the President's quarters ever since. A steady flow of cablegrams had been coming in all morning. Prettyman, concerned that the President had barely touched his breakfast, had taken it upon himself to call down for a luncheon tray. He held the door open as they brought it through and indicated with a nod of his head that they were to take it to the far side of the room and set up a table.

The President, haggard, savagely jammed a cigarette into his holder. "How *many*, General Marshall? How many taken prisoner?"

For all the control, the coolness of command bred into him, General George Marshall was a man badly shaken. "Mr. Stimson has those figures, Mr. President."

Stimson consulted the cable that had just been handed him. "Over eleven thousand, Mr. President, we don't have the exact numbers."

"And dead . . . wounded?" the President demanded.

"Two thousand or more, near as we know."

"What about General Wainwright? Is he alive?"

"Yes, sir," General Marshall said heavily. "The Japanese will keep him alive. You may be sure they'll capitalize on the fact that they have him."

Roosevelt wheeled his chair sharply one way, then the other: his only means of pacing. His advisers waited.

At the other side of the room Roach, setting out plates and flatware, whispered anxiously to Coates. "Did I hear him? He say Wainwright? We lose Corregidor?"

Coates nodded. "Seems like."

"My boy's out there someplace . . . on a ship . . ." For a moment Coates thought Roach was going to drop a plate, but he didn't; he put it down carefully and went about his work.

"Mr. President, we'll recapture Corregidor . . . and the rest of the Pacific, sir," Admiral Leahy assured.

"I'm certain, Admiral Leahy . . . certain we will . . . with time . . ." The President removed his glasses. There were painful red marks on his nose from the pince-nez. He rubbed them, closing his eyes against the weight of office. "Henry," he said to Stimson, "call a full cabinet meeting within the hour."

"Yes, Mr. President."

"We've got a long road back." He was speaking more to himself than to them. "A long, brutal road . . . And the cost . . . My God, the cost in lives . . ."

There was a long silence, as though a prayer was being observed.

THE BATAAN DEATH MARCH

THE BATTLE OF MIDWAY

TOBRUK FALLS

Every twist of the radio dial brought battles into the house. Maggie was torn; she could never really turn them away; they were out there, on the airwaves, one more horrible than the other, but there was only so much agony a person could endure. Her days of forced inactivity were long. Without the sound of a human voice hours on end, the silence of her life was sometimes suffocating. There were neighbors to visit with, and grocery shopping to do, but everywhere was the same depressed mood. The demands of the White House on Lillian's time had narrowed the hours they shared to mighty few; it was the same with Mercer and Mays. Maggie found herself walking back and forth in the small rooms and wondering what was happening over at 1600 Pennsylvania Avenue. That was another "old lady" development, she thought: talking out loud to herself: "Woman, don't let yourself turn into one of those old chair rockers. You want people pointin' their finger, sayin', 'Look at that crazy old woman, jib-jabbering away at herself'?"

She set aside her memento box as too much looking back into the past, and turned on the radio to Henry Aldrich. His cracked, adolescent "Coming, Mother" rang through the parlor and made her laugh. She settled down in the armchair to listen.

Fraser came up the stairs and hesitated outside Maggie's door before knocking. Through the door, he could hear the radio he'd brought to the apartment with him back in Mr. Hoover's time, and had left behind as a gift to Maggie when Lillian married and he'd moved out. *Everything changes,* he thought. For a moment his mind played back on some of the good times, the lighthearted, untroubled times. There didn't seem to be too many of those, when you added it all up. *I guess they're just the sweetenin',* he thought, *to make the rest of what you have to swallow go down.* Maggie's laughter was rich and full. He hated to take that away from her, but he had to. He knocked.

"Jus' a minute, I be comin' . . ." The words were said through a chuckle that died as she opened the door to find Fraser in the uniform of a Red Cross staff aide, carrying a B-4 bag. She shook her head vigorously, everything about her crying out "NO." He gently moved her back into the room, closing the door.

"I saved sayin' goodbye to you till last, Maggie."

Henry Aldrich's antics didn't belong in such a moment. Maggie turned him off. *"Why,* Fraser . . . why? You almost past the age of bein' drafted, they never goin' get to you . . . Why you got to go?"

"Been tryin' to figure that out myself, Maggie . . . and while I was puzzlin', the Red Cross said yes to my application . . ."

"But you fixin' to be a teacher . . ."

"I'll get to that, college be here when I get back . . ."

"But, Fraser, you always sayin' time not come yet for you to worry . . ."

He smiled with effort. "I did say that, didn't I? Well . . . things are different. Time has come . . . I'm not goin' 'cause I care for war. I don't. I been tryin' to puzzle out why I am goin' . . . It come down to, I got to *do* somethin' . . . Never got that Bonus Army out of my mind . . . soldiers needin' help. Somebody's got to be there, Maggie, help 'em when they get hurt . . ."

Maggie could no longer accurately see him. The tears in her eyes blurred him, turned him into Emmett Junior. "I remember so well," she said, "Emmett goin' off. Said that was goin' be the last war."

Fraser opened his wallet. "Want you to have my ration stamps, Maggie."

"That's real generous of you, Fraser." As he bent to pick up the B-4 bag she grabbed his arm, offering refreshments—anything to delay his departure. But there was no more time.

"Got a train to catch, Maggie. I'll write to you . . ."

"We be countin' on that, Lil'yan and me."

He gave the room a lingering, affectionate look. "I'll always think of this place as home." He leaned down, kissed her on the cheek. For an instant her arms held, then released him.

"Now don't you go gettin' yourself hurt, y'hear?"

"Nothin' to worry 'bout." His fingers touched the Red Cross patch on his sleeve. "Couldn't be safer with Florence Nightingale . . ." A broad, reassuring smile, and he was gone. She stood at the top of the stairs, listening to his footsteps. The sound of the front door closing came to her, and with it an overwhelming sense of loss. She went back into the apartment and sat in the chair.

"A *gun?*" Lillian said. In the alcove of the staff dining room, she watched Mercer prepare a tray and couldn't believe what he'd just told her. "A gun?" she repeated.

He put a lace doily on the tray and wrapped black bread in a napkin. "Right there in his suitcase. I was unpackin' Mr. Molotov, lifted his shirts out to put 'em in the drawer, and there it was—a pistol, big and ugly . . ."

"What'd you do?"

"Didn't touch it, guarantee you that. Informed the Secret Service, don't know what they goin' do 'bout it."

"He say anythin' to you 'bout it?"

"Mr. Molotov? Wasn't there when I was unpackin'— him or his aide either. One of the chauffeurs said he took 'em over to their embassy."

"Then who's the tray for?"

"His valet. Know what else was in the commissar's suitcase? A big hunk of dried salami and black bread— guess he didn't figure we goin' feed 'em . . ." Mercer checked the items on the tray. "Lessee . . . caviar, black bread, raw onion, one hundred proof vodka."

"You'd think a valet would come down for his own tray," Lillian said.

"Wouldn't you, though . . ." Mercer went out the door, shaking his head. What was the world coming to . . . Bolsheviks in the White House. As he ascended the back stairs to second floor and traversed the length of center hall to the rooms reserved for royalty and world figures, he was practicing the minimal Russian that had been given him by Chief Usher Crim. "Lessee now . . . *Da* . . . 'yes.' *Nyet* . . . 'no.' *Da da, nyet nyet.*" With a "here goes" shrug, he rapped on the door. The valet's voice came to him, slightly muffled. *"Da?"* Then, puzzlingly, *"Pazhahlista zeedyech."* Mercer, unsure whether he'd been bade to enter or not, opened the door slightly, " 'Scuse me . . ."

He knew the instant he opened the door that he should have turned around and closed it behind him. But there were times in a man's life when his reflexes just don't take orders from his brain.

The valet, female, stood in the center of the room, stark naked. Toweling her short-cropped hair, she gave him a pleasant smile and gestured him forward. *"Zeedyech pazhahlista . . . Da . . . Da . . ."* "Yes, sir," he said, "no, ma'am . . . thank you, sir, ma'am . . ." and finally was able to put the tray down and leave the room posthaste. He chortled all the way down to the changing room.

"And there she was," Mercer recounted, "wearin' nothin' but a towel—on her head."

"Was it one of ours or theirs?" Jackson wondered.

Mays wised him up. "Haven't you heard? We got lend-lease . . ."

"Tell you the truth, Jackson, didn't have my glasses on," Mercer said. They chuckled to themselves, shaking their heads. Mays sat on the bench, crossing one foot over onto his knee, rubbing his ever bothersome foot. "Fraser goin' get a kick out of . . ." He stopped, remembering that Fraser was gone. "Forgot . . ."

"Mays, you got no memory at all," Jackson chided, it being easier on the emotions to kid around than to talk about the realities. But once Fraser's name was spoken, he was in the room with them. "Fraser's a good man, goin' miss him," Mercer said. Mays and Jackson nodded. "How long has he been here, anyway?"

"Come in with Mr. Hoover," said Jackson.

"Now who's got no memory?" said Mays. "Was Mr. Coolidge, don't you recollect? Taught the Coolidge boys to dance."

Mercer reflected that it was a long time back. "Sure

don't seem the same around here without Maggie . . .
Fraser . . ."

"No, sure don't . . ."

"Funny thing 'bout years," Mays mused as he put on
his shoe and tied the laces. "They don't seem to be
movin' at all, then one day you look up, and they all
jus' kind of ambled right 'round the corner . . ."

They finished dressing, all acutely aware of their
geriatric status. To keep from dwelling on their diminishing ranks, Mercer made an attempt at lightness.
"Think I ought to go back, see if it was our towel or
theirs?" The others smiled, but the mood couldn't be
salvaged.

"Hope Fraser goin' be all right," Jackson said as they
put on their hats and went to the door. Mays assured,
"Oh, he goin' be fine . . . fine . . . fine . . ." They left
the room. Mercer, the last one out, turned off the light.

The days were lengthening; it would soon be winter
again. The only chance Lillian had of enjoying the daylight was to occasionally go out on the south grounds
and watch the turning leaves fall. Piles of autumn leaves
would always remind her of Emmett and Charlie Taft.
She took her lunch out under a tree that President Polk
had planted, and after that went back to finish her day's
work. It was dark when she left the White House at
six thirty: darker than dark, with no moon, no street-
lights; ghostly streetcars, automobiles creeping along
with headlights taped up except for a sliver across the
middle, like a sinister eye. Windows behind which people were beginning to have their dinner, blacked out.
No welcoming light anywhere made the streets seem
hostile, frightening.

Lillian had gotten a ride home with one of the office
workers, and promised herself she wouldn't go through
that knuckle-chewing experience again. "Thanks a lot,"
she called. The crutch was an advantage, in that she
could thrust it out for obstacles before she ran smack
into them. She picked her way to the curb, across the
sidewalk, up the stone steps, and into the apartment
vestibule. The hanging light fixture was draped with

black crepe paper but gave off enough illumination for her to find her way up the stairs. It was with relief that she came into the lighted apartment.

"Mama?" In the kitchen two plates were set out for supper, and a pot still steamed on the stove. "Mama . . ." Lillian checked the spare bedroom and bathroom, but Maggie wasn't in the apartment. She picked up her purse and started for the door when it opened and Maggie, out of breath from the stair climb, came in.

"Where have you been?"

"Thought I'd walk up and meet you."

"I got a ride home." Lillian helped her mother off with her coat. "You shouldn't be out on the street this time of night . . ."

"Can't expect me to sit cooped up all the time . . . Minute dark comes, got to close the blackout curtains, can't even look out the window evenin's, anymore . . ."

As they went into the kitchen, Lillian continued the scolding, as to a child who hasn't learned a lesson. "Streets not safe . . . no light out there, you could hurt yourself."

Maggie scoffed. "You sound like that air-raid warden I run into . . . Frettin' me for walkin' around in the dark in my own neighborhood. I told him, I'll have you know I have worked from kin-see to cain't-see, walked back and forth to that White House before the sun come up, and way after it come down—night, day, rain, hot, cold, snowdrifts so high . . . you name it." She lit the flame under the coffeepot, and dished stew, with its allotted meager ration of meat, onto their plates. Lillian got milk, bread, and a smidgen of rationed butter from the refrigerator.

"You were a lot stronger then, Mama."

"You tryin' tell me I'm not as able as anybody else over there? Why, Mays, Mercer, and Jackson, they my age, they still workin' . . ."

"That's 'cause the younger men all got drafted, Mama."

"Well, what happened today?" Maggie, now that she had her feet under the table and conversation going, was ready for news bulletins, but Lillian's fatigue was catalyst to irritation.

"Mama, I am dog tired."

Maggie puffed her cheeks in annoyance and loudly exhaled. "Sure don't tell me much. Wouldn't have known the Prime Minister Mr. Churchill been there, hadn't I read it in the papers."

"Took us by surprise, too, Mama."

"You could at least said they were layin' in supply of brandy and see-gars and let me form my own conclusions."

Lillian smiled absently and continued to eat. Maggie tried again. "The Pres'dent ... how's he farin'?"

"Workin' terrible hours ... seems he's always catchin' the influenza ..."

"You didn't tell me he was sick again."

"Didn't I, Mama? Shows you how tired a body can be, thought I told you ... Well anyway, he hardly ever jokes or smiles like he used to."

"Not surprisin', Americans fightin' in Africa and the Pacific both."

Lillian got up and poured coffee. "Was there any mail today?"

"From your brother ..." She brought the letter from her apron pocket.

Lillian unfolded it and tried to keep her question casual. "This all that come?"

"That's all. Postcard yesterday from Fraser, you read that. You still expectin' to hear from Wheatley?"

"I think 'bout him, wonder ... worry ..." As Lillian read the letter she realized how very much she missed Emmett.

Maggie must have read her thoughts. "Miss him myself so bad, sometimes in the night I wake up, hearin' his voice—jus' as plain, like he was in the room. Worry so about him, gettin' wounded ... in those trenches ... in the rain ..."

Lillian looked at her in alarm. Was Mama caught up in a memory? Or a memory lapse?

"Funny ..." Maggie mused, moving to the table with

the coffeepot. She saw the full cups, and took the pot back to the stove, continuing with a chuckle, "So funny there in the letter, 'bout him and the other doughboys pourin' water on that hard cake and eatin' it out of their helmets like mush . . ."

"Mama, this is *now* . . ."

"What?" Maggie seemed startled, disoriented.

"Mama . . . Nineteen forty-two. Another war altogether."

"Well . . . 'course . . . 'course it's forty-two. What did you think it was? I'll get out there, Arizona, one of these days, visit Emmett and his wife." Her attention returned to the letter, but not to the extent that she failed to see Lillian pick up the medicine bottle from the table. "And quit countin' those pills every day."

"Didn't take 'em, did you, like you s'posed to? Or go back, see the doctor."

"What I want to bother him for? He got enough to do, tendin' the Pres'dent and people over there that—" A sharp gasp; Maggie's breathing was suddenly short, her manner apprehensive. Recognizing the symptoms, Lillian handed her a pill and moved quickly to the sink. Maggie took the medication, drank the water, and calmly went back to rereading the letter.

It bothered Lillian more than she would admit. The fear was always there that she'd go to work some morning and Mama'd get taken sick, or worse; so she paid a neighbor lady to keep an eye on her mother, an arrangement which Maggie tolerated only a short time, complaining she couldn't stand "that woman hangin' 'round, talkin' my ear off."

There were frequent reminders after that of Maggie's disturbing memory lapse. She took to losing her glasses with regularity, misplacing things from her memento box and accusing Lillian of having put them somewhere without telling her. Small things, but frequent. Mercer assured Lillian there was nothing to worry about. "People get older, Lil'yan, they tend to get mixed up now and again. Do it myself sometimes, don't mean a thing . . . nothin' to fret about your mama . . ."

The war dragged on, but that winter of '42–'43 some light appeared on the bloody horizon. The Americans drove the Japanese off Guadalcanal and once and for all wrenched the Kasserine Pass from Rommel. The last of the Germans at Stalingrad surrendered. Every hopeful headline had its effect on the staff at the White House. If, when the President was rolled through, he smiled or waved, Mercer and Mays would check the paper thoroughly to see if there was some news about the war they'd missed.

For three days running the mood had been fairly high in the White House. Even the new maid, Evalina, who carped about Lillian riding the elevator when others had to walk, had been surprisingly civil. Mercer, on a ladder, cleaning crystal wall sconces, hummed to himself. Lillian was damp-ragging the leaves of a rubber plant in center hall when she heard the familiar footsteps and looked up to see Maggie, in maid's day uniform, coming out of the backstairs corridor. Lillian dropped the rag and hurried to her. "Mama," she whispered, distressed. "What you doin' here?"

"I was sent for," Maggie said pridefully. "I am needed."

"Mama, you are mixed up . . . don't you remember? You retired . . ."

"I got to see the First Lady."

"Come on, Mama . . ." Mercer hurriedly came down the ladder to help Lillian get Maggie out of there before she came back to the present and realized her predicament.

"What do you say, Maggie, we go down, get a nice cup of coffee?"

She resisted the pull on her arm. "No, Mercer, no. I have you to know I was sent for . . ."

They were both gently, if insistently, tugging at her when the door to west sitting hall slid open and Mrs. Roosevelt stepped out to witness what to Lillian was about to be the most humiliating experience of her life. "Oh, Maggie," Mrs. Roosevelt called. *Here it comes,* thought Lillian. *Mama's goin' to die when she realizes what she's done.* But the First Lady was moving toward them, a welcoming smile on her face. "I'm so glad you could come on such short notice. There is no one else I would trust to handle Madame Chiang Kai-shek's visit. Now if you'll come along downstairs with me," Mrs. Roosevelt went on, "we'll discuss some of the details. I want you to be thoroughly familiar with Madame Chiang's needs and wants." Mrs. Roosevelt went ahead to the elevator. Maggie, just a step behind, paused to run a finger across a table. For the briefest instant she turned and faced Lillian and Mercer, holding the accusing finger aloft. "Dust," she mouthed. Then she disappeared after the First Lady. Mercer and Lillian knew when they'd been had. Shaking his head, he went back up the ladder. Lillian whipped a dustcloth from her apron pocket and dusted the offending table.

During the elevator's descent Mrs. Roosevelt impressed upon Maggie the diplomatic importance of Madame Chiang's visit. "I've arranged some special personal comforts for her. As a matter of fact, I'm preparing one right now in the staff dining room."

The room was empty when they arrived. Mrs. Roosevelt moved directly to the hot plate where a kettle was already steaming. From an antique tea tin she took a heavy pinch of leaves and dropped them into a teapot to let them steep. "Hundred-year-old tea, Maggie. Madame Chiang will be flattered we've gone to these lengths to please her." She strained the tea, pouring it into two cups. "Would you care to taste it?"

Both Maggie and the First Lady, braving the pungent odor, took it unsweetened. Which was just as well, in Maggie's opinion. Even sugar couldn't mask the staleness. She swallowed some, hoping her distaste didn't show. Mrs. Roosevelt smiled gamely. "I'll admit, it's not really my cup of tea . . ."

"Not bad though, ma'am," Maggie assured, "for hundred years old."

Mrs. Roosevelt took another sip. "But then each culture has its own ways, we should try to understand their tastes."

Maggie's good manners prevailed, and she took another sip. "Yes, ma'am."

On the table was an exquisite antique tea set, translucent and fragile as eggshells. "Now these dishes," Mrs. Roosevelt said, as she carried her cup to the table, "they're for Madame Chiang's personal use; her embassy sent them over. They're—I've forgotten which dynasty they said . . . I just hope we don't break any."

"Give you my word, ma'am, no one will touch 'em but me."

"That's why I wanted you, Maggie, and no one else." Mrs. Roosevelt lifted and rolled her shoulders to relieve the tension in her back. "My, it's good to sit, I'm still not over my last trip . . ." Determined to find something palatable about the tea, she sampled it again. Maggie followed suit. "Sit down, Maggie, good heavens, sit down." Maggie sat, stiffly, self-conscious about being at table with the First Lady, but Mrs. Roosevelt made it seem the most comfortable circumstance, sipping tea and chatting. "Oh, and the embassy will probably be sending over a cook. I don't know if he speaks English, or even if he understands it . . . But please," she implored, "see that peace is kept in the kitchen."

"Yes, ma'am, I will surely do that."

Mrs. Roosevelt looked reflectively into the cup. "We can certainly use peace somewhere in this world."

"We all prayin' for that, ma'am."

"So much destruction . . ."

"If I might say, ma'am, I been readin' and hearin' on the radio 'bout you . . . how you been movin' 'round, travelin' . . . seein' the soldiers—bringin' back all those letters to their mothers. That was a blessin' you did, ma'am."

Mrs. Roosevelt shook her head sadly. "So many boys in the hospitals . . ."

"Your sons come to my mind, ma'am—all bein' in the war. I pray for 'em every night."

"That's kind of you, Maggie." She sighed deeply. "They're never out of my mind, no matter where I am or what I'm doing."

"I know that feelin', ma'am. Remember when my son was fightin' in World War I."

"I never knew that, Maggie."

"Oh, yes, ma'am. He was decorated—promoted to second lieutenant on the battlefield."

"I'm sure he was a fine soldier. Where is he now?"

"Arizona, ma'am. Mr. Coolidge arranged it. You see, my boy was gassed."

"Oh, I'm sorry to hear that."

"Yes, ma'am."

"If the mothers of the world ever formed a coalition there'd never be a war."

"For a fact."

"Something to think about, isn't it, Maggie?"

"It is that, ma'am . . . Who knows? Look what the suffragettes did with their marchin'."

Mrs. Roosevelt smiled and got to her feet. Maggie pushed her chair back to follow.

"No, no, you stay. Finish your tea." But Maggie was glad to be rid of the bitter obligation. "Thank you, ma'am, I've had enough." She accompanied the First Lady to the door and reached to open it for her, but Mrs. Roosevelt already had it.

"Maggie, I'm counting on you."

" 'Deed I know that, ma'am."

"Oh, one more thing. *Silk* . . . Madame Chiang sleeps only on silk sheets . . ."

Lillian discovered it was to be a round robin of silk sheets. The wife of the Generalissimo, the youngest of the celebrated Soong sisters, not only required silk on her bed, but a blanket had to be sewn between the sheets, its corners mitered by hand so that no wool would touch her body. After having been used once, the combination had to be ripped apart, the sheets and blankets washed, and the process begun all over again. Lillian spent her mornings on the floor of the sewing room, shoeless, with the delicate pastel sheets spread out on clean paper as she meticulously hand-stitched a fresh blanket into its silk covering.

Maggie, climbing the stairs, paused at the landing,

her chest tight for lack of breath; then, eased somewhat, continued on up to Lillian's room.

"Mama . . ." Lillian's involuntary shout of protest caused Maggie to quickly close the door for fear the whole house would hear it. "What you tryin' to do, kill yourself? Why didn't you send somebody else up with this stuff . . ." She took the blanket, silk sheets, and laundry bag with which Maggie was laden and sat her down in a chair. "That Madame Chiang's runnin' you ragged."

"My job to take care of Madame Chiang, and I'm doin' it." Indicating the bedding she'd brought up with her, she reminded Lillian that the Madame also required silk sheets for her nap.

"Never get one set done before I get another," Lillian groused. "Four a day, washed, ironed, and sewed in a blanket. No way I can keep up."

Lowering herself to cross-legged position on the floor, Lillian resignedly went about her work, but kept an eye on her mother, sitting there, breathing carefully so as not to betray how hard the walk up had been. Finally Maggie put her hands on her knees to boost herself to a standing position.

"Mama, rest a bit."

"No time, got to do Madame Chiang's hand laundry."

"Tirin' yourself out and for what? That hundred-year-old tea got a complaint from the embassy, only supposed to be used as medicine, they said."

"That's the onliest mistake we made. Miz Roosevelt's very pleased, way things are goin'." She picked up the embroidered silken laundry bag and turned to leave.

"Mama, you goin' all the way down to the laundry, at least ride the elevator."

"No orders for me to ride."

"But the Pres'dent ordered me to ride, I'm sure Miz Roosevelt jus' overlooked offerin' it to you—she'd want you to, knowin' your health . . ."

"You don't go 'round to the First Lady with all

your personal little aches and 'plaints." From the door-way Maggie advised Lillian, "You keep workin'. Like Miz Roosevelt said, Madame Chiang is international relations—silk sheets or no."

Lillian listened to her descend the stairs, one careful foot after the other.

Mercer, putting away the vacuum and oil mops in the service closet on second floor, heard Maggie coming and smiled at her as she appeared at the foot of the stairs.

"Sure nice havin' you 'round again, Maggie."

She leaned close, to speak confidentially. "Hate to tell you this, Mercer, but this house is in bad shape. You're head houseman, your responsibility . . ."

"I know, Maggie . . . there's a war on. No money for repairs."

"War no excuse to be slovenly."

"Yes, Maggie . . . " He took the chastising with ex-aggerated solemnity. "Was sayin' to Mays the other day, war's no excuse to be slovenly."

"Oh, Mercer," she said, exasperated, "You never change, always jokin', never change . . ."

"Yes, Maggie, you right . . . never change." Enjoy-ing her chiding, he went down the stairs with her to the laundry, accommodating to her slowed descent.

Lillian didn't see Maggie again during the rest of the day. The sheets kept her in the sewing room except for the brief time she spent at Miss LeHand's bedside, watching her during the nurses' time off. Miss LeHand was in fitful sleep the entire time Lillian was there, and no words passed between them.

When the day was finished, Lillian went to the changing room. She dressed, hung up her uniform, and waited. Sevilla came through the door and began to change. "You see my mother?" Lillian asked her. "She was s'posed to meet me here . . ."

"Last I saw her, she turned down the Madame's silk bed and left the floor. Probably up with Miss LeHand."

"No, I was jus' up there."

"Maybe she stopped to get a cup of coffee."

"Maybe she did."

Mercer, the only person in the staff dining room, was wrapping a couple of pieces of leftover chicken and some bread into a piece of newspaper for totin' when Lillian opened the door. "Mercer, you seen Mama?"

"No, not in quite a while," he said. "Why?"

"She was s'posed to meet me in the—" She didn't wait to finish the thought, but turned and hurried down the corridor. Mercer, sensing her fear, left the food where it was and followed her.

On her way up in the elevator, Lillian tried to rationalize. Sevilla had said Mama had opened the bed and left the floor, but Sevilla could be wrong. Mama could still be on the floor . . .

But she wasn't. Not in center hall, or in the rooms assigned to Madame Chiang. Lillian found herself practically sprinting to the back stairs. "Mercer," she called down the stairwell. "You down there?"

His anguished voice came up to her. "Lil'yan . . . you'd best come."

Moving as fast as the crutch would take her, she went down the steps. As she made the turn she could see Maggie, just below the first landing, sitting, leaning against the wall. Pale, her breathing labored, she clutched her chest with both hands as though to keep it from exploding.

"Mama . . ." Lillian cried in alarm.

Maggie's voice was barely audible. "Take me home, chile."

There would be no more returning to the White House for Maggie Rogers. The doctor saw her, pronounced her unfit for physical labor, proposed caution, and left the bedside table covered with prescriptions. Lillian stayed home for two days until assured her mother's condition was stable, then she hired another neighbor lady who talked little and was more to Maggie's liking. Mercer came mornings and evenings until the critical time passed.

Lillian hadn't gotten much sleep these last harrowing days, but still she sat up half the night in the small Victorian chair beside Maggie's bed, working by the dim light, sewing.

Maggie stirred, "Lil'yan, you got to get your rest ..."

"It's all right, Mama ... you go back to sleep ..."

"What you workin' on?"

"Bed jacket for Miss LeHand. Want to get this to her in the mornin' ... maybe make her feel some better. You get to sleep, Mama."

"You doin' too much, chile ... Don't let that White House swallow you ..."

"Yes, Mama ..." Lillian soothed, "I'll do same as you did ... won't let it swallow me." Maggie dozed off. Lillian sewed until four in the morning, finishing the jacket.

Missy LeHand's door was closed when Lillian reached the top of the stairs the following day with the bed jacket packaged in tissue paper. She rapped at the door. "Miss LeHand ..."

A nurse should be walking across the room now, opening the door. But no sound came from within. Lillian rapped again, lightly, then carefully opened the door. There was no one in the room. The bed was made up. All of Missy's photographs, medicines, wheelchair—everything that was part of her was gone. Like she'd never been there at all.

"They took her away yesterday."

Lillian turned to find Sevilla holding an armload of napkins. "Said she was too sick to stay here anymore, took her to Boston ... got kin there."

"Took her away?"

"Where you want me to put these napkins? Miz Nesbitt say they all got to be mended again."

Lillian barely heard Sevilla. She stood in the doorway and looked at the untenanted room, bereft. "I didn't even get to say goodbye ..."

Handy set flatware and dishes for breakfast and brought in the tureens for the hot table. That first hour in the morning a servingman didn't have a minute to stop and think, what with getting all the butlers, maids, housemen, gardeners, doormen coffeed, fed, and off to their workday. He was just as glad he hadn't time this morning to dwell on his own problems, else he would be stewing about that paper in his pocket from Selective Service. There would be time enough for that. He served coffee all around, carefully dished up one egg each, one piece of bacon, as decreed by White House economy. When everybody was settled and eating, he went to the flag-draped THOSE IN SERVICE bulletin board and added one more blue star to the growing row.

"Who's that for?" Jackson asked.

"Me."

Mercer turned in his chair. "You? Thought you 4-F, Handy."

"Thought I was too. Draft Board got different ideas. I am now 1-A . . ."

Lillian looked up from her plate. He was a good boy, Handy, with the softness of childhood still in his trusting face. A soldier . . . *What will it do to him?*

"Got to give you a big send-off, goin' miss you, Handy," Mays told him.

"Wait'll the enemy learns Handy's in the war—get it over real fast." As Mercer said it he felt the echo of another time and vaguely remembered having spoken similar words back in that other war when Michaels went off, and stayed in France, one of a row of white crosses.

"How long you been here?" Handy asked Mays, as he refilled his coffee.

"Me? Oh, lessee . . . celebrated my twenty-fifth, celebrated my thirtieth . . ." he paused, calculating, "Comin' up on thirty-five . . . Me and Jackson both."

"I got three weeks on both of 'em," Mercer added.

"Looks like a good permanent job," Handy said. "Think they'll hold it open for me?"

"Tell you what," Mays assured. "You promise to get the war over with in a hurry and come right back, I promise to be on the door to welcome you."

"You got a deal." They shook hands.

Howell Crim came into the room. It was unusual for

the chief usher to visit, except for the occasional retirement party, or special instructions. They all waited to learn the reason for his presence. He was obviously uncomfortable, and hesitant. He straightened his tie and his vest. "I . . . I don't mean to interrupt . . . but I . . ." Unable to speak any further, he walked the few steps to the THOSE IN SERVICE bulletin board, picked off a blue star, and replaced it with a gold one.

They sat, fearful. Coates tightened his hand around the pocket that held the recently received letter from his son. Mercer broke the silence. "Would you be kind, Mr. Crim, sir, and tell us who that star is for?"

Crim tried to clear his throat of a lump that refused to go away. "Fraser . . . killed in a bombing raid, in London. They'll be bringing him back . . . I'm so sorry . . ." He turned suddenly and left the room. The food went untouched. Mays and Jackson put on their uniform jackets. Almost simultaneously they reached into their pockets, blew their noses hard, wiped the tears from their eyes. "Damn that Hitler." They went to their posts.

The others left the room until only Mercer and Lillian remained. He got up, moved unsteadily to the door, shaking his head in disbelief. "Fraser . . . he not even a soldier . . ."

Lillian sat alone. *Can't be you, Fraser . . . Not you . . . You goin' be a teacher . . .*

The weather, never a respecter of Presidents or Kings, chose to be inclement when Franklin Delano Roosevelt took his oath of office for the fourth time. Leaning more heavily than ever on the arm of his son James, he came out to the south portico of the White House and there, without the Inaugural trappings, the silk hat, the drive down Pennsylvania Avenue, the parade, he swore, as he had on three previous occasions, to preserve, defend, and protect.

The staff, shivering, huddled together under umbrellas and newspapers, stood on the south grounds and heard their much beleaguered President's failing voice, remembered the rich, vigorous timbre it once had, and worried about him being exposed to this kind of weather. When he went off to Yalta newsreels and newspaper photos brought his image home: lined, hollow-eyed, shrunken in the Inverness cape he favored. Rumors of his deteriorating health weren't allayed in Washington circles when he permitted himself to be wheeled into the House of Representatives and addressed Congress sitting down, publicly admitting, for the first time, the burden of the heavy steel braces he wore on his withered legs.

"You goin' to the movie?" Mercer asked Mays at the end of a day late in March, as they changed into their street clothes.

"Not me, goin' home, get off my feet and stay off 'em."

"They botherin' much, Mays?"

"Wish you'd quit askin' all the time 'bout my feet."

"You brought it up."

"Then wish you'd quit answerin'."

Mays went home. Mercer went into the East Room and found a seat with Dixon and Roach just before the lights dimmed and the movie started. There was a cartoon of Tom and Jerry, just like in the theaters. The President was wheeled in by Prettyman and sat up in front, having a drink, while Tom and Jerry tried to blow each other up with dynamite.

Lillian hadn't gone to the movie. Everybody in the White House was invited, but she had few opportunities when she could get into the presidential suite and make needed repairs.

She sat on a straight chair, the bottom of a drape across her lap, trying to hold together fabric weakened by twelve years' exposure to the sun. At the sound of the door opening, she looked up, startled to see the President wheeling in, and began gathering up her sewing basket.

"Little girl, what are you doing here?"

"Sorry, sir ... lost track of time ... didn't realize the movie'd be out."

"It's not ... didn't stay for it ... I'm just sick and

tired of war movies . . . wish they'd send around a good western, lots of horses . . ."

"Yes, sir . . . Excuse me, sir." She picked up her crutch to leave.

"No, no, go ahead, finish what you're doing, if you want . . ."

"Thank you, sir . . . won't take more than a minute." She went back to her work, cutting little strips of adhesive tape, applying them to the back of the drape where the material was weakened to the point of shredding.

"You know you should be downstairs, relaxing, with everybody else . . ."

"After hours, sir, only time I get to catch up with my sewin' . . . Did some hems for Miz Roosevelt, and while I was here, thought I'd patch this drape."

He wheeled closer to her, examining what she was doing. "With adhesive tape?"

"Hard these days to get requisitions."

"I've had the same problem with Congress for years . . ."

"Besides, these drapes fallin' apart, need somethin' strong to hold 'em together."

"Westerns are the best movies. You like horses?" he asked.

"Yes, sir, I do, very much, sir . . ."

"Nothing like a good mount," he said wistfully.

Prettyman busied himself preparing the President's bed. Lillian continued with her work, thinking how thin Mr. Roosevelt looked, shirt collar three sizes too big now.

"Yes," he said finally, looking around the room. "Guess with all the conflicts we've let the house fall apart . . . Should take better care of the old place."

"If I may say, Mr. Pres'dent, it's nobody's fault. Happens, durin' war. The British burned it down . . . Durin' Mr. Lincoln's time, when the downstairs was a hospital and morgue, the carpets and wallpaper got all ruined . . ."

With trembling hand, he put a cigarette into the

holder, lighted it. "Sounds like you'd make a fine tour guide, little girl."

"I'd enjoy that, sir—would they take ladies?" She smiled at him. "You know there are ghosts in this house . . ."

"I've heard of the Lincoln ghost . . . but we've never met."

"Oh, he's here all right, always lookin' for his bed."

A rare, easy laugh escaped the President. "When my time comes," he said pensively, "I may just reappear . . . walk through the place . . ."

The "walk" wasn't lost on her. "Yes, sir." She put away her equipment, picked up her sewing basket and crutch. "Thank you, sir, for the time. I be goin' now." At the door, she turned, looked back at him. "Goodnight, Mr. Pres'dent."

For a flickering instant there was the ghost of his former self: the familiar toss of the head, cigarette holder at a jaunty angle in his mouth. His hand raised in a wave. "Good night, little girl."

It was the last time she saw him. He left for Warm Springs the following day. Fifteen days later they brought him back on a lonesome, mournful train. He lay in state on a catafalque in the East Room. His widow sat alone beside the coffin, as had Florence Harding, Mary Lincoln, Ida McKinley, others. The White House wept.

14

⛩ ⛩ ⛩

They came out of the elevator, escorted by Howell Crim, and stood, grouped closely together in this awesome new environment as though gaining strength from each other. Harry S. Truman, in his natty double-breasted suit, bow tie, steel-rimmed glasses, receding gray hair neatly parted on the side, was one month short of sixty-one years. A Vice-President thrust into the seat of power, he stood erect, as befitted a former artillery officer, with his bride of thirty-six years, Bess Wallace Truman, a matronly, compactly plump lady, and their comely daughter Margaret at his side.

"They're so small," Mercer said of the Trumans as he first glimpsed them. Lillian's initial impression was that they looked anything but comfortable.

Center hall was in an uproar, with the Truman possessions being moved in and the Roosevelt household being gathered together. It would take weeks to weed it all out, twelve years of Roosevelt occupancy, and pack for the exodus. Which is what it was: an exodus—with most of the staff feeling that Moses had just departed.

"You folks go on about your work," the new President said. "Don't worry about us, we can take care of ourselves." Picking their way through the obstacle course of trunks, boxes, cartons, the Trumans went into their private quarters, but not before Bess Truman and Margaret had given the staff somewhat uncertain but welcoming smiles.

"Pres'dent?" Dixon questioned later in the staff dining room. "I never will get used to callin' him that."

"Well, that's what he is, you better work on it . . ." Butlers, Mercer had found over the years, had a tendency to take on airs. It was all that mingling with heads of state at those galas in the East Room. Now that Coates had retired, Dixon was head butler. The years had whitened him, eyebrows and all. Still had a full head of hair (Mercer noted with envy), and carried himself like an ambassador. *Gettin' as highfalutin' as those British servants,* Mercer thought.

"They sure not the Roosevelts," Dixon went on, breaking his toast into polite-size bites.

"Give 'em a chance," Mercer objected. "They brand spankin' new."

"You the one said they was small . . ."

"Now hold on . . . Was jus' reflectin' on their size. Bein' small don't mean they not up to snuff . . ."

Jackson laconically added his comment. "Somebody got to keep the office warm till election time." He looked down the table, expecting approbation, but got blank stares for his trouble. "Well, that's what it says in the paper," he finished lamely.

"Don't care a hoot what the paper say," Mays spoke up. "He is my kind of Pres'dent. Comin' through the door, walked right up and shook my hand. 'I remember you, Mays,' he said, 'from when I was Vice-President, good to see you again.'"

Prettyman found that astonishing. To Dixon, for a President to behave with such familiarity was beyond belief.

Once they got going, everybody had an opinion about the new occupants. "When Mercer and I unpacked him," Roach said, "he called his suitcase a 'grip.' Not heard that since I was down home."

"Well, maybe that's how they do in Missouri," Mercer said. Mrs. Garvey, a cook who had come in during the Roosevelt tenure, looked down her nose. "And *she* brought her utensils right down to the kitchen, said she's used to doin' her own cooking."

"Be nice," Sevilla added, "she likes to do her own dusting too."

Lillian shoved back her chair with such irritation it almost toppled. "Wouldn't be so high and mighty, was I some of you," she said. "I have you to remember you are speakin' 'bout the Pres'dent of the United States."

Not only were the Trumans under the scrutinizing eye of the staff, but of the public. The Roosevelt mystique was a tough act to follow, but Mr. Truman didn't seem cowed by that from the moment he entered the White House. Newspapers, commentators chipped away, never bothering him unless they criticized his "womenfolk," then he let them have it. "Mrs. Truman looks just like she should look," he fired off when the gossipmongers complained of her poodle cut. "Nobody's damn business what she does with her hair." He won Lillian over the first morning. She was just coming through the gate on her way to work when three sets of rapid footsteps overtook her. She stepped aside as the President swept by, at his Army-paced walk, two breathless Secret Service men in his wake. A few steps beyond, and without breaking his pace, the President looked back and winked at her.

It was Margaret Truman who livened up the place. She was twenty, a college girl, and just to see her bounding down the stairs to greet her friends made you feel younger. Been a long time since people that age were around; made you think back to the Roosevelt young people before they were all married, had children, went off to the war. Took you back to the Coolidge boys before the sorrow struck. *Kept you smiling,* Lillian thought.

"Come on up," Margaret called down from the landing. "I'll give you the grand tour before class."

Mays grinned away as he watched the two young ladies he'd just admitted trot up the grand staircase in their cardigan sweaters, saddle shoes, bobby socks, carrying their schoolbooks. Seemed to him, between the President, Margaret, and her friends, this was going to be one fast-walkin' administration.

"Wow ..."

"You can say that again ..." The girls' heads swiveled to take in every detail. "Sure beats the YWCA."

"Wait till you see the Queen's room," Margaret said as they reached her, "knock you out." One of her friends stopped suddenly. "What's the matter?" Margaret asked.

"I feel guilty, running up these stairs ..." Pointing the toe of her saddle shoe like a dance slipper, she took a mincing minuet step. "What would Martha Washington say?"

"Don't let Martha bother you," Margaret assured her. "She never lived here. Come on, I'll show you the Lincoln bed."

"Can we sleep in it sometime?"

"If you're game ... Oh, my aching back ..." The three young women sprinted across east sitting hall. Their voices, exclaiming over the lushness of the royal suite, came back to the staff. Center hall was alive with movement—a feeling of regeneration, energy. The walls had been painted, furniture was being moved in: not elegant, but warm with color and a feeling of comfort. Prettyman and Jackson, rolling in a chintz sofa, paused to listen to the girls' laughter. "Now ain't that the nicest sound," Jackson said.

The door to the President's room opened and the President, buttoning his vest, popped out. "That my baby I hear?" he asked Lillian, who was nearest.

"Yes, sir, Miss Margaret and some of her school friends."

"What's your name?"

"Lillian, sir."

He gave her a slight wink, acknowledging their previous meeting. "You take good care of my womenfolk now." And popped back into the room. Mercer was on the floor when he came in, on all fours, peering under the bed.

"Mercer, what in God's name are you doing?"

Embarrassed, Mercer got to his feet, reaching out to help the President into his suit jacket, but Mr. Truman was already into it.

"Your socks, sir . . . couldn't find them."

"Don't wonder. I already washed them. Among the many things my mother taught me, don't ever ask anybody else to clean your socks or underwear." He adjusted an immaculately folded handkerchief in his breast pocket so that the four points showed equally and was about to pick up his briefcase and desk sign when two bells rang out.

"What the hell is that?"

"Two bells, sir, means the First Lady's on her way up . . ."

"Oh, good." Truman stepped out of the room, calling to the staff, "Hurry up, everybody . . . sweep the dirt under the rug, the Boss is coming"—only to realize there was no one there. Just moments before, the hall had been a beehive of activity; now cleaning equipment and furnishings had been abandoned as though Patrick Henry had just ridden through with the British at his heels. "Where'd everybody go?"

The ritual of the bells had somehow been abandoned these past days during the chaotic changeover, and the staff had been caught off guard. The President reached the backstairs hallway just in time to see Lillian, a little slower than most, squeezing into an already people-filled closet. He opened the door, confronting the startled staff. "Everybody out, what is this? Nobody hides when we come around, that's an order . . ."

They went back to their chores, but the President realized what that gardener fella had been doing this morning, hiding behind a bush as he went by; tomorrow he would tell him to straighten up. Everybody was to work in the open when Harry Truman was around.

Bess Truman came up from the kitchen in the elevator, accompanied by housekeeper Mrs. Nesbitt, with Howell Crim at the controls. "You don't have to stop your work to take me up and down, Mr. Crim," Mrs.

Truman told him firmly. "I can run an elevator. Of course it's likely to bounce a few times." She laughed, a free open laugh to which Crim responded; but Mrs. Nesbitt's face, ever since the Trumans had moved in, had the look of someone who'd just bitten into a lemon. Bess Truman had noticed it, but it was not her nature to instigate confrontations. If there was a problem here, it would come out. "Have a muffin?" She offered the plate to Crim and Mrs. Nesbitt. He took one. She did not.

"What did you make, Boss?" the President inquired as the First Lady stepped from the elevator.

"Muffins . . . blueberry. Take one." He took two. "Just *one*, Harry." He put one back. "See you at lunch," he said. The First Lady and housekeeper went on to center hall. As Truman, munching on the muffin, stepped into the elevator, he asked Crim, "Do I get bells too?"

"Yes, sir. Three for you—whenever you leave or return . . ."

Truman listened as the three bells sounded. "Well now, if that isn't the damnedest thing." He went on to the Oval Office, his desk sign THE BUCK STOPS HERE under his arm.

Bess Truman passed out muffins to everybody working in center hall. "Take some, come on, have them while they're warm." Urging everybody not to work too hard because it was likely to be a hot day, she gestured Mrs. Nesbitt and Lillian to follow her.

It was the same room that Mrs. Roosevelt had used as a sitting room, but that all previous First Ladies had used as a bedroom. It looked much the same as during Mrs. Roosevelt's tenure, except for the face-lifting paint job, the brightened upholstery, and new draperies. A small workmanlike desk was the principal addition. "This room is turning out fine for me, Mrs. Nesbitt. Thank you for your help. And the small bed in the dressing room will do nicely for me."

"It served Mrs. Roosevelt well," Mrs. Nesbitt commented.

Mrs. Truman paused, wondering if she'd caught a

hint of partisanship in her tone, but chose to ignore it. Moving behind the desk, she said, "Lillian, there's a dress on my bed that needs doing. They tell me you're good with a needle, I wonder if you'd be kind enough to alter it for me?"

"Yes, ma'am, I be glad to." Lillian went into the smaller room for the dress.

"Sit down," Mrs. Truman cordially urged Mrs. Nesbitt, who chose to perch on the edge of the chair. Mrs. Truman was aware of this bit of resistance too. "We're an easy family to please—chicken, a good roast, simple foods"—Mrs. Nesbitt made no notes on her clipboard —"but we're going to have to pare down the budget. And, regretfully, we'll have to discontinue serving breakfasts to the live-out help." In the smaller bedroom, Lillian heard this directive and mentally calculated what it would do to *her* budget. "I wish we didn't have to make such a decision," Mrs. Truman went on, "but one meal a day is as much as the house can afford . . ." She picked up a sheaf of papers, consulting some figures. "I will supervise all menus, keep the books, pay our personal bills . . ."

"Mrs. Roosevelt did things differently," Mrs. Nesbitt said. "Never troubled herself with budgets and menus."

Bess Truman deliberately didn't answer. "You find the dress, Lillian?" she called. Lillian stepped into the doorway, holding a sedate black crepe. "This the one, ma'am?"

"That's the one." Continuing pleasantly to Mrs. Nesbitt, she said, "My mother will be moving in with us permanently. Mr. Truman's mother is coming for a visit. Since they're both quite elderly, it would be nice if we could fix up a hot plate or something, so we can fix their food up here."

"Oh, we installed a nice little diet kitchen on the third floor for the convenience of the President."

"That's very thoughtful, Mrs. Nesbitt, but Mr. Truman doesn't require any special cooking."

"I was referring to Mr. Roosevelt."

There it was again. Bess Truman's face set. "Thank you, Mrs. Nesbitt, that will do for now." She watched her leave the room with the awareness that she had acquired an adversary.

Not one to dwell on things or to waste time, as she went into the dressing room-bedroom for the fitting, she picked up a paperback book that was pages down on the desk. Lillian, zipping her into the dress, saw that it was a paperback mystery, *The Case of the Three-Headed Corpse*. While Lillian set pins and corrected the hemline, Bess Truman found the dog-eared page where she'd left off, near the end of the book. Reading avidly, turning pages rapidly, she came to the last, brief page. Finishing with a gasp, she said, "Well, never would have suspected *him* . . ."

You could hear her delighted laughter the length of center hall.

It was not hard to develop affection for the Trumans: the pleasure they found in each other's company was contagious. Backstairs, the staff very soon found themselves exchanging anecdotes.

"Anyway, when I was servin' em dinner, Margaret was making those little doughballs out of bread and flippin' 'em at the Pres'dent. And you know what? He's a better shot . . ."

"What did Bess do 'bout it?"

"Well, she sat through 'bout four shots and put a stop to it. But she was laughin' . . . My, that lady can laugh . . ."

"Well," Mercer recounted, "when I was packin' Harry's suitcase for his weekend at Key West, the First Lady said, 'Harry, you're not takin' those awful red trousers and that Hawaiian shirt?' "

"And what did he say?"

"You know him, poker face. He said, 'Oh, no, Boss, I don't know how they got in there . . .' He took 'em right out the suitcase, but somehow when they showed him on the news, he was wearin' 'em in Florida . . ."

Dixon was the holdout. Having expressed himself so forcefully, it would be eating crow to admit he'd been wrong. Besides, in his view, it took more than just being a friendly fellow to make a President.

The newspapers also reserved their judgment, waiting to see what the thirty-third President would accomplish.

It was a fine June evening. Lillian opened the windows of the Lincoln room to let in the fragrance of flowering trees, and turned down the bed. Mrs. Truman had put the Lincoln room back almost the way it had been for its original occupant, and with the rosy lamplight glow in the room—discounting, of course, that there was now electricity—Lillian almost had the feeling she was preparing the room for Abraham himself.

Instead it was Martha Ellen Truman who walked through the door. More accurately, barely stepped across the threshold, holding back, as though fearing contamination.

She was ninety-one years old, rock-ribbed, strong-willed, spare of body and speech, and the mother of Harry Truman.

"Well, Mother, isn't it a beautiful room?" he said from the doorway. "Go on, Mother, go on in."

"Oh, no, you don't get me in that man's bed . . ."

"But, Mother, it's the finest bed in the house . . ."

"I'm surprised at you, Harry. Ashamed. You, from the great border state of Missouri where we were burned out by Yankees . . ."

"Mother, the Civil War's long gone . . ."

"Not for me . . . Young woman," she said to Lillian, "just you spread up that bed."

"Yes, ma'am," Lillian said, forcing a straight face. Martha Ellen Truman marched ahead of her son, waving off his assistance at the two steps down from east to center hall. "This house has fooled a lot of people into thinking they're something they're not. You bear that in mind, Harry."

"Yes, Mother," he said humbly. "I think on it every day."

"I'd like a small room with a plain bed." This reverberating comment was clearly heard by Bess Truman, who was sitting at the coffee table having tea with *her* mother, a redoubtable eighty-six-year-old who agreed with Grandmother Truman, and let it be known

that Harry ("Is that clear, Harry?") should have more
respect for his mother's wishes. Caught between the
two old ladies, the President could do nothing more
than turn in mute appeal to his wife, who accepted her
job of keeping peace with good-natured equanimity.
"Now, Mother . . ." she said, putting period to any
further discussion of the matter.

Harry Truman was relieved when Mercer came to
him, informing that there was an important phone call
in his quarters.

"Take it in here, Harry, we're family," said his
mother-in-law.

"No, thank you, Mother Wallace. These are affairs
of state." As he reached the door of his room, Margaret
was just coming out of west sitting hall in a party dress,
with a gardenia in her hair, "Don't leave," he said to
her.

"But Dad, I have a date."

"Don't leave till I get back."

Margaret was immediately surrounded by her mother
and both grandmothers, surveying her dress and hairdo
like so many duennas. The First Lady found the dress
a little too colorful. Grandmother Truman pulled the
neckline up a bit: "Not going out with a Yankee, I
hope." Grandmother Wallace surveyed her from the
rear and found the dress too snug: "Or anybody in
show business. Can't trust those people."

"Help." Margaret laughed, and Bess Truman came
to her rescue. Calling Lillian, she instructed her to
please show Grandmother Truman the small maid's
room at the end of the hall, the smallest, plainest room
in the house.

"Yes, ma'am."

"And Mother . . ." The First Lady urged Mrs.
Wallace out of her chair. "Why don't you go along,
help Mother Truman decide."

Mrs. Wallace gave her daughter a baleful eye. " I
know when I'm being sent from the room," she said.

Margaret threw a glance at her watch. "Will Dad be
long?" The First Lady picked up a western paperback

from the cushions of the sofa. "He said wait, you'd better wait. And that dress *is* too much . . ."

When the President returned from his phone call, it was with vigorous step and a smile. "Well . . . good news for a change. That SOB Hitler is dead."

"Harry," his wife chastised. "Did you have to put it that way?"

"Only way to put it, better than he deserved. I'd say it plainer, believe me, if I was with the fellas from D Battery."

"Dad, does that mean the war's over?"

"Getting closer, baby . . . but still Japan to sweat out. I'll be happiest when it's all over."

Grandmother Truman's strong voice came from the bedroom down the hall, "Bess . . ."

"Now what?"

"Better go tend to Mother," the President urged. "Give her some good old Southern Comfort."

"Harry . . ."

"A little libation might do the old rebel good."

"Harry Harry Harry . . ." Bess Truman went to join the old ladies, shaking her head at his incorrigibility. The President walked his daughter to the elevator.

"Who are you going out with, hm?"

"Just a fellow from school."

"Is he an upstanding fella? Somebody you can trust?"

"Dad . . . it's just a date. For once, just say 'Have a nice time.' "

"Have a nice time. Well, is he upstanding?"

She laughed, then paused before ringing the elevator. "Dad . . . I read what the papers are saying about you filling Roosevelt's shoes—but I know who's the President."

"So do I, baby."

They shared a warm look. "Mr. President, could you do a constituent a favor?"

"Long as it's not political."

"Will you call off those Secret Service men?"

"Uh-uh, no . . ."

"Dad, I can't leave this place without being trailed

. . . I'm surprised anybody even wants to date me—
shadowed everyplace I go . . ."

Truman bristled. "Any fella worth his salt should
be damned proud to take my baby out."

"That's not what I mean . . . I have no freedom.
I hate to complain, knowing what you have to put up
with, but sometimes I feel like a prisoner."

"This is a big white jail," he said heavily, "and no
time off for good behavior."

The elevator doors were open. Crim was waiting to
take her below. "Did you ever go out on a date," she
said to her father, "with two watchdogs around all the
time?"

The President nodded emphatically. "Oh, yes. My
mother and your mother's mother." Margaret stepped
into the elevator; Crim covered a grin with his hand.

"Now you get home—" Truman admonished.

"I know, I know—*at a decent hour*. Just do me one
favor? If I'm a little late, don't send out the Marines?"

"The Marines? Crackerjack idea, why didn't I think
of that?"

Her "Oh, Dad" echoed as the elevator took her
away. He smiled at the image of her youth and bright-
ness that stayed behind with him, but as he turned back
to his rooms the smile slid from his face. Hitler was
dead, the war in Europe was, to all intent and purposes,
over. But there was still Japan . . .

The Three Musketeers, as the staff had dubbed the
Trumans, breakfasted together. The President always
found time to crowd in a little music. Lillian especially
liked to hear them when the President played piano
accompaniment and Margaret sang "Ah Sweet Mystery
of Life" or "Vilia" from *The Merry Widow* and Bess
Truman applauded. There were times, though, when
the President went into his room and played Chopin
for himself alone; the staff came to recognize these as
times when he worried.

The ping-pong table was set up midway in center
hall. Every day after lunch that summer, Margaret and

the First Lady played for an hour or so. Margaret had longer legs and a longer reach, but Bess Truman had a wicked backhand. It would have surprised them to know that a little polite wagering was going on backstairs. Lillian, farther down the hall dusting the breakfront, listened to the erratic *pong* of the ball from one side of the table to the other and thought, *Margaret's off her game.* The score was 8–5, Margaret didn't usually let her mother cream her, but something had thrown her off.

She swung wide and missed an easy return.

"I could beat you with my hands tied behind me," Bess said.

"Well, did you see the morning paper?" The ball rolled down the hall to Lillian. She brought it back to the table. "Thank you, Lillian . . ." Margaret put the ball back into play. "They practically have me married off to Adlai Stevenson . . ." Lillian, listening to the *pong—pong* thought, *No, not Adlai Stevenson.* Anthony Eden was her choice for Margaret.

"I was Adlai's dinner partner exactly once," Margaret went on as she hit a too strong return and missed the table altogether, "and the most intimate thing he said to me was 'Please pass the salt' . . ."

"I can see why the papers picked that one up." Bess Truman's backhand serve caught the corner of the table. Margaret swung and missed. "You must admit that's pretty racy conversation." Bess deadpanned. "Twenty-one and game." She moved to put away the paddle.

"Oh, no," Margaret said. "You've got to give me a chance to get even."

The game that followed was more closely played. Lillian, keeping tabs from overheard sounds, was aware the score was tied when Mrs. Nesbitt came out of east sitting hall with her clipboard. She paused beside the linen cart, made a notation, conferred briefly with Lillian about the conduct of the other maids, and continued on through center hall, eyes straight ahead. A schooner, bow into the wind, she sailed past the ping-pong game as though it weren't there.

Bess Truman caught the ball in her hand, paused in the game. "Mrs. Nesbitt . . ."

Mrs. Nesbitt hesitated, poised to move on. "Yes, madam?"

"My Spanish class meets today. My contribution to refreshments is a stick of butter. I'll stop for it on my way out."

"Oh, I'm sorry, madam, but butter is rationed. We never permit anything rationed to leave the White House." She sailed on. Bess Truman, holding ball and paddle in her hand, looked after her calmly. Too calmly. Margaret, observing, was not surprised by her mother's next move.

Bess Truman turned back to the game and vented her anger by whacking the ball the length of center hall.

The President was livid. He rang for Crim, then sat at his piano, waiting, without playing a note. Crim had no sooner knocked and opened the door than the President turned from the piano bench and pointed at him.

"Might as well get used to it right off the bat, Mr. Crim. Anybody insults my womenfolk has me to answer to—so just tell your Mrs. Nesbitt, maybe she can't spare a stick of butter but we can spare her. Do I make myself clear?"

"Yes, Mr. President . . . sorry, sir . . . I'll see that she's dismissed at once."

The President felt better. Turning back to his piano, he immersed himself in the Chopin A-Flat Waltz, Opus 42. It reached him as no other piece seemed to do. He needed the personal consolation of the music this evening. His mind and heart were burdened by greater problems than a stick of butter.

Out in the hall, Mercer heard the familiar notes that heralded the President's mood. He knocked softly, waited a proper moment, then entered the room with a tray that held a bottle of bourbon, a pitcher of water, and a glass. The President turned his head, but continued playing.

"I took the liberty, Mr. Pres'dent . . . thought you might be wanting your slight libation."

"Mercer, you are a man among men."

Mercer poured the drink, the President downed it.

"I want you to pack my grip for tomorrow morning."

"Yes, sir. Flowers and red pants, sir, for Key West?"

"No, *business suits* . . ." Mercer replenished the drink, then went about laying out clothing for travel. Harry Truman went back to Chopin. Yes, business suits, for the serious business of sitting down at a table with that old bird Stalin and Prime Minister Churchill. A high-stakes game, with peace, continued war, or the carving up of the Pacific in the pot. He held an ace, but hadn't decided yet how he would play it . . . *if* he would play it or if the move would be forced upon him. A hell of a big ace . . . A monstrous responsibility.

He left the next day for Potsdam.

It was the absence of breathing that awakened Lillian. Even in deepest sleep, she was sensitive to any change in the rhythm of her mother's breathing, but there was no sound from the other bed. In a panic she sat up reaching for the lamp switch; only partly relieved, when the light came on, to find the other twin bed was empty. These days, with Maggie's forgetfulness, it was hard to tell what she'd be up to. She might even have left the apartment.

Quickly pulling on a robe, Lillian stepped into slippers.

There was a light on in the kitchen.

"Mama . . . you got to quit scarin' me like this."

Maggie was at the kitchen table, her scrapbooks, clippings, treasures spread over chairs, kitchen cabinet, and drainboard. She was sorting her possessions with the zeal of an alchemist.

"What are you doin' up?"

"Captain Butt, chile," she said impatiently as she wrote in a notebook.

"What?"

"Did he go down with the *Titanic* before or after

Teddy Roosevelt started his Bull Moose party against Pres'dent Taft?"

Lillian emptied Maggie's cup into the sink. "When are you goin' to start takin' care of yourself? With your blood pressure, you know you not s'posed to be drinkin' coffee . . . And sitting out here, this time of night, no heat in the house . . ."

"And the bridesmaids . . ."

"Bridesmaids?"

"For the Wilson girls."

"Mama, please come to bed . . ."

"I got to finish this." Her search back through notebooks was compulsive. "Lessee, Jessie was married first . . ."

Lillian gathered clippings from the drainboard and put them back into the memento box. "I cain't work all day and worry about you not sleepin', not takin' care of yourself . . ."

"Lil'yan, I want you to read everythin' I got . . . everythin' I wrote, everythin' in the scrapbooks. Learn it, know it, so's it won't be forgotten if anythin' happens to me . . ."

Lillian helped her to her feet. "I will, Mama, I will . . . soon as I find the time."

"You make time, chile. Every day we work over to the White House, we part of history."

"Well, if history's mostly long hours and short pay, we part of it all right."

"Got to put my treasures away . . ."

"I'll do it, Mama."

"Don't you lose anythin' now . . ."

"I'll be careful."

Maggie pushed Lillian's hand off her arm. "I have you to know I can still get myself off to bed."

Lillian watched as Maggie made her way alone, then picked up the scrapbooks, pausing over her mother's notes, reading some of the entries. The handwriting had changed drastically. The first notebook, pages almost brown with years, bore the date 1910. The handwriting was strong, legible. In the most recent entries, she noted sadly, the handwriting trembled like the veined, bony hand that held the pencil, words not always completed, dwindling off, as Maggie's thoughts sometimes did these days. Lillian closed the notebooks and put the memento box away.

August 6, 1945, a mushroom cloud appeared over Hiroshima: the atom-bomb blast that shook the world. August 9, the second bomb was dropped on Nagasaki. August 14, the war in the Pacific was over. The atomic age, with all its profound implications, was born.

And a new kind of war came into being: the cold war. "Known of a lot of wars," Mays said as he read the paper, "but this the first one ever heard of bein' cold . . ." Mays interpreted the Truman Doctrine for those staff members who were interested, most of whom were, considering the ramifications. "As I see it," Mays said, "the Pres'dent sayin' to Stalin and the boys, 'Fellas, you jus' keep cool, 'cause if there's a war, you goin' be responsible. You got enough now, you jus' stay put . . .'"

In 1948 the Russians blockaded West Berlin. The United States, Britain, and France sent in an airlift with supplies. This was nuclear saber rattling. The world held its breath.

"That Mr. Truman is one tough, straight man," Dixon admitted.

"Well, so you finally come 'round," Mays gloated.

"What you mean, finally? I recognized my Pres'-dent's qualities a long time back, I jus' don't make myself known much as you do, Mays."

Elias, the young new servingman, brought the President's luncheon tray from the kitchen. Dixon put on his white gloves, carefully checking each item on the tray. "You didn't touch any of this food with your hands?" he challenged Elias.

"Oh, no, sir."

Dixon picked up the tray and carried it off to "his President," Mercer chuckling as he watched him leave.

"Would you like some more coffee, Mr. Mercer?" Elias asked.

"Elias, you got to get used to callin' me by my

name, Mercer. You got the job, don't worry 'bout holdin' on to it, jus' do your work."

"Yes, sir."

Mercer liked this young man. He was the same size and color as Fraser. Didn't quite have his style or grace . . . Mercer wouldn't expect Elias to dance in from the front door, or tap a few steps like Bojangles Robinson. But he brought a feeling like Fraser had, with his nice smile and cheerful ways. Lillian had noticed, too, and mentioned it.

Elias looked up from pouring Mays' coffee. "What was that?"

Both Mays and Mercer, the only ones left at the table, had also heard the sound. A creak, kind of a groan, somewhat like the timbers of an old wooden ship complaining against the tide. Mays didn't even look up from his paper. "Haven't you got used to it yet? The house been full of creaks for years." In a while, the sound repeated, heavier this time. They all looked up.

"That's more than a creak," Elias said, "sounds like this buildin's in pain."

"Ghosts," Mercer said wryly. "Place full of ghosts." Mays, turning a page of his newspaper, commented the building was in about the same condition as President Truman's political future.

"Sad to say, you're right," Mercer agreed. Mr. Truman's future did look pretty shaky, what with labor down on him for seizing the coal mines, the Eightieth Congress resenting being called "do nothing," the South resisting him on civil rights, even Senator Fulbright calling for his resignation. "Barrin' a miracle," Mays said, "Mr. Truman don't stand a chance. Looks like we goin' get Mr. Dewey." He shared a section of his newspaper with Mercer. They read in silence for a while.

"Think Jackson'll be comin' back to the door?" It was a question Mercer had delayed in asking, not wanting to hear the answer. Mays looked up from his paper with a sigh that carried on it the loss of Jackson's presence. "Don't seem so . . . talked to his family, he's feelin' right poorly . . . You know, Mercer, we pretty old roosters—you, Jackson, and me—pushin' seventy."

Mercer set aside his dishes for Elias to pick up, and rose from his chair, straightening first his neck, then his back, and finally his knees. "Well, now, wouldn't say I was *pushin'*, mind you . . . Jus' kind of *stroolllin'* along with it . . ." He did a semblance of the cakewalk to the door, paused, and looked back. "Now . . . could an old rooster do that?"

The look they shared encompassed thirty-nine years spent together. Mercer made his way up the back stairs to center hall, grateful that it was an easy workday. Perhaps Mays was right about them bein' old roosters.

There was no ping-pong game. The First Lady was in her sitting room, going over household accounts. Margaret could be heard from her room, playing the piano and vocalizing scales, arpeggios.

"Miss Margaret sure sounds nice, don't she?" Lillian said to Sevilla as they dusted.

"I like it better when she sings songs, 'stead of that ah-ah-ah-ah-ah . . ."

"That's what it takes to become a singer, practice . . ."—and for an instant, Lillian had a flash of herself at the *barre,* in dancing school. She and Sevilla finished with the tables and began to help Mercer and Prettyman remove books from the shelves, dusting and returning each one to its place. If the papers and radio were right, they'd soon be packing these books in cartons. It was pleasant, working for this administration, and Lillian hated to see it coming to an end, but if Mays' interpretation was correct, they'd soon be losing the Trumans.

They felt it before they heard it. The floor under their feet, suddenly unsteady, vibrated. The chandeliers moved, as though caught in a sudden wind; then came the horrendous tearing sound.

"The buildin'—it's fallin' down," Mercer cried out.

Downstairs in the dining room, where he was sharing a luncheon tray with an adviser, President Truman heard the grinding sound and looked up to see the chandelier dance, as if from a shock wave. "Get out from under that thing," he ordered his guest—and came charging up the grand staircase two steps at a time, his napkin still in his hand.

"What the hell's goin' on up here?" he shouted. Margaret, at that instant, came running out of west sitting hall, frightened. "Dad . . . Come see what happened." On a dead run, he joined her, as the First Lady rushed out of her room, anxious. The three of them got to the door of Margaret's room to see her piano at a drunken tilt: one leg had gone through the floor through the ceiling below, and threatened to catapult itself down into the dining room where, moments before, the President had sat.

"Get this building cleared," he ordered. "This place is a national disaster. We're getting the hell out of here . . ."

With speed worthy of volunteer firemen, the building was quickly cleared of personnel. But it didn't fall. Groans and creaks increased, doorjambs shifted, and Mays remembered reading that even back in President Grant's day the ceiling of the East Room had to be shored up against sagging timbers.

President Truman and his family left for Missouri and his whistle-stop campaign that the smart money said was useless; he didn't have a prayer, they said. The staff was called to a meeting by Howell Crim. His face telegraphed the dire news. Lillian, standing with Mays and Mercer, felt the ax coming and tried to block it out, but enough of his words penetrated to make it a certainty: ". . . with great regret, but there is no alternative . . . Already let some of the staff go, you are the last . . . Blair House will be the interim residence . . . However, whoever occupies it—whether Mr. Truman or his successor, it is a small dwelling and can only support a skeleton staff . . . No one to blame, I guess, except the original architects of this building for constructing it without a foundation . . . Mrs. Truman wants you one and all to know how sincerely sorry she is . . ."

Only Mays and Mercer, because of their long years of service, were being kept on, at the President's request: Mays to function on the door to the Oval Office in the sound west wing of the White House, Mercer at Blair House. If Dixon hadn't retired a few months back, having been even longer in service than Mercer, he would have surely been offered the job. Had that happened, Mercer didn't know what he would have done: hard to find work when you get up in years and all you've ever done is serve, or open and close doors.

The White House looked like one of those bombed Berlin buildings in the newsreels, Lillian thought as she walked past it: windows boarded up, steel scaffolding supporting its outer walls. She'd managed to get close enough to get a good look before being shooed off by a foreman. Inside, rooms, halls, ceiling, floors were gone. Crisscross bars of steel, like a giant erector set, held up the roof. *Depressin' . . . just plain depressin' . . .*

She continued on down the block, walking over to Lafayette Park. As she waited out the light on the corner, she waved. Mays and Mercer, sitting on a park bench having a sack lunch, saw her and waved back.

"Poor Lil'yan," Mays said.

Mercer nodded. It was tough enough pounding the pavements, looking for a job, when you were a youngster and had two stout legs to walk on. Seeing her come across the avenue on that crutch gave him a feeling of uselessness at not being able to help her. But as she neared them, any sag in her shoulders was gone. She greeted them with a big smile; sat down and shared their lunch.

"Made up your mind yet?" Mercer asked.

"Made up for me . . . I'm goin' to Treasury . . ." She made a face. "Not my style, filin' cards all day . . . but Mama's pension so small, we always needin' money. It's a job, and Treasury's on the same car line to home. Sure tells you somethin', don't it? Twenty years and they let me go jus' like that . . ."

"I remember when you first come in," Mercer said. "Depression time, we all sittin' there in the dinin' room. Lot of spunk you had. 'I have come to take the veil,' you said."

"To think I used to pick on Mama, way she took on 'bout the White House. Twenty years . . ."

"You still young," Mays encouraged.

"Goin' on fifty."

"Cain't be . . . Won't have it. You got to stay young. You don't, what does that make the rest of us?"

"You ought to see all the forms I got to fill." She opened her purse and took out a pair of reading glasses and a thick packet of forms.

"When did you put on glasses?"

"Oh . . . awhile . . . In triplicate," she said of the forms, "Jus' to file cards. You'd think I was runnin' for Vice-Pres'dent."

"Talkin' 'bout that, Mr. Truman keeps sayin' he goin' to win. Surprised he don't see the light, Mr. Dewey way in the stretch . . ." Mays got up to drop the brown paper sack into a trash can and grimaced as he put his weight full on his foot.

"Mays, you still usin' a razor to pare your corns? Wasn't blood poisoning once enough for you?"

"I'm careful, Lil'yan, I'm careful."

Mercer shook his head in disgust. "No use talkin' to that stubborn old man, he's got to do things his way, no matter . . ." They walked Lillian to the streetcar, Mays treading gingerly on the bothersome foot.

"Give 'em hell, Harry," they told the President out in the boondocks. But in Washington, cabinet members were making private plans for the future; some even had their household goods packed to ship. Election night, Maggie was asleep by nine. Lillian, who would begin the dreaded drudgery of filing cards in the morning, stayed up for the dismal returns. At ten, defeat for Truman seemed certain and remained unchanged with each succeeding report. Lillian dropped off to sleep on the sofa sometime around midnight, but the radio droned on. At 4:00 A.M., H. V. Kaltenborn announced that, much to the surprise of the entire country, Harry S. Truman was leading by 2 million votes. Lillian didn't hear this. She came to sufficiently sometime later to reach over and turn off the set. Mag-

gie shook her awake at six, distressed to find she'd
spent the night uncomfortably on the sofa. First day
at a new job she should be on her toes, and look at her,
barely able to open her eyes . . .

Lillian had showered and was just zipping herself
into a "business" dress, her spirits as drab as her garb,
when Mercer telephoned to inform her that Harry S
Truman was still the President of the United States.

"Mama, Pres'dent Truman won," Lillian called into
the kitchen.

"Won? But you said he lost."

"Never mind breakfast for me, got to change my
clothes." She bolted back into the bedroom, Maggie
following her.

"Will you please tell me what's goin' on?"

Lillian pulled off the business dress and reached for
something with more color. "We got an inauguration
comin' up, Miz Truman wants me back." Her smile
was radiant. "Mama, I am needed . . ."

They came out of a room in the office wing set aside
for storage—Lillian, Mercer, and Mays—laden with
pots, pans, pillows, blankets, and made their way single file, like some nomadic tribe, across Pennsylvania
Avenue to the four-story yellow stucco town house
known as Blair House, Siamese twin to Blair-Lee
House. At the sentry box that jutted forward at the
side of the building, Officer Leslie Coffelt smiled and
saluted. The parade of utensil bearers passed through
the ground-floor door into the cellar, level with the
street, of the nineteenth-century house. Through an
open doorway Lillian could see the kitchen, a cramped,
ancient arrangement, and steep, narrow stairs that led
to the floors above.

They deposited the things they'd brought on a trestle
table and benches that, along with the usher's desk and
chair, were the main furnishings of the stark room. A
cook and helper they hadn't met before came out of
the kitchen for the utensils they'd set down and took
them back in. Mercer and Mays started back for another load, but Mrs. Truman detained Lillian. She

came out of a door that Lillian would have thought was
a closet, but which concealed the gate to the elevator.
"Lillian, glad you're here," Bess Truman said, on the
move, gathering up blankets and bed pillows, handing
some to Lillian. "We got a lot to do to get this house
in order. Come on, I'll take you up to your room, it's
on the fourth floor."

Lillian hadn't been far wrong in thinking the door
led to a closet—which was an exact description of the
elevator: a closet, with barely room for the two of
them. It jerked its way to the fourth floor and deposited them in a narrow hallway at the top of the
house. Mrs. Truman guided Lillian around a carpenter
who was cutting a doorway between the two houses,
explaining as they went that with a door cut between
the two houses on each floor, Blair and Blair-Lee
would now be one house, with two kitchens, two dining
rooms, two of everything except the elevator, which
Blair proudly possessed. On the Blair-Lee side was a
narrow steep stairway, which Lillian soon discovered
was the trickiest passageway devised by man.

"This is your room, Lillian, next to my office." The
First Lady handed some of the bedding she'd carried
to the plump, pleasant, middle-aged dark lady who was
moving an ironing board out of the way so that she
could unpack a carton of linens. "You remember
Vietta, my mother's hired girl, she's going to be with
us."

"Glad to see you again, Vietta."

"Me, too, Lillian."

"Do the best you can, Lillian, get this room in order
—your sewing machine's in that mess somewhere—
we're going to be needing curtains and I don't know
what-all . . ."

"Yes, ma'am."

"Oh, and Lillian, when you have a moment—would
you please stitch up a pillowcase to put coffee grounds
through—makes the best drip coffee. Come, Vietta,
we've beds to prepare." The First Lady and Vietta,
carrying bed linens, took the elevator to the rooms
below.

Lillian looked around the cluttered little room. It was a dusty mess. She moved a box out of the way, wiped off the dirty window, and looked out. From where she stood she could see the White House across the street. Aside from some of the scaffolding visible from this angle, it looked as it always had. Pulling back from the window, she hit her head on the low-slanting roof. It was even lower, she realized, than the old White House attic before Mr. Coolidge's remodeling. As Mrs. Truman had promised, her sewing machine was somewhere in this mess. She pulled boxes and cartons away from it, and wiped it off. Out of her uniform pocket, she took her scissors and pincushion and put them on the machine. She was home.

It was All Saints' Day, 1950, and although the saints would have wished for it, there was no peace. The Korean conflict was four months old. The President spent long worrisome hours in the Oval Office, and again there was a constant procession of generals, cabinet members, statesmen. The blood of American soldiers once more stained foreign soil.

On the fourth floor of Blair House in Lillian's sewing room, the war seemed remote. It was a pleasant place to work, with bright curtains at the windows, and theatrical photos of Margaret Truman, at a radio microphone or backed by a concert piano, tacked to the walls. Lillian especially enjoyed it when the First Lady came up to her small office next door to do her accounts and read her paperbacks; they would sit for hours sometimes, Lillian hand-sewing, and talk about what to do with their mothers, getting up in years and sometimes difficult to handle. Nice thing about Mrs. Truman, she talked to you and she listened.

This particular morning Lillian and Vietta were working on evening gowns for Margaret, who had lost weight since being in show business; Lillian making alterations and Vietta pressing.

"Hear Miss Margaret singin' on the radio last night?" Vietta asked.

"Sure did. Give my mama so much pleasure . . ."

Lillian tissue-folded a gown and placed it in a packing box. "I wonder, do you think the Pres'dent's goin' put these dresses on the train himself like he did Miss Margaret's hats?"

"You know the Pres'dent . . . Anything his baby needs up there in New York, he's goin' see it gets done right." They talked for a while about the closeness of the Truman family, then Vietta inquired after Lillian's mother.

"Got good days and bad. Scares the life out of me sometimes, I come home, can't find her, she off someplace on her own for a walk . . ." Lillian opened the window. "Ever see it so warm for November? Almost like summer." She took a deep breath, savoring the day. "Things sure more easygoin' over here to the Blair House."

"Well, I'm in no hurry to go back to that big old White House, tell you that . . ."

"That won't be for another year or more," Lillian told her. "Walked over there the other day, those guards—you'd think I was some kind of secret agent, way they took on . . . But I got a peek. The inside still lookin' like one of those bombed-out buildin's after World War II."

"Fine thing, they got to number the wars . . ."

"Wonder if this Korea thing will come to a World War III . . ."

"Oh, I hope and pray not . . ." Lillian leaned out the window, resting her arms on the sill. "Hard to believe there's fightin' anywhere in the world, day like this . . ." From the street came the sudden unexpected staccato crack of gunfire . . . One gun, then another . . .

"What's that?" Vietta asked, startled.

"Oh, my God, they killin' people . . ."

From where she looked down, she saw the confused blur of men running, shooting at each other. Two strangers in dark suits, then Secret Service men and police coming from everywhere. Officer Coffelt, running out of the sentry box, firing, was instantly felled by a bullet. Secret Service men had wrestled one of the assassins to the ground, disarming him. When it was over, it seemed to her there were three or four crumpled bodies on the sidewalk. Lillian's heart was beating like a trip-hammer.

Everyone in Blair House heard the shooting. Mercer, who'd been mopping the floor of the ground-floor room with just a door between him and the shooting, stood frozen as the President, closely followed by Crim, came running down the steep narrow stairs.

"What's going on?"

Crim grabbed the President by the arm. "Mr. President, please, don't go out there . . ."

The door to the street burst open, a Secret Service man quickly entered, closing the door behind him. "Get that pail and mop aside," he ordered Mercer. "Mr. President, please, get back upstairs, sir . . ."

The President resisted the order. "I've heard gunfire before." It was his intent to go out to the sidewalk and investigate, but Mrs. Truman delayed him by stepping out of the elevator. "Harry," she said in relief. "You're all right . . ."

"Nothing to worry about, Boss. Go on back upstairs."

"Are you sure?"

"Please . . ." Gently but firmly he guided her back into the elevator. When he saw her on her way up, he turned back to the business at hand. "Anybody hurt out there?" was his first concern. Sirens screaming urgently up to the front of the house answered part of his question. The Secret Service man filled in the details. "Two officers wounded. One of the assassins killed. Officer Coffelt dead."

The President's distress was enormous. "Terrible, terrible . . . nice man, Officer Coffelt . . ." He reached for the doorknob; the Secret Service man blocked him.

"Please, sir . . . I can't let you go out there. They were after *you*. If you'd come out the door, as they expected, I hate to think what might have happened."

Truman checked his watch. "I have a speech to make at Arlington."

"I recommend you cancel, sir, you'll be out in the open there . . ."

"I remind you, we're at war. Any comfort I can give, that's my duty. I appreciate what you Secret Service fellas do, but I made a commitment . . ." The Secret Service man continued to plead. "Mr. President, they were here to kill you . . . It's too much of a risk."

The President nodded. "Goes with the job," he said. Accepting a compromise, he allowed himself to be taken out the back door and into his car. He made the speech. No one who heard him knew at that time that he'd been a hairsbreadth away from assassination.

After that, life at Blair House was no longer easy-going. Guards were tripled. Bulletproof glass was put on the windows, shades were drawn when the lamps were lighted. Until she took herself in hand, Lillian, jumpy at the slightest sound, would stop sewing, go to her door, and look down those long, treacherous steep stairs. She wasn't sure what she was looking for, and she most certainly didn't want to come face to face with it.

Everyone showed the effects of that frightening experience, except the President. If he felt fear, he kept it well disguised. His lifelong habit of brisk morning walks was curtailed. Every move he made was with a cordon of Secret Service. But one day, when a phone call came to the Oval Office informing him that his wife wasn't feeling well, he bolted out at a dead run across Pennsylvania Avenue to get to her. Drove the Secret Service crazy. That's the way he was, when it came to his family.

They were tense days. Over two hundred thousand Chinese "volunteers" crossed the border into North Korea and drove the American troops southward. And President Harry Truman, as Commander-in-Chief, ultimately crossed swords with the commander of the United Nations forces, General Douglas MacArthur, over the conduct of the war. The country divided into pro- and anti-MacArthur camps.

Not so at Blair House. They were pro-Truman right down the line.

"The Pres'dent sure comes right to the point." Mays read from the newspaper during lunch. "Paper quotes him as sayin', 'General MacArthur was insubordinate, and that's all there was to it' . . ." He chuckled knowingly. "Sure would like to hear what he have to say 'bout it in private."

Elias, who'd been kept on as kitchen helper, cleared the table and read over Mays' shoulder. "You think there'd be World War III if the general had had his say, and go into China?"

"Don't know, but I sure wouldn't want to hang around to find out."

Later, when his cleanup work was completed, Elias sat down with the paper and read it thoroughly. Mercer, observing him, was reminded again of the resemblance to Fraser.

That Friday, when Lillian came to work, she was surprised to find Elias setting the table for lunch. "What's the big rush?" she asked.

"Goin' to the game, I got time off."

"What game?"

"Baseball. First day of the season, Lil'yan, you ought to keep up with these things . . ." As she went about her housekeeping chores, dusting the delicate porcelain figurines and crystal sconces above the fireplace of the sitting room, she realized she hadn't been keeping up. And remembered how, when she was working at the Dunbar Theater, and watched from the box office as the crowds surged to and from Griffith Stadium, she knew 'most every ballplayer by sight, and 'most every prizefighter, and reminded herself to keep track of these things; not to do so was to admit the years were creeping up on her. And that wasn't her style.

It was still early in the afternoon when Elias came back to Blair House. Lillian had just come down to have a cup of coffee with Mercer and catch a few minutes of television on her break.

"What you doin' back so soon?" Mercer asked. "Ball game cain't be over . . ."

Elias was in an agitated mood, not like him at all. Hanging up his jacket and cap, he couldn't hold back his distress. "The Pres'dent was there to throw out the first ball of the season . . . I could see him fine from where I was, and I thought, this goin' be one big moment for me . . . Then he stood up—people 'round him started throwin' paper cups at him and yellin' at him for firin' MacArthur—then the crowd began to *boo*. It started low, and got so loud . . . He had the ball in both his hands—don't know what he was feelin', must been somethin' awful . . . He finally threw the ball, then he turned 'round and climbed up the steps and went down the ramp. I couldn't stay after that . . . I jus' walked out, too . . ."

The sound of hysterical shouting brought their attention back to the television set. On the tube was General MacArthur, sitting high in the back of an open limousine, exulting in the hero's welcome of a ticker-tape parade. Lillian turned off the set.

By the time election day came around, another general had captivated the public's interest and its votes to win the election and become the thirty-fourth President of the United States: Dwight David Eisenhower, heretofore undeclared politically, sought by both parties, had swept into the Republican nomination over Robert A. Taft. The same wave of popularity brought him to victory over Adlai Stevenson, the Democratic nominee. His charm, his smile, and the fact that he was *the* American hero served him well and made him impossible to beat.

The Trumans and a full staff had settled back into the newly restructured, refurbished White House, whose ghosts, if any, no longer made creaking sounds when they moved about.

But Mr. Truman was making plenty of noise his last morning in residency. Dressed in the traditional Inaugural garb, he paced up and back near the ushers' office, waiting for Mays to bring him the latest bulletin from outside the front door, where President-to-be Eisenhower sat in the back of a limousine, refusing to come into the White House and escort the outgoing President to the Capitol.

"The nerve of that bird out there . . ." Truman said to Howell Crim. "Asked the President of the United

States to come to the hotel and pick him up, can you imagine that? Never been done . . ."

Mays came back in.

"Well, Mays?"

"I'm sorry, sir, but he jus' sittin' . . . don't look like he's goin' change his mind and come in, escort you out, sir."

"It's not me he's insulting, it's the presidency . . . And for one more hour I hold that office . . . Who the hell does he think he is, breaking tradition? I've had two generals in my life I could've lived without— MacArthur and that bird waiting out there . . ." He stood just inside the door a moment. If General Eisenhower had turned his head, he could have seen him. "Well . . ." the President finally said. "It has to be done. Mercer?"

Mercer moved to him with his overcoat, helped him on with it. The President offered his hand to Crim. "Thank you for everything, Mr. Crim."

"Thank you, Mr. President."

"Mays . . ."

"Pleasure to serve you, sir." The President shook Mays' hand, then Mercer's. "Thank you, Mercer."

"May I speak, sir?"

"Now what the hell kind of question is that? 'Course you can speak."

"Mr. Pres'dent," Mercer said, "you got class, sir."

The slightest smile crossed Harry Truman's face. Mercer handed him his hat, Mays held the door for him. Just before he went out, he paused, turning the homburg over in his hand, studying it a moment.

"I used to run a haberdashery back home," he said to them in parting. "This is not really my kind of hat." With that, he left the White House.

15

☒ ☒ ☒

Whatever the new President had in mind in terms of administration was yet to be found out. But on one political issue, there was no equivocating. The official portrait of Harry S Truman was taken off the wall and carried up to the attic by Mercer. Lillian saw it go by her door. "Wait . . . wait a minute, Mercer, where you goin' with Mr. Truman's picture?"

Mercer came into the room, rested the portrait on a chair, and sat down. "Our new Pres'dent wants it removed from the main entrance foyer."

"But it's tradition, the last four Pres'dents to hang there."

"Guess Mr. Eisenhower got his own tradition . . ."

Lillian went over to the portrait and touched it with affection. "I don't understand . . . jus' don't understand . . ."

"That's not all," Mercer said. "There's also Mr. FDR."

This distressed her even more. "Took him down, too?"

As soon as they heard Mays plodding up the stairs, lugging the Roosevelt portrait, Mercer moved into the hall. "Mays, I told you I be comin' back for that . . .

Shouldn't be walkin' all the way up here, those grievous feet of yours . . ."

"Now Mercer, don't make a to-do, they not botherin' me." But he moved Mr. Truman's portrait from the chair and sat down, taking off his shoe. " 'Scuse me, Mr. Truman."

Lillian studied the Roosevelt portrait, remembering the last time she'd seen him, then went back to working on the massive king-size bedspread that covered her sewing machine. "Who's goin' up in their place? Can't leave the wall blank; every tourist comin' to the White House expects pictures."

"Oh, they be pictures," Mercer said, "Mr. Washington, Mr. Lincoln, they goin' hang there with Mr. Coolidge and Mr. Hoover."

Mays made a dry snorting noise that expressed his feelings. "Never knew before Mr. Washington to be a Republican . . . but then, everythin's movin' too fast for me . . ."

Lillian picked up the phone on the first ring. "Linen room. Yes, Miz Walker, I be right down." She hung up and reached for her crutch. "First Lady's askin' to see me."

Mays and Mercer expressed surprise. "You mean, personal? You must be important. Rest of us get orders by chain of command."

"Well, gentlemen," she called back at them as she left the room, "you all just better treat me respectful . . ."

Chain of command . . . A new phrase to Lillian. The only other general, to her knowledge, who'd occupied the White House was Ulysses S. Grant, and from what she'd learned about him, things weren't all that spit and polish. As she went down the stairs and across center hall she thought about Mrs. Walker; Lillian remembered how smoothly she had taken over when Mrs. Nesbitt "retired" after the butter incident with Mrs. Truman.

Rapping lightly on the door of the First Lady's bedroom, Lillian waited a moment and was admitted by the housekeeper. Mabel Walker was unique, in Lillian's opinion. Brisk, efficient, expert with a broom herself, if need be; but it was her open, ingratiating smile that had won everybody on the staff from the day she appeared. "Come on in, Lillian," she whispered in her gentle Tennessee drawl.

It was the same room that Mrs. Roosevelt and Mrs. Truman had used as a sitting room, but with a quick influx of painters, decorators, it had been transformed into an ice cream sundae. The drapes, the same fabric as the bedspread in Lillian's machine, were floral, primroses lavish on a vine. The upholstered chairs were pink, the coverlet, the sheets. And so was the slight, somewhat delicate lady in the king-size bed. Mrs. Mamie Eisenhower, wearing a fluffy pink bed jacket, candy-pink hair ribbon tied in a bow over her bangs, a breakfast tray on her lap, nibbled at her breakfast.

"Mrs. Eisenhower, ma'am, you wanted to know which one was the maid who sews." Mrs. Walker brought Lillian forward, "This is she. Lillian."

"Delighted, madam." The Eisenhowers had been in residence several weeks now, but it was Lillian's first direct encounter with the First Lady, although she'd helped unpack her extensive wardrobe and set up garment racks for the overflow in the bedroom across the hall that now looked like the back room of a gown salon. And they were still trying to figure where to put her two hundred hats.

Mrs. Eisenhower picked up the bedside telephone. "Connect me with Mrs. Doud, please." As she waited for her mother's voice, she nodded and smiled at Lillian.

"I'm already workin' on your bedspread, ma'am, to match your drapes."

Mrs. Eisenhower addressed herself to the housekeeper: "Mrs. Walker, it has come to my attention that one of the servants used the word 'okay' the other day. I will not have slang in my house. And the word is not 'drapes,' it is 'draperies.'" Into the phone, she said: "Mother? Having your breakfast, dear?" Nibbling a bit of sweet roll, the First Lady agreed, "Oh, my, they are delicious, aren't they? Just the right amount of cinnamon . . . Um . . . Well, if you're not comfortable, dear, I'll have you moved to the Lincoln Room—or bring the bed to you. Let me know what you prefer. When I'm bathed and dressed, I'll pop in. 'Bye, dear." She replaced the telephone. "Or nicknames, Mrs. Walker. No nicknames in my house."

Mrs. Eisenhower's questioning look was directed to Lillian. Mrs. Walker translated the look. "Lillian, do you have a nickname?"

"No, ma'am . . ." Lillian couldn't resist adding, "But my mother still calls me 'chile.' "

Mrs. Walker looked anxiously to Mrs. Eisenhower for her reaction to this.

"That's hardly a nickname." The First Lady smiled pleasantly. "Mrs. Walker, do you have the menus?" Mrs. Walker gave them to her, waiting while she studied them. Lillian knew she should have remained silent, but the imp in her that had never been completely exorcised reared its head. "And backstairs," she continued to Mrs. Walker, "they call you the Tennessee Darlin' ' . . ."

Mrs. Walker almost went through the floor, astonished both at Lillian's audacity and the nickname she'd never before heard.

"Flattering, Mrs. Walker," Mrs. Eisenhower said, "but we can dispense with it."

Mrs. Walker flushed. "Yes, madam . . . The menus are for your tea . . . your bridge club . . . and dinner."

"I can see that. You've indicated it quite plainly, thank you."

As Mrs. Eisenhower studied the menus, Mrs. Walker threw Lillian a look to please not make matters worse. Lillian looked at the hundreds of perfume bottles on the floor, waiting for special cabinets to be built to house them. Elsie, Mrs. Eisenhower's personal maid, laid out exquisite lingerie, hosiery, then went back into the dressing room for a bouffant afternoon dress and piquant Sally Victor hat, matching the accessories on the chair. From all indications, Lillian thought, the White House was going to be the center of fashion.

"You'll find she sews quite well, madam," Mrs.

Walker billboarded Lillian's talents. "She can do anything you require."

"Have her make slipcovers for my draperies," Mrs.
Eisenhower said, without looking up from the menus.

Mrs. Walker exchanged a puzzled look with Lillian,
"Slipcovers, madam?"

"Yes, like pillowcases on the bottom of each one,
tied on . . . or something . . . You know, to keep them
from getting dirty at night."

"Yes, madam," Mrs. Walker said, not quite certain.
Lillian raised her shoulders in a questioning gesture,
Mrs. Walker's eyes warning her, *Don't speak, don't
move.*

"Now," said the First Lady, handing the menus back
to the housekeeper. "Leftovers. They seem to have a
way of disappearing. You can change that, I'm sure.
Leftovers make nice lunches . . . sandwiches for the
staff. I don't want anything thrown out."

"Yes, madam, I'll watch out for that."

The First Lady turned her attention to the wardrobe
her maid was arranging for the day. "Oh, Elsie," she
enthused delightedly, "the dress is beautiful. Isn't it
beautiful, Mrs. Walker?"

"Yes, madam. Beautiful."

"Lillian?" The First Lady's open look invited a reply. "Yes, madam," Lillian agreed. "Beautiful."

A brisk knock at the connecting door brought the
President into the room. First time Lillian had seen
him up close, too, since the day of the changeover.
She'd known his face well from newsreels during World
War II, in his battle jacket, overseas cap and welcoming grin. He came into the room dressed for golf, and
carrying a shocking-pink carnation.

"Mamie, are you receiving?" Lillian thought he
sounded like Clark Gable. "For you," he handed the
First Lady the flower. "New carnation—called Mamie
Pink." She tucked it into her hair ribbon and asked him
to please not come through the house on his way back
from the putting green: it wouldn't do for her luncheon
guests, especially the press, to see him in golf clothes.
Mrs. Walker tapped Lillian on the elbow, and they

left the room, but not before Lillian heard the President compliment the First Lady on her choice of costume for the day. "It'll look great on you, Mamie—class A . . ."

"How can drapes get dirty in the night?" Lillian asked Mrs. Walker as they came out into west sitting hall. The housekeeper drew Lillian to the cleaning cart, out of earshot of Moaney, the President's valet who waited in center hall with golf bag and golf shoes. "Lillian, you deliberately antagonized the First Lady with those—nicknames."

"Wasn't meanin' to antagonize, ma'am," Lillian said, with an innocent smile. "Informin' her . . ."

The President walked through, past them. Moaney fell into step behind him, and they both left by the elevator. Mrs. Walker waited out the three bells, then quickly grabbed the vacuum cleaner, turned it on, and began to vacuum the rug.

Lillian reached for it. "Miz Walker, I'll do that . . ." But as she stepped onto the rug from the bare floor, Mrs. Walker waved her back, "No, no, don't walk over the rug! Have to get the President's footprints off . . ." She vacuumed backward, to remove her own prints. "One thing Mrs. Eisenhower can't stand is footprints on a carpet . . . even her own . . ."

Lillian thought back on the advice she'd received when she first came to the White House: "Every administration is different." *You could say that again.* "Best get back to my sewin' room," she said. "Keep puttin' my foot in it down here . . ." Walking on the bare floor so as not to sully the rug, she reached the door. Mrs. Walker turned off the vacuum cleaner.

"Lillian . . ."

"Yes, ma'am?"

"Do they really call me the Tennessee Darlin'?" Lillian grinned, nodded, and went on her way. Mrs. Walker turned the vacuum on again, smiling as she worked.

That year, more than any previous one, Lillian found herself tied to the machine. For months, without letup, she sewed slipcovers, curtains, dressing table skirts. It was always rush-rush. Cut down draperies, take out linings for "silent cloths" to deaden the sound of small round tables for a hundred ladies at luncheon . . . take old pillowcases apart, and cover the bed ticking so that the stripes would not show through the pillowcases. And when these worked out successfully for the White House, Mrs. Eisenhower ordered that they be done for Gettysburg, too. Not a feather was wasted. The President ordered a small pillow to fit under his neck for sleeping and enjoyed it so much, another had to be made for the farm.

"Stop what you're doing, Lillian . . ." Mrs. Walker hurried up to the sewing room, pushing the piles of unfinished jobs off the worktable. "All this can wait for now," she said, making room for an enormous amount of white silk material that the two Filipino housemen, whose job it was to serve the First Lady's needs, put down. "Mrs. Eisenhower wants you to get to work right away on new curtains for the second floor."

Lillian waited to explode until the housemen were on their way back downstairs. Then, in deference to her job, which she badly needed to keep, she kept her voice down. "New curtains? Didn't you explain to her that Mrs. Truman had new ones made before she left?"

"I mentioned it."

"And she had 'em done by a decorator, they still brand-new . . ."

"Mrs. Eisenhower wants them replaced."

"But that's thirty-two pairs and I got all this other stuff to finish . . ."

"All new curtains for the second floor, Lillian. Those are my orders."

Snorting her impatience, Lillian leaned on her crutch, to examine the stacks of white material. She ran a section of it through her fingers, her curled nose implying that she didn't think much of it. "What is this stuff, anyway?"

"Parachute silk . . ."

"Parachute silk? Workin' with this slippery material, I'm goin' be here till doomsday . . . Thirty-two pairs," she said accusingly to Mrs. Walker, who merely held up her hands in surrender and went back down the stairs.

In the days that followed, as she worked herself almost snow-blind with the dizzying stark white material, she tried to imagine herself on a cloud bank each time she lifted and snapped a completed panel. Light as it was, it billowed, floated for a brief instant.

She was in the midst of one of those cloud banks when she heard the voice. "Would you like to buy the story of my life?"

The puff of silk settled down for her to see over it. A young boy was standing in the doorway.

"Hi," she said.

"I'm selling the story of my life, would you be interested?"

"Well, now . . ." She took off her glasses and studied this serious young man, who couldn't have been more than ten. "We ought to have some conversation 'bout this, don't you think?"

"All right," he said agreeably.

"How much were you figurin' on askin' for this story?"

He frowned over the problem. "Haven't decided exactly, but it should be a pretty fair amount. Mimi says prices are going up something terrible."

"Who's Mimi?"

"My grandmother, Mrs. Eisenhower. You know, the First Lady."

"Oh . . . then you must be David."

"Yes, ma'am, David Eisenhower. What's your name?"

"Miz Lillian Rogers Parks."

"Well, Mrs. Parks." He was all business. "It's a good story—lot of exciting things happened to me. We're in the Army, you know—lived a lot of places. And Ike —that's my grandfather—he's the President."

She nodded with him over the enormity of it. "That does sound like a real whiz . . . Have you thought of goin' to a publisher with it?"

"Well, I was kind of hoping for a quick sale . . ."

"Oh, I understand that feelin', believe me, I do . . ."

"I was hoping you would, ma'am."

"How long is this story?"

"Four pages . . ."

"You know, seems to me a story as excitin' as all that deserves a few more pages . . ."

He nodded gravely, "Yes . . . I thought about that . . . Thank you, Mrs. Parks." He walked away. She called to him as he started down the stairs. "You come back and see me . . ."

"I will."

"And be sure to write more pages."

That stopped him. But only momentarily. "I'll have to wait till something more happens to me."

Feeling lighter in spirit, Lillian went back to her sewing.

Maggie put on her coat and hat and came out of the apartment, carefully closing the door. Clutching her pocketbook to her breast, she descended the two flights of stairs, holding onto the banister. She moved quickly and with purpose, because she had somewhere to go and didn't want to be late. As she reached the vestibule she was aware of someone coming in from the street, but with her eyes to the floor, hurrying as she was, she didn't look up to see who it was.

"Mama . . ." Lillian cried, keeping her voice low so as not to disturb the neighbors. "Where you goin'? It's past midnight . . ."

Maggie resisted the tug on her arm, "Got to go back . . . my lady needs me . . . Miz Wilson very sick . . ."

"Mama . . ." Lillian said gently, "Miz Wilson's long time ago . . . It's Miz Eisenhower First Lady now . . . *Miz Eisenhower . . .*"

Maggie looked at her, not comprehending. For an instant, Lillian wondered if she recognized *her.* Then the cloud lifted from her eyes. " 'Course, Miz Eisenhower . . ." She looked around, puzzled. "What am I doin' down here, chile?"

Lillian helped her back upstairs. "You jus' tired, Mama . . . sleepy . . ." They proceeded slowly, stopping at the landings. "Nice," Maggie said of the fading carpet, the scarred banisters.

"Yes, Mama, very nice . . ."

Lillian found her key and opened the door to their apartment. Maggie stood like a child, waiting to be told what to do.

"You never tell me a thing about the Pres'dent," she said.

Lillian went ahead of her, turned on the light. "Mama, I told you a half-dozen times . . ."

"Never tell me a thing . . ."

"Not much to tell . . ." Patiently guiding her back to the bedroom, Lillian repeated the oft-told tale. "He's a very private man . . . don't think he knows the name of anybody, 'cept his valet Moaney. Hardly knows we're there, any the rest of us . . ."

Maggie nodded wisely. "Mr. Hoover . . . Mr. Hoover . . ." Lillian helped her out of her wraps, thankful she'd met Mama downstairs before she could get out to the street, wearing her flannel nightgown under her coat.

"And the First Lady?"

Lillian sat her on the bed, took off her hat, and removed the black lace-up shoes. "Nice lady, Mama. Sometimes months go by, I don't see her at all." It seemed useless to go over it again, but Maggie wanted to hear it all. "She don't come out of her room till afternoons, most times . . . delicate in health, you know . . . Got her own personal maid . . . likes pretty clothes, got racks of 'em . . ."

"Now that's Miz Hoover . . ."

"And very fussy 'bout her house. 'My house,' she calls it."

Maggie smiled, confiding, "That's Miz Taft, all right . . ." Lillian urged the aging body into the bed. "Now you get to sleep, Mama. I got a long day tomorrow . . ." Lillian tucked the covers around her, but Maggie was not ready to settle into the pillow. "What happened with the powder room? You didn't tell me about the powder room tonight . . ."

"Nothin' special . . . a party, you know. Tips only

fair. Miz Eisenhower's against tippin', you know. I stood by with my needle and thread, handed out towels, sewed up a zipper . . . heard a lot of gossip."

Maggie held up a hand in agitation, "Don't want to hear it. Every time they gossip 'bout a First Lady means they want to be somebody they not . . ."

"It's all right, Mama, I didn't hear a thing."

"That's right. Never talk about anythin' that's not in the papers."

"Good night, Mama." Lillian lowered the light and started to leave the room.

"You not goin' out again?" Maggie asked fearfully.

"No, Mama . . . jus' goin' get me a cup of tea before I come to bed . . ."

Maggie nodded, closed her eyes. Lillian stood awhile in the doorway, looking at her, wishing people didn't have to get old.

The President, as he had promised the electorate, went to Korea. That war came to a close. The President had a heart attack, but recovered. A small number of military advisers were sent to a place called Vietnam; not many gave it much thought. Lillian, ascending the back stairs, ran into the First Lady coming out of the elevator, and realized she hadn't seen her in a year. The First Lady laughed. "Guess we just keep different hours, Lillian." Lillian agreed they did.

When David Eisenhower came for a visit, Lillian remarked on how tall he was getting to be, and asked how his biography was coming along. "I gave that up," he said. "Things weren't happening fast enough. Changed my mind, I'm going to be a ballplayer." Whipping some baseball cards out of his pocket, he wanted to know if she'd like to trade. She said she'd buy some bubble gum and catch him next time.

The President was reelected.

For Lillian, one day followed another. The ever necessary cleaning, bed making, linen mending went on. The worktable in her sewing room was never without fabric of some kind—usually pink—waiting to be made, repaired, remodeled. She had just turned out new dressing table skirt and mirror ruffle for the ground-floor powder room and was leaning back in her chair, shoes off, thinking she'd go into the room set aside for resting and lie down, when she heard the staccato of Mrs. Walker's high heels on the stairs. For an instant it took her back to Missy LeHand, so vigorous, always rushing everywhere she went, and thought maybe that was why she liked the housekeeper so much.

"Oh, no, I don't believe it," Lillian groaned, as Mrs. Walker came through the door burdened with piles of pink material.

"New banquet cloth and napkins, Lillian."

"But I repaired two good cloths—why aren't they being used?"

"No more mended linens. From now on, everything new." Lillian leaned over to the worktable to look at the pink material. "Can't understand why they don't buy a new banquet cloth instead of havin' one made."

"Couldn't, not in time. Not the right size and color."

Lillian shook out the material and started to measure the yardage, nose to arm length. "How much time have I got?"

"Not much."

"Meanin' I won't be gettin' home tonight . . ."

"Or the weekend, I'm afraid." Mrs. Walker was genuinely sympathetic. "Formal VIP reception—Tuesday . . . Oh, and Lillian . . ." said from the hallway, "a *hundred* napkins?"

Lillian measured and cut until the inside of her hand was bruised by the scissors handle. She basted, stitched. Whoever invented napkins was an enemy of the people. Should have stayed with the old ways and used birch bark, dry leaves, your petticoat . . . *Lillian,* she said to herself, *you do nothin' but complain anymore . . .* Then she realized she'd said it aloud. "Oh, boy . . . they'll be sendin' the boys in white coats for me, I don't watch out . . ." For a while she worked feverishly, running the fabric through the machine, but it barely put a dent in the work. Pausing for needed respite, she took off her glasses, closed her eyes, and leaned back in her chair, her mouth open in a big yawn.

The President chose that moment to appear in her doorway. "Come," he said urgently, "I need you."

"Yes, sir, Mr. Pres'dent." As she put on her shoes and picked up her crutch to follow him, it dawned on her he was wearing a barbecue apron. When she came out into the hallway he'd disappeared, but by following the pleasant aroma, she found him in the small Pullman kitchen down the hall where a large pot of soup steamed. As though he'd forgotten she was in the room, he stirred the soup, then ladled some into a bowl and handed it to her.

"Taste it."

"Yes, sir."

"Careful, it's hot."

He watched avidly for reaction as she took a sip. "How is it?" he asked.

"Oh, fine, sir. Very tasty . . ."

"Doesn't need a touch more bay leaf?" She sipped again, and again he studied her. This was obviously a critical matter with him. "Take your time, don't be impulsive . . . I want the truth."

She savored it, mulled the question, then: "Fine, sir . . . doesn't need a thing. Couldn't be better."

"That's what I thought. If I do say it myself, I make the best soup in the world, thank you." He turned back to stirring the pot. It was a dismissal. She looked around for a place to put down the soupspoon and bowl, but every inch of table was taken up with condiment bottles of one sort or another. Catching her indecision out of the corner of his eye he urged her to take it with her, finish it, enjoy it. Flashing his celebrated smile, he said, "Don't work too hard now . . ."

It was the following day, with Lillian little more than a quarter of the way through with the banquet cloth and napkins, when Mrs. Walker again came up the stairs. This time, Lillian braced for it.

"Don't tell me to stop what I'm doin' . . ."

"Sorry, Lillian, sudden change of plans. They're going to Gettysburg for the weekend, need a dozen sheets and pillowcases, two dozen towels. The houseboys will be up shortly to get them."

"But they didn't bring back all the sheets from the farm last time," Lillian protested. "How am I supposed to keep track what's here, what's at the farm, what's at the laundry if I don't get things back? I'm the one responsible for the inventory . . ."

"That's the order."

What was the use? Lillian went to the shelves and started counting off the items required, checking them against a clipboard.

"Oh, and the First Lady wants to see you right away."

"What does she want to see me 'bout?"

"You'll have to ask her."

"Probably wants me to take down the curtains, make 'em all over again . . ." Now that Lillian was started, she couldn't stop. "Never get a chance to finish anythin', always another job—I'm kept hoppin' like I'm four people. What does she think I am, one those Indian goddesses with twelve arms?"

"You're absolutely right, Lillian . . ."

"You know, one of these days I'm goin' take my scissors and pincushion and walk out of here. Got a notion to go down right now and say, 'Get yourself somebody else' . . ."

"Why don't you, Lillian?"

She was taken aback by this. "What?"

"No reason why you shouldn't, wouldn't blame you in the least. If I were you I'd go right now and tell her. I'll be with you all the way . . ."

"All right, that's what I'll do." She took off her glasses, put scissors and pincushion in her purse, and walked out of the room. On the way down, with Mrs. Walker on her heels, she began to realize she'd steamrollered herself into it, and wondered, for a fleeting instant, if she was doing the right thing. But no, she told herself emphatically, there has to come a time to call a halt.

She stepped into center hall, and she stopped in her tracks.

"SURPRISE . . ." The word hit her first. Then the sight. A portion of center hall was decorated for a

birthday party—hers. There were pink crepe paper
streamers, balloon-festooned wall sconces and chandeliers. A table, covered with pink cloth, supported a
pink birthday cake, candles, candy baskets. It was all
more than Lillian could absorb, but one thing was
obvious: Mrs. Eisenhower had arranged all this for her.

"Happy birthday," the First Lady said, with obvious
pleasure. "Come on, everybody . . ."

"Happy birthday," the group joined in, raising punch-
bowl toasts to her, and Lillian sorted out who-all was
there: Mercer, Mays, the maids, the girls from the
kitchen, Moaney, Elsie, the Filipino housemen. Mrs.
Eisenhower brought out gaily wrapped packages: "Wait
till you see all the pretties we have for you . . ." Mrs.
Walker, sidling up to Lillian, gave her a little nudge:
"Well, go ahead, Lillian. Tell her. Tell her what you
came down to say . . ." Lillian, feeling foolish, shrugged.

"Open one," Mrs. Eisenhower was saying, "you must
open one right away . . ." She waited, with almost
girlish anticipation, as Lillian opened the gift the First
Lady had personally selected for her.

Lillian took the lacy, hand-crocheted stole from the
box. "I don't know what to say, ma'am."

Later, when Lillian sewed herself bleary-eyed
throughout the weekend, she thought, *What can you
do with a lady like that?*

One morning soon after, Lillian came to work to
find the downstairs corridor looking like some kind of
evacuation exercise. Storage files, stacks of papers
crowded the corridor, and Mrs. Walker was lugging a
huge cardboard carton out of her office.

"Good mornin', Miz Walker."

"Oh, I wish it were." She sighed, pushed an errant
strand of hair out of the way, and went back into her
office, Lillian following.

"Somethin' wrong, Miz Walker? Somethin' I can
do?" The office was in the same turmoil as the corridor. File drawers were open, papers, pads, stapled
notes strewn all over. Mrs.Walker was saying, "It's like
trying to find the proverbial needle in a haystack."

"What is?"

"I know they had hot dogs, but it was a picnic."

"Who?"

"The King and Queen of England—that is, the present Queen Mother and her late husband."

"Oh, I remember that, I was here. Pres'dent and Miz Roosevelt took them up to the Hyde Park for that picnic . . . was fretful hot that day . . ."

Mrs. Walker fanned out a sheaf of newspaper clippings. "Oh, there's plenty recorded on that event— every newspaper of the world made note of it. 'PRESIDENT SERVES HOT DOGS TO ROYALTY' . . ."

"Miz Walker, how can I help you if I don't know what you're lookin' for?"

"A menu. The Queen Mother is coming again—we can't serve her what we served last time and there doesn't seem to be a record anywhere of that state dinner."

"A menu?" Lillian laughed. "Oh, if that's all you need, I can get that for you easy."

A limousine was summoned. Mays held the door for Lillian, and she drove off in high style. The limousine caused the same stir of excitement in her neighborhood as had Mrs. Jaffray's the day she brought Maggie the calf's-foot jelly. While the chauffeur held the door for her, and Lillian went up the steps into her apartment, neighborhood children were already gathering, to walk around, touch it, peer into it. The chauffeur watched them with a hawklike eye, but he understood; he had kids, and he lived in such a neighborhood himself.

Maggie was resting on the couch listening to her radio when Lillian hurried into the room. Maggie was confused for a moment; couldn't quite understand why Lillian, who had just gone to work, was returning. But when she learned the reason for the foray, her mind focused, sharp as ever.

"Don't get up, Mama, tell me where it is and I'll find it . . ." But Maggie was on her feet, proprietary, as Lillian brought the memento box out and placed it on the end of the sofa. "You jus' move that box over to me, chile . . ."

"But, Mama, I can . . ."

"No, no you cain't . . . I'm the onliest one knows where to look . . ." Adjusting her glasses, tilting the box toward her, she began to search. "Should be—jus'— 'bout—middleway—here . . ." Pausing briefly, she looked up at Lillian over the rim of her glasses. "And you and your brother always chidin' me 'bout keepin' these things . . ."

"Mama, could you hurry?"

Maggie moved and spoke deliberately. "Everythin' in this box . . . history . . ." Her stiff fingers parted the papers, and from the center pulled out a printed menu. "Here 'tis . . . June . . . 1939." Lillian reached for it— "I'll take it, Mama"—but Maggie put up a staying hand. Adjusting her glasses, she read aloud: "State dinner for Their Royal Highnesses, King George VI and Queen Elizabeth of England . . . Calf's-head soup . . . Maryland terrapin . . . boned capon . . ." She nodded approvingly. "Nice menu. "

Presenting the menu to Lillian, she said, "Mind you, chile . . . I want it back . . ."

"Yes, Mama."

"And remind them over there not to use the Wedgwood. We served on that, last time they come to visit . . ."

Lillian went out the door, smiling. "Yes, Mama, I'll be sure to tell 'em." Long after the limousine drove away and the street returned to normal, Maggie sat with her box of treasures. Eyes closed, she gave the slightest bow of her head, remembering a handsome young Prince of Wales, Mrs. Edith Galt Wilson on his arm, and Mr. Wilson standing there, on his cane. "Yes, Your Majesty . . . Yes, Your Royal Highness . . ."

In September 1957 the subject of Little Rock wasn't much discussed in the staff dining room, but it was on everybody's mind. Mays, looking up from his newspaper, put it into words: "The Pres'dent's the one goin' have to move on this, 'cause Governor Faubus don't run the country . . ."

It was a distressing thought, the Arkansas National Guard standing in doorways and on the steps of Central

High School in defiance of a court order to integrate.

"We been waitin' a long time to go to school together," was all Mercer said. "Ever since Mr. Lincoln."

Lillian and Mercer, with the help of two new maids who hadn't yet learned the routine, were cleaning the second floor when the three bells rang. The Filipino housemen, who up to that moment had been casually sitting on chairs on either side of the First Lady's door, quickly got to their feet and stood at attention, heads thrust back, hands at their sides, eyes straight ahead, as though the order " 'Tenshun!" had been shouted.

The President came out of his room followed by his valet, who carried his briefcase. Whereas normally they might expect a brief nod or even the flash of a smile, this morning he was dour. "Place is always dirty," he commented to his valet. "See up there? Get 'em." He headed to the elevator. Moaney paused and spoke to Mercer, indicating the wall sconce as the President had. "Mercer . . . see up there? Cobwebs. Get 'em." And Moaney marched off. Mercer looked after them, shaking his head. Reaching into his back pocket for the feather duster, he attacked the offending cobweb.

Lillian, who had observed this exercise, left the linen cart and came to Mercer. "You get the feelin' sometimes we're in the Army?" She started to plug the vacuum cleaner in.

"No, no," Mercer said, "cain't use that . . . First Lady still sleepin' . . ."

"Got to get the Pres'dent's footprints up . . ."

"Have to use the carpet sweeper . . . cain't make noise."

Lillian's sigh was heavy with irritation. The new maids, slow to catch on, made her wonder what was happening with the labor force. In her earlier days, if you dawdled the way they did you'd get your walking papers fast. But then, she'd been broken in by Maggie Rogers. And although salaries still weren't anything to write home about, there wasn't a depression now. The President was right, the place wasn't as clean as it should be, but how could she and Mercer keep it up? She looked over at the Filipino housemen, who had returned to their casual posture.

"Cain't get used to those two," she said to Mercer, "sittin' 'round like statues. You twice their age, they don't move a finger to help you."

Mercer was more tolerant. "Oh, now, Lil'yan, that's their orders. Stand by, do the First Lady's biddin' . . . You can see they military, they from the Navy. Give 'em an order, that's just what they follow."

Lillian wasn't impressed. "Jus' hangin' 'round, day in, week out, waitin' on her hand and foot . . ."

"Lil'yan, no use gettin' riled . . . Come on, I'll go with you, get the carpet sweeper. Can use some fresh rags anyway." Together they walked into the backstairs corridor, which, it suddenly occurred to Lillian, was the central core of their lives. "Is it me, Mercer? Am I jus' gettin' old and cranky?"

"You still a child, Lil'yan . . ."

Lillian smiled: *a child* . . . pushin' sixty. "Things different than they used to feel, Mercer . . . kind of like we here but we not here . . ."

He caught her meaning. "Gettin' to me somewhat, too. Started me thinkin' on callin' my time in . . ."

"You mean retire, Mercer? What would Mays and I do without you?"

"Has to come sometime. Lil'yan, you got to recognize I'm way up there in years." He leaned on the handle of the carpet sweeper. "Been lookin' at a little duplex . . . too far away from the White House while I'm still workin'—but time comes I retire, I might buy a little place like that—got a bit of money laid by . . . Live in one apartment, rent the other . . ."

"Your own place, Mercer? My, I am glad for you . . ."

"Do I get a place of my own, I'd be proud you and your mama come live upstairs . . ."

"Oh, Mama'd have to get a lot better before I can make a move . . . but I do thank you . . ." She touched his hand affectionately. He smiled at her, thinking that in a way she was like a daughter to him. "Well, let's go," he said. "Let's get the Pres'dent's footprints off the rug . . ."

But before they had a chance to move from the service closet, Mrs. Walker came hurrying up the back stairs. "Lillian, drop whatever you're doing . . . Another birthday party, you're going to have to make party favors . . ."

There were many parties in the White House these days, one more elaborate than the other. Many evenings the south and north grounds were illuminated by the lights of the State Dining Room, the East Room, the Green, Blue, and Red Rooms, the Diplomatic Reception Room. Chauffeurs waited beside limousines and listened to the music. Sometimes people from the kitchen brought cakes out to them.

On the second floor Mercer stood by, in full livery. The two new maids, he noted, were properly garbed in their black moiré uniforms, white lace aprons tied just so, and he thought Lillian had finally got through to them. He would have to speak to them later about the proper way to stand. He adjusted his own waistcoat, white gloves. Straightening his back, he placed his hands behind him.

The doors to west sitting hall were opened by Moaney, and the President, looking splendid in tails and white tie, was joined by the First Lady. Glamorously attired in a beaded, bouffant, low-cut gown, with matching slippers and evening bag, Mrs. Eisenhower paused to indicate to her maid where a fold in the skirt needed adjusting. Moaney stepped forward, giving the President's tailcoat a last brush.

From the grand foyer below came the first notes of "Ruffles and Flourishes." The President, a touch impatient, extended his arm to the First Lady. Evincing the excitement of a belle at a cotillion, she tucked her hand into his crooked elbow.

As they started down the grand staircase, Mrs. Eisenhower made a final check of her gown and gloves for perfection. At the landing their heads were high, their smiles radiant. They descended the rest of the way and made the traditional grand entrance to "Hail to the Chief."

The instant they were out of view, Mercer urgently beckoned to the new maids, who hurriedly ran back to the service closet, returning to Mercer with two carpet sweepers. Mercer took one, Moaney the other. Together, as the sounds of the gala came up to them, they swept away the footprints of the President and the First Lady, carefully backing down the center hall as they did, to eliminate their own.

Lillian, working in the cloakroom, listened to "Hail to the Chief," and when the high hum of voices receded from the grand foyer to the State Dining Room, she knew she had a few hours to be off her feet. Checking that all of her clients' wraps and hats were properly placed on rods and shelves, she sat on the stool. Intending only to close her eyes for a moment, she put her head down on her arms.

Mays woke her.

"Oh, good heavens, how long have I been sleepin'?"

Mays checked his pocket watch. "Well, it's comin' up on 'Good Night, Ladies' time . . ."

Lillian got up, adjusting her uniform and hair. "You mean, they had dinner and gone into the ballroom, music's been playin' and I didn't hear a thing?"

Mays pulled up a chair and sat on the other side of the counter from her and removed his shoe. He was limping worse than usual, she noticed, but didn't speak of it. His grimace, as he sat down, spoke of his discomfort, and there didn't seem any point in adding to his burden by reminding him of it.

"You workin' yourself into the ground, Lil'yan," he said. "They askin' too much of you . . ."

"Don't I know it . . . Tell you, Mays, if I didn't have so many bills—doctor, medicine, ladies to come in, watch over Mama when I'm not there . . . I'd jus' go upstairs, get my scissors, my pincushion, and be on my merry way . . ."

"Heard you say that before, don't believe you, Lil'yan. You got too much time in this place—like me —to walk out." Out of her view, he felt his toe. It was sending shooting pains up his leg. Last week when he'd cut his corns with the razor, he'd slipped and gone just a little too deep, and it hadn't healed like it usually did. When he got home, he promised himself, he'd soak it in hot water and some Epsom salts, and keep it elevated during the night. That always worked.

Mercer, having finished extra duty in the pantry, came out with a napkin-wrapped packet of pastries. "Yep, been around a long time," he heard Mays saying, as he went through the swinging gate into the cloak-room and put the pastries on the counter.

"You right, Mays. You been 'round too long, you gettin' stale . . ."

"Don't you go spreadin' that rumor now. You got three weeks on me, remember. You and me here by the grace of Mr. Truman extendin' our time. Be thankful nobody's noticed we still 'round."

"And that's another thing that bothers me," Lillian spoke up, "the feelin' of not bein' noticed anymore . . ."

"Well, I notice you, chile . . ." He handed her the napkin packet. She opened it and found the half-dozen tiny squares of pastry.

"My goodness, petits fours . . ." She shared them, her face warm with memory. "I remember . . . we were livin' over the undertakers, first time I saw one of these. Mama had just started workin' here . . . brought 'em home . . ."

"Those days, we all new here ourselves," Mays said.

"And young," Mercer added.

Lillian looked from one to the other of their bur-nished, lived-in faces. "I can still see you two, all duded up, takin' Mama dancin' to the butlers' ball."

"Turkey trot, huh?" Mays reminded Mercer.

"Oh, you have got a memory . . ." The two men chuckled, but Lillian felt irritated at herself. "I'm gettin' like Mama . . . talkin' 'bout the past."

"That's what we got a whole lot of—past."

"You know, Mays," Mercer said, "between us we got in better than eighty years . . ."

"And Mama gave thirty." Hard to believe, Lillian was coming up on thirty years herself.

"And Jackson, rest his soul."

It was like Mercer to try to lift the mood. "On the pool table of life," he said, "we have racked up a lot of time."

"I didn't know you a philosopher, Mercer."

"Picked it up from you, Mays."

Lillian was sorry they'd got off on this nostalgic tack. Usually they could laugh it away, but tonight—maybe they were all just tired—it just lay there.

"Yes," Mays mused, "things are changin' . . . It's jus' not the same place, but I'm stayin' here long as they let me. What else would I do, this place come to be my life . . . My time comes to go, I want to be openin' the door sayin', 'Good evenin', Mr. Pres'dent' . . ." From the East Room came the strains of "Good Night, Ladies." Mays put on his shoe. "Oh-oh, they be comin' out now." Adjusting his livery, he went back to the door. Mercer put the bowl for tips up front on the counter, and he and Lillian stood by at attention, waiting for the guests to come out.

There was an air of tension, distress, in the atmosphere of the second floor. A butler came up with the President's tray, as ordered, and was sent away. Moaney and Elsie remained inside the presidential suite, not even going down for breakfast as they usually did, and Mrs. Walker had been in the First Lady's bedroom much longer than usual.

The ultrachic New York lady who was sitting on a banquette in center hall with the dress designer box beside her began to get edgy. She had an appointment for a fitting with the First Lady; never before had she been kept waiting this long.

Lillian was descending from the third floor with a ruffled blanket cover she'd just finished, and was about to continue on down to run it through the mangle, when Mrs. Walker came out of west sitting hall. Pausing briefly, she gave the New York lady the message that Mrs. Eisenhower hoped she'd be patient a little longer, and intercepted Lillian, who was about to descend the stairs.

"The President's taken sick again, we've got to get him to the hospital without anybody knowing it. You see that lady in center hall?"

"Oh, yes, ma'am, I know her. Dress designer from New York. Name's Amanda Vincent, she's been here before."

"You've got to get her up to your room, keep her there, while they take him out . . ."

Lillian took another peek at the lady, whose impatience was now reflected in the drumming of her heel. "How am I goin' do that?"

"I have faith in you."

"Miss Vincent?" The New York lady raised her eyes to Lillian, who stood before her, smiling pleasantly. "We've met before, I'm Lillian Rogers Parks, you know, the seamstress."

"Yes?" The word was crisp.

"In my sewing room upstairs now, I received a phone call from the First Lady's social secretary, askin' me to inform you that she regrets the delay . . ."

"The housekeeper just told me that, thank you . . ."

"There's more. Since the First Lady is involved in very high-level protocol at the moment, it was suggested —*requested*—that you wait up in my sewin' room . . ."

"Your sewing room? Why should I wait there when I can wait here? I don't like to rush the First Lady, but I have a plane to catch back to New York . . ."

Lillian latched on to this. "That's jus' the point. To expedite matters, the social secretary says the First Lady requests that you do the preliminary fitting on the gown, on the dress form in my room."

Miss Vincent consulted her watch. "All right, if I must." She followed Lillian reluctantly up the stairs.

Center hall stayed empty for a brief moment, except for Mercer, then two medical corpsmen double-timed up the grand staircase, carrying a gurney. At Mercer's direction they rushed it into the President's room, and moments later, wheeled him out. With him were his doctor and the First Lady. Blanket-wrapped, visibly ill, the President tried for a smile of reassurance to his wife, who walked anxiously alongside him, comforting him, holding his hand. At the grand staircase, they raised the wheels of the gurney and carried the President carefully down the stairs. Mercer watched them out of sight, worrying. It was the third time the poor man had been struck ill since he'd come to office.

Lillian was doing her level best to keep the New York lady calm, but Amanda Vincent was used to having clients wait for her. First Lady or no, she found it hard to accept being relegated upstairs to the sewing room. Lillian helped her put the dress on the form, and set some of the pins.

"Would you call down, please, and find out how much longer it's likely to be?"

"I'll have to check with the social secretary."

"Fine."

Lillian asked for an extension on the phone, and was connected with the housekeeper's office. Mrs. Walker knew immediately, when Lillian identified herself as Mrs. Parks, that they were playacting.

"When do you think Mrs. Eisenhower will be free from her present obligation?" (Mrs. Walker was saying, "Keep her there, don't let her out until the President is safely away.") "Oh, *that long,* I see . . ." She hung up and informed that the First Lady was sorry for the delay, but wanted her to finish pinning the dress before she left.

"You mean, I'm being asked to come back?"

"Not till you finish pinnin' . . . You know how much the First Lady admires you—and she's a trend setter, that's why she wears your clothes."

"I get the distinct impression you're stalling . . . trying to keep me here . . ."

"No, ma'am . . . now why would I do that, ma'am?"

The siren blasted the quiet, diminishing only slightly in its raucous wail as it pulled away from the building. Amanda Vincent rushed to the window, peering out in time to see it turn into traffic. "Ambulance! Someone's sick . . . the President? Again?"

"Oh, Lord," Lillian said in exasperation. "Try to keep anythin' quiet in this place . ."

There was no picture or sound on the screen—just snow and horizontal and vertical lines. Lillian fiddled with the knobs on the front of the twelve-inch set, then chanced a tug at the aerial wire, but nothing materialized. It was a new set, she'd just had it delivered as a gift for Mama, company for her during the long hours she had to spend alone, and it was aggravating that the thing didn't work. Maggie directed the operation from the chair where she sat, an afghan over her knees. "Try that bottom one."

"Mama, that's the thing that turns it on."

"The kitchen set up?"

Lillian adjusted the horizontal. The lines stayed a moment, then turned into herringbone.

"I asked you 'bout the kitchen."

"Mama, everythin's ready—dinner's in the oven, soon as they get here, we'll eat."

"You set the table?"

"Yes, Mama, but don't get upset—I had to move your clippin's . . ."

"You study the notes I made?"

"I will, Mama . . . later."

"You always say later . . . Oh, you got it!" The set cleared. For an instant they had the face of the news commentator, then lost him.

"This knob supposed to do it . . ." A twist, and Lillian got the sound along with the commentator: "President Eisenhower, whose first term in office was beset by illnesses, and who is recuperating in Palm Springs from the stroke he recently suffered"—she lost the picture. Now there was only snow with the voice—"is expected to be back at his desk." She changed stations, the set cleared miraculously, and there was Milton Berle in a lady's hat and dress. They both settled back to watch the program.

Maggie laughed. "That fool man is a caution."

It was good to see her enjoying herself, laughing and talking back to the screen. Lillian got up to check the oven. Mercer and Mays were late, unusual for them. Sunday dinner was almost a ritual. She hoped they'd arrive before the meat dried out, and was relieved to hear the knock at the door.

"Come on in, Mercer, we got Uncle Miltie . . ." She looked past him to the stairs. "Where's Mays?"

He came into the room and stood there, his hat in his hand, face stricken. Maggie, in the middle of a laugh, looked up to see him. "Mays is in the hospital," he said. "They goin' take off his leg . . ."

It was a gray day when they buried John Mays. They stood around the grave, the handful of people who knew him, and tried not to look at that yawning hole waiting to receive him. Tried to remember him as he had been. ". . . and we commit the soul of your loving servant, John Mays, into your everlasting, loving care, dear Lord . . . Amen . . ."

"Amen," from the mourners. And again, "Amen . . ."

They remained until he was lowered, not wanting his last moment to be tended only by strangers. Mercer dropped in a handful of earth. So did Lillian. Maggie, unable to lean over, held out her hand. Mercer put a bit of earth into it. She let it fall, like sifting sand. The wind picked up the last bit and carried it away.

Maggie failed rapidly after that. Lillian tried to stimulate her with news from the White House: "You know who's there now, Mama—Emperor Haile Selassie and his grandchildren. Imagine that, Mama—Negro royalty . . ." But she showed only casual interest. When she no longer wanted to be helped into a chair to see Red Skelton or Milton Berle, Lillian knew she'd lost the desire even to laugh. At Maggie's bidding, the neighbor lady waited evenings, at the top of the stairs, to hurry Lillian along.

"Mama all right?" Lillian asked anxiously.

"Same. Jus' anxious for you to get home, always anxious to see her little Hop-Skip . . ."

"Hop-Skip? Mama calls me that?"

"Didn't you know?" the neighbor lady said. "Always calls you that, when speakin' 'bout you. 'My little Hop-Skip,' she says . . . 'always was the dancin'est chile,' she says."

Mercer came faithfully, mornings and evenings. Sat by her bed when she allowed him, and out in the parlor when she was too fretful for company.

The weather turned nice. Maggie expressed interest in a soft-boiled egg and some tea. Lillian prepared it and was feeding it to her. Mercer opened the window so she could see what a nice day it was. A bird lighted on the sill and captured her attention.

"Soon as you're feelin' able, Maggie," Mercer told her, "we goin' start walkin' out to the park on Sundays like we used to . . ."

Maggie, tired of eating, waved away the spoon. "Mays is gone . . ." Her eyes drifted, and with them, her thoughts. "Lil'yan, why doesn't your brother come?"

"He wants to, Mama . . . soon as he well enough to travel, he be here . . ."

"He died, and you didn't tell me," Maggie accused.

"No, Mama . . . Emmett's been in the hospital again, but he's recoverin' now . . . I'll get him on the long distance, you can talk to him . . ."

With a strength she hadn't shown in days, Maggie raised from the pillow. "Your papa? He on the telephone?" Lillian eased her back. "No, Mama . . . Papa's been gone a long, long time . . ."

"Oh, I know that, chile . . ." She smiled. "Your papa jus' kind of walked by jus' now . . ."

"Maybe you'd like some broth? I've got some on the stove . . ."

"Yes, chile . . . I would like that." She lay quietly, smiling at her own images. When Lillian went into the kitchen, Mercer moved over and took the chair she had vacated.

"You get well now, y'hear, Maggie . . ." He took her hand in his, "You know that little duplex I talked 'bout? I put my name to a piece of paper and give in some money . . . When you ready, I fix up an apart-she roused, she was completely lucid, saw him clearly. ment for you and Lil'yan . . ."

"An' Emmett . . . got to have my babies with me . . ."

"Sure, Maggie, sure." Her eyes closed briefly. When

"Mercer, you see that Lil'yan writes my book now . . ."

"What you talkin' 'bout? You goin' write it yourself . . ."

She shook her head. "There comes a time . . . comes a time . . ." She reached out tremblingly, and put her hand over his. "Mercer . . . I come to know this 'bout you, that you always been there . . ."

Her hand felt cold as ice. He took it in both of his to warm it. "Well, Maggie," he said. "Plain truth is, I always been secretly courtin' you . . ." He felt her leave him. The hand relaxed, and the tired eyes closed. She gave a little sigh, and she was gone. He held the dear hand a moment, then he lay it gently back on the bed and moved to the window, unable to hold back his tears.

Lillian stepped into the doorway with the bowl of broth, and she knew. Putting the bowl down on the table, she moved to the chair beside the bed, and sat, stroking the lifeless hand. *Good night, Mama . . .*

They went on, Lillian and Mercer, serving the White House until one day it was almost the end of 1960. A new President, John Fitzgerald Kennedy, captured the voting population with his youth and his vigor, and it would soon be time again for the changeover.

Mercer had wakened that morning, knowing the time had come. As he sat in the staff dining room and looked down the table at all the new, younger faces, he wondered what he was still doing there.

Later that day, when he finished cleaning the Treaty Room and came out into center hall, he looked the crew over again. Only one he really knew of all these people was Lillian, coming out of the First Lady's room, stuffing pink sheets into the laundry cart.

"Lil'yan," he called, "you have a minute . . ."

She came forward. "You all right, Mercer?"

"I been lookin' 'round," he said. "You know any of these people workin' this floor?"

"No closer than to nod, say good mornin' . . . Nobody left here I really know, 'cept you, Mercer. And Miz Walker, of course."

He drew her around the corner where they could speak in privacy. Where they stood they could look down the graceful steps of the grand staircase that had borne so many up and down over the years. It seemed a fitting place to say what he had to say. "I been thinkin' on it, quite a spell . . . why I stayed on this long. Tell myself what I'm doin' is important . . ." He shook his head, puzzling it out. "Last eight years with a Pres'dent never talked to me, now a new one's comin' in young enough to be my grandson . . . but the truth is, like Mays, I don't really want to go, this place been my life, my family . . ."

"I know what you mean, Mercer. Things changin'. You and me the only ones left."

"In times gone by," he resumed the thought, "when the farmer got old and the children took over, there was a place for the old folks . . . they kind of lived out their lives in the house . . . But that time's passin', Lil'yan . . . I can't stay here no more. I'm goin' down, tell Miz Walker."

"I've been givin' lot of thought to that myself, Mercer, but I'm not quite ready . . . my house too empty these days . . . I need to keep busy . . . feel I got work to finish."

"You Maggie's daughter, all right."

She smiled.

"My offer's open. Want you to have that apartment upstairs from me . . ."

"I'll think 'bout it, Mercer."

"You got my phone number now, and you know what bus line gets you there . . ."

"You'll be hearin' from me . . ."

They stepped back where they could look down and see all of center hall. How many times they'd turned this long room upside down, getting one family out, another in. "A man stays better than half his life in a place," Mercer said, "then suddenly one day it comes on him, he don't belong."

"Oh, you belong . . . the Pres'dents, their families, they jus' the tenants, we the ones lived here . . ."

"I'll remember that." He smiled at her. She watched

him walk the length of the hall, his back slightly stooped, his step slowed, but still steady, for all his eighty years.

One of the last things Mama had said was "There comes a time." But to make the decision just when that time was plagued Lillian after Mercer left. There was an irony in all this, now that she had a new assignment mornings, manning the tourist desk. Every day she came in, went directly to the little table on the other side of the drape where, for four hours, she checked the public's cameras, packages, pocketbooks (for guns? bombs?)—so close to her original ambition in the White House, that of being a tour guide, and yet so far.

"And this is a portrait of Julia Tyler, second wife of John Tyler, tenth President of the United States . . ." the uniformed, crew-cut, Ivy League young man was saying. "A very ambitious woman, said to have had delusions of grandeur. Now, we'll move on . . ."

Lillian beckoned to him. "Excuse me, could I see you a moment?" Puzzled, he asked the group to wait and moved to the desk. "Yes, Lillian, what is it?"

"You're a bright young man, Tom, I been watchin' and listenin' to you, but if I might make a suggestion . . . be a good idea you look at the picture before you start talkin'."

He flushed. "What do you mean?"

"Miz Tyler's portrait went to the shop yesterday for a new frame. That lady you talked about is Abigail Fillmore, wife of Millard Fillmore, thirteenth President, a very intellectual lady who created the White House library."

He stammered in embarrassment. "Thanks for pointing that out to me." She grabbed his sleeve before he could leave. "And I've been noticin', you not givin' much time to the story 'bout Dolley Madison when the British put the torch to the White House. Now that story's a real barn burner . . ."

He smiled sheepishly. "Okay, Lillian," and moved quickly to his group. She could hear him, a few yards away, calling the tourists' attention to the fact that this was not the original building and although President Truman had had it completely restructured, the rooms were identical in size, shape and in most cases faithful to the original design. (*The boy has promise,* she thought.)

A late-arriving tourist, an attractive young woman in her early thirties, hurried past the desk to join the others. "Sorry, ma'am," Lillian stopped her, "I have to check through your purse, that's the rule." The tourist, showing some anxiety, put the purse on the desk. "Don't worry, you'll catch up to them."

"I'm anxious to go through. You see, my grandfather was here."

"Oh? Who was your grandfather? Maybe I knew him."

"President Taft."

Lillian smiled warmly. "Oh, yes, indeed, I knew Pres'dent Taft."

"You did? Then maybe you knew my father . . . Charlie Taft."

"No, I didn't really know him, but my brother did. Knew him well, they were friends . . ." For an instant, she could hear Emmett saying, *"I'm not s'posed to do these things 'cause I got the best blood in Virginia in my veins . . . what kind of blood has Charlie Taft got?"*

"Really? That's nice . . ." The young woman looked anxiously down the long corridor where the tour had paused in front of a portrait of Mary Todd Lincoln. "Go on, you go ahead, ma'am, catch up to 'em." The tour turned the corner, out of sight, but Lillian could still hear the guide, noting with interest that he'd added a new touch to his spiel, the White House ghosts.

It was true, she realized. The place was filled with ghosts. Everywhere she turned these days, she saw herself: as a child, in the big bathtub, in a plethora of tropical plants, while the gentle giant, President Taft, helped her out of it; coming up the stairs, carrying a repaired, folded American flag to find the Coolidge boys learning the Charleston from Fraser, joining in a few steps of the dance with them; crawling around on the floor, pinning blackout curtains together, Mr.

Roosevelt wheeling out, tracking them up and laughing when she called him on it; on the stairs, and Missy LeHand saying *"Stop in anytime, for a cup of coffee, tea, whatever, I'd offer you a drink but there's Prohibition . . ."* And Mama . . . *"Young woman, I have you to remember you may sass your mama at home, but here I am First Maid Maggie Rogers."*

Ghosts . . . It may have been that, the realization that ghosts belong to the past, that did it. Or perhaps— just perhaps—it was the thought of possibly having to make thirty-two new pairs of curtains. Whatever, like Mama said, *"there comes a time . . ."*

Lillian was cleaning out her desk when the young guide returned from his tours. "Want to thank you, Lillian, for pulling me up on my toes. I'll be boning up tonight, wait'll you catch my act tomorrow."

"Won't be here tomorrow, Tom. This is my last day." Actually, she stayed another week at Mrs. Walker's request until they got a replacement.

Her final day dawned cold, crisp. She worked her full hours, helping in the changeover, packing Eisenhower possessions for their imminent departure. It was early evening when she went upstairs to her sewing room, tidied that up, closed her machine, put her pincushion and scissors into her purse, and started down, for a brief moment pausing in center hall. Deluged by memories, she quickly turned to the back stairs and descended them for the last time. In the changing room her open locker door blocked her from the view of two new kitchen helpers who'd come in to change. "I had to give a dollar for her present," one of them complained, "and I don't even know her."

"Well, when we been here thirty years," the other answered somewhat cynically, "we get our dollar back." Lillian waited them out while they dressed and left, rather than embarrass them.

Mrs. Walker was at her desk, harassed, hurriedly wrapping the traditional silver tray as Lillian came into you know I'd run out of tissue paper? New family the office. "Oh, Lillian, you're too soon . . . wouldn't coming in, hardly know what I'm doing . . ."

"That's all right, Miz Walker, you don't have to finish that, I know what it says anyway . . . 'thirty years . . . faithful service . . .'" She accepted the half-wrapped farewell gift. "Thank you, and thank everybody for me that chipped in . . ."

"Wish you'd let us give you a retirement party, Lillian."

"Thank you very much, but hardly anybody left here knows me . . ."

"Well, if you change your mind, come back . . . we'll have a small party just for those of us who do . . ."

"Might just do that, one of these days."

"Thank you, Lillian, for your good work."

"Thank you, Miz Tennessee Darlin' . . ."

Lillian came out of the White House onto Pennsylvania Avenue where the reviewing stand was set up and ready for the Inauguration tomorrow. In just a few hours, hardy souls would be out in their sleeping bags, and bucket fires would line the avenue. Waiting at the bus stop, she watched one couple, wearing blankets and carrying a pup tent and Coleman stove, set up camp on the sidewalk.

The pneumatic brakes of the bus gave their gasping moan as it came to a stop. A few people got off, Lillian got on, thinking how much warmer the buses were than those old streetcars. She settled into the first available seat where she could be alone. There was time, from now on, to do a lot of thinking. Perhaps she'd call Mercer in the morning and ask him to kindly set up that apartment for her.

Looking out of the window, she admired the symmetry of the bleachers all along the way that would be alive with people by dawn. There'd be a new President tomorrow. She wouldn't be in center hall, to welcome him, but she'd see him, and hear his words on television . . .

"And so, my fellow Americans . . ."

Her face reflected back at her from the window, and she realized how much like Mama she'd come to be.

"Ask not what your country can do for you . . ."

It had begun to snow. She felt strangely calm, for having just turned her back on thirty years, and realized it was because she knew what she had to do. She'd write Mama's book. In the back of her mind she'd kind of known that all along.

"Ask what you can do for your country . . ."

She got off at her stop and walked up the block to her apartment. Just before she went in, she looked up at the moon. There were no scattered clouds, no wind. Yes, she thought, it should be a fine day tomorrow for the Inauguration.

Ed Friendly Productions Presents

BACKSTAIRS AT THE WHITE HOUSE

AN NBC-TV BIG EVENT

WHITE HOUSE STAFF

LESLIE UGGAMS ....Lillian Rogers Parks
OLIVIA COLE ....Maggie Rogers
LOUIS GOSSETT, JR. ....Levi Mercer
ROBERT HOOKS .... Mays
LESLIE NIELSEN ....Ike Hoover
and
CLORIS LEACHMAN ....Mrs. Jaffray

FIRST FAMILIES
(in order of appearance)

JULIE HARRIS ....Helen "Nellie" Taft
VICTOR BUONO ....Wm. Howard Taft
ROBERT VAUGHN ....Woodrow Wilson
KIM HUNTER ....Ellen Wilson
CLAIRE BLOOM ....Edith Galt Wilson
CELESTE HOLM ....Florence Harding
GEORGE KENNEDY ....Warren G. Harding
ED FLANDERS ....Calvin Coolidge
LEE GRANT ....Grace Coolidge
LARRY GATES ....Herbert Hoover
JAN STERLING .... Lou Hoover
EILEEN HECKART ....Eleanor Roosevelt
JOHN ANDERSON ....Franklin Roosevelt
HARRY MORGAN ....Harry Truman
ESTELLE PARSONS ....Bess Truman
BARBARA BARRIE ....Mamie Eisenhower
ANDREW DUGGAN ....Dwight Eisenhower

Teleplay
Gwen Bagni and Paul Dubov

Director
Michael O'Herlihy

Executive Producer
Ed Friendly